SEX IN THE MIDDLE AGES

GARLAND MEDIEVAL CASEBOOKS
(VOL. 3)

GARLAND REFERENCE LIBRARY OF THE HUMANITIES
(VOL. 1360)

GARLAND MEDIEVAL CASEBOOKS
Joyce E. Salisbury and Christopher Kleinhenz
Series Editors

Sex in the Middle Ages
A Book of Essays

Joyce E. Salisbury

GARLAND PUBLISHING, INC. • NEW YORK & LONDON
1991

Library of Congress Cataloging-in-Publication Data

Salisbury, Joyce E.
  Sex in the Middle Ages : a book of essays / Joyce E. Salisbury.
    p. cm. — (Garland reference library of the humanities ; vol. 1360.
Garland medieval casebooks ; vol. 3)
  Includes index.
  ISBN 0-8240-5766-X
  1. Sex customs—History—Europe. 2. Europe—Social conditions—To
1492. I. Title. II. 2. Series: Garland reference library of the humanities ;
vol. 1360. III. Series: Garland medieval casebooks ; vol. 3.
HQ14.S25 1991   91-3959
306.7'094'0902—dc20   CIP

Printed on acid-free, 250-year-life paper
Manufactured in the United States of America

To
Ziad-Aaron

CONTENTS

Public Implications

ACKNOWLEDGMENTS

The credit for this book must go to the contributors. I appreciate the willingness of established and busy scholars to interrupt their research projects to write these essays contributing to the growing body of knowledge on sexuality. The talent represented in this book is matched by the intellectual generosity of these scholars.

Even with fine contributors, producing a work like this requires resolving a good of technical problems (converting programs and the like). I offer my thanks to Rita Logghe for helping me arrange all the details involved in bringing this work to press.

Finally, the dedication is for my new grandson who has brought the promise and fun of a new generation to all of us.

INTRODUCTION

A definitive work synthesizing medieval beliefs about sexuality has not yet been written. While there have been many fine studies exploring aspects of the history of sexuality, we still seem as proverbial blind scholars describing the elephantine subject. In the Middle Ages, as now, sexuality included questions of biology, morality, sociology, and of course, passion. Thus, medievalists interested in sexuality study texts from science, theology, law, history, and literature. Each discipline brings certain insights into the expression of human sexuality. Whatever the discipline, it seems to me that studies of sexuality revolve around three main questions: What were people doing? What did they think about what they were doing? What did they think about what other people were doing? This collection of essays contributes to our understanding of medieval responses to these questions.

This collection draws scholars from many fields. Each essay is a specialized look at some aspect of sex in the Middle Ages approached from the perspective of a particular discipline. All address sexual practices and attitudes. By collecting these essays diverse in theme and method, I hope that the puzzle of medieval sexuality will be made a little more complete. In time, we will have a clearer picture of our sexual past that cannot help but influence our sexual present.

There are any number of ways to arrange such a collection—by discipline, chronology, geography, etc. I have chosen a thematic organization that will throw into focus certain facets of sexuality, and look at each from several perspectives.

Courtship

This seemed a reasonable place to begin a study of sexual intercourse. Jenny Jochens reminds us that physical attraction remains at the core of sexual attitudes and practices. Yet, our understandings of sexual attraction cannot be imposed uncritically on the past. In her essay, "Before the Male Gaze," Professor Jochens carefully and creatively studies Old Norse texts to consider perceptions of corporal beauty which shaped interactions within that society. She discovers then, as now, the sight of the beloved was stirring. However, in contrast to modern texts, the Old Norse sources show that the female body was not the measure of sexual attractiveness. In the cold north, clothing, hair, and men's bodies drew the eye. Professor Jochens forces us to re-look at the glances that begin the sexual process.

Even glances expressive of mutual attraction did not always lead to fulfillment of sexual desire. Richard Kieckhefer's article on "Erotic Magic" reminds us with wit and compassion that people will try almost anything to gain the objects of their desire. In an exhaustive survey of the practices of erotic magic, Professor Kieckhefer describes how people used natural magic, demonic magic, and magical use of religious objects to try to do everything from inducing someone to have sex to improving the sexual experience between consenting partners. In addition, Professor Kieckhefer describes the use of magic to prevent sexual intercourse and inclinations, and finally considers the literary tradition of erotic magic. The mind reels in contemplating all these recipes for sexual success, yet as one laughs at the images some of these conjure up, one can't help but wonder at the power of sexual attraction that would drive people to think of some of these techniques. Surely, it would be easier to find another partner.

One way or the other, people did come together. The first sexual experience of an individual, particularly a woman, was seen as transforming. Medieval societies from families to theologians valued virginity as a heavenly physical state. Esther Lastique and Helen Lemay edit, translate, and comment on a scientific treatise on the defloration of virginity. In "A Medieval Physician's Guide to Virginity," Professors Lastique and Lemay show that defloration was considered a medical problem, unnatural and warranting medical intervention. Their analysis ranges far more widely than the text itself to consider the valuing of virgins in a larger context. Texts like these seem to point to a society in which sexual intercourse was seen as somehow unnatural. Perhaps such attitudes would contribute to people resorting to the recipes described by Professor Kieckhefer.

Disclosure

Possibly one of the most influential insights offered by Michel Foucault in his *History of Sexuality* was to note the importance of sexual discourse as part of the human experience. For all that sexual intercourse is a private matter, we spend a good deal of time talking about it. Contrary to frequent modern perceptions, this desire to discuss was common in the Middle Ages, too. The three articles collected in this section reveal three strikingly different kinds of sexual disclosure. Yet all reveal the seemingly universal need to praise, analyze, and confess our sexual activities.

Romantic and erotic literature may be the most familiar form of sexual disclosure. Christopher Kleinhenz analyzes Italian poetry and prose, exploring this literary expression of sexual activity. In "Texts, Naked and Thinly Veiled," Professor Kleinhenz looks at a range of literary expression with which writers discuss sexual activity. Some writers veil their references in symbol and double entendre, while some discuss sexuality in terms as blunt as the most modern expressions. Professor Kleinhenz's essay shows both that the range of sexual expressions in literature has always been broad and diverse, and that questions of the limits of freedom of sexual disclosure have always been part of such expression.

Margaret Schleissner studies the translation and transmission of the medical text *Secrets of Women*. She studies the function of the text rather than simply its contents and, in doing so, illuminates both the "eroticization of medical discourse" and the "male to male discourse" that marks the transmission of such texts. Professor Schleissner sees this process as part of Foucault's recognition that the history of sexuality has been marked by a proliferation of discourse on sex. It would seem that preservation of medical texts is as much a part of sexual disclosure as erotic poetry.

Pierre J. Payer looks at sexual disclosure in the religious texts studying the important thirteenth-century confessional writings. By decreeing that everyone must confess at least once a year, the Fourth Lateran Council institutionalized religious sexual disclosure. Professor Payer shows how questions of sexuality dominated the confessional literature, and reflects upon some of the reasons for such domination. Of all the sins and wrongs that plague society, it always surprises me that the medieval church focused its attention so strongly on sexual sins. The power of sexuality and the lure of its disclosure retained a strong hold on the imaginations of both laity and clergy.

Diversity

Perhaps one of the most prevalent sexual myths of each generation is the belief that it has invented some new form of sexual expression. A study of the history of sexuality reveals this to be false. The variation across time is not so much in what people were doing, but in the changing attitudes toward what people were doing. The articles in this section point to some of the diversity of sexual expression in the Middle Ages, and considers changes in attitudes toward some of these practices.

Professor Payer's observation that the medieval church was not very successful in imposing its sexual morality on the whole society is borne out by Cathy Jorgensen Itnyre's cataloguing of sexual activities in the Icelandic sagas. In "A Smorgasbord of Sexual Practices," Itnyre shows that saga writers boldly (and often playfully) described fornication, adultery, incest, seduction, genital size, castration, bestiality and sex with monsters. This overview of the broad range of medieval sexual practices introduces this section, which then looks more closely at some specific practices and considers changing attitudes toward these practices.

There have been a number of excellent works exploring the history of homosexuality, but Professor Norman Roth's essay demonstrates that there is still a great deal more to be said, and that there is still a good deal of controversy over interpreting the texts. In "Fawn of My Delights," Professor Roth demonstrates the existence of love of pre-pubescent boys in Hebrew and Arabic society, and analyzes the expression of this love in the elegant, sensitive poetry. This poetry includes an expression of beauty that has echoes of Jochens's recognition that the "male gaze" was more often than not directed at male beauty.

In spite of the values articulated in the beautiful poetry expertly analyzed by Professor Roth, the medieval church pressed to consider homosexual intercourse unnatural. By the thirteenth century, laws were passed that attempted to punish such "sins against nature." Intercourse with animals joined sodomy as a "sin against nature" in the eyes of the church. In my article on "Bestiality in the Middle Ages," I explore the changing attitudes toward bestiality that led from classical mythology's praise of the practice to thirteenth-century scholastics who considered it the worst of the sexual sins.

Ideas of acceptable sexual behavior certainly changed over time, and at any given time everyone did not share a uniform sexual morality. Many of these essays have shown that the medieval church tried repeatedly with little success to impose such a uniform morality. One area of diversity that the church could not ignore was when sexual practices were given religious significance. Such worship seems fairly quickly to disappear from the texts, yet remnants of such practices are glimpsed in folklore and some unusual documents. Professor Peter Nelson translates an account of one of these sexually charged religious practices (or religiously charged sexual practices) written in Germany. The original article explores the worship of a preserved horse penis and the subsequent conversion of the household to Christianity. Here we can see evidence of old fertility worship that may have been preserved in the text because of the happy ending of the tale (the destruction of the venerated object). Yet, recollection of people's worship of such a fetish item perhaps is an appropriate way to close this section on diversity.

Public Implications

We usually think of sexuality as a private matter, a matter of choice that is nobody else's business. It may be that we are kidding ourselves even in the twentieth century, but it is certain that people in the Middle Ages believed sexuality to be a matter of public interest. Early in the Middle Ages, penance for sexual sins was a public penance. Late in the Middle Ages, execution for bestiality was a public execution. For them, private acts had public implications, and this last section considers some such implications.

Jane Tibbits Schulenburg's article "Saints and Sex, ca. 500–1100" brings forward one of the more unexpected public implications of sexual activity. Extraordinarily pious sexual activity can contribute to the public veneration of that person as a saint. Saints were perceived to have been conceived in unusual fashions (often extra-vaginally), they were able to resist sexual temptation in extraordinary ways, and they used their expertise in these matters to counsel the faithful in their own sexual lives. The sexual lives of the people who most belonged to the public sphere were also part of the public domain.

Just as unusually "licit" sexual expression could cause public veneration, unusually illicit activity could lead to public humiliation. I have reprinted two short articles under the title "Penis Captivus" to illustrate this point. The two articles cite medieval references that described couples who engaged in inappropriate sexual activity, then were unable to part until they received help from the community. All these anecdotes tell of a public humiliation that accompanied the embarrassing situation. These articles reveal a good deal about medieval fears of sexuality and the female body. In part I chose to reprint them because they also reveal that such fears have endured well into the twentieth century. Both articles were written in the 1930s and appeared in respectable medical journals. However, both treat the notion of couples being joined together as a real possibility, in spite of common sense experience and medical wisdom to the contrary. Old fears shape even science long after we should know better.

James A. Brundage demonstrates that sexual activity can lead to results worse than public humiliation. In "Politics of Sodomy," Professor Brundage describes a trial for sodomy, and shows how charges of sexual variation were tied to larger political issues in the Middle Ages. That which seems to us to be the most private activity can have public implications of the largest sort.

I hesitate to draw many conclusions from these thought-provoking essays. One of the things they all show is how complex expressions of human sexuality have always been, and for all the answers that are presented here, more questions remain. Certainly, we see that there are constants within the human experience of sexual passion. Human imagination and inclination were as varied 1,000 years ago as they are today, and people's expressions of sexuality are as varied as people themselves. Beyond the stirring of passions, however, attitudes toward gender have changed. Notions of beauty and roles have shaped expressions of passion. Ideas about what was "natural" have changed. Furthermore, privacy as the realm of human sexuality is a relatively new concept. People in the Middle Ages lived in a more public arena, whether sharing beds or doing public penance for sexual "sins." Such publicity could not help but shape their attitudes toward their private passions. These essays have contributed toward illuminating important aspects of medieval life and thought, and perhaps cause us to reflect somewhat upon the implications of our own inclinations. These are only a few thoughts that occur to me as I reflect upon this collection. I am sure readers will be drawn to many more considerations and conclusions as they read these essays. I am pleased to bring them to you.

Courtship

BEFORE THE MALE GAZE: THE ABSENCE OF THE FEMALE BODY IN OLD NORSE

Jenny Jochens

As perceived in the Western tradition, beauty has been a quality particularly associated with the bodies of women, although most often articulated by men who contemplated their beloveds' visual attractiveness, signaling thereby their own emotional and sexual arousal. With roots in Ovidian love poetry and fully developed in courtly love, this tradition has been at home in the West at least since the twelfth century. In our generation feminist film critics have coined the term "the male gaze" and uncovered its pervasiveness throughout all aspects of our culture.[1]

Although the Germanic parts of early medieval Europe eventually were engrossed in this articulation of the male gaze, the perceptions of beauty that originally obtained here were less gender specific. Whereas the early Germanic evidence from the Continent and the Anglo-Saxon materials are too sparse to permit more than a rudimentary analysis, the Old Norse sources, in particular the so-called family sagas, are sufficiently rich to allow a more thorough investigation of the problem.[2] The purpose of this article is to examine perceptions of corporal beauty, particularly as they relate to sexuality, in the Icelandic society depicted in these narratives where, as we shall see, the male gaze did not yet dominate the general optic. Undoubtedly all composed by men, these stories offer the advantage of providing a genuine representation of a masculine outlook.[3] The reader should be forewarned, however, that the main interest of the sagas is in "Bloodtaking and Peacemaking," in the title of a recent study of the field, and information of genuine interest to our investigation is most often given inadvertently.[4] Furthermore, the sagas do not offer long formal portraits in the manner of, for example, Chrétien de Troyes.[5] As a consequence, we need to fly like hawks, surveying the entire landscape of the forty-some family sagas and short stories (*þættir*) and diving for details wherever they appear. Furthermore, since we want to pursue particular themes in a logical manner, we are obliged to skip back and forth between the narratives.

Beauty

As elsewhere, beauty was an important human asset, and scopophilia, the pleasure of beholding, is often attested, but in Old Norse society the gratification was derived from handsome men as well as beautiful women. This is clear from the fact that both men and women were described in such terms as *væn(n)*, *fríð(r)*, and *fagr* (*fǫgr*), all denoting beauty.[6] Hofskuldr, described as "a handsome and capable man" (*vænn maðr ok gǫrviligr*; [*Lax*, 5.7.14]), married Jórunn who was a "beautiful woman" (*væn kona*; [5.9.16]). In the same saga Guðrún's second husband þórðr was a "handsome man" (*vænn maðr*), whereas the characterization, "she was neither beautiful nor capable" (*ekki var hon væn kona né gǫrvilig*; [5.32.87]), described þórðr's first wife Auðr. Ingólfr þorsteinsson was known as "the most handsome man in the Northern parts of the country" (*vænstr maðr norðan lands*; [*Hallfreðar saga*, 8.2.141]), and in the same area the young Hrefna was "the most beautiful woman" (*vænst kvenna*; [*Lax*, 5.40.113]). Originally suggesting "promising," *vænn* implies both outer and inner qualities. The full meaning of the term is ascertainable from the characterization of Guðrún who was "the most beautiful woman" (*kvenna vænst*) in Iceland at that time, "as to both her looks and her intelligence" (*at ásjánu ok vitsmunum*; [*Lax*, 5.32.86]).

In contrast, *fríðr* was firmly linked with visual beauty, which is clear from the near automatic addition of *sýnum*, "by sight." Thus, among many descriptions of the handsome Oláfr Hǫskuldsson, one stated that he was "the most handsome man people had ever set eyes on" (*allra manna fríðastr sýnum, þeira er menn hafi sét*; [*Lax*, 5.20.49]).[7] The word can be qualified by prefixes. A man lacking in beauty was called "not handsome to look at" (*ófríðr sýnum*; [*Hávarðar saga Ísfirðings*, 6.8.318]), whereas two young girls in *Egils saga* were deemed "exceptionally beautiful" (*allfríða*; [2.7.16 and 2.48.120]).

Less frequent than the two preceding terms, *fagr* was also associated with physical beauty. Not yet aware of his paternity, Helga's father declared her to be "the most beautiful girl" *fegrst miklu*; [*Gunnlaugs saga*, 3.3.57]) and nicknamed her "the beautiful" (*in fagra*). Later she was described as "so beautiful that knowledgeable men said she was the loveliest woman there has ever been in Iceland" (*svá fǫgr, at þat er sǫgn fróðra manna, at hon hafi fegrst kona verit á Íslandi*; [3.4.60]). Rather than signifying beauty in general in the manner of *vænn*, *fagr* often referred to hair. In the previous passage the author continued by describing Helga's hair—so long that it "could envelop her entirely" (*hylja hana alla*) and "as fair as beaten gold" (*svá fagrt sem gull barit*). As a nickname, however, *fagr* was more often applied to men than to women.[8]

Although male and female beauty is identified by the same semantic range, the terms are elaborated in far greater detail for men than for women. Without doubt the most admired male attribute was physical strength. Almost every man credited with good looks was also said to be "a large and strong man" (*mikill maðr ok sterkr*) at some point.[9] Old Norse heroes likewise conformed to timeless standards of male beauty. Crediting Hrútr with the usual strength, the author of *Lax* added that the young man, whom the Norwegian Queen Gunnhildr later considered to be irresistible, "was better built than anyone, tall and broad-shouldered, slim-waisted and straight-limbed," and concluded with the standard formula that he was "the most handsome of men to behold" (*allr manna fríðastr sýnum*; [5.8.16]). Several male heroes require descriptions of half a page to enumerate the qualities of their physical beauty, often including vivid details, particularly about their noses. Gunnlaugr's was not very becoming (*Gunn*, 3.4.59), young Bolli's and Gunnarr's were turned at the end (*Lax*, 5.63.187; 12.19.53), and Arngrímr's was large (*Eyrbyggja saga*, 4.12.21).[10]

In comparison to men, the linguistic markers of feminine beauty rarely added physical traits, and they are, therefore, much shorter. Only two women in the family sagas receive detailed physical portraits and even these are meager by any standard. Since these portraits concern an older woman and a young girl whom the author specifically characterized as not being beautiful, they are not animated by masculine desire and do little to identify a potential male gaze, the linguistic barometer of sexual yearning. Because of their rarity, however, these sketches are worth examining in more detail.

According to *Eyr*, a ship arrived in Iceland the year Christianity was accepted, bringing a woman from the Hebrides named þórgunna. She

> was a large woman, both tall and broad, and getting stout. She had dark eyebrows and narrow eyes, brown and full hair. . . . People thought she was in her fifties, but she was still a very active woman (4.50.139).

þórgunna was also the only woman in the narratives to appear naked, albeit as a ghost. Being Christian, she had stipulated that she be buried at Skálaholt, the future see of the bishop. When the men who were transporting her body—"wrapped in an un-stitched linen shroud"—were refused hospitality at a farm, þórgunna herself, "stark-naked, not a stitch of clothing on her," appeared in the kitchen to prepare a meal for them (4.51.144). Under these circumstances—needless to say—þórgunna's nakedness elicited only fear from her inhospitable hosts, but her age, added to her looks, may have inhibited men from desiring her during her later years. At this time, however, she herself was smitten by a young boy, attesting to a recurrent theme of an older woman's love for a young man. Among all the people on the farm þórgunna felt close only to the young Kjartan whom she "loved . . . dearly" (*elskaði . . . mjǫk*; a rare word). At age thirteen or fourteen he was "both large of size and manly to look at" (*bæði mikill vexti ok skǫruligr at sjá*). Her attention "made him keep his distance," however, a fact that caused her to become "irritable" (*skapstygg*; [4.50.139]). In other words, this rare portrait of a woman's body, rather than conveying male desire, reveals only an equally rare glimpse of female passion.[11]

The other woman earning a relatively full description is the young þorbjǫrg. Encountered by þormóðr in *Fóstbrœðra saga* as he paid a visit to her mother's farm, she appeared as

> a well-bred and elegant (*kurteis*) woman, though not particularly beautiful (*eigi enkar væn*), with black hair and eyebrows, wherefore she was called Kolbrún. Her face had an intelligent expression and good color. She had shapely limbs and was slender and of average height. Her toes pointed out a little when she walked (6.11.170).

A modern reader will perhaps agree that the gait suggested by the position of her toes may not have been very becoming, but otherwise it is hard to see why Kolbrún earned the authorial comment of not being particularly pretty. We shall see, however, that the author shared the Old Norse convention of considering black hair as unattractive. Kolbrún apparently possessed other chemistry to attract þormóðr, with whom she and her mother were *kátar*. This word is normally translated as "merry," but it may also suggest sexual arousal as in modern Norwegian and Swedish (*kåt*). In fact, the narrative provides a rare glimpse of two young people falling in love, a process in which scopophilia, visual pleasure, played a determining role as they let their eyes roam over each other. Despite the author's original disclaimer, þormóðr pronounced Kolbrún beautiful (*lízk honum vel á hana*) at the end, and she reciprocated by finding him handsome (*verðr henni hann vel at skapi*; [6.11.170]). It was even alleged that þormóðr had composed love poetry to her.[12] This episode not only illustrates the phenomenon—undoubtedly normal in any society, although not necessarily articulated—that young men and women enjoyed the physical contemplation of each other, but it also demonstrates that scopophilia could occur even when customary standards of beauty were not met.

Clothing

In contrast to men, the women described by the adjectives denoting beauty were not credited with attractive features of face or body. The only exception is their hair, to which we shall return. What made a woman beautiful, instead, was her clothing, but clothes were equally important for men. The sagas contain numerous passages depicting fine male attire. For men, however, clothing supplemented their physical features whereas women's fine clothing alone constituted their beauty.[13] The standard expression stated that the woman was "well dressed" (*vel búin*). Having been described both as "pretty to look at" (*fríð sýnum*; [*Nj*, 12.1.6]), "beautiful" (*fǫgr*; [12.1.7]), and "the most beautiful woman to behold" (*kvenna fríðust sýnum*; [12.9.29]), Hallgerðr was further identified as "most well-dressed" (*bezt búin*) among a group of women, all of whom were "finely attired" (*vel búnar*), when she and Gunnarr met for the first time. Furthermore, her finery was described in great detail (12.33.85).[14] Likewise, when Oláfr—who himself was well-dressed—arrived at Egill's booth to persuade þorgerðr to agree to his marriage proposal, he immediately spotted her sitting on the bench as the woman who was "beautiful and distinguished and well dressed" (*væn ok stórmannlig ok vel búin*; [*Lax*, 5.23.65]).[15]

Since marriages were primarily based on property and politics, it is extremely rare to find references to love and beauty in the negotiations leading to marital unions between two families. When they do occur they carry authorial disapproval, as suggested in the two episodes just mentioned.[16] In the first case it is obvious that at Hallgerðr's and Gunnarr's first encounter at the Thing they were attracted to each other through scopophilia resulting from physical and sartorial beauty as well as by the pleasure of conversation. When Gunnarr quickly asked how she would consider a marriage proposal, she referred him to her father and uncle. Because of Hallgerðr's unsavory character, however, her uncle Hrútr felt obliged to advise Gunnarr against the match, but he realized with dismay that he would not be able to prevail because the two young people were obsessed by *girndarráð* ("mad desire"; [*Nj*, 12.33.87]).

In the second case þorgerðr was correct to resist Oláfr's proposal of marriage because, as she pointed out, his illegitimate birth raised the obstacle that he and she were not "of equal social status" (*jafnræði*), the most important qualification for successfully negotiating a marriage. Neither was she persuaded by her father's argument that the original position of Melkorka, Oláfr's mother—a woman whom we shall encounter again—as daughter of an Irish king was more important than her later role as a slave, her condition when she had given birth to Oláfr. þorgerðr admitted that the young man was "handsome" (*vænn*) and a "showy dresser" (*mikill áburðarmaðr*; [*Lax*, 5.23.63]; here used pejoratively).[17] As in all traditional societies, male beauty was most certainly never considered by fathers as they pondered marriage proposals for their daughters, and even female beauty was rarely acknowledged explicitly as a qualification for marriage.

It must be conceded, of course, that certain physiological conditions had to be met if marriage was to succeed in the ultimate goal of reproduction. The woman had to be, or at least become, of reproductive age and to please the man enough to arouse him sexually. Without mention of age limits, the law code *Grágás* stipulated that an engagement was legal if the woman in question had no physical impediment that would have devalued her had she been a slave, (*ambátt*, "female slave"), but one manuscript further clarified that possible flaws should be determined only by the age of sixteen, supposedly the time of menarche (*Gg*, 1b.35; 2.162).[18]

Within this broad definition of femaleness, however, men undoubtedly could not refrain from looking at the women they considered marrying, a fact occasionally admitted in the sources. *Brandakrossa þáttr* contains a rare case of a marriage in Norway that was celebrated immediately when a father noticed that a visitor was taken by the beauty of his young daughter (11.2.189). In another text, Ofeigr questioned Gellir about the best marriage prospects in the western parts of Iceland, and was surprised to find that Gellir did not include his own daughters among the candidates, since—to flatter the father—Ofeigr argued from Gellir's own good looks, that nobody could be "more beautiful" (*fríðari*) than his daughters, in Ofeigr's eyes apparently an important qualification.[19] Ofeigr arranged a marriage between his own son and Gellir's daughter Ragnheiðr, but nothing further is said about her looks.

In a few other cases, however, female beauty was acknowledged, but again associated with clothing. Suggesting marriage for his brother Hrútr, Hǫskuldr proposed Unnr as a candidate. Since she was also present at the meeting of the Thing the two men were attending, he offered that Hrútr could "see her" immediately. Pointing to a group of well-dressed women the next morning, Hǫskuldr singled out Unnr and asked his brother "how do you like her" (*hversu lízk þér á hana*; [*Nj*, 12.2.8]; the verb *líta* indicating impression through sight).[20]

Unnr's physical beauty was apparently not sufficient to warrant authorial comment, but in addition to wealth and excellent family, her clothing assured her acceptance as a suitable marriage candidate. Other women, likewise not described as being pretty, used clothes to enhance their attractiveness. When Ásdís, formerly described as being "a generous woman and rather proud-tempered" (*drengilig kona ok heldr skapstór*; [*Eyr*, 4.18.33]), wanted to arouse two berserks, she put on "her best clothes" (*sinn bezta búnað*; [4.28.73]).[21]

This importance of clothing can be further detected in the Melkorka episode in *Lax* (5.12.22–25). While in Norway on a business trip Hofskuldr went with some men "to amuse himself" (*at skemmta sér*), a frequent euphemism for sexual intercourse. Deciding to buy a "female slave" (*ambátt*), he entered a tent where twelve women were for sale. Hǫskuldr's eyes were caught by one who was "poorly dressed" (*illa klædd*), but whom he thought "beautiful to behold, judged by what he could see" (*fríð sýnum, ef nǫkkut mátti á sjá*). Bedding down with her that same night did not elicit further comments about her beauty, but the next morning he gave her "a good dress" (*góð kvenmannsklæði*), and "it was everybody's opinion that fine clothes became her well." Melkorka's physical beauty, barely noticeable in ragged clothing and earning no comment from the state of nature, was fully perceived only when she was well-dressed.[22]

In current anthropology women are often associated with nature and men with culture.[23] In the Old Norse context, however, men's looks partook both of nature and of culture because their features and bodies were enhanced by fine clothing, but female beauty was most likely to be perceived primarily through the cultural optic of clothing, but—it should added—a culture of the women's own making.[24]

Clothes as Gender Markers

The identification of female beauty with clothing rendered clothes as important markers of gender. Since Old Norse society was dominated by the masculine activity of feuding, gender roles were clearly defined by necessity. It is not surprising, therefore, that the law confirmed gender distinctions by making it illegal for men and women to wear the clothing of the opposite sex:

> If a woman dresses in male clothing (*karl klæðom*) or cuts her hair like a man or carries weapons in order to be different from others, the punishment is the smaller outlawry (expatriation for three years). . . . The same is the case if men dress in female (*Gg*, 1b.203–04).[25]

Although the saga literature furnishes few examples to substantiate this paragraph, two episodes in *Lax* (chs. 34–35) provide gender-specific details about clothes. Married against her will to þorvaldr, Guðrún received with pleasure the attention of þórðr who did not care for his own wife.[26] When þorvaldr slapped Guðrún, þórðr advised her to make her husband a shirt described as having a *brautgangs hǫfuðsmátt* (literally, "neck opening that gives cause for leaving") and declare herself divorced. The saga author continued: "Guðrún raised no objections to this, and they dropped the subject. That same spring Guðrún declared herself divorced from þorvaldr and returned home" (5.34.94). Although no details were provided, we must assume that Guðrún made the offensive shirt and that by wearing it þorvaldr gave her sufficient reason for divorce.

The exact nature of this shirt becomes clear in the next episode where Guðrún persuaded þórðr that he should likewise use the accusation of dressing across-gender in order to get rid of his wife Auðr. Guðrún insinuated at length that Auðr had been wearing male pants. Claiming that he was unaware of his wife's behavior, þórðr was slow to react. Only days later did he return to the subject and asked Guðrún "what a woman *varðaði* (a legal term meaning "would receive in penalty") if she often appeared in pants like men." Guðrún replied:

> The same penalty (*víti*) applies to women in a case like that as to a man who wears a neck-opening (*h ǫfuðsmátt*) so wide that his nipples (*geirvǫrtur*) are exposed. Both are grounds for divorce (*brautgangss ǫk*; [5.35.96]).

In other words, at þórðr's instigation Guðrún had made a shirt for her husband cut with such a wide neck-opening that he had exposed his nipples and thereby given her sufficient reason for divorce.[27] The rule reflects the obvious that the sight of a man's nipples demonstrates that he is not a woman. A man was not allowed to wear a shirt with a wide neck opening for fear that he, at least at a distance, might be mistaken for a woman. Does it then follow that Icelandic women wore décolleté? We shall return to the problem, but for the moment we notice that climate would hardly encourage such a practice. The few itemized descriptions of full female clothing in the family sagas do not suggest such a style. Guðrún's attire, described in some detail after the murder of her third husband, included a "tight bodice" (*vefjarupphlutr þrǫngr*; [*Lax*, 5.55.168]), a feature that would be sufficient to reveal her female figure.[28] One might speculate that women wore a décolleté undershirt only when inside the house, but needed to cover themselves when they went outside. The shape of a low-cut shirt underneath might still allow their nipples to be contoured against the tight outer layers in moments of extreme cold or sexual arousal. We may have to be content to conclude, however, that women were allowed to exhibit their breasts, but most often revealed this most visible sign of their femaleness through tight bodices, while men were supposed to keep their nipples covered.

Returning to the male pants which Guðrún accused Auðr of wearing, we encounter an equally sex-specific piece of male clothing. According to Guðrún, Auðr dressed so often in "pants equipped with inserts and with cross-garters almost down to the shoes" (*brókum, ok setgeiri í, en vafit spjǫrrum mjǫk í skúa niðr*), that she was called "Breeches-Auðr" (*Bróka-Auðr*; [5.35.95]). Apparently, two features distinguished these pants; they were equipped with *geiri* ("insert" or "gore") and they were pulled tightly around the ankles with bands called *spjarrar* or *vaf*.[29] Suggesting that the pants were long, the latter feature combined the pants and the stockings into a single unit, a purpose also served by the *leista brókum*, pants to which stockings were permanently attached in a style adopted especially for walking.[30]

Before examining the feature of the insert and trying to determine what made these pants male, we must take note of the fact that women also wore trousers, at least occasionally. This is not surprising since the only mode of locomotion faster than walking was riding, for which pants were more practical than skirts. In spite of þórðr's general disbelief of his wife's male attire, Auðr did, in fact, don pants at least once. Describing her mounting the horse before her furious ride to þórðr's hut when she intended to kill or harm her former husband, the author commented with approving sarcasm that "at that time she certainly was in pants" (*var hon þá at vísu í brókum*; [5.35.97]).[31] As suggested by Hallgerðr's nicknames, *longbrók* ("long pants"; *Nj*, 12.9.29) or *snúinbrók* ("turned pants"; *Landnámabók*, 1.S105.143), women in pants were not an uncommon sight.[32]

The best evidence for female pants, however, comes from a scene in *Nj* that also illustrates the mixed signals that could be conveyed by clothing. A difficult arbitration had been arranged between two feuding parties represented by Njáll and his sons on the one side and Flosi on the other over the murder of Hǫskuldr, Njáll's foster son and the husband of Flosi's niece Hildigunnr. The guilty Njálssons were to pay treble indemnity to Flosi. At the dramatic moment when the enormous sum was to be handed over, Njáll added a pair of boots (*bóta*) and a piece of clothing called a *silkislœður* (the word is plural) for good measure (12.129.312). No objections were raised over the boots, but the latter caused problems. The word suggests a garment made of silk and so long that it trailed on the ground.[33] This expensive piece of clothing is occasionally encountered elsewhere in the literature. On his return from England Arinbjǫrn gave Egill a *slœður* of silk, custom-made to fit his friend's ample size (*Eg*, 2.67.213). Years later Egill's son þorsteinn wore it at the meeting of the Thing with his mother's connivance but without Egill's knowledge. Since þorsteinn was shorter than his father, he soiled the cape which angered Egill (2.79.274).[34] In the prose narratives such garments were worn by men, but in the Edda poem *Rígsþula*, Móðir, the female representative of the third, aristocratic class of society, was seen in *síðar slœður* ("a long cape"), suggesting that it could also be worn by women.

This conclusion is confirmed by Flosi's reaction. Picking up the cape, he demanded who had donated it. Nobody answered and he continued: "you do not dare tell me," using an expression (*þoriðþér eigi at segja mér*) that always signals impending trouble. When Skarpheðinn, one of Njáll's sons, asked him whom he thought the donor might be, Flosi accused Njáll, "because many do not know whether he is man or a woman when they see him,"—a clear reference to Njáll's lack of a beard. Calmly referring to Njáll's fathering of sons with his wife—the final proof of manhood, Skarpheðinn snatched up the cape and threw down a pair of "blue pants" (*brókum blám*) on the pile, claiming that Flosi was more in need of these. Responding to Flosi's question and claiming he was simply repeating a rumor, Skarpheðinn accused Flosi of being the lover of the Svinafell Troll who used him as a woman every ninth night (12.123.314), thus subjecting Flosi to the ultimate insult against a man, that of passive homosexuality.

It seems clear that the purpose of the cape was not to humiliate Flosi. It strains imagination that Njáll himself would have done anything to jeopardize the settlement which he desired more strongly than anyone else. The cape was intended for a man, or, at most, it was sexually neutral as an androgynous piece of clothing.[35] But Flosi thought otherwise. We shall return to an earlier scene in which Flosi's niece Hildigunnr had urged him to take revenge for her murdered husband by challenging her uncle's "courage and manhood" (*manndóm ok karlmennsku*; [12.116.291]). For the moment we notice that the implied insult in her words, suggesting that Flosi perhaps did not possess these qualities, had stung him and made him sensitive to the gift of the cape. Perceiving a new innuendo to his manhood in this garment, Flosi latched out against Njáll with a sexual insult. Njáll's lack of a beard had earlier been the butt of Hallgerðr's taunts but it had not been used in an overtly sexual manner (12.35.91, 41.107, 44.113). Flosi's self-doubt was further sharpened by Skarpheðinn's blunt accusation and reinforced by the blue pants. In other words, although nobody shared his opinion, Flosi's initial reaction indicates that in his mind femininity was attached to the cape. While the cape thus was open to different interpretations, there was no ambiguity about the pants. They were clearly understood to be female. The sexual insult intended by Skarpheðinn was perceived both by the audience and by Flosi, as he kicked apart the pile of money, refusing arbitration and swearing blood revenge (12.123.314).[36]

These female trousers were apparently not distinguished by any special style.[37] Let us now return to the pants worn by Auðr. As we recall, Guðrún described them as being long with straps at the end and with inserted triangular gores. It was the last feature that distinguished them as male. Following Guðrún's advice, þórðr went immediately to the Law Rock at the Thing and divorced Auðr by using as his sole reason that "she wore pants with inserted gores" (*setgeirabrœkr*).[38] It has been suggested that the *setgeiri* was a single insert sewn into the seat of the pants, whereas women's pants were open in the crotch, both features supposedly for reasons of elimination.[39] This assumption might be correct in case of the female trousers, and it would also fit Skarpheðinn's innuendo, enabling the wearer to be available sexually. It is difficult, however, to see why men would need an insert in the rear, especially since it was sewn and could not be easily opened. This fact can be deduced from an episode in the life of the Norwegian pretender Sigurðr slembidjákn. Swimming ashore to escape captors sometime in the 1130s, he was forced to spend the night in wet clothes hiding in a cave. He avoided freezing to death by removing one pair of pants, "cutting a hole in the inserts" (*rauf á setgeiranum*), slipping the pants over his head and putting his hands though the holes.[40] Male anatomy requires extra room in the front, not in the back. This episode in *Lax* is the only saga passage to deal with the insert at any length, and since this morsel of information about tailoring is juxtaposed with a trait that designates female identity through clothing by focusing on women's most visible sexual feature, it seems likely that the *setgeiri* has the same function. I submit that the *setgeiri* was a piece of material inserted in the front of either half of the pants in order to accommodate the male genitalia. In other words, like female dresses, male clothing was also sex-specific. Women were no more allowed to wear male pants than men to appear in low necklines. An attitude of "truth in advertisement" prevailed, demanding that clothing be separated by the most obvious and visible sexual markers of differentiation for both sexes, the breasts and the penis. We recall that the law had been formulated as a negative injunction stating in a general way what men and women were not supposed to wear. Adding specificity to this broad rule, these saga episodes defined, in a similarly negative manner, two pieces of gender-specific clothing not permitted by the opposite sex, thereby permitting a few observations on male and female attire.

Hair

We have seen that hair was the one natural feature of female beauty singled out for comment. Reinforcing good looks for men, however, the male mop also received its share of attention. Men's hair was noticed far more frequently than their beards, and it exhibited more variety than women's tresses. At times a man's hair was included in an abbreviated characterization; thus, Helgi Njálsson was said to be "a handsome man with a good head of hair" (*fríðr sýnum ok hrœðr vel*; [*Nj*, 12.25.70]). More specifically, another Helgi was "a handsome man with beautiful light blond hair" (*vænn maðr og vel hærðr, hvítr á hárslit*; [*Fóst*, 6.12.181]). In fact, men's hair displayed the full palette of colors ranging from white to black.[41] The change caused by aging was noticed occasionally: Asmundr had "the best head of hair" (*hærðr manna bezt*), but turning prematurely "grey" (*hærur*), he became known as *hærulangr* or *hærulagðr* (*Gr*, 7.13.33–4).[42] Men's hair could be "curly" (*skrúfhárr*; [*BjHít*, 3.32.197] or *hrokkinnhærðr*; [*Fóst*, 6.23.236, 24.250]). Steingerðr considered "curls on the forehead" a blemish on the otherwise handsome appearance of Kormakr (*Kor*, 8.3.210). In contrast to women, men cut their hair. Outside poetry the term "hair-cut" (*skǫr*) refers only to male hair styles, but, nevertheless, some men had long hair. Kjartan's "hair was long and fine as silk, falling in curls," and young Bolli's locks "fell to his shoulders . . . and were cut in bangs above his eye brows" (*Lax*, 5.28.77; 5.63.187).[43]

As in the case of men, women's hair could also be characterized in a general way, for example, when Steingerðr was said to be "a woman with wonderful hair" (*hærð kvenna bezt*; [*Kor*, 8.3.212]). In contrast to the masculine variety, however, ideal female hair was blond, long, and straight, and only this caught the attention of saga authors. Never shorn, it grew throughout the woman's life. In the case of Hallgerðr we can follow its descent from the time she was a young girl when it reached to her belt (*Nj*, 12.1.6) until as a grown woman she could wrap it entirely around herself (12.9.29). Its length was still evident many years later when her husband Gunnarr asked for, but was refused, "two locks from your hair" to replace his broken bowstring in his final battle (12.77.189). Equally impressive, as we saw, was Helga's mane (*Gunn*, 3.4.60).[44]

Since the law prohibited women from cutting their hair in the male style, hair became the most important gender determinant (*Gg* 1b.203–04).[45] We shall see that married women in Iceland, like their sisters elsewhere in medieval society, normally tied up their hair and hid it under a piece of cloth or a bonnet called a *faldr*, whose elaborateness could vary with the social occasion. This meant that women only showed their hair when they were on the nuptial market, either as young girls or as marriageable widows, or on the rare occasion when they were seen in the privacy of their bed or bedroom. In other words, comments about women's hair indisputably carry overtones of sexuality.

These familiar images were the lenses through which Norse men viewed the entire world, mythical as well as foreign. Fulla—one of the lesser known goddesses—was described by Snorri as "a young girl with untied hair (*laushár*) and a gold band around her head."[46] Recounting the visit of Rǫgnvaldr, Earl of the Orkneys, to Countess Ermingerðr of Narbonne in the 1150s, the author of *Orkneyinga saga* likewise described Ermingerðr's beauty: "She was dressed in the best clothes, her hair was untied as is the custom of young girls, and she wore a golden band around her forehead" (34.86.210).[47]

Because of the sexual connotations it not surprising that hair figured prominently in love poetry, for which a few examples will suffice. Rǫgnvaldr, just mentioned, was so taken by Erminger∂r's beauty that he composed love stanzas to her in which he mentioned her hair cascading upon her shoulders (*Ork*, 34.86.210). Einarr Skúlason, the well-known Icelandic poet, devoted a stanza to how a blond woman lets her "head-snow" float down loosely.[48]

The focus on hair for both men and women and the privileging of men's hair over their beards may be the result of a culture where men's genetic make-up—undoubtedly then as now—made them prone to baldness. Except in an unusual case like Njáll's, beards could have served as the most indisputable gender divider, but little attention was paid to facial growth.[49] Lasting throughout life, beards were less favored than the more ephemeral masculine manes. Treasuring their own capillary splendor while it lasted, men were impressed by the quantity and permanency of women's hair, making it the most important female identification marker.

The Head-dress (*Faldr*)

For women the cultural element of clothing melded with the natural feature of hair to produce the special female head-dress known as the *faldr* which became the most important social indicator of female gender. When the French artist Auguste Mayer made his famous drawings of Iceland and its inhabitants during Paul Gaimard's expeditions in the 1830s, he depicted all grown women with a head-dress (*skotthúfa*).[50] It seems probable that this was well-established among Icelandic wives already during the Middle Ages. At least, this is how medieval writers and artists perceived all married women, including goddesses, in the past. Recounting the hilarious story of how þórr retrieved his hammer, the Edda poem *þrymskvi∂a* noted that he was persuaded to go to Giantland in female disguise in pretense of marrying the giant. Included among his female paraphernalia was the head-dress, as suggested in the expression that he should be *hagliga um hǫfu∂ typp∂r* ("suitably attired in the bridal head-dress"; str. 16, 19). The last word, from the verb *typpja*, is related to *toppr* ("point" or "top"), in this case another word for *faldr*, the female head-dress, that would bring the final touch to þórr's female disguise.[51] That the *faldr* also was used in iconography is suggested by the story in *Nj* in which a statue of the goddess þorger∂r hǫldabrú∂r was thus described: "She was as large as a grown man; on her hand she had a large gold ring and a *faldr* on her head."[52] Half-way between goddesses and ordinary women were the three mythical women representing the female half of the social classes in the poem *Rígsþula*. Each was adorned with the head-dress (str. 2, 16, 29).

In medieval Iceland the wearing of the head-dress was closely associated with marriage. The Norwegian princess Ingibjǫrg presented Kjartan with a particularly beautiful specimen, called a *motr*, as a parting gift, instructing him to give it to his intended wife Guðrún as the customary first bridal present.[53] Its precious quality—it was white and woven with gold threads—would, the princess hoped, both reflect on the giver and make Guðrún "look wonderful" (*hølzti gott*) as she "wrapped it around her head." When Kjartan arrived home, however, Guðrún was already remarried, but we next encounter the precious item as Kjartan and his shipmate invite their two sisters, þuríðr and Hrefna, to go through their treasures on board ship. Tempted to try on the *motr*, the unmarried Hrefna was encouraged by þuríðr. When Kjartan showed up unexpectedly, he approved of her looks and added—stung by Guðrún's remarriage and without enthusiasm for any union—that he should probably have both "the head-dress and the maiden" (*motr ok mey*; [5.44.133]). It is likely that the wedding feast offered a woman the first opportunity to wear the *faldr*. During the ceremony celebrating Guðrún's fourth marriage we get a glimpse of the bride and other women on the bridal bench, all "wearing linen head-dresses" (*hǫfðu lín á hǫfði*; [*Lax*, 5.69.202]).[54]

From the sources it is impossible to be sure how often married women wore these bonnets thereafter, but it seems to have been frequent, if not constantly. *Svarf* contains the arresting story of twice-married Yngvildr whose beauty was evident from her nickname *fagrkinn*. Aroused from her bed by an intruder during her husband's absence, she attempted to dress before she was dragged outside, but she managed only to get into her slip. "She was without her head-dress (*faldlaus*) and had long and beautiful hair" (11.25.197). This story demonstrates at the same time both the sexual connotations of visible hair and the practice of married women covering their heads during the day. From the Orkneys comes the story of two aristocratic wives engaged in the normal activity of preparing fine cloth. Less habitual was their application of poison to the fabric. When the wrongly intended person draped himself with the cloth and suffered immediate pain, thus revealing the murderous scheme, they pulled off their head-dresses in despair and tore their hair (*Ork*, 34.55.118).

Likewise, during the murder of Bolli, Guðrún—who had instigated the deed—went about the everyday business of her laundry. After the crime had been accomplished Guðrún's outfit was described in detail, including her "large head-dress on her head" (*sveigr mikill á hǫfði*; [*Lax*, 5.55.168, *sveigr* being another word for *faldr*]). Since Guðrún's attire at this moment may have been dictated by her near ritual role of inciter, this does not necessarily permit the conclusion that a woman wore her head-dress during such normal activities as laundry. We shall see, however, that several cases of cross-gender dressing suggest, nonetheless, that the *faldr* was part of everyday gear.

There is no doubt, however, about the festive use of the *faldr*. A special part of the house was reserved for women at weddings, where they "put on their head-gear (*fǫlduðu sér*"; [8.44.118], as reported in *Vatn*. Since the infamous *motr* was perhaps exceptional and too precious for ordinary use, it was carried back and forth between Kjartan's and Guðrún's farms for the celebration of feasts. Although Hrefna was hesitant to wear it because of Guðrún's obvious jealousy, her mother-in-law insisted that she bring it to Bolli's and Guðrún's farm: "When are you ever going to use that wonderful treasure, if it is kept hidden in a chest whenever you go to a feast." When the women went to get dressed the next day, however, the *motr* had disappeared. Guðrún all but admitted that she had destroyed it (5.46.140–44).

When a woman divorced or became a widow she appears to have discarded the *faldr*, because her loose hair once again signaled her reentry into the marriage market.[55] This is the most satisfactory conclusion that can be drawn from several references to the visible and beautiful hair of heroines during times intervening between marriages. During two different periods of widowhood Hallgerðr was praised for her thick and beautiful hair—long, flowing across her bosom in two streams, and fastened under her belt—as new suitors asked for her hand (*Nj*, 12.13.44, and 33.85). Also from *Nj* comes the arresting story of Hildigunnr, Hǫskuldr's widow. We recall that her hope for revenge of her husband's murder was focused on her Uncle Flosi. Preparing for his visit, she, therefore, readied her farm for a feast, ordering "the women to clean the house, put up the wall hangings and prepare a high-seat for Flosi." With such careful staging of the festivities, it seems altogether likely that Hildigunnr herself would have worn the *faldr* if her new status of widowhood had not enjoined it, but, she was clearly bareheaded. Appearing before Flosi when he had finished his meal, she "pushed her hair away from her eyes and wept," as she urged her uncle to take revenge (12.115.289–90).[56] It was not likely that Hildigunnr was thinking about remarriage at this moment, but she was still young, and custom required her to be maritally available, as announced by her unbound hair. And remarry she did. In *Nj* the final gesture of reconciliation is the union between her and Kári, the avenger of Njáll and his sons, the men who had been burned in retaliation for the murder of Hildigunnr's first husband. In this marriage, moreover, she produced children.

That the *faldr* is seen to represent marriage is confirmed from its metaphorical use in a famous scene in *Lax* (5.33.88–90). Perturbed by many dreams, Guðrún asked her relative, the wise Gestr, to explain four particularly troubling ones. Gestr interpreted them as Guðrún's four future marriages. In the first she was wearing a "crocked head-dress" (*krókfaldr*) which she did not think was becoming to her.[57] Despite being warned, she tore it off and threw it in the water. Identifying the *faldr* with her first husband, Gestr explained that this marriage would not be a "love match" (*girndaráð*; the term is used sarcastically), and that she would leave her husband. The last dream also involved a head-gear, this time a golden helmet inset with precious stones, its beauty marred only by its weight. In her dream Guðrún was relieved of this caricature of a *faldr* when the helmet slipped from her head and fell into the water. According to Gestr, the helmet represented Guðrún's fourth husband, a man whom he predicted would overpower her (*bera heldr ugishjálm yfir þér*) until his untimely death by drowning.[58]

The *faldr*, however, was not necessarily a tailored hat or bonnet under which the woman's hair was hidden. The proximity between the strong verb *falda* ("to put on the head-dress") and the weak homonym *falda* ("to fold") suggests that the hair instead could be wrapped in a soft cloth. In fact, instead of *faldr* the word *hǫfuðdúk* (literally, "head-cloth") is used often. Since the hair was already tied up in a knot, the effect of such a scarf would be turban-like, similar to the *faldr*. This is particularly clear from an episode in *Ork*. Visiting Earl Rofgnvaldr, Ragna arrived with a red "hat" (*gaddan*) made of horsehair on her head. When the earl ridiculed this attire, instead "she wrapped (or 'hatted') herself with a silk scarf" (*[h]on tók þá silkidúk ok faldaði sér með*; [34.81.184–85]). The impression of a soft untailored cloth is also conveyed by Vesteinn's gift to his sister of a precious piece of *hǫfuðdúk* about thirty feet long, acquired in England and woven with gold thread (*Gísla saga*, 6.12.42).[59]

Cross-gender Dressing

There is little doubt that the regulations against cross-gender dressing were normally obeyed. No examples occur in the literature of saga heroes flaunting the rules in drag. Medieval Iceland was undoubtedly too poor to be able to stage the sartorial carnivals so beloved by modern ethnographers. Since female clothing—the *faldr* in particular—proclaimed sexual identification, it is not surprising, however, that people occasionally used cross-gender dress to escape difficult situations. Since these scenes aid our understanding of gender distinctions in clothing, they are worth examining. When Helgi Harðbeinsson was surprised by a group of hostile men at his mountain hut where he was in company only of a shepherd boy and women, he ordered the latter to "dress in male clothing" (*snarask í karlfǫt*) and ride as fast as possible to the main house for reinforcements in the hopes that the enemy would not notice "whether they were men or women" (*Lax*, 5.63.190).[60] The late *Víglundar saga* contains the story of Olof who during her husband's absence foiled an attempt of rape by dressing a servant woman in her own cape to receive the would-be rapist. Donning blue male clothing, carrying a sword, and feigning rage, she scared the assaulter off (14.8.77–78). Cases of women dressing like men, however, are rare.[61]

More frequent is the opposite cross dressing. The law prohibited a man from "disguise himself in the female head-dress or dress in female clothing [in order to seduce a woman]" (*feldr sér til vélar við kono, eða fer han i kvenklæðe*; [*Gg*, 2.176]; see also [1b.47]). The punishment was lesser outlawry. The saga literature, however, yields no examples of disguise for sexual advantages. That a man might don female clothing to escape a hopeless situation is seen on occasion, however, although not necessarily approved. During the burning of Bergþórshváll the women were allowed to leave, as was customary under the circumstances. Ástríðr told her brother-in-law, Helgi Njálsson, that she would "throw a female cape over you and wrap a scarf around your head" (*kasta yfir þik kvenskikkju ok falda þér við hǫfuðdúki*; [*Nj*, 12.129.329]) to enable him to leave safely with the women.[62] Although refusing at first, Helgi eventually acceded to her entreaties. Ástríðr arranged the scarf around his head and another sister-in-law put the cape over his shoulders. When he emerged between the two women, however, Flosi ordered "the tall woman with the broad shoulders" to be apprehended. Discarding his disguise, Helgi fought to his death.[63] Helgi's uneasiness over being caught in female clothing was reechoed by two young brothers in *Víg*. When Víglundr received a nasty wound in the forehead, his brother bandaged it with a piece of cloth torn from his shirt. Upon returning home, Víglundr's appearance elicited the greeting of "brother and sister" (*systkin*) from their father. To the question "Why do you call us by a female term?" (*Hvárn okkar kvenkennir þú*), the father answered that the one who wore the *faldr* must surely be a woman. Víglundr answered curtly that this was indeed not the case (14.14.89).[64]

By piecing together disparate episodes from the puzzles of *Vatn* and *Hall* a mini-drama can be reconstructed in which two men were saved through female clothing. At a wedding celebration þorkell Krafla killed a certain Glæðir. During the ensuing confusion þorkell headed toward the area where, as we saw, the women were putting on their head-dresses. He explained his predicament to Hildr who helped him escape through the *skot* (a covered passage running around the house; [*Vatn*, 8.44.118]). Hoping for repayment, Hildr reminded þorkell several years later that she had "saved his life" by pushing him under her *skikkjuskauti* ("lap of the cape"; *Hall*, 8.10.190), suggesting that he had escaped by first hiding under her skirt.

Hildr needed þorkell's help at this moment because her son had killed a man.[65] Because of kinship ties with the victim, þorkell felt obligated to take revenge.[66] Heading straight for the booth where he knew he would find Hildr's son, þorkell encountered the mother. Reminded of his debt, he responded brusquely that it had happened a long time ago. He ordered the women out so the men could search for the young man. The fuller version in *Vatn* recounted that Hildr "took off her head-dress and placed it on [her son]; she then took his seat so no more women would go out than was expected" (8.45.123). The shorter *Hall* added the important detail that since the son "was *faldinn*, he escaped and was not discovered" (8.10.190). In spite of þorkell's initial firmness, however, the author of *Vatn* suggested that Hildr understood that þorkell had devised a secret plan to help her. He urged the women to hurry so that Hildr would not have to witness the slaying of her son, but when the men thronged to perform their bloody act, he warned that they might kill each other in the confusion and proposed that they settle instead. In other words, not only did Hildr save her son's life by personally placing on his head the female identification badge, her *faldr*, but, according to one version, if þorkell's plan of settling had not been accepted, she risked her own life by joining the men on the bench where, presumably, her uncovered head with her hair tied up might have caused her to be mistaken for a man.[67] We notice that Hildr's lack of beard did not cause comment, again indicating the lack of importance of this safe gender marker.

Although cross-gender dressing is an infrequent theme in the sagas, individual identification through clothing was a common phenomenon—to be expected in a society where wardrobes were limited. Saga authors on occasion dress one character in another's clothes to produce dramatic effect through mistaken identity. Gísli thus saved his life twice by swapping clothes with a slave (*Gí*, 6.20.64–65; 6.26.81). The same trick was used by þormóðr who on another occasion avoided identification—and death—by turning his cloak inside out, thereby changing the color from black to white (*Fóst*, 6.23.231–39). As would be expected, clothes provided individual as well as sexual identity.

Ugliness

Before taking leave of the beautiful people in the sagas we should also note that their opposites, the ugly, likewise can be found. Although women were more likely to be described as "not particularly beautiful," than "ugly," as we saw in Kolbrún's case, the stronger term *ljótr* ("ugly") not only described certain men but also could be used as a nickname—even as a regular name. Although occurring more rarely, it was also affixed to women, as shown by the sorceress named Ljót in *Vatn*.[68] Men were considered handsome even when old, but, not surprisingly, old women were often designated ugly. Although Bjofrn was old enough to have trouble with his eyesight, he was still considered to be "a handsome . . . man" (*maðr . . . vænn*; [*BjHít*, 3.32.197]), whereas a certain þórdís was said to be "old, and both ugly and dark" (*gǫmul, bæði ljót ok svǫrt*; [*Drop*, 11.10.161–62]).

This last statement raises the discomforting observation that according to the oldest evidence Nordic people, along with their Continental contemporaries, identified beauty with blondness and considered dark skin and hair to be ugly. The nickname Ljótr "the black" (*inn svarti*; [*Nj*, 12.12.36]) is rare because it was redundant, while Ljótr "the Pale" (*inn bleiki*; [*Eg*, 2.64.201 and *Svarf*, 9.8.145]) deserves notice. It is important to recall that Kolbrún's lack of beauty was associated with her dark hair and eye brows. Two women in *Land*, both named Ljót, were known to be of partial or full Celtic origin. Wolfgang Krause suggests that their Pict genes may have given them a foreign look that occasioned the unflattering name.[69]

A Nordic origin for dark complexion, however, is given in *Geirmundar þáttr Heljarskinns*, the connecting link between the contemporary Icelanders portrayed in *Sturlunga saga* and their mythical Norwegian ancestors. The twin brothers Geirmundr and Hámundr eventually settled in Iceland and became important men, but in Norway they had been repudiated by their mother, the queen, at birth because of their appearance:

They were both extraordinarily big and hideously ugly in appearance
(*furðuliga ljótir ásynis*). But the worst thing about their ugliness was that
no one had ever seen darker skin than on these two boys.

Since the children were born during the king's absence, the queen
exchanged them with a slave's wife who had just given birth to an
exceptionally beautiful son. As the three boys grew up and the royal nature
of the twins became evident, however, the queen arranged a re-exchange.
Finally presented with his sons, the king conceded that they looked like his
offspring but added that he had never seen such "Hell's complexion"
(*heljarskinn*; [*Stur*, 1.1.5–6]), thus providing them with a permanent
nickname.

Conclusion

Although not nearly as rich and detailed as in Continental literature,
physical descriptions of men and women can be found in the Old Norse
sources. We have seen that they separate people into blond and dark,
beautiful and ugly, granting men a dominant presence in the first half of
these two binary groups. This is particularly well illustrated from the first
and the last chapters of *Egils saga*. Framing, as it were, his entire narrative
with an analysis of human beauty and its contrast, the author introduces two
Norwegian brothers, þórólfr and Grímr, in the first chapter. The older,
þórólfr, was "the most handsome of men" (*manna vænst*) whereas Grímr was
"a dark, ugly man like his forefathers" (*svart maðr ok ljótr, líkr feðr sínum*;
[2.1.5]). Although þórólfr died without progeny, his favored genes
nonetheless reappeared in his brother's offspring after Grímr settled in
Iceland. Nicknamed Skalla-Grímr (because he lost his hair), the latter
became the progenitor of a vast clan, known as the *Mýramannakyn* after the
place, Mýrar, where he settled upon arrival (2.28.73). Summarizing the
qualities of this clan in the last chapter of his narrative (2.87.299), the
author linked the offspring of þorsteinn, Egill's youngest son, to this
ancient clan. That Snorri Sturluson himself, who was perhaps the author of
Egils saga, also belonged to this lineage adds special poignancy to the
chapter as it joined the contemporary audience to the characters in the story.
The people of the *Mýramannakyn* were praised as being good poets, strong
men, good fighters, and, occasionally, wise individuals. In what seems like
a conscious effort to conclude the saga in the manner it began, the author
continued by describing the most remarkable feature of the clan: the
Mýramenn included both "the most beautiful" (*fríðastir*) and "the most ugly
people" (*ljótastir*) in Iceland. Providing no examples of the latter, the
author admitted nonetheless that they were more numerous. Among the
beautiful, however, four individuals were singled out: þorsteinn Egilsson,
Kjartan Oláfsson, Hallr Guðmundarson, and Helga in fagra, representing the
three generations succeeding Egill himself. We are already aware of the good
looks of Kjartan and Helga, and Hallr's praise was sung in *Lax* (5.45.136).

Þorsteinn, the pivotal figure between the old and the new branch of the *Mýramannakyn*, was described in the following way: "the most handsome in appearance of all men, light blond of hair and bright of countenance" (*allra manna fríðastr sýnum, hvítr á hár ok bjartr álitum*; [2.79.274]). Snorri—if he indeed was the author—used the masculine plural (*fríðastir, ljótastir*) when referring to the appearances of both groups. Among these three handsome men, however, he included only one beautiful young girl, Helga. We can hardly find a better illustration of the emphasis of males over females when the saga authors considered human beauty.

Although admitting to the importance of human attractiveness in general, the sources are, as we have seen, reticent about founding beauty on specific bodily or facial features. This is especially true for women. We recall that the physical descriptions of women are exceedingly few and short. We have culled practically all references to female beauty extant in the literature, and we have learned that beautiful women are characterized by a single adjective or identified by brief references to hair or clothing.

The use of the family sagas invariably raises the vexing problem of their historical context, also when the subject is corporal beauty. Written in Iceland during the Christian era of the thirteenth century, their stories are set in the pagan tenth and eleventh centuries. Those themes we have been pursuing—perceptions of the body and beauty—do not lie on the surface of the narratives but must be distilled by paying close attention to inadvertent details. It would of course be too much to find in these scattered phrases attitudes or traits attributable to the characters of the tenth and eleventh centuries. Rather, they articulate the tastes and opinions of the thirteenth-century society that inscribed the narratives.

This should not lead to the conclusion, however, that Christianity in medieval Iceland imposed ascetic restraints which prevented writers from revealing the female body. The absent female body in the Norse literature is the result neither of modesty nor of morality but, most likely, of meteorology. In Mediterranean cultures both sexes wore togas. The thinness and suppleness of the fabric and the looseness of the fit permitted by the mild climate revealed the body underneath and identified its sex more readily than in the North, particularly in Iceland, where people of both sexes needed heavy cloth and fur to keep warm. Multiple layers of coarse wool in the shape of a toga would effectively have hidden the body and made gender identification virtually impossible. Germanic people, therefore, did not wear togas. The process of sexual identification was removed from the body and attached to clothing. The need to distinguish between male and female clothes directed the focus to the most apparent sexual distinctions between men's and women's bodies. Allowing room for the penis, tailored pants—the Germanic gift to the world of fashion—were worn by men. Following the contours of the body, women's clothes acknowledged their breasts. While it would seem doubtful that women in Iceland indulged in decollete outside the house, they may have worn, as we have suggested, an inner shirt of this shape that permitted the nipples to be perceived through the fitted outer covering. At least it is clear that female clothes clung closely enough to the upper torso to reveal the female body.[70] As Icelanders came in contact with the larger world of Western Europe they became progressively susceptible to foreign fashions.[71] If, however, we accept the premise that gender differentiations in clothing were originally dictated by climatic conditions, the basic traits of body and beauty we have identified in the sources may be applicable to pagan Iceland of the tenth and the eleventh centuries, the purported context of the sagas, as well as to the authors' own age.

Regardless of time, however, the greater attention to male than female beauty would suggest that Old Norse culture had not yet constructed a fully developed male gaze, even by the thirteenth century. When men did take a look, climate forced them to notice female clothing rather than the body. We have also seen that male attire elicited more comment than female. The shadowy existence of the female body masked beneath layers of clothing caused its presence to be understated in literature. The attention devoted to female hair and its head-dress, however, does suggest that these attributes became the primary focus of Nordic men as they looked at women. Perhaps masculine awareness that men might lose their own manes sharpened their consciousness of female "otherness" as women's locks kept growing. The identification of female beauty with abundant hair—still an important feature in perceptions of female beauty—may have constituted the first step toward a male gaze in the North.

Notes

Shorter versions of this article were presented at the 26th International Congress on Medieval Studies, Kalamazoo, Michigan, May 1991 and at the Eighth International Saga Conference, Gothenburg, Sweden, August 1991. Support toward travel expenses from Towson State University History Department and Faculty Development Office is gratefully acknowledged.

The saga texts are quoted mainly from the editions in the series Íslenzk fornrit (ÍF) (Reykjavik, 1933–) giving volume, chapter, and page. Those infrequent sagas not extant in this series are quoted from the older Samfund til Udgivelse af Gammel Nordisk Litteratur (SUGNL). For the numerous sagas available in English translations, see Donald Fry, *Norse Sagas Translated into English: A Bibliography* (New York, 1980). The first time a text is quoted, whether in the main body or in the notes, it is given in full. Afterward, the following abbreviations are used:

Bjarnar saga Hítdœlakappa	ÍF 3	BjHít
Droplaugarsona saga	ÍF 11	Drop
Egils saga	ÍF 2	Eg
Eyrbyggja saga	ÍF 4	Eyr
Fóstbrœðra saga	ÍF 6	Fóst
Gísla saga	ÍF 6	Gí
Grágás		Gg

Grettis saga	ÍF 7	Gr
Gunnlaugs saga	ÍF 3	Gunn
Hallfreðar saga	ÍF 8	Hall
Hávarðar saga Ísfirðings	ÍF 6	Háv
Heiðarvíga saga	ÍF 3	Heið
Jómsvíkinga saga		Jóms
Kormáks saga	ÍF 8	Kor
Landnámabók	ÍF 1	Land
Laxdúla saga	ÍF 5	Lax
Njáls saga	ÍF 12	Nj
Orkneyinga saga	ÍF 34	Ork
Svarfdœla saga	ÍF 9	Svarf
Sturlunga saga		Stur
Vatnsdœla saga	ÍF 8	Vatn
Víglundar saga	ÍF 14	Víg
Vǫlsunga saga		Vs

1   As far as I know, the first to use the term was Laura Mulvey, "Visual Pleasure and Narrative Cinema," *Screen* (1975), rpt. Laura Mulvey, *Visual and Other Pleasures* (Bloomington, 1989), 14–26; 19.

2   For Anglo-Saxon poetry, see Paul Beekman Taylor, "The Old English Poetic Vocabulary of Beauty," *New Readings on Women in Old English Literature*, ed. Helen Damico and Alexandra Hennessey Olsen (Bloomington, 1990), 211–21.

3   Helga Kress has suggested that *Laxdœla saga* was authored by a woman; see her "Meget samstavet må det tykkes deg. Om kvinneopprør og genretvang i Sagaen om Laksdölene" (Swedish), *Historisk tidskrift* (1980), 266–80.

4   William Ian Miller, *Bloodtaking and Peacemaking: Feud, Law, and Society in Saga Iceland* (Chicago, 1990).

5   See Alice M. Colby, *The Portrait in Twelfth-Century French Literature* (Geneva, 1965).

6   For this investigation Wolfgang Krause, *Die Frau in der Sprache der altisländischen Familiengeschichten* (Göttingen, 1926) is invaluable. For this section, see in particular 79–83. Occasionally less specific terms are used as when the young Bjǫrn is said to be "pleasant to look at" (*sœmiligr at sjá*; [*Bjarnar saga hítdœlakappa*, 3.1.112]).

7   Further descriptions of Oláfr's good looks are found in the same text in 13.28, 20.49, 22.62–63.

8   See for example, Þorsteinn fagri in *Þorsteins saga hvíta* (11.3.7) and ǫnundr inn fagri in *Njáls saga* (12.72.176).

9   Thus when the author of *Háv* stated about Hallgrímr Asbrandsson that he was "big and strong" (*mikill ok sterkr*) but "not handsome" (*ófríðr sýnum*), he quickly added, "but still manly" (*en þó karlmannligr*; [6.8.318]). For a similar formula, see Herjólfr in *Lax*, 5.7.15.

10   See, for example, the long description of Kjartan in *Lax*, 5.28.76–77. For an unusual and detailed description of a man, see Klaufi in *Svarfdœla saga*, 11.15.162. Although outside the family sagas, *Vǫlsunga saga*—the prose retelling of the complete Sigurðr story—illustrates most vividly the contrast between long descriptions of male beauty and short references to the same qualities in women; Sigurðr's own looks command more than a page, whereas the women in his life, the valkyrie on the mountain, Brynhildr (in this version these two women are identical), and Guðrún each receive only one of the adjectives denoting beauty; Magnus Olsen, ed. *Vǫlsunga saga ok Ragnars saga Loðbrókar*, SUGNL (Copenhagen, 1906–08), 23.55–56 (Sigurðr), 21.48 (Brynhildr on the mountain), 25.58 (Brynhildr in the tower), and 26.60 (Guðrún).

11   In the same saga the middle-aged Katla's obsession with the young Gunnlaugr is almost palpable; see especially 4.15.28 and 4.16.29. The aging Queen Gunnhildr's appetite for young men is attested in several sagas.

12   On this problem, see Bjarni Einarsson, "Um þormóð skáld og unnusturnar tvær," *Gripla* 5 (1983), rpt. *Mælt mál og forn fræði* (Reykjavik, 1987), 137–49; Jenny Jochens, "He Spat on þórir's Portrait and Kissed Ástríðr's: Manifestations of Male Love in Old Norse," to appear.

13   See, for example, the scattered descriptions of Oláfr Hǫskuldsson in *Lax* chs. 22–23 (5.22–23.69–66) and of Kjartan (5.44.134–35). We also notice that weapons formed part of a man's attire; in fact, weapons were often mentioned first in a fixed formula: "he was well attired in weapons and clothing (*hann var vel búinn at vápnum ok klæðum*; [*Lax*, 5.20.49 and 5.22.62]). See also Hrafn in *Vatnsdœla saga*, who "paid great attention to weapons and clothes" (*bjósk mjǫk at vápnum ok klæðum*; [8.17.47]). Details for the two groups of attire can be found, for example, for Geirmundr in *Lax*, 5.29.79.

14   On the only occasion when Guðrún's true love Kjartan (*Lax*) talked about her notorious beauty, he referred to the importance of clothes; after the precious *motr* ("head-dress;" see below) had disappeared at Guðrún's farm, Kjartan's wife made a snide remark that Guðrún had worn it and that it became her well. Blushing with anger, Kjartan answered that Guðrún did not need the head-dress to "look better in clothing" (*sama betr*) than all other women (5.47.145).

15   In this connection the word *kurteiss*, the Icelandic form of the French *courtois*, is of interest. In certain cases "well-dressed" should be added to a list of several possible translations. This is thus the case when the author of *Lax* stated about Guðrún that she was "so well-dressed that at the time whatever fineries other women wore, they seemed like cheap trinkets besides hers" (*kurteis kona, svá at í þann tíma þóttu allt barnavípur, þat er aðrar konur hǫfðu í skarti hjá henni*; [5.32.86]). Likewise, when Hǫskuldr in *Nj* invited þorvaldr to inspect Hallgerðr's *yfirlit . . . ok kurteisi*, he undoubtedly had her physical beauty and her dress in mind; this reading is reinforced by a variant text that for these words substitutes the expression "her looks" (*ásjónu hennar*; [12.9.31]).

16   *Gunn* demonstrates that love caused by beauty could lead to disasters that kept unfolding for years. Gunnlaugr's infatuation with Helga was reciprocated as Helga was smitten by Gunnlaugr's good looks; observing her at a feast after her wedding to another man, the author remarked that "she could not keep her eyes from Gunnlaugr, thereby proving the old proverb that 'eyes can not hide a woman's love for a man'" (3.11.89). Passion caused by beauty was noticeable in *Eg* in the match between Bjǫrn and þóra. Finding her to be "a beautiful girl to whom he took a great fancy" (*mey fagra, þá er honum fannsk mikit um*; [2.32.83]), Bjǫrn asked for her in marriage, but her brother turned him down. He abducted her twice, and although they eventually were formally married, their union and their daughter's inheritance continued to pose serious problems throughout the saga.

17   Generally, fine clothes were admired also for men, but this is not the only case where criticism against excessive male interest in clothing was noticeable. More strongly, in *Eyr* Snorri's frugality in not spending his money on clothes while abroad turned out to his advantage, although he was laughed at by his fellow travellers (4.13.23).

18   The various manuscripts of *Grágás* are available as follows: *Gg* 1a, b: *Grágás: Konungsbók*, ed. Vilhjálmur Finsen (Copenhagen, 1852); *Gg* 2: *Grágás: Staðarholsbók*, ed. Vilhjálmur Finsen (Copenhagen, 1879); *Gg* 3: *Grágás: Skálholtsbók*, ed. Vilhjálmur Finsen (Copenhagen, 1883); *Gg* 1–3, rpt. (Odense, 1974). The first half of *Konungsbók* (*Gg* 1a, 1–217) has been translated; Andrew Dennis, Peter Foote, and Richard Perkins, *Laws of Early Iceland: Grágás* [Winnipeg, 1980]).

19   *Bandamanna saga*, 7.9.339; the passage is found only in the longer text in the Möðruvallabók.

20   In the same saga, at the negotiations concerning Hallgerðr's second marriage Hǫskuldr explained her inner qualities to þorvaldr and his brother, but invited them to see for themselves about "her looks and behavior" (*yfirlit hennar ok kurteisi*; [*Nj*, 12.9.31]); see also note 15.

21   A slight variation is found in 4.28.70. In this text it is not clear whether Ásdís acted on her own behalf or at her father's instigation, but in *Heiðarvíga saga* where the same story is told, the father was in charge: "Styrr tells Ásdís to get dressed in her best clothes" (*lætr Styrr A'sdísi búa sik sem allra bezt*; [3.4.222–23]). In *Grettis saga* a woman was characterized simply as "young and all dressed up" (*ung ok skrautbúin*; [7.63.208]).

22   Women's bodies seemed to shine through their clothes, as it were, only in the episodes describing the illicit visits of berserks. Since these fearsome intruders invariably demanded women, a nervous sexuality is almost palpable. The women were not described by the usual epithets of beauty but rather by the terms "grown enough to be ready for marriage" (*gjafvaxta*; [*Heið*, 3.4.221; *Gr*, 6.40.135] or *frumvaxta*; [*Gr*, 7.19.62]), suggesting sexual availability for any taker strong enough to overcome the family's objections. The berserk episodes are identified in Benjamin Blaney, "The Berserk Suitor: The Literary Application of a Stereotyped Theme," *Scandinavian Studies* 54 (1982), 279–94.

23   See, for example, Sherry B. Ortner, "Is Female to Male as Nature Is to Culture?" *Woman, Culture, and Society*, ed. Michelle Zimbalist Rosaldo and Louise Lamphere (Stanford, 1974), 67–87.

24   On the importance of women's cloth making in Iceland, see Nanna Damsholt, "The Role of Icelandic Women in the Sagas and in the Production of Homespun Cloth," *Scandinavian Journal of History* 9 (1984), 75–90.

25   A similar passage is found in *Gg* 1b.47 where male clothing is referred to as *karlfötom*.

26   This episode does not fit the theme of "the illicit love visit" and the relationship should not be translated as an "affair," as done by Magnusson and Pálsson (Penguin, 124). The legality of the situation is suggested by the expression that þórðr "paid court to þorvaldr and Guðrún . . . and people talked about love between þórðr and Guðrún" (*gerði sér dátt við þau þorvald ok Guðrúnu . . . ok fel þar mǫrg umræða á um kærleika þeira þórðar ok Guðrúnar*; [5.34.93]). The first half of this expression (*gerði sér dátt við*) can have either a woman or a man as its object; see *Eg*, 2.35.88 and 2.41.105, respectively. On these visits, see Jochens, "The Illicit Love Visit: An Archaeology of Old Norse Sexuality" (*Journal of History of Sexuality* 1 (1991), 357–92.

27   William Miller has suggested that the shirt's low neckline reappeared, this time as a bloody seam on þórðr's body, when Auðr, seeking revenge for her divorce, slashed him across both nipples as he was lying in bed alone. Since she also wounded his right hand, the curve would seem to be bending in the wrong direction; William Ian Miller (note 4), 354, note 35.

28   See also the description of Hallgerðr wearing a "tunic" (*kyrtill*) covered with a "cloak" (*skikkju*). Referring to her hair as falling across her "bosom," the author used the term *bringa*, a word applicable to both sexes, thus suggesting that on this occasion when she was dressed in all her finery, her shape was noticeable but her breasts were covered (*Nj*, 12.33.85).

29   In *Gull-þóris saga* a man is nicknamed Vafspiarra-Grimr because of his habit of wrapping his white pants around his ankles with these bands (SUGNL 26.10.21).

30   For these, see also *Nj*, 12.134.349, *Gunn*, 3.6.68 and *Eyr*, 4.45.129.

31   See the brief reference in *Ljósvetninga saga* to a certain þórhildr in pants; since she also was equipped with a helmet and an axe and was about to predict the future, her outfit was probably ritualistic and does not reflect normal female attire (10.11[21].59).

32   *Barðar saga* knows of a slave woman known by the name of *Skinnbrók* ("Leather pants"); Jón Skaptason and Phillip Pulsiano ed. and tr., *Barðar saga* (New York, 1983), 3.12.

33   In *Vatn* a man was wearing a "a cape of fine cloth" (*slæður af góðu klæði*) so long that he got it dirty from riding and cut a piece off the hem the width of a span (8.31.84).

34   The Swedish Princess Ingigerðr gave her fiancé at the time, the Norwegian King Oláfr a "fur cape" (*slæður af pell* [*Oláfs saga helga*, 27.80.117]).

35   A different case could be made for the boots, although nobody objected to them; Hjalmar Falk, *Altwestnordische Kleiderkunde* (Videnskapsselskapets Skrifter. II. Hist.-Filos. Klasse, 1918, No. 3 (Kristiania, 1919), 138, argues from the Norwegian legislation that *bóta* were for female feet, whereas men used "shoes" (*skoar*); see R. Keyser, P.A. Munch, eds., *Norges gamle love*, 5 vols. (Christiania, 1846–95), 3.13 for 1282.

36   Two other saga passages refer to men being used as women every ninth night, but they do include specific clothing; see *þorsteins saga Síðu-Hallsonar*, 11.3.308 and *Króka-Refs saga*, 14.7.308. On this subject, see Preben Meulengracht Sørensen, *The Unmanly Man: Concepts of Sexual Defamation in Early Northern Society*, tr. Joan Turville-Petre (Odense, 1983).

37   The color blue is associated with vengeance and often worn by men as they set out on their expeditions. In rare cases women on similar occasions were dressed in blue; see the story in *Eyr* of the magician Geirríðr out to unmask the magic of her colleague Katla; (4.20.53). This association is undoubtedly also behind the author's choice of color here.

38   On the use of the unique expression, "as masculine women" (*sem karlkonur*; [5.35.96]) at this place, see Krause, *Die Frau*, 67.

39   The suggestion was first presented by Valtýr Guðmundsson, "Ur sögu íslenzkra búninga," *Afmælisrit til dr. phil. Kr. Kálund* (Copenhagen, 1914), 66–87; 72, 74 and repeated by Falk, *Kleiderkunde*, 122, note 2. Neither provide a reason. The latter argues that the first syllable of the word (*set*) refers to the noun for 'seat,' but it could as well be related to the verb *setja*, to 'place' or 'insert.'

40   *Morkinskinna*, ed. Finnur Jónsson, SUGNL 53 (Copenhagen, 1932), 412. The passage is cited by Falk, 120, note 1, who argues for the normal use of two pair of pants. We know from other texts that men pulled down their pants to urinate and thus were used to getting cold; see *Jómsvikinga saga*, ed. N.F. Blake (London, 1962), 36.41.

41   Light blond was also þorsteinn's in *Gunn* (3.1.51), whereas young Bolli was "blond" (*gulr*; [*Lax*, 5.63.187]), Arngrímr "red-blond" (*rauðbleikr*; [*Eyr*, 4.12.21]), Snorri in the same saga "auburn" (*bleikhárr*; [4.15.26]), Gunnlaugr "light-brown" (*ljósjarpr*; [*Gunn*, 3.1.51; 3.4.59], and Kormakr and þormóðr "black"; (*svartr*, [*Kormáks saga*, 8.2.206 and *Vatn*, 8.2.124]). Klaufi even had "coal black eyebrows and hair" (*svartastr bæði á brynn ok hár*; [*Svarf*, 9.15.162]).

42   Likewise, Egill's hair had been black when he was a child, but it turned "wolf-grey" (*úlffrátt*), and he early become "bald" (*skǫllóttr*; [*Eg*, 2.31.80; 2.55.143]).

43   When Bróðir, a berserk who was a lapsed Christian, was said to have "hair so long that he tucked it under his belt" (*hár svá mikit, at hann vafði undir belti sér*) it seems to be a case of Viking romanticism, especially since the author added, for good measure, that "it was black" (*þat var svart*; [*Nj*, 12.155.446]).

44 Another Hallgerðr was killed by her husband as she was "combing her hair that fell all around her to the floor" because she refused to go with him; *Land*, 1.S152/H122.192–93. In *Droplaugarsona saga* a woman washed her hair that was "long and beautiful and well arranged" (11.1.138).

45 Although outside the scope of the family sagas, it is worth noticing the encounter between Sigurðr and the woman on the mountaintop as described in the prose before the first stanza of the Edda poem *Sigrdrífomál* and repeated almost identically in the prose rendition of the full Sigurðr story in *Voflsunga saga*. Attracted by the light on the mountain, Sigurðr climbed to the top and found "a *maðr* ('man' or 'person') asleep in full armor. He took the helmet off this person's head. Then he saw it was a woman" (*Vs*, 21.48). It seems that Sigurðr was not puzzled by the person's lack of a beard, and we must assume that he perceived the female identity only as her long hair was freed from the helmet.

46 *Edda Snorra Sturlusonar*, ed. Finnur Jónsson (Copenhagen, 1931), 38.

47 There is an extensive literature on this visit, pertaining, in particular, to the countess's marital status for which her hair would be an important indicator. For a comprehensive treatment, see Rudolf Meissner, "Ermengarde, Vicegräfin von Narbonne, und Jarl Rögnvald," *Arkiv för Nordisk Filologi* 37(1925):140–191, esp. 161–66 for her hair. The normalcy of long hair for young girls is also clear from *Kjalnesinga saga* where a giant's daughter named Fríðr was said to have "loose hair in the custom of young girls" (*slegit hár sem meyja síðr er*; [14.13.29–30]).

48 Finnur Jónsson, ed., *Den norsk-islandske Skjaldedigtning*, 2 vols. (Copenhagen, 1908–15), 1B, 456; str. 10. See also Snorri Sturluson's stanza describing a woman who was combing her hair; ibid. 2B, 90. Admiring Steingerðr's hair as she was combing it, Kormakr estimated it at a high price (*Kor*, 8.3.212–13).

49 On medieval beards, see *Apologiae dvae*, ed. R.B.C. Huygens, *With an introduction on Beards in the Middle Ages* by Giles Constable; Corpus Christianorum 62 (Turnholt, 1985).

50 Paul Gaimard published his work, *Voyage en Islande et au Groenland*, in eight volumes in Paris 1838–52. Reduced and enhanced with colors, Auguste Mayer's pictures have been reproduced in *Íslandsmyndir Mayers 1836*, ed. Arni Björnsson and Ageir S. Björnsson (Reykjavik, 1986). Executed before the technique of photography was available, they are particularly valuable. The comment to picture 21 suggests that women at this time put their headgear on in the morning and left it on until they went to bed at night (50).

51 See Richard Perkins, "*þrymskviða*, Stanza 20, and a Passage from *Víglundar saga*," *Saga-Book* 22 (1988), 279–84.

52 Both items were stolen by the disreputable Hrappr who later offered them to þráinn (12.88.214–16).

53 Such a present was known as a *bekkjargjoff* if the woman had been married before. Mentioning Guðrún who was both divorced and widowed, Ingibjqrg used this word, but when Kjartan finally gave it to the previously unmarried Hrefna, it was termed *línfé* (*Lax*, 5.43.131, 45.138).

54 It is probable that the expression about Hallgerðr at her second wedding that she "sat on the bench and *samði sér vel*" referred to her looks and clothing (including the *faldr*) and not to her behavior, as translated by Magnusson and Pálsson (12.14.45; tr. 67).

55 Enlarging his analysis beyond the Norse world, Meissner (note 47) attempted to show that visible hair was not associated with marriage but was related more to fashion and social status. It is, of course, dangerous to draw conclusions from silence, but the Norse evidence is consistent in associating visible hair with marital availability or limiting it to the privacy of the bedroom.

56   For a ritual interpretation of this scene, see Carol J. Clover, "Hildigunnr's Lament," *Structure and Meaning in Old Norse Literature*, ed. John Lindow et sl. (Odense, 1986), 141–83.

57   Eggert Olafsen and Bjarne Povelsen, *Reise igiennem Island*, 2 vols. (Sorøe, 1772), 1, tab. 7, presents a drawing of a woman wearing a *krókfaldr* (reproduced in Falk, *Kleiderkunde*, 100). Also in Perkins (note 51).

58   It is of interest to notice that Guðrún's two middle husbands were represented by rings, the Christian symbol of marriage, although—as pointed out by Gestr—Christianity did not arrive officially in Iceland until well into her third marriage.

59   Falk, 102, suggests that the cloth was intended to serve as head-dresses for the three women in the family; each of them would thus receive about ten feet, ample to make a turban-looking head-dress. Occasionally such a cloth may have been used as a veil to hide the woman's face; see the story in *Jóms* (Blake, 25.27) of a double wedding where the brides were *síðfaldit* in the evening, but the next morning they did not *skupla*. Both *síð* and *skupla* refer to face masks, but since the whole story deals with deceit, it does not permit Falk's conclusions about the general use of veils at weddings; see Falk, *Kleiderkunde*, 102–10.

60   One is reminded of Paul the Deacon's famous story of how the Lombards received their name.

61   On the importance of the color blue, see note 37. For an authentic case from the contemporary sagas, see the story of Yngvildr þorgilsdóttir who in 1158 "cut her hair in the style of a man and donned male clothing" in order to escape with her lover, for whom she secretly had borne a daughter; *Sturlu saga*, in *Sturlunga saga*, ed. Jón Jóhannesson et al., 2 vols. (Reykjavik, 1946), 1.9.72–73.

62   There is no further information of the features that distinguished a "female" cape.

63   As a rare admission of female pleasure in an attractive male, we notice that these two women attempted to help their brother-in-law, but paid no attention to their own husbands who also were present and who perished in the fire. It is difficult to find any other reason than Helgi's physical attractiveness—he was the best looking of the three Njálssons—to explain their behavior. The brothers are described in 12.25.70.

64   On this passage, see Richard Perkins (note 51).

65   The son was called Hermundr in *Vatn* and Brandr in *Hall*.

66   The man was the son of þorkell's wife's sister. þorkell's marriage had taken place after the incident at the wedding and is mentioned in *Vatn* (8.45.122), but his wife's name and family relationship is found only in a variant text of *Hall*; see 8.10.188, note 1.

67   On the complicated relationship between the two sagas, see the introductions to the ÍF edition (8.xv–lxxix) and Bjarni Einarsson, *To skaldesagaer* (Oslo, 1976), 159–77).

68   In *Færeyinga saga* þóra is characterized as "not very pretty" (*ekki dávæn*; [ed. Halldórsson (Reykjavik, 1987), 35.81]). Concerning men described as *ljótr*, see *Fóst*, 6.23.229, 238, *Háv*, 6.15.343, *Eyr*, 4.15.27. As a regular name for men, Ljótr occurs close to two dozen times in the family sagas.

69   See Krause, *Die Sprache*, 79–80. The two women in *Land* are found in 1.S257/H221.284–85 and 1.M13/S349/H308.354–55.

70   Kormakr's sudden infatuation with the young Steingerðr was prompted by his having had a glimpse of her ankles; although she was hiding behind a door at the moment, this was the only part of her body he would ever be able to appreciate. It is characteristic that he praised in poetry the visible parts of her body, her ankles, her eyes, and her hair; (*Kor*, 8.3.207–15). In the same saga a woman, described as "beautiful and shapely" (*væn ok vel at sér*) was nicknamed *mjóbeina* "slender-ankle" [8.15.257]),

suggesting an almost Victorian focus on this part of the female anatomy. On this subject, see William A. Rossi, *The Sex Life of the Foot and Shoe* (London, 1977).

71   That this particularly Icelandic item was exposed to foreign, especially French, influence is suggested by the term *franzeisfaldr* found in a Norwegian charter from 1352, quoted in Falk, 100.

EROTIC MAGIC IN MEDIEVAL EUROPE

Richard Kieckhefer

A case might be made that the expressions "love-magic" and "sex-magic" are tautological, since most cultures recognize love and sex as ideally mysterious and magical in themselves, even without amulets and philtres. But precisely because of this inherently mysterious nature, erotic states and activities are distinctly vulnerable to magical intrusion: magic operates most powerfully at moments when one feels seized by unfamiliar forces at least partly beyond one's control. No doubt for this reason, virtually all types of sources at our disposal for the history of medieval magic—magicians' own handbooks, laws and treatises condemning magic, judicial records, and fictional literature—give erotic magic a significant role. The authors of the *Malleus maleficarum* proposed that "inordinate love of one person for another," which they call "philocaption," is "the best known and most general form of witchcraft." Elsewhere they argue, "God allows the devil more power over the venereal act, by which the original sin is handed down, than over other human actions."[1] And while the *Malleus* is not in all respects typical of late medieval thinking on the question, its emphasis on erotic magic is not altogether idiosyncratic.

People at various levels of medieval society appear to have had recourse to magic for sex and love. Erotic magic could play a role in court intrigue: in the early fourteenth century Mahaut of Artois was accused of accidentally killing Louis X with a love potion designed to restore his love for his wife, and in 1376 a tribunal tried a friar for providing Alice Perrers with magical means to obtain the love of Edward III.[2] The lower strata of society were no less tempted by amatory magic: Gabrina degli Albeti, sentenced to mutilation by a town court at Reggio in 1375, and Matteuccia Francisci, burned for sorcery by a municipal court at Todi in 1428, seem to have specialized in love-magic, and provided amatory counsel for the abused and forsaken women of their towns.[3]

A disproportionate number of the people tried for use of erotic magic were women—probably not because women were more inclined to this offense than men, but because women's manipulation of male affections was more intensely feared, and because men would be more likely to explain their irregular liaisons by charging their mistresses with bewitchment. Here as elsewhere in Western culture, women seemed the more likely sources of temptation. Late medieval men accused women of bewitching them, much as men in early America invoked the stereotype of the primitive temptress, the "sable Venus," to excuse their sexual liberties with Black women.[4]

Yet male fascination manifested itself not only in its etymological sense of "bewitchment": men might fear female charms, but they could not resist at least a horrified curiosity, as became clear in 1016 at the town of Trier. The local archbishop, Poppo, had commissioned a nun to make a pair of liturgical footgear for him. The nun made these slippers, but allegedly she bewitched her handiwork, so that the prelate had no sooner put them on his feet than he found himself inflamed with passion for her. The archbishop proceeded to conduct a series of experiments: he had other clerics and finally a local secular official don the footgear, and they too were immediately infatuated with the nun. Eventually she was expelled from the monastery, while the archbishop, fearing divine condemnation for whatever guilt he had incurred in the incident, sought to expiate his offense with a pilgrimage to Jerusalem.[5]

Fear of erotic magic led to its condemnation and prohibition by ecclesiastical and secular authorities alike. As early as the sixth century, the penitential of Finnian prescribed six years of penance for anyone who administered a potion "for the sake of wanton love."[6] Secular legislation tended to be less specific about the magic it was prohibiting, but rulers could sometimes be quite detailed in their legislation, especially when they were influenced by clerics: Louis the Pious issued a capitulary in 829 condemning the use of love potions, enchanted foods, and charms worn on people's bodies to influence the minds of others.[7] Burchard of Worms, whose eleventh-century *Corrector* is more concerned with superstitious belief than with superstitious practice, repudiated the idea that a woman "through certain spells and incantations can turn about the minds of men, either from hatred to love or from love to hatred."[8] For the most part, however, authorities were concerned with use rather than erroneous beliefs about magic. In their minds erotic magic threatened private morality and public order just as much as bodily harm and death, destructive storms, or theft. Because it violated the free will of those it ensnared and disrupted the social order, erotic magic was categorized not with the white magic of healing, prevention of misfortune, and recovery of goods, but with the black or maleficent magic of sorcery.

The Purposes of Erotic Magic

Erotic magic could be used to induce a person to become a sexual partner ("sex-inducing magic"), to encourage an intimate and lasting amorous relationship ("love-magic"), or to enhance the sexual experience of partners who were already willing ("sex-enhancing magic"). Magic could, of course, also serve various gynecological purposes such as contraception, abortion, promotion of fertility, and ease of childbirth.[9] It was also used to discern whether or not a woman was a virgin, or whether she was faithful.

But this article will be limited to magic relating directly to love and sex, not to their consequences, however interesting and important the latter may be.

The simplest and most basic distinction to be made in the realm of erotic magic is that between magical aphrodisiacs (or sex-inducing magic) and love-charms (or love-magic).[10] As we will see, this distinction need not be reckoned absolute, but one must grant a *prima facie* distinction between superficial, fleeting attraction and heartfelt, enduring commitment.

Theoretically, people might use magic simply to incite passionate desire for sex, even without any specific sexual partner in mind. Thus, Albert the Great said that the allectory "has the power to arouse sexual desire, to make one pleasing and constant, victorious and distinguished" and the *Book of Secrets* falsely ascribed to Albert prescribed carrying henbane on one's person to make the bearer "pleasant and delectable" so that he would be "loved of women," which probably means sexually appealing to women generally.[11] Even more blunt are the Ashmole ad Peterborough lapidaries, which say that allectory makes a man lecherous or "excites the service of Venus."[12] Such indiscriminate application, however, is rare. Sex-inducing magic is generally a means of arousing desire for a specific partner, either for the magician or for the magician's client.

More often than not (despite the stereotype in the judicial record) the purpose indicated in the magical manuals was to make a woman pliable to a man's desire. The lapidaries of high and late medieval Europe, following Marbode of Rennes, said the "hawkstone" could serve this purpose; presumably it was carried on one's person, as vervain was borne for the same purpose.[13] Or a woman's passion could be aroused by approaching her in her sleep and placing under her head a wad of wool soaked in bat's blood.[14] A yet more exotic way to arouse a woman sexually was to put ant eggs in her bath, which would so inflame her womb that willy-nilly she would be driven to copulation. To this formula is added the instruction to write out the nonsense words "amet lamet te misael," but it is not clear where one is to write this inscription, or what connection if any it has with the use of ant eggs.[15] The purpose of all this business with ant eggs and gibberish might be taken as ambiguous, since the manuscript gives the heading "Nota ad coitum, ad amorem," which suggests an equation of sex-magic with love-magic, but in this context it is probably safe to take amor as referring to passion. So too, when a manuscript enjoins its reader to write the words "pax + pix + abyra + syth + samasic" on a hazelwood, hit a woman on the head three times with the stick, then kiss her at once to obtain her "love," we are probably safe in assuming that the love in question is a matter of immediate sexual passion, not "esteem enlivened by desire."[16]

At times it is a woman who is attempting to arouse a man. Thus, the penitential of Egbert of York requires a three-year fast for a woman who "mixes pepper seed in her food and thereby hopes to be the more attractive to a man,"[17] but usually the practitioner is male—even in the case of a married couple. Thus, the Mirabilia mundi ascribed to Albert the Great advises that if "a woman desireth not her husband, he should "take a little of the tallow of a buck Goat, . . . and let him anoint his privy member with it, and do the act of generation afterward with any [other]."[18]

One might conclude from this evidence that many people in medieval Europe were desperate for sexual encounters. The distance between medieval culture and our own was surely not so great that putting ant eggs in a woman's bath, or hitting her head with a magically inscribed stick, would then have seemed normal and reasonable behavior. Anointing one's phallus with goat-grease might seem marginally less odd, but this too suggests a high degree of fervor, conviction, and perhaps deprivation. No doubt many people were indeed desperate, and did not trust their own powers of attraction; medieval Europe had no monopoly on such problems, and surely there are individuals today who would use such techniques if they thought they might work. That such procedures were actually used is clear enough from the trial records, which show that some people would perform extravagant deeds in hope of spectacular success. Indeed, it may have been easier to expect success from a dramatic and even clearly transgressive act than from a milder and more nearly conventional one.

We must also reckon with the possibility, however, that not all these prescriptions were written seriously, even if at times they were seriously read and used. Magical formulas sometimes read like self-parody, and it is difficult to know when the comic elements were intended. It is not impossible—nay, it is perhaps likely—that the writer who suggested tapping a prospective lover with a magical stick did so in jest.

Even devices meant in earnest may sometimes have been more theoretical than practical in intent. When Marbode of Rennes and others wrote their lapidaries, their main concern was to unfold the marvelous powers of the gems rather than to recommend the actual use of all these *virtutes*. Such works were more analytical than prescriptive. Thus, the authors are often vague in specifying just how the wondrous powers of the gems are to be exploited, and the very organization of their works (according to the various stones, rather than by functions) suggests that they were not meant as a reference guide for people with practical needs. The same might be said about the Pseudo-Albertine *Book of Secrets* and other such works. It was in any case possible, of course, that some readers would attempt in practice what was meant as theory.

Whether theoretical or practical in intent, magic could serve as a means not only to induce sexual desire but also for the second of our purposes, to arouse love.[19] To be sure, this distinction between sex-magic and love-magic might be challenged on various grounds. One might argue that love is of its essence a free commitment of the will, and that the idea of magically induced love is thus self-contradictory, in which case love-magic could be little more than a means for lasting sexual arousal, however sublimated it may be. When the *Malleus maleficarum* laments the fate of a man "so bound in the meshes of carnal lust and desire" that he cannot be reformed, but "puts away his beautiful wife to cleave to the most hideous of women," whom he visits at night "by devious ways," the condition might be mistaken for love but could scarcely be distinguished from obsessive sexual attraction.[20] Indeed, D.W. Robertson has argued that the term amor is routinely used for lust in medieval literature, in contradiction to the purely spiritual caritas that Augustine recommended.[21] Without following Robertson in this implausibly sweeping claim, we must admit that the relevant forms of magic blur together. We have already seen formulas in which the word "love" is surely used for lust, and in fact some texts use the term interchangeably. Pseudo-Albert, for example, says that philtres taken from the dove and the sparrow are useful for arousing amorous affection, particularly when these birds themselves are found in a state of "love, or carnal appetite."[22]

When medieval manuscripts give magical formulas for engendering love, they almost always specify that the intent is to ensure—or more commonly to restore—love between spouses. Whether the authors are being virtuous or merely discreet is impossible to gauge. According to the *Book of Secrets* ascribed to Albert, periwinkle has power to induce love between husband and wife when imbibed in food, while the eaglestone could accomplish the same end if suspended on one's left shoulder.[23] Thomas of Cantimpré in his *De natura rerum* told how the allectory could make wives appealing to their husbands if they carried it in their mouths (perhaps a misogynist joke?).[24] Marbode of Rennes credited moonstone with the capacity to procure love, and beryl with the power to bind marital affection. Magnetite, on the other hand, had ambiguous potency: it could reconcile quarreling spouses, but might also destroy the marital love, and presumably would thus have to be used with great caution.[25] And when a manuscript says that a concoction with mashed earthworms can arouse love between a man and a wife if she uses it in cooking, one can imagine that this recipe too might for purely nonmagical reasons have had quite the opposite effect.[26] Amorous magic within marriage is often explicitly remedial: if man has fought with his wife, a series of characters written out and hidden beneath their threshold will restore amicability,[27] and Pseudo-Albert says (citing the obviously pertinent *Book of Cleopatra*) that if a wife does not love her husband he should bear on himself marrow from the left foot of a wolf, which will cause her to love him and him alone.[28]

In the two Italian trial records mentioned above, women were prosecuted for love-magic of this sort on behalf of their clients. Matteuccia Francischi at Todi gave women various prescriptions to regain the lost affection of their abusive husbands (or, in one case, of a priest's concubine). In at least two instances the formulas allegedly had some success: one woman's husband became infatuated with her "as if in frenzy" for at least a few days, while in another case the man began fawning upon the woman and doing whatever she wished.[29] But when a woman with similar problems went to Gabrina degli Albeti at Reggio she received less satisfaction, and her husband kept mistreating her.[30]

In other cases prosecution was directed against women who on their own behalf had used love-magic to ensnare men. In 1375 a prominent Florentine merchant accused a woman of bewitching his brother with a wax image, thereby gaining his love, causing him to neglect both family and business, and inducing him to give her a substantial sum of money.[31] It is obviously hazardous to generalize, but women were probably most liable to prosecution when they used love-magic for adultery or when they provided it as a professional service for other women, while women who used it for their own purposes, especially to improve their own marriages, were comparatively safe.

Distinct in principle from both sex-inducing magic and love-magic is sex-enhancing magic, intended to enhance sexual desire, sexual performance, or the frequency of sex between partners who are already willing. The distinction between sex-inducing and sex-enhancing magic might be challenged on the grounds that performance is correlative to desire, but the correlation is far from absolute. The Old English version of Sextus Placitus's *Medicina de quadrupedis* gives three relevant prescriptions: to increase a woman's sexual pleasure, a man should mix incense, roebuck's bile, and nettle seed, and anoint his genitals before intercourse; anointing the genitals with boar's bile will give the man himself immense delectation; and to make a person more eager and more keenly aroused in intercourse, one should administer wine to which the pulverized testicles of a bull have been added.[32] Less wondrous in its effects but still useful was the stone *exebenus*, which, crushed and drunk, guaranteed untiring energy for *venerias voluptates*.[33]

Heightening the intensity of sexual relations was a matter in which either partner could take the initiative: it was presumably men who anointed their own genitals, but it was women in particular who could stimulate more passionate love-making, and thus deepen their husband's affection, by wearing the gem allectory.[34] Vervain, too, was said to be a potent stimulus "in venereal pastimes, that is, the act of generation," presumably regardless of who procured it.[35]

For some, the goal was not intensity of pleasure but frequency of performance. Drinking the juice of a plant named *Polygonum aviculare* "maketh [a man] to do often the act of generation,"[36] which could be construed as meaning that the potion makes the man compulsive and oversexed, but probably means he is enabled to do what he would otherwise only wish. And Michael Scot prescribed carrying jasper or topaz as a means for having frequent sex without injury to one's health.[37] One might doubt the efficacy of these prescriptions, but one early fifteenth-century magician in Lorraine boasted of having relations with eighteen women on the same day thanks to the help of love philtres.[38] In the realm of sex-magic it is difficult to distinguish physiological effects, but sometimes magic attained the purely psychological result of delusion: William of Auvergne tells of magicians who claimed they could cause a woman to think she had had intercourse fifty or sixty times when it had in fact occurred only once or twice.[39]

Closely allied to these procedures were magical techniques for overcoming impotence; here too the point was not so much to arouse desire as to make performance possible. To take a single example, one version of a tract on vulture-magic recommended mixing the bird's lung with must and citron, or drying and pulverizing its kidneys and testicles and administering them with wine, as a cure for impotence.[40]

The Techniques of Natural Magic

The techniques used in magic generally fall into broad categories: natural and demonic. Natural magic relies on hidden powers (or "occult virtues") within nature. It assumes that certain plants, animals, gems, ceremonies, and verbal formulas have power that cannot be explained in ordinary terms but is nonetheless part of their natural condition and not due to supernatural intervention.[41] To be sure, it is often difficult if not impossible to distinguish sharply between ordinary and magical causes. If the powers exploited were manifest, the operation was in principle nonmagical; if they were occult, the procedure was magical. But the sources at our disposal do not tell us explicitly how these powers were conceived, and thus we must distinguish in a rough-and-ready way on the basis of whether symbolic or otherwise occult factors seem to have been at work. More often than not it is the context that will help in making this decision: the mere fact that a prescription appears in a book of "secrets," for example, suggests (although perhaps not infallibly) that the powers invoked were thought of as occult.

The substances most obviously powerful for arousing passion were those derived from animals in heat. Thus, William of Auvergne speaks of sorcerers (*malefici*) who observe the mating of animals so they can kill them when they are in heat and thus obtain bodily parts or powders with which they can inflame libidinous love in those they desire.[42] The *Book of Secrets* ascribed to Albert the Great reflects on this link:

> [T]hey which will move love look what beast loveth most greatly, and specially in that hour in which it is most stirred up in love, because there is then greater strength in it in moving to love; they take a part of the beast, in which carnal appetite is stronger, as are the heart, the stones, and the mother or matrix. And because the Swallow loveth greatly, as Philosophers saith, therefore they choose her greatly to stir up love. Likewise the Dove and the Sparrow are holden to be of this kind, specially when they are delighted in love, or carnal appetite, for then they provoke and bring love without resistance.[43]

Even when an animal is not immediately aroused, the organs physiologically or symbolically associated with its sexuality were thought to have powers of arousal: the testicles of a stag, a bull, or a dog, for instance, or the tail of a fox, could arouse a woman to sexual desire.[44] Yet the sexual pharmacology of the animal world was not limited to such obvious cases. From the works of Paulinus, medieval Europeans learned of various animals whose magical virtues could incite amorous feeling: not only the testes of a hare or stag, a donkey's penis, the semen of a stag, and the vaginal secretions of a sow were recommended, but also the urine of bull, and the droppings of a hen, and the blood and brains of a sparrow.[45]

Substances directly connected with human sexuality would serve, perhaps even more effectively, for amorous arousal. The seventh-century penitential of Theodore condemns any woman who mixes her husband's semen into his food so that he will love her more fervently.[46] And Gabrina degli Albeti advised one woman to heighten her husband's love for her by putting her hand on her genitals while they engaged in sexual relations, then touching her mouth and kissing him with her *labiis pudibondis.*[47]

People eager to find aphrodisiacs have experimented over the millennia with various plants and plant products. Anglo-Saxon manuals recommend St. John's wort, valerian, and vervain.[48] (The power of vervain was ambiguous: it had "great strength in venereal pastimes," but if powdered and sprinkled between two lovers it could induce strife between them.[49]) A fifteenth-century manuscript prescribed French lavender for arousing venereal desire.[50] Also taken from a plant was a gum known as "dragon's blood," although according to a legend reported in Pliny it was extracted from a dragon or serpent crushed by a dying elephant; this gum is said to have been used for love into at least the tenth century.[51] These vegetable aphrodisiacs are, however, the least obviously magical of the means we have discussed.

The trial records mention numerous substances not only prescribed but actually used for erotic purposes: powders (made from bird-bones, toads, snakes, and so forth), ashes from burned reeds, water used for washing one's feet, herbs and herbal extracts, hair, menstrual blood, human excrement (the *Malleus maleficarum* speaks of a woman who drove several abbots mad with love by feeding them her feces), and in one case a mixture of water and wine served up in a skull.[52] One sorceress told a woman to place one of her pubic hairs and some of her husband's fingernails in the heart of a black hen, then perform a simple ritual with the fowl's heart tucked into her genitals, then extract the heart and feed it (along with some powdered plants) to her husband.[53] All of which corroborates what was suggested above—that extravagant and transgressive measures were the common refuge of the desperate.

One reason the authorities frowned upon erotic magic is that some of the substances used might accidentally cause physical harm. Indeed, the court records contain cases of love potions administered in food and drink with lethal or otherwise harmful effect. Mahaut of Artois was charged with killing Louis X with a love-potion composed of powders from toads and snakes. Another French woman allegedly killed a man by giving a potion meant to restore his love for his wife. And when a woman at Putten gave a man a potion to arouse his passion, he lost his senses for a period of time.[54] The accident might only appear to be such; an enemy might have procured a poison and claimed it had erogenous qualities. Thus, when the count of Foix quarrelled with his wife, his disaffected brother-in-law provided a powder which, sprinkled on his food, would allegedly reconcile him to her—but the count discovered the powder and administered it to a dog, which immediately died, showing that it was no love-potion at all.[55]

Often the magical effect was attained not so much by erogenous substances as by procedures or rituals, with gestures and words thought to have occult power. One manuscript, for example, gives two procedures for gaining the love of a woman: First, one may take some pieces of broom, put them in a satchel, attend mass on three (presumably consecutive) Sundays, then put the broom into one's mouth and kiss any woman at all; one will immediately have one's desire with her. Alternatively, one can write out a series of characters in one's own blood, on Thursday before sunrise, and carry them around until Saturday, then touch these characters to the naked flesh of a woman one desires, or merely show them to her, and "you will gain your wish."[56] A third ceremony, from a different source, is like these first two in its simplicity, and once again the emphasis is on touching the beloved with a magical object. Starting before sunrise, a man should carry a scrap (of presumably either paper or parchment) containing the letters HLDPNAGU, and he should touch the left hand of a woman, and "she will follow thee"; the same works for a woman if she uses the letters HLNPMQUM and surreptitiously touches a man's neck.[57] An "experiment" for mutual love ascribed to a King Behentatus requires inscribing a series of numbers, from 220 to 284, on wood or on bread.[58] When the inscribed material is administered to the intended couple in food or drink, evidently ground or crumbled, it will arouse them to keen love for each other. The author boasts that he has often used this formula, indeed he is an expert in it, and he has found it reliable.[59]

Rather different procedures, more complex than the above, involved image-magic with virgin wax for the love of a woman. One required a wax candle into which are worked three hairs from a man's own head and a thread spun by a virgin on a Friday. The man must write (presumably on the candle) the name of the intended woman, with the blood from a cocksparrow. Then he must light the candle, taking care that it not drip on the earth, and "she shall love thee." The candle is identified with the woman through the inscription of her name; when it burns, she too will burn with love. In another procedure the man makes a wax image of a woman, sprinkles it with holy water, then writes her name on the image's forehead and his own name on its breast. While saying a conjuration, he pierces the image with four new needles. Finally, he lights a fire and writes the woman's name in the ashes produced. He places a bit of mustard seed and salt on the image, then places it on the coals, and "as they leap and swell, so shall her heart be kindled."[60]

The trial records allude at times to the use of such wax images in love-magic. One Italian woman was supposed to have bewitched a man by placing an image of him (probably either transfixed with pins or inscribed) in his own bed. Matteuccia Francisci used images in different ways for erotic magic: she might place a wax image of a man over a fire while she recited incantations, or else she would wrap an image with a virgin's girdle, then have her client place it at the head of a bed while reciting a threefold incantation. And wax images were said to have succeeded (along with herbs and charms) in gaining Alice Perrers the love of Edward III.[61]

The occult or hidden powers in nature exploited by natural magic are often thought to derive ultimately from the stars and planets; animals, plants and minerals are reservoirs of astral power that they have accumulated. This notion of putting astral *virtutes* to practical purpose is nowhere more explicit than in the use of astral images, generally carved on stone or metal. Several medieval treatises, usually translated from Arabic, told how to use such images, which could be either conventional astronomical signs for planets and constellations or representations of the deities associated with the planets. Venus—both the goddess and the planet—specialized, naturally, in amatory functions. To take one fairly simple example from *Picatrix,* the Latin version of an Arabic manual of (mostly astral) magic:

> If, among the forms of Venus, you make (at the hour of Venus, on lapis lazuli) the form of a naked girl, holding a chain around her neck and having a man next to her, and on the reverse side the form of a small boy holding up a sword, whoever carries this image on himself will be loved by women and will do whatever he wishes.[62]

Astral magic often entailed the use of conjurations addressed to astral spirits, whom orthodox theologians—and sometimes the magicians as well—would spontaneously have identified as demons. At this point, therefore, we stand on the threshold between natural and demonic magic.

The Techniques of Demonic Magic

While natural magic invoked hidden powers in nature, demonic magic invoked the power of evil spirits.[63] To be sure, what one person took to be natural magic another might represent as demonic: a theologian might argue that procedures using plants, animals, and mysterious verbal formulas were nothing but a set of signals to the demons who (whether the magician knew it or not) were the agents responsible for the magical effects.[64] In other words, while the formulas given above contain no explicit reference to demons, many writers in medieval Europe would have assumed that they were in effect specimens of demonic magic. Even when the trial records speak of invoking demons, the charge may be doubtful. Thus, a woman tried at Innsbruck in 1485 had allegedly taught others to invoke the devil for the sake of either love or illness, and Alice Kyteler was accused in 1324 of using "the intestines and innards of cocks sacrificed . . . to demons, along with certain horrible worms and various herbs" and various other substances, mixed and boiled in the skull of an executed thief, for amatory and other magic—but in both cases natural magic may have been interpreted *in pessimum.*[65] Indeed, even if everyone was agreed that a certain magical procedure did involve invocation of spirits, further confusion could arise over the question *which* spirits were being conjured: the magician might claim to be invoking angels, but could anyone be sure whether the spirits bidden were fallen or unfallen? Occasionally, however, the formulas for erotic and other magic make it quite clear that the magician was conjuring demons. Explicitly demonic magic, known in the later Middle Ages as necromancy, could serve for a wide range of ends—necromancy covered a multitude of sins—but erotic purposes were among the most prominent. Stories about demonic magic go back to much earlier times. Hincmar of Rheims in the ninth century, for example, reproduced a story from the life of St. Basil about a young man who signed a pact with the Devil to gain a young woman's love. The Devil sent demons to incite fornication, and they tortured the woman with passionate desire for the man—but rather than plunging into an affair she married the youth, then discovered what he had done, and in horror took him to the local bishop, who by his intercession retrieved the written pact.[66] Like the Theophilus legend, this one gives dramatic warning against demonic wiles, although the focus is on the saint's power to counteract the demons even in so difficult a case. In any case, documents of this sort are not likely to tell in detail how one goes about conjuring demons; it is only from the late Middle Ages that we have manuscripts with precise necromantic instructions.

A Middle Dutch manuscript of the fifteenth century shows how necromancy might be used for erotic ends. Very early on a Friday morning, under a waxing moon, one must draw a human figure on a freshly baked tile while saying, "I, N., draw this picture in the form and likeness of the person N., daughter or son of so-and-so." One invokes the aid of Venus, and implores God for power over certain fallen angels who can bind man and woman together. One then conjures the demon (and sometime fertility goddess) Astaroth to execute the desired effect. At this point the experiment breaks off abruptly in the manuscript, so we do not know precisely how its various elements fit together.[67] We may have indirect evidence for the sequel, however, in the account of a trial: in the second half of the fifteenth century a priest at Tournai allegedly tried to seduce a girl with a procedure at least partly similar to this one. He drew her image on tile with a piece of charcoal, then baptized the figure and sprinkled it with holy water. He made a second image out of wax and baptized it as well. Then, following the counsel in a book of magic, he invoked demons by reciting various conjurations.[68] The Dutch manuscript gives in its entirety another "experiment" involving making a wax image, filling its belly with a magical concoction, piercing it, wrapping and binding it tightly, placing it in a jar, burying it under the floor of the victim's house, and invoking certain spirits while casting incense onto a fire.[69] The woman will be tormented by the conjured spirits, and will be unable to rest or do anything else until she yields.[70] This correspondence between the case history and the prescriptive document is particularly important; the mutual corroboration of the texts suggests that necromancy was taken quite seriously and actually attempted.

A fifteenth-century necromancer's manual from Germany gives more varied procedures for erotic magic.[71] To seduce a woman one must draw an image of her and write the names of demons on various parts of the image so that the corresponding parts of her body will be affected until she yields. At one point the magician says, "By this image I have drawn the heart and mind of so-and-so, and by a strong invocation I arouse her to love, desire, and yearn for me, and to think of me all night even in her sleep." He fumigates the image and conjures the demons, then hangs the image to blow in the wind. If the necromancer encounters any obstacle in approaching the woman (a rare admission of potential difficulty!) he can conjure the demons to transport the woman to a magic circle, where he may have his will with her. Alternatively, this handbook has the necromancer fashion a wax image and baptize it in her name. Then he traces a circle with the names of Belial and other demons inscribed. The core of the procedure involves piercing specified points on the image with nine needles, while reciting relevant incantations (for example, "As this needle is fixed in the heart, so may the love of N. be fixed on N., so that she will burn with love of me and not be able to sleep, wake, lie down, sit, or walk without burning for love of me"). He then conjures each part of the woman's body, causing her to languish until she becomes compliant to his "libidinous will." Finally he melts the image over burning coals while saying, "as the raven longs for carrion [!], so may you desire me, and as this wax melts before the fire so may N. desire my love." The passion all this arouses will cause the woman to wail, lament, beat her breast, and so forth, until she succumbs.[72]

All these necromantic experiments rely heavily on some form of image-magic; whether the image is made of wax or drawn on skin or tile, and whether it is pierced, burned, or subjected to other abuse, the basic assumption is that the affliction of the image will cause suffering in the desired woman until she yields to the magician. This form of magic is thus inherently violent, and more overtly than other forms of erotic magic it constitutes a kind of magical rape of the victim. If the necromancers rely on demonic support in this project, their doing so reveals little about their character that could not be gathered from other elements in their magic.

Those who used such necromancy, usually clerics, were at times brought to court for their misconduct. A case at Carcassonne in 1329 amply supports the impression that this sort of magic tended toward violence. The necromancer here was a Carmelite friar named Peter Ricordi, who had seduced three women by uttering conjurations of demand over images of wax, pouring various noxious substances over these images (including blood extracted "in a terrible and horrible manner" from a toad), then burying these images under the women's thresholds. On one occasion he pierced one of the images in the stomach, and blood had come out. To celebrate his triumphs he had sacrificed a butterfly to Satan. Apprehended and tried by an inquisitor, he was sentenced to life imprisonment on bread and water—not a light sentence, but more lenient than he would probably have received in later centuries.[73]

Magical Use of Religious Objects and Formulas

In theory, magic and religion can be distinguished easily enough: magic appeals to occult virtues in nature or demons, while religion appeals to God (directly or through the intercession of other good spirits). In practice, however, this distinction sometimes becomes blurred. At times a holy object or formula is used for so unholy a purpose that its holiness seems to be perceived as a kind of morally neutral potency, exploitable for either good or evil ends. When this happens the object or formula seems to possess residual holiness, assimilated to the powers (likewise morally neutral) in nature. Thus, a Florentine sorcerer sought a woman's love by writing a psalm on a slip of parchment and depositing it where he expected her to walk by, [74] and a twelfth-century source tells of a woman who held a consecrated host in her mouth while kissing her husband, to gain his love.[75] Medieval theologians would typically have branded these practices as superstitious (involving the misuse of holy things) rather than magical (entailing invocation of demons or use of occult powers in nature). This distinction is entirely coherent. Yet in form and intention these procedures resemble magic so closely that it would seem pointless to deny the correspondence.

The border between religion and magic is further tested by a fourteenth-century manuscript from Poland, which gives a prayer-cum-conjuration enabling a woman to secure her husband's love. The complicating factor here is that the first part of this long formula is a prayer, clearly addressed to God, asking his aid in securing "such love between me and my husband Theoderic as there was between Adam and Eve, between Abraham and Sarah, between Mary and John, between Christ and the Church"—but then the formula turns to a conjuration, addressed neither to God nor to any spirit, but to the woman's husband himself, who is charged by the power of various divine names to come to the wife and "carry out all my will." The document concludes, "The preceding words are written for Elizabeth and her husband Theoderic."[76] Both the prayer and the conjuration are written in Latin, and this fact, along with the concluding sentence, suggests that some cleric provided them for Elizabeth, either for recitation or for use as a talisman (borne on her person or placed near her husband). Particularly if the document was indeed meant as a talisman, it would furnish a clear case of religion being conflated with magic.

Perhaps the most striking case of such religion-turned-magic arises in the "Leiden Lorica," which mimics the litany forms of Celtic loricae but uses them for a magical rather than religious end: in Peter Dronke's words, "it is a poet-magician's attempt to achieve tyrannic sexual subjugation of the woman he desires, by casting a spell over her." The formula begins, "Let my love descend upon her:/ may all her limbs be hunted out for my love's sake. . . ." After listing the parts of her body to be thus "hunted out" and afflicted, the magician beseeches, "May God take the heart of N. from her, for love of me, N." He then adjures the archangels (including Uriel, Sariel, and Panagiel) and the other angels, patriarchs, confessors, apostles, martyrs, virgins and widows, heaven and earth, and so forth, enjoining them all with the refrain, "take N.'s heart from her for my love's sake!" The lorica contains reminiscences of the Psalms and the Canticle of the Three Children from Daniel, but holy words are clearly applied to unholy ends.[77] Elements of religion are being used as if they were magical formulas, perhaps on the assumption that they are yet more powerful than ordinary magic.

While the Polish conjuration and the "Leiden Lorica" both test the boundary between religion and magic, they do so in different ways. The conjuration in the Polish manuscript more closely resembles the conjurations elsewhere used for demonic magic, but its purpose is praiseworthy within the context of medieval morality; the person who gave it to Elizabeth might have been charged with superstition (as Gabrina degli Albeti was tried for sorcery), but none would have found fault at Elizabeth's own motives. The "Leiden Lorica," on the other hand, more closely resembles a liturgical prayer but extravagantly infringes Christian ethical norms. The one is in this sense a moral conjuration; the other is an immoral prayer.

Anaphrodisiacs and Countercharms

If one wanted to divide the magicians of medieval Europe into two groups, one could do worse than to distinguish those who wanted people to have sex from those who did not. For the latter group, various forms of magic could frustrate either sexual desire or sexual performance. Consuming the flowers of a willow or a poplar could diminish one's sexual appetite, as could the heart of a turtledove carried in a wolfskin pouch.[78] And Pseudo-Albert told how a man (presumably a husband) could keep a woman (presumably his wife) from wanting sex with other men:

> If thou wilt that a woman be not vitiate nor desire men, take the privy member of a Wolf, and the hairs which do grow on the cheeks or eye bright of him, and the hairs which be under his beard, and burn it, and give it to her in a drink when she knoweth not, and she shall desire no other man.[79]

Elsewhere the point was to impede not sexual desire but sexual performance. Peter of Abano tells of a kind of fascination that can take away a person's bodily powers and thus impede sexual intercourse.[80] Albert the Great says that if a knot is tied around the phallus of a wolf in the name of a man or woman (the wolf being presumably dead, and the phallus removed), that person will be incapable of copulation until the knot is untied.[81] Elsewhere Albert reports that an emerald cannot endure for intercourse to occur in its presence:

[T]he present King of Hungary [Bela IV?] wore this stone on his finger
when he had intercourse with his wife, and as a result it was broken into
three pieces. And therefore what they say [of this stone] is probable—that
it inclines the wearer toward chastity.[82]

And the Hermetic *Liber lune* tells how to impede sexual relations throughout
an entire area by means of an engraved image.[83] While these measures
evidently had temporary effect, imbibing forty ants boiled in daffodil juice
could have more lasting impact, causing permanent impotence.[84] All such
procedures might well have had psychological effect, which would of course
be more easily attained with men already anxious about their sexual
performance and thus vulnerable to the power of suggestion.[85] A far more
drastic measure was magical castration—but this seems to have been a
relatively uncommon fantasy, the best known manifestation being in the
Malleus maleficarum.[86]

Two forms of sympathetic magic appear in the trial records as means
for afflicting men with impotence. Two women of Durham were charged with
binding "virile members" (presumably meaning images thereof) for that
end. And when a young man of Todi found his beloved married off to another
man, Matteuccia Francisci instructed him to go to a crossroads and
extinguish a lighted candle at the time of the wedding, recite a prayer
(described as "diabolical"), then break the candle and deposit it on the spot.
Until it was removed, the hapless husband would remain unable to
consummate his marriage.[87] Interestingly, while Matteuccia prescribed
love-magic for women, it was for a man that she provided this impediment.
In the latter case it must have been particularly easy to identify the client; in
most such cases we can only speculate about the poisoned interpersonal
network that might have given rise to anxieties and sexual inabilities.

Impotence through bewitchment was a matter with far-reaching legal
and theological as well as medical implications, since it gave rise to the
question whether the marriage could be dissolved and whether the man could
then remarry. The solution which may seem obvious, and on which some
consensus emerged, was that dissolution was permitted if the impotence was
permanent while remarriage was allowed if the impotence was selective.[88]
Such bewitchment could arise in any of several situations, but one that leapt
quickly to the medieval mind was that of the abandoned lover wishing to
prevent marriage out of jealousy. Burchard of Worms referred to adulteresses
who, on learning that their paramours want to marry other women, used
magic to "extinguish the male desire, so that they are impotent and cannot
consummate their union with their legitimate wives."[89] And the twelfth-
century penitential of Bartholomew Iscanus gave penance for a woman who
used magic "to prevent the consummation of a legal marriage."[90] But Peter
Mamoris in his *Scourge of Sorcerers* spoke of husbands and wives who
pretend to be bewitched and incapable of sex with one another, only as an
excuse to have relations with other partners.[91]

Not surprisingly, however, there were some in medieval society who
seem to have thought of magical anaphrodisiacs as essentially a good

thing, a God-given means for abatement of lust and promotion of virtue. The lapidaries, in particular, often mention this function among the noble services of the gems, and they pass not unduly subtle judgment on sexual desire when they speak of certain stones as guarding against "tempest and lechery."[92]

When a person felt threatened by a magical charm intended either to promote or to inhibit sexual relations, that person might have recourse to a countercharm. To be sure, theologians might argue that it was sinful to fight magic with magic,[93] but because the boundaries between magic, medicine, and religion were somewhat fluid such prohibitions were difficult to interpret. Thus, for example, Hildegard of Bingen said that a woman could counteract a love potion by drinking plantain juice or by putting betony leaves in her nose and beneath her tongue, which might be taken as a purely medical and nonmagical solution if one construed the anaphrodisiac qualities of plantain and betony as manifest rather than occult. But Hildegard also advised that a woman could rid herself of a diabolically incited suitor by pouring wine over a sapphire thrice while asking the gem itself to spare her from the man's lust, then having the man drink the wine—and the magical element in this prescription seems harder to ignore.[94] Perhaps more commonly cited were cases of magically induced impotence that might be remedied through magical or quasi-magical means. One writer who devoted much thought to this problem was Arnold of Villanova, who distinguished in effect between impediment through natural magic (such as cock's testicles, placed beneath the marriage bed, or an inscription in bat's blood) and impediment through demonic intervention; if the obstacle entailed natural magic, it could be overcome by such a simple and purely natural means as removing the magical object, but if demons were involved one would have to resort to exorcism.[95] In countermagic as in magic, therefore, the distinction between natural and demonic causation was vital.

Erotic Magic in Literature

We have encountered no major differences of type between the magic prescribed in medieval manuscripts and the magic alleged in medieval court records—which suggests that the accusations made in court may have reflected actual magical practice fairly faithfully. Indeed, we have seen one instance in which the account of a trial seems to supplement a prescriptive document that is incomplete. When we turn from these bodies of material to the rather different realm of fictional literature, however, we find conceptions of erotic magic that are significantly distinct.

Erotic magic occurs in various literary genres. A German Spielmann epic, for example, which appears in various other languages in different forms, told how King Fore gained the love of Solomon's wife Salome by means of a magic jeweled ring, then arranged for her to eat a root that caused her to seem dead, and after she was buried he had her safely exhumed.[96] Another tale, which migrated from the Orient and became reworked in various forms, ranging from fabliau to sermon *exemplum,* concerns a man (in some versions a lecherous cleric) who obtains the aid of a go-between to obtain his desires with an unwilling paramour. The go-between feeds pepper or mustard to a dog to make it weep, and persuades the obstinate woman that the dog was previously a woman and was transformed into its present shape because she had refused a lover (identified in one version as a Jewish sorcerer). Fearing a similar fate, the woman relents.[97] Strictly speaking, however, what we have here is not erotic magic but erotic manipulation by mere threat of magic.

Not surprisingly, however, the form of literature most useful for such a study is the romance, in which love often serves as a pivotal theme, usually complicating the plot by posing an obstacle to its otherwise expected progression.[98] The romances sometimes portray love as induced or suppressed by magical gems,[99] but far more often the medium is a potion, usually concocted with herbs. The use of such means contrasts markedly with the forms of courtly behavior that Andreas Capellanus recommended as ways to gain affection.[100] Courtly manners serve to enhance one's personal attractiveness in the amatory quest—but when potions come into play what usually ensues is unwanted, problematic love.

The earliest relevant interest is Chétien de Troyes's *Cligés,* where the purpose is not to induce love but to create the illusion of sexual activity. The heroine, Fenice, has been compelled to marry the emperor but loves Cligés instead, and so that she can remain faithful to her beloved her nurse provides for her a potion that causes the sleeping emperor to think he is passionately engaged with his wife.[101] Similarly, in the chanson de geste *Raoul de Cambrai* there is a lady who has been coerced into marriage and who maintains her chastity (out of regard for her true love) by putting an unspecified plant into her mouth, which prevents her unwanted spouse from doing anything but kiss and embrace her.[102]

The most famous instance of a potion that does not arouse love is that in *Tristan.* In the version of the romance by Thomas of Britain, when Iseult is departing to marry King Marc her mother gives her a potion with flowers and herbs that they may drink on their wedding night, but Iseult accidentally shares the potion with Tristan instead and they fall lastingly and tragically in love. While on one level the potion causes their love; however, Thomas seems to downplay the causal element and make the drink more a symbol of a love to which they are already inclined. Another version of the story, by Béroul, has the sharing of herbed wine much more clearly and abruptly causing the love—although, paradoxically, the potion itself lasts only three years, and the love continues even when the potion has worn off.[103] Johannes de Alta Silva's *Dolopathos* refers to a powerful herbal beverage, reinforced with charms and incantations, with which a queen intends to gain the love of Lucinius, but the victim discerns her plot and refuses to drink the potion: "He shielded his ears against her poisonous incantations, and he would not drink the love potion."[104] If Tristan and Iseult are driven by fate to an affair that neither they nor the brewer of the potion intended, Lucinius evades a potion that clearly is intended for him. In neither story does the intention behind the potion succeed.

Love-magic in the romances is thus not always an aid to romance, but often an impediment. Indeed, it is in the nature of the romance tradition to require that virtue, prowess, and love be tested by encounter with natural or magical obstacles, and it is only by overcoming such difficulties that these values can be promoted. Thus, a character in *La Violette* drinks an herbal potion that causes him to forget his love, but eventually his love overcomes this magical impediment and regains its strength.[105] If love is an affliction that can be caused by magic, it is not surprising to find that it may also be relieved through magical remedies. Thus, the love-sick Orgueilleuse in *Blancandin* seeks plants from a physician of her acquaintance that will cure her affliction, and in *Guillaume de Palerme* there is a certain root that can heal Melior of the sickness that she suffers out of love.[106]

If the magicians' writings and the judicial record alike suggest that love can be manipulated more or less straightforwardly by magic, it is literature that sets the record straight by showing love as an independent force, overcome at times by magic, but also overcoming it—and even when magic succeeds, its power is seldom quite within the control of its user.

Notes

1   [Heinrich Krämer and Jakob Sprenger], *Malleus maleficarum*, tr. Montague Summers (London: Rodker, 1928; rpt. London: Pushkin, 1948), ii.2.3, ii.2.2 (Summers, 170, 187). I am grateful to my wife Barbara Newman for her help with my work on this article.

2   Paul Lehugeur, *Histoire de Phillippe le Long, roi de France, 1316–1322*, 1 (Paris: Hachette, 1897), 168–74, 415; *Chronicon Angliae . . . auctore monacho quodam Sancti Albani*, ed. Edward Maunde Thompson (Rolls Series, 64) (London: Longman, 1874), 97–100; Jeffrey Burton Russell, *Witchcraft in the Middle Ages* (Ithica, N.Y.: Cornell University Press, 1972), 172; George Lyman Kittredge, *Witchcraft in Old and New England* (Cambridge, Mass.: Harvard University Press, 1929), 78, 105. For other cases at the English court see the incident involving Eleanor Cobham, fully recounted in H.A. Kelly, "English kings and the fear of sorcery," *Mediaeval Studies*, 39 (1977), 219–29; and the case of Elizabeth Grey, given in Kittredge, *Witchcraft*, 84f. For general discussion of erotic magic in the court records see Richard Kieckhefer, *European Witch Trials: Their Foundations in Popular and Learned Culture, 1300–1500* (London: Routledge & Kegan Paul; Berkeley: University of California Press, 1976), 57–60.

3   Candida Peruzzi, "Un processo di stregoneria a Todi nel 400," *Lares: Organo della Società di Etnografia Italiana-Roma*, 21 (1955), fasc. I–II; Aldo Cerlini, "Una strega reggiana e il suo processo," *Studi storici*, 15 (1906), 64f.; Giuseppe Bonomo, *Caccia alle streghe: La credenza nelle streghe dal secolo XIII al XIX, con particolare riferimento all'Italia* (Palermo: Palumbo, 1959), 119; Russell, *Witchcraft*, 209f. For the shift from sorcery to diabolism in the trial of Matteccia Francisci, see

Kieckhefer, *European Witch Trials*, 73f. In 1446, women at Durham cleared themselves of the charge of obtaining husbands for their clients (in the latter) by magic: James Raine, ed., *Depositions and Other Ecclesiastical Proceedings from the Courts of Durham* (Surtees Society, 21) (London: Nichols, 1845), 29; Kittredge, *Witchcraft*, 113.

4   Winthrop D. Jordan, *White Over Black: American Attitudes Toward the Negro, 1550–1812* (Chapel Hill: University of North Carolina Press, 1968), 150f.

5   *Gesta Treverorum*, ed. G. Waitz, in *Monumenta Germaniae historica, Scriptores*, 8, ed. Georg Heinrich Pertz (Hannover: Hahn, 1848), 176f.; Hansen, *Zauberwahn*, 116f.

6   John T. McNeill and and Helena M. Gamer, *Medieval Handbooks of Penance: A Translation of the Principal* Libri poenitentiales *and Selections from Related Documents* (New York: Columbia University Press, 1938), 90. More obscurely, the slightly later penitential of Columban refers to "a magician for the sake of love," who is culpable even if he "destroys nobody" thereby, which suggests that practitioners of love-magic might well be suspect of causing bodily harm and that the denial of such a link had to be explicit (ibid., 252). The reference is essentially duplicated in the Burgundian penitential of the eighth century (ibid., 274), in the so-called Roman Penitential of Halitgar from the ninth century (ibid., 305).

7   *Monumenta Germaniae historica, Leges,* sec. 2, 2, ed. Alfred Boretius and Victor Krause (Hannover: Hahn, 1897), 44 (the text is somewhat ambiguous: "Dubium etenim non est, sicut multis est notum, quod a quibusdam prestigiis atque diabolicis inlusionibus ita mentes quorundam inficiantur poculis amatoriis, cibis vel fylacteriis, ut in insaniam versi a plerisque iudicentur, dum proprias non sentiunt contumelias"); Hansen, *Zauberwahn*, 67.

8   Ibid., 331.

9   For one spectacular example, see the advertisement of the stone *orites* in the Hellenistic lapidary of Damigeron (translated into Latin in late antiquity and influential in medieval Europe), in Joan Evans, *Magical Jewels of the Middle Ages and the Renaissance, Particularly in England* (Oxford: Clarendon, 1922), 210: "reges concubines suis ut non deformentur aut ut filios minus generent aut minus pariant vel non concipiant, hunc lapidem circumligant eis. Tantam efficatiam sterilitatis ei dedit natura ut si gravide mulieri imposueris, coget eam per posteriora infantem eicere."

10   For the general history of aphrodisiacs, including magical types, see Alan Hull Walton, *Aphrodisiacs: From Legend to Prescription: A Study of Aphrodisiacs Throughout the Ages, with Sections on Suitable Food, Glandular Extracts, Hormone Stimulation and Rejuvenation* (Westport, Conn.: Associated Booksellers, 1958), and P.V. Taberner, *Aphrodisiacs: The Science and the Myth* (Philadelphia: University of Pennsylvania Press, 1985). While both of these books present medieval material, however, neither distinguishes rigorously between medieval and postmedieval sources.

11   Albertus Magnus, *Book of Minerals*, trans. Dorothy Wyckoff (Oxford: Clarendon, 1967), 73; Michael R. Best and Frank H. Brightman, eds., *The Book of Secrets of Albert Magnus of the Virtues of Herbs, Stones and Certain Beasts, also A Book of the Marvels of the World* (Oxford: Clarendon, 1973), 21; This use of allectory can be traced to Damigeron: see Evans, *Magical Jewels*, 197.

12   Joan Evans and Mary S. Sergeantson, eds., *English Mediaeval Lapidaries* (Early English Text Society, orig. ser., 190) (London: Oxford University Press, 1933), 59, 68.

13 For the use of a hawkstone see John M. Riddle, *Marbode of Rennes' (1035–1123) De lapidibus, Considered as a Medical Treatise*, with C.W. King's translation *(Sudhoffs Archiv: Zeitschrift für Wissenschaftsgeschichte*, Beiheft 20) (Wiesbaden: Steiner, 1977), 69, lines 445–46. Regarding vervain, see Henry Ellis, "Extracts in prose and verse from an old English medical manuscript, preserved in the Royal Library at Stockholm," *Archaeologia*, 30 (1844), 395f.

14 British Library, Sloane MS 3132, 56r–56v, and Bodleian Library, Oxford, MS e Mus. 219, fol. 187v.

15 W.L. Wardale, "A Low German-Latin miscellany of the early fourteenth century," *Niederdeutsche Mitteilungen*, 8 (1952), 11.

16 Bodleian Library, Oxford, Wood empt. MS 18, fol. 33v. James Thompson's phrase "esteem enlivened by desire" is the title of a forthcoming book by Jean Hagstrum on the history of marital love.

17 Taberner, 58 and 267f. Oswald Cockayne, ed., *Leechdoms, Wortcunning, and Starcraft of Early England*, 1 (Rolls Series, 35/1) (London: Longman, Green, 1864), xlv, refers to the formula in Egbert as "so filthy, that I must leave it in the obscurity of the original old English." Whether this practice counts as magical in any strict sense is difficult to say.

18 Ps-Albert, MW, 87. Further "experiments for love" are given in British Library, Sloane MS 3851, fols. 140–44; see Lynn Thorndike, *A History of Magic and Experimental Science*, 2 (New York: Macmillan, 1929), 808.

19 For the general theme see the *Malleus maleficarum*, i.7, "Whether witches can sway the minds of men to love or hatred" (Summers, 48–54), and ii.2.3, "Remedies prescribed for those who are bewitched by being inflamed with inordinate love or extraordinary hatred" (Summers, 170–73).

20 Ibid., ii.2.3 (Summers, 170f.).

21 E.g., D.W. Robertson, *A Preface to Chaucer: Studies in Medieval Perspectives* (Princeton, N.J.: Princeton University Press, 1962).

22 *The Book of Secrets of Albertus Magnus, of the Virtues of Herbs, Stones, and Certain Beasts: also A Book of the Marvels of the World*, ed. Michael R. Best and Frank H. Brightman (Oxford: Clarendon, 1973), 81.

23 Ibid., 8, 45.

24 Evans, *Magical Jewels*, 226.

25 Marbode, 65, line 389; 50, line 198; and 58, lines 306–07. For beryl's ability to foster and restore marital affection see also Evans, *Magical Jewels*, 198, 218, 226. The lapidaries edited by Evans and Serjeantson, *English Mediaeval Lapidaries*, recommend five stones as love charms: allectory is especially valuable for "a woman that would be loved of her lord" (31); beryl "nourishes love between man and woman" (28, 125; magnetite does the same, makes "marriage betwixt man and woman," and "reconcileth and accordeth love" between them (33, 52f., 99f.); diamond "accordeth man and woman of love together"(121); selenite "keepeth love betwixt man and woman" (126). According to the Peterborough lapidary, "If thou bearest [beryl] in a ring, put a little savin under the left knee, and thou shalt never be wroth with the woman that thou hast wedded" (73).

26 British Library, Sloane MS 3564, 35v–36r.

27 Bodeleian Library, Oxford, MS e Mus. 219, fol. 186v.

28 *Book of Secrets*, ed. Best and Brightman, 91; see Thorndike, *History of Magic and Experimental Science*, vol. 2, 736. A Florentine sorcerer of the early fifteenth century anointed his genitals with some unguent before he engaged in sex with his mistress, to prevent her from being attracted to other men; see Gene A. Brucker, "Sorcery in Early Renaissance Florence," *Studies in the Renaissance*, 10

(1963), 10, and Brucker, *The Society of Renaissance Florence* (New York: Harper & Row, 1971), 266–68.

29   Peruzzi, "Un processo di stregoneria," 9–11.

30   Cerlini, "Una strega reggiana e il suo processo," 64f.

31   Brucker, "Sorcery in Early Renaissance Florence," 9f.

32   Cockayne, *Leechdoms, Wortcunning, and Starcraft*, pt. 1, 351, 359, and 369. Cockayne translates these prescriptions from Old English not into Modern English, but into Latin, "pudoris causa." The second of them appears again, e.g., in a fifteenth-century manuscript, British Library, Sloane MS 3132, 56r–56v. Whether most contemporaries would have thought of these recipes as specifically magical is difficult to say.

33   Evans, *Magical Jewels*, 202.

34   Riddle, *Marbode of Rennes' De lapidibus*, 40, lines 89–91.

35   *Book of Secrets*, ed. Best and Brightman, 22f.

36   *Book of Secrets*, ed. Best and Brightman, 19. The same book, 21, is somewhat vague in its recommendation of henbane: "it is profitable to them that would do often the act of generation; and to them that desire to be loved of women, it is good that they bear it with them, for it maketh the bearers pleasant and delectable." This prescription could arguably be construed as belonging to any of our three categories: as an inducement to sex, as a means for enhancing sexual performance, and perhaps even as a means for love.

37   Thorndike, *History of Magic and Experimental Science*, vol. 2, 331 (where the wording is somewhat unclear).

38   Jacques Bournon, *Chroniques, lois, moeurs et usages de la Lorraine, au moyen-âge*, ed. Jean Cayon (Nancy, 1838), 23; Maurice Foucault, *Les procès de sorcellerie dans l'ancienne France devant les jurisdictions séculières* (Paris: Bonvalot-Jouve, 1907), 294.

39   Guilielmi Alverni, *De universo*, ii.3.25, in *Opera omnia*, 1 (Paris: Pralard, 1674; rpt. Frankfurt am Main: Minerva, 1963), 1072: one can find "in libris experimentorum" that "ludificationes mulierum . . . quidam malefici et attentaverunt et scripserunt, posterisque reliquerunt, si tamen eis de talibus creditur. Scripserunt enim experimentum ludificatorium, quo apparere dicebant mulieribus se multo pluries cognosci, quam cognoscerentur"; Thorndike, *History of Magic and Experimental Science*, vol. 2, 353.

40   Loren C. Mackinney, "An Unpublished Treatise on Medicine and Magic from the Age of Charlemagne," *Speculum*, 18 (1943), 495f. It is not altogether clear whether these are two separate prescriptions or two elements of a single one.

41   For this distinction see Richard Kieckhefer, *Magic in the Middle Ages* (Cambridge: Cambridge University Press, 1989), *passim*, esp. 9f.

42   *De legibus*, c. 4, in *Opera omnia*, 1, 35 (William uses the imperfect tense— "malefici explorabant coitus, seu commixtiones quorundam animalium"—suggesting that he thinks of such practices as historical); Thorndike, *History of Magic and Experimental Science*, vol. 2, 353.

43   *Book of Secrets*, ed. Best and Brightman, 81.

44   British Library, Sloane MS 3132, fol. 56r–56v; W.L, Wardale, "A Low German-Latin Miscellany," 17.

45   Walton, *Aphrodisiacs*, 99.

46   McNeill and Gamer, *Medieval Handbooks of Penance*, 196, no. 15 and n. 94 ("quae semen viri sui in cibo [eius?] miscens ut inde plus amoris accipiat").

47   Cerlini, "Una strega reggiana," 67.

48   Taberner, *Aphrodisiacs,* 58. Pseudo-Albert also recommended verbena as a means to induce love; see Thorndike, *History of Magic and Experimental Science,* vol. 2, 555.

49   *Book of Secrets,* ed. Best and Brightman, 22f., 16.

50   W.L. Wardale, "A Low German-Latin Miscellany," 17.

51   Taberner, *Aphrodisiacs,* 47.

52   Kieckhefer, *European Witch Trials,* 57f.; *Malleus maleficarum,* i.7 (Summers, 51); Brucker, "Sorcery," 16f.

53   She gave substantially the same prescription to two different women; see Aldo Cerlini, "Una strega reggiana e il suo processo," *Studi storici,* 15 (1906), 64f.

54   Joseph Hansen, *Zauberwahn, Inquisition und Hexenprozess im Mittelalter, und die Entstehung der grossen Hexenverfolgung* (Munich: Oldenbourg, 1900; rpt. Aalen: Scientia, 1964), 357; Chassaing, *Spicilegium brivatense,* 442; Joseph Hansen, *Quellen und Untersuchungen zur Geschichte des Hexenwahns und der Hexenverfolgung im Mittelalter* (Bonn: Georgi, 1901; rpt. Hildesheim: Olms, 1963), 576. See also E. Hoffmann-Krayer, "Luzerner Akten zum Hexen- und Zauberwesen," *Schweizerisches Archiv für Volkskunde,* 3 (1899), 22f. and 93. When a woman in Florence put bread, charcoal, salt, and a coin in a neighbor's bed to gain his affections he suffered pains in heart and elsewhere: Brucker, "Sorcery," 10. For discussion of the legal implications of such magic see Hansen, *Zauberwahn,* 290. For the classic instance of such an accident in literature see *Hercules Oetaeus* in Seneca, *Nine Tragedies,* tr. Frank Justus Miller, rev. ed., 2 (Cambridge, Mass.: Harvard University Press, 1987), 186–341, esp. 222–33.

55   Barbara W. Tuchman, *A Distant Mirror: The Calamitous 14th Century* (New York: Knopf, 1978), 344.

56   Bodleian Library, Oxford, Wood empt. MS 18, fol. 31v.

57   Taberner, *Aphrodisiacs,* 50.

58   W. Braekman, "Magische experimenten en toverpraktijken uit een middelnederlands handschrift," *Verslagen en mededelingen van de Koninklijke Vlaamse Academie voor Taal- en Letterkunde,* 1966, 53–118; also published separately (Ghent: Seminarie voor Volkskunde, 1966), no. 19, 43f. Pagination here used is from the separate edition. This experiment echoes a passage from *Picatrix: The Latin Version of the* Ghāyat Al- Ḥakīm, ed. David Pingree (London: Warburg Institute, 1986), 16, no. 6.

59   If the same numbers are written on clothing, the wearer will be unable to part from the magician, and if the appropriate number of raisins or pomegranate seeds is consumed the person who eats them will likewise attract the person he wants.

60   Ibid., 51–54. A third prescription is similarly involved. Before sunrise on a Friday one writes his own name and the intended woman's name in wax on parchment. Then he burns this inscription over a fire, along with hairs from the woman. Finally he administers the remainder to the woman in food or drink, "and she shall be so much taken with thee that she shall take no rest." Taberner ascribes the last of these three formulas to the thirteenth century.

61   Brucker, "Sorcery," 9f.; Peruzzi, "Un processo di stregoneria," 9–11; *Chronicon Angliae . . . auctore monacho quodam Sancti Albani,* ed. Edward Maunde Thompson (London, 1874), 97–100.

62   *Picatrix,* 70; cf. ibid., 16, 21, 70–72, 113, 115f., 130–32 (a conjuration or "prayer" to Venus), 156f., 229, 233. Another source recommended a procedure for compelling a person to come running in the heat of passion: on the day and in the hour of Venus, when the face of Taurus is rising and Venus is in the ascendant, one should inscribe certain figures and the person's name on a linen cloth; see Braekman,

"Magische experimenten en toverpraktijken," No. 23, 52f. See also Thabit B. Qurra, *De imaginibus*, vii.62–71 "Ad coniunctionem et dilectionem ac separationem aliquorum"), in Francis J. Carmody, *The Astronomical Works of Thabit B. Qurra* (Berkeley and Los Angeles: University of California Press, 1960), 190–92. The Hermetic *Liber prestigiorum* gives information on using such an image to regain a husband's affections: Lynn Thorndike, "Traditional medieval tracts concerning engraved astrological images," in *Mélanges Auguste Pelzer; Etudes d'histoire littéraire et doctrinale de la Scolastique médiévale offertes à Monseigneur Auguste Pelzer* (Louvain: Bibliothèque de l'Université, 1947), 229.

63   On this distinction see Richard Kieckhefer, *Magic in the Middle Ages* (Cambridge: Cambridge University Press, 1989).

64   The *locus classicus* for this argument is Augustine, *Concerning the City of God, Against the Pagans*, xxi.6, trans. John O'Meara (Harmondsworth: Penguin, 1972), 974–76.

65   Hartmann Ammann, "Der Innsbrucker Hexenprocess von 1485," *Zeitschrift des Ferdinandeums für Tirol und Vorarlberd*, ser. 3, 34 (1890), 29; Thomas Wright, ed., *A Contemporary Narrative of the Proceedings against Dame Alice Kyteler* (Camden Society, 24) (London: Nichols, 1843), 2.

66   Hincmarus Rhemensis, *De divortio Lotharii et Tetbergae*, resp. ad interr. 15, in J.-P. Migne, ed., *Patrologia Latina*, 125 (Paris: Migne, 1852), 721–25; Russell, *Witchcraft*, 83f. The story comes not from Jerome (*pace* Russell) but from the *vita* of Basil falsely ascribed to Amphilochius of Iconum, iii.43–48, in *Acta sanctorum*, Jun., 3 (Paris and Rome: Palmé, 1867), 428–30. For a hagiographic parallel see Jerome, "Life of St. Hilarion," c. 21, in Roy J. Deferrari et al., tr., *Early Christian Biographies* (Fathers of the Church, 15) (Washington, D.C.: Catholic University of America Press, 1952), 259f.

67   Braekman, "Magische experimenten," 38–40.

68   Paul Fredericq, ed., *Corpus documentorum inquisitionis haereticae pravitatis Neerlandicae*, 1 (Ghent and The Hague, 1889–1906), 428f.

69   Braekman, "Magische experimenten en toverpraktijken," No. 20, 45–49.

70   One further experiment in the manuscript (pp. 12f.) contains names clearly referring to spirits who will prevent a wife from loving another man. One should take the tail of a gray lizard and stroke her *conte* all over while saying, "Ysak, Belyal, Ninniker, Magod, perhibiu iam." When this is done, no man will be able to have sex with her.

71   Bayerische Staatsbibliothek, Munich, Clm 849. See Kieckhefer, *Magic in the Middle Ages*, esp. 6–8 and 158–64, and Richard Kieckhefer, *A Necromancer's Manual from the Fifteenth Century* (forthcoming).

72   Clm 849 contains two other relevant experiments: one involves inscribing names (of demons, of the magician, and of the desired woman) on a rib and then burning the rib and conjuring the demons; the other, which can be used for purposes other than erotic magic, also entails inscribing and burning a bone.

73   H.C. Lea, *A History of the Inquisition of the Middle Ages*, 3 (Philadelphia: Lea, 1888), 657–59.

74   Brucker, "Sorcery," 10f. For a Syriac parallel see C. Kayser, "Gebrauch von Psalmen zur Zauberei," *Zeitschrift der Deutschen Morgenländischen Gesellschaft*, 42 (1888), 460: one writes Psalm 34 on a cistern so that the woman and man who drink from it will fall in love.

75   Peter Browe, "Die Eucharistie als Zaubermittel im Mittelalter," *Archiv für Kulturgeschichte*, 20 (1930), 134–54. For similar use of holy chrism see Cerlini, "Una strega reggiana," 67.

76   Jerzy Zathey, "Modlitwa z XIV wieku o charakterze zaklęcia, mająca zapewnić żonie miłość męża," *Biuletyn Biblioteki Jagiellonskiej*, 34/35 (1984/85), 63–64.

77   See Peter Dronke, "Towards the interpretation of the Leiden love-spell," *Cambridge Medieval Celtic Studies*, 16 (1988), 61–75, for text, translation, and interpretation.

78   British Library, Sloane MS 3132, fol. 56v; W.L. Wardale, "A Low German-Latin miscellany of the early fourteenth century," 16.

79   *Book of Secrets*, ed. Best and Brightman, 87. A Florentine sorcerer of the early fifteenth century anointed his genitals with some unguent before he engaged in sex with his mistress, to prevent her from being attracted to other men (Brucker, "Sorcery," 10).

80   Thorndike, *History of Magic and Experimental Science*, vol. 2, 901: "fascinatio animalis occupans vires ut sui compos esse non valeat, actum venereum impediens."

81   Albert the Great, *Man and the Beasts: De animalibus* (Books 22–28), trans. James J. Scanlan (Binghamton, N.Y.: Medieval & Renaissance Texts & Studies, 1987), 158; Thorndike, *History of Magic and Experimental Science*, vol. 2, 561.

82   *Book of Minerals*, 119f.; Thorndike, *History of Magic and Experimental Science*, vol. 2, 546.

83   Thorndike, *History of Magic and Experimental Science*, vol. 2, 224.

84   British Library, Sloane MS 3132, fol. 56v The Peterborough lapidary warns of the effects of drinking powdered magnetite, which can make a woman barren or cause a man (who drinks it four times) to lose his "genetralis" (Evans and Serjeantson, *English Mediaeval Lapidaries*, 99). The Old English version of the *Medicina de quadrupedis* of Sextus Placitus (Cockayne, *Leechdoms*, pt. 1, 365) warns, "Beware thee that thou mie not where the hound mied; some men say that there a mans body changeth so that he may not, when he cometh to his wife, bed along with her." On magical impotence generally, see Cockayne, xli–xliv, and the *Malleus maleficarum*, i.8, "Whether witches can hebetate the powers of generation or obstruct the venereal act" (Summers, 54–58), ii.1.6, "How witches impede and prevent the power of procreation" (Summers, 117f.), and ii.2.2, "Remedies prescribed for those who are bewitched by the limitation of the generative power" (Summers, 167–70). The authors' conclusion in the first of these passages is that "a man can obstruct the generative powers by means of frigid herbs . . ., therefore much more can the devil do this. . . ."

85   For a recent exploration of such psychological processes see J. Finley Hurley, *Sorcery* (London: Routledge & Kegan Paul, 1985).

86   *Malleus maleficarum*, i.9, "Whether witches may work some prestidigitatory illusion so that the male organ appears to be entirely removed and separate from the body" (Summers, 58–61), ii.i.7, "How, as it were, they deprive man of his virile member" (Summers, 118–22), and ii.2.4, "Remedies prescribed for those who by prestidigitory art have lost their virile members. . . ." (Summers, 173–75). The second passage contains the classic castration fantasy: "witches . . . sometimes collect male organs in great numbers, as many as twenty or thirty members together, and put them in a bird's nest, or shut them up in a box, where they move themselves like living members, and eat oats and corn," as was seen, for example, by a man who tried to reclaim a large one and was told it belonged to a priest.

87   Raine, *Depositions and Other Ecclesiastical Proceedings*, 27; Peruzzi, '"Un processo di stregoneria," 11.

88   For the legal question see Hansen, *Zauberwahn*, 88–95, 153–64, 285–90. The theological issues are concisely summarized by Thomas Aquinas, *Quodlibet* XI, ix. 10, given in Alan C. Kors and Edward Peters, *Witchcraft in Europe, 1100–1700: A Documentary History* (Philadelphia: University of Pennsylvania Press, 1972), 72f.

89   McNeill and Gamer, *Medieval Handbooks of Penance*, 340.

90   Ibid., 349 (wording partly in brackets).

91   Thorndike, *History of Magic and Experimental Science*, 4 (New York: Columbia University Press, 1934), 301.

92   The lapidaries edited by Evans and Serjeantson, *English Mediaeval Lapidaries*, recommend various stones for reduction of lechery: allectory (51), crystal (76), diamond (31, 83), sardonyx (105), and especially balas (29, 49, 123) and emerald (20, 85); the last of these "voideth lechery, for God gave it such virtue" (121).

93   See especially *Malleus maleficarum*, ii.2.6 (Summers, 179–88).

94   Barbara Newman, *Sister of Wisdom: St. Hildegard's Theology of the Feminine* (Berkeley: University of California Press, 1987), 149f.

95   Hansen, *Quellen*, 44–47; see Kieckhefer, *Magic in the Middle Ages*, 85.

96   Alfred Karnein, ed., *Salman und Morolf* (Tübingen: Niemeyer, 1979), 30–32 (stanzas 92–99), 34–36 (stanzas 109–11), 40 (stanzas 125–26), 41–43 (stanzas 129, 133, 135), 46 (stanzas 145–47); John Revell Reinhard, *The Old French Romance of Amadas et Ydoine; An Historical Study* (Durham: Duke University Press, 1927), 83.

97   George H. McKnight, ed., *Middle English Humorous Tales in Verse* (Boston: Heath, 1913), 1–24 ("Dame Siriz"); the versions are compared ibid., xxi–xliii; see Kittredge, *Witchcraft*, 104.

98   See Reinhard, *The Old French Romance*, 27–30, 33, and especially 72–97, for a survey of erotic magic in the romance tradition; De la Warr Benjamin Easter, "A Study of the Magic Elements in the *Romans d'Aventure* and the *Romans Bretons*" (Johns Hopkins University dissertation, 1905); and Joan Nancy Ricardo-Gil, "The Practice of Witchcraft and Magic in Fact and Fiction During the French Middle Ages" (Boston College dissertation, 1980). Easter's dissertation was published in part (Baltimore: Furst, 1906), but the relevant material is only in the original typescript.

99   Reinhard, *The Old French Romance*, 33; Ricardo-Gil, "The Practice of Witchcraft," 313).

100   *Andreas Capellanus on Love*, ed. and tr. P.G. Walsh (London: Duckworth, 1982).

101   Chrétien de Troyes, *Cligés*, tr. L.J. Gardiner (New York: Cooper Square, 1966), 85–90, 176f. (lines 3248–58, 3333–72, 6610–21, 6631–38); see Easter, "A Study of the Magic Elements," 70f.

102   *Raoul de Cambrai*, ed. Paul Meyer and A. Longnon (Paris, 1882), lines 6848–91, 7222–41, 7258–67; Easter, 123f. For the theme generally see Reinhard, *The Old French Romance*, 33.

103   Thomas of Britain, *The Romance of Tristram and Ysolt*, c. 46, tr. Roger Sherman Loomis (New York: Dutton, 1923), 129–35; Béroul, *The Romance of Tristran*, ed. and tr. Norris J. Lacy (New York: Garland, 1989), 67, 69, 101–05 (lines 1384, 1412ff., 2133–2220, 2300ff.). See Geoffrey N. Bromiley, *Thomas's Tristan and the Folie Tristan d'Oxford* (London: Grant & Cutler, 1986), 12f.; Alberto Varvaro, *Beroul's Romance of Tristan*, tr. John C. Barnes (Manchester: Manchester University Press, 1972), 74–81; and Easter, "A Study of the Magic Elements," 72f. Varvaro compares the potion in Béroul to "a mechanism through which a single impulse has been transmitted, a hand which on a single occasion has rearranged the

pieces on the board. All the subsequent action will be determined by this impulse, by this rearrangement. . . ."(p. 77).

104 Johannes de Alta Silva, *Dolopathos, or The King and the Seven Wise Men,* tr. Brady B. Gilleland (Binghamton, N.Y.: Medieval & Renaissance Texts & Studies, 1981), 33; Easter, "A Study of the Magic Elements," 73.

105 *Roman de la Violette,* ed. Gibert de Montreuil (Paris: Michel, 1834), lines 3406–27, 3456–60, 3551–3612, 4124ff., 4295–4305, Easter, 73.

106 *Blancandin et Orgueilleuse d'Amour,* ed. H. Michelant (Paris, 1867), lines 1437–40; Easter, 124. *Guillaume de Palerme,* ed. H. Michelant (Paris: Firmin-Didot, 1876), 32 (lines 1085–92); see Easter, "A Study of the Magic Elements," 122f.

A MEDIEVAL PHYSICIAN'S GUIDE TO VIRGINITY

Esther Lastique and Helen Rodnite Lemay

Introduction

In a Latin manuscript located in the public library at Lille, the fifteenth-century Florentine physician "Nicholus"[1] sets down instructions for treating a virgin who has just been deflowered. He describes anatomically the defloration process, presents virginity tests, and guides the doctor in treatment of injuries that inevitably result from this act. In the course of his discussion, Nicholus gives us a brief survey of medieval medical thinking on virginity, and indicates that the loss of a woman's maidenhead normally requires medical intervention.

Lille manuscript 334 is a fifteenth-century book on the Diseases of Women (*De passionibus mulierum*),[2] which has never been published and exists, so far as we know, only in this codex. The author, Nicholus, also composed another medical work, *Sermones medicinales,* published in Venice in 1607.[3] The *De passionibus mulierum* was dedicated to Guillaume de Naste, a doctor practicing at Lille in the fifteenth century, and this copy is personally annotated by him, along with four other volumes in the Lille library that were in his possession.[4] The text consists of 221 folios, divided into 33 chapters. Chapter 30, *De defloratione seu violatione virginis* (On the Defloration or Violation of a Virgin), is one of the shortest sections of the book, extending from fol. 216v–217v.

Nicholus's treatise deals with the complexion of the womb, sterility, conception, the fetus, pregnancy, birth, abortion, disorders of the womb (mole, suffocation, ulcers) and the menstrual period. The work is encyclopedic in character; Nicholus makes a point of discussing every aspect of each topic, including signs, causes and treatments of every malady. The author's method is to cite a number of authorities on a subject, and then continue to the next. We do not hear much of Nicholus's voice in this text; the authorities are prominent.

Nicholus is widely read in medieval medicine. His favorite authority is Avicenna, who is mentioned on almost every page of the codex, but he also quotes frequently Galen, Hippocrates, Aristotle, Bernard de Gordon, "Haly,"[5] Johannitius, and many others.

Nicholus makes four specific references to authorities in the chapter on defloration: to Gilbertus Anglicus, Avicenna, Musahan and Galen, in that order. The third citation is problematic; the text advises the physician that a sitz bath in styptic waters will help heal injuries resulting from defloration, "as Musahan says in the commentary on the *Continens*." The name "Musahan" is clearly written out, and is found in a number of other places in this manuscript, usually with reference to the same writing.[6] From similarity of name, one possibility is Misusun, who composed in Arabic a synopsis in question-and-answer format of Soranus's gynecological work. Although Misusun's *Book of Midwives* is no longer extant, Rhazes cites it numerous times in the *Continens*,[7] and thus the possibility for confusion exists here.

The problem with this conjecture is that Misusun is not mentioned in the passages of the *Continens* referred to by Nicholus. Rhazes's volume contains a chapter in Book V entitled "On Substances that Constrict the Vulva," which begins with a recipe of herbs to be mixed in wine. This chapter is a possibility for this reference, if we take the phrase "as Musahan says in the commentary on the *Continens*" to refer only to the immediately preceding clause; "it is necessary that she sit . . . in cooked wine or sap or oil." This would be stretching the text, however, for Rhazes prescribes here soaking a cloth in the mixture and inserting it in the vulva, not sitting in the solution as Nicholus does.[8]

If for *commentario* we read *nono* (for the abbreviations could be identical), that is, if we interpret the text to say "as Musahan says in the ninth book of the *Continens*," we still find no reference to Misusun in any of the chapters of the *Continens* that refer to the female reproductive system. There is a recommendation that a woman sit in an herbal concoction for prolapse of the uterus or the anus, but the base of this recipe is water, not "wine or sap or oil" as we read in the Nicholus passage.[9]

We know that three commentaries were made on Rhazes, and his works were taught in the medical faculties of Paris and Montpellier,[10] so the name "Musahan" could possibly refer to any of these glossators. As of now, however, we have not been able to identify this author.

Nicholus's other three references in this passage are fairly straightforward. The passage from the thirteenth-century physician Gilbertus Anglicus is almost a word-for-word quotation,[11] as is the material from Avicenna and Galen.

The chapter on defloration, although among the shortest in the treatise, is interesting because this topic is not a standard part of medieval gynecological writings, and because the subject of virginity is a focus for societal prejudices and sheds light on cultural presuppositions. We shall first present a translation and explication of Nicholus's chapter, then discuss virginity in historical perspective, and finally provide an edition of the text.

Translation and Explication de Texte

I. The determination of whether a virgin is violated and corrupted is made by the sight and touch of the midwife.

The term used here for "midwife" is *obstetrix*, and the definition of this word has been the subject of some recent scholarly discussion. A midwife is a woman, a trained healer who cares for other women in obstetrical and gynecological matters, although the questions of just how far this care extended and whether men were also allowed to give it are still unsettled.[12]

We know that midwives assisted in childbirth, baptized newborns, and prescribed abortifacients, for records of these activities are found in judicial proceedings.[13] Similar traces of virginity testing have not as yet been uncovered for the Middle Ages, although theoretical treatises on medicine sometimes contain information on this topic. William of Saliceto, for example, states in his thirteenth-century medical treatise that ocular inspection of a woman in question is carried out by the midwife, who has received instruction in anatomy from a doctor.[14] The individual records that do exist are associated with notorious cases, Joan of Arc being a prominent example. Joan was examined many times to ascertain if she was a virgin: the Queen of Sicily, the duchess of Bedford and numerous matrons all took their turn during the course of her trial.[15] It is not until 1560, however, that we find a formal connection with the medical profession in a Paris regulation that states that "matrons or expert midwives will not make a report by themselves on the chastity, corruption, or pregnancy of girls or women without the presence of a physician, two official surgeons of the King . . . or one of them . . . since they (midwives) are not instructed in this matter, added to which is the need to write and sign those reports, and few of them know how to write."[16]

Although midwives came to exercise a monopoly on manual inspection and manipulation of the genitals in the Middle Ages, in the ancient Greek and medieval Arab worlds, males carried out these procedures as well. Once again, however, this "sight and touch" did not include determination of maidenhood. In the Hippocratic writing, *Diseases of Women*, the author informs us that the presence of an obstructing membrane in the uterine passageway is to be determined by manual inspection,[17] and the first-century Roman medical writer Celsus instructs the male physician to examine a woman for bladder stones by inserting a finger into her vagina or, if she is a virgin, into the anus. Similarly, the Arabs Abulcasis and Rhazes recommend to men that they deal with some gynecological disorders; in the *Continens* Rhazes advises the practitioner to use an instrument similar to the modern speculum to widen the vulva and the cervix.[18]

In the Latin west, manual inspection was much less emphasized in the medical literature, and, so far as we know, not practiced by males until the fifteenth century. Renate Blumenfeld-Kosinski has demonstrated in a recent study that it was not until the 1400s that male doctors invaded the lying-in chamber by taking responsibility for Caesarean births; before this, obstetrical matters remained the midwife's province.[19] Consequently, the chances of a university-trained physician carrying out an internal examination for virginity are slim, even though some learned treatises on the womb do deal with the anatomy of virginity. In the fifteenth century, the Pavian physician Anthonius Guainerius alludes to the possibility of a doctor performing a pelvic examination on a female patient, but the reason for this procedure would be to determine causes of sterility, not whether the patient is in a virginal state.[20]

Although it is virtually impossible to determine whether a woman has had her first sexual encounter even today, with the help of the modern speculum, electric lighting, and other technology, clearly in the time of Nicholus "sight and touch" were considered to be authoritative. On the basis of the scanty records we have of this procedure, however, we must assume that virginity testing by pelvic examination did not form a regular part of the medieval midwife's role.

II. Before defloration, as was discussed earlier, the mouth of the womb is covered with a membrane woven with veins and arteries which are broken when she is deflowered and as a result the woman bleeds.

The use of the term *panniculus*, defined as "membrane,"[21] leads us to interpret this text to read that a girl possesses a hymen before defloration. Giulia Sissa has demonstrated that the existence of this particular membrane was not acknowledged in ancient medicine, although she alludes in a footnote to a passage from Augustine recounting how a midwife destroyed a virgin's maidenhead during manual examination,[22] and suggests that the Church fathers accepted the hymen's existence.

If we move to the medieval period, we find evidence that the hymen was incorporated into western anatomical understanding by way of Arabic medical sources. The late ninth/early tenth-century physician Rhazes tells us that the opening of the vulva in a virgin is contracted and wrinkled, and in the folds of this virginal neck five subtle veins are woven. These are broken when the woman is corrupted and the wrinkles are smoothed out.[23] Later, in the eleventh century, Avicenna ends his chapter on the anatomy of the womb with the statement that before the violation of a virgin girl there are membranes (*panniculi*) in the mouth of the womb woven from veins and extremely delicate ligaments issuing from every member. The violator destroys these and the blood in them runs out.[24] In the twelfth century, Averroes repeats part of this description of a wrinkled vulva.[25]

The translations from the Arabs appear to be the source for medieval Latin understanding of the hymen. Rhazes and Avicenna were translated by Gerard of Cremona after 1150,[26] and Nicholus cites both these authors in our text. If we look at an early Latin gynecological writing like Muscio's sixth-century rendering of Soranus[27] we see a description of the orifice of the womb of a virgin who has not yet been deflowered as "fleshy and soft."[28] The Salernitan *Anatomia Cophonis* (1100–1150), which also predates the Latin versions of the Arabic treatises,[29] simply gives a description of the womb as a concave organ with two orifices; the exterior one is the *collum matricis* (neck of the womb), and here coitus is accomplished. There is no mention in these texts of blood vessels or a membrane.[30] When we move to a later author like Albertus Magnus, however, who used Avicenna's writings extensively and was familiar with Rhazes's *Continens* as well,[31] we see Albert describe in the entrance to the womb of virgins "membranes made of a tissue of veins and extremely loose ligaments which are destroyed by the [sex] act or even by inserting one's fingers; whereupon, the small quantity of blood in them flows out."[32] The thirteenth-century scientist and philosopher follows the Arab description closely, and this becomes a pattern in medical texts as well.[33]

William of Saliceto, a Bolognese physician and surgeon who was roughly Albert's contemporary, presents us with his own adaptation of this passage. William, who normally relies very heavily on Avicenna,[34] tells us that "the knot of virginity is tightly tied and wrinkled with veins and arteries that stand out like creases on a chickpea."[35] The fourteenth-century anatomists Henry of Mondeville and Mondino de Luzzi are less independent of their source; they describe "veins which are torn at the moment of deflowering" and "a subtle and venous membrane" which breaks at the time of defloration. Danielle Jacquart and Claude Thomasset, who have examined this problem, note, however, that we do not find the term "hymen" used for this membrane until Michele Savonarola in the fifteenth century.[36]

Thus, medieval Arabs and Latins generally accepted the concept that some sort of rupture occurred to a virgin at the moment of defloration, resulting in vaginal bleeding, and Nicholus's account here is fairly standard.

III. This blood is to be distinguished from menstrual blood because it is clear, not muddy, and because it is small in quantity. Further, it is shed only at the moment of defloration, and not beforehand or afterward.

This passage, which is very close to William of Saliceto's account,[37] points to the significance of menstrual blood in medieval scientific thought. According to medieval doctors, menstruation is a sign of female inferiority. In the Trota text, for example, we find the traditional account from the Greek physician Soranus of monthly purgation: women are cold, wet, weak creatures who are unable to burn up the moistures that collect in them, and so are purged every month by the menstrual period.[38] Another theory is that menses consist of food which the woman has not been able to digest.[39]

However the actual composition of menstrual blood may have been conceived, there is a long tradition affirming the venomous nature of this substance, and it is for this reason that Nicholus is careful to distinguish it from the blood of defloration. The menses is poisonous and infects the body; if it touches the twig of a green tree the twig immediately dries up; a fetus generated from it becomes leprous; and it will cause great harm to the male member.[40] Women who have their menstrual periods are so filled with poison that they can kill babies merely by glancing at them; their hair, too, is venomous and serpents can be generated from it.[41] Since menstrual blood and the blood of defloration flow from the same area of the body, Nicholus points out the differences between the two types of flow.

The pollution caused by a woman's menses leaves an indelible mark on her body; she is permanently unclean. Even after she has been "cleansed" by the flow, she must take steps before meeting with a man. Gilbertus Anglicus prescribes aromatics before sexual activity because of the size of the female organ and its heavy odor. Women should moderate nature with artifice, he states lest they appear improper and disgusting to men.[42] A similar prescription to improve the woman's odor is contained in one of the Salernitan texts.[43] Thus, the "muddy" flow to which Nicholus refers plays an important role in the medieval medical conception of women.

IV. The urine of a virgin is thin and clear because the passages of the womb and vulva are narrow, so nothing descends into the urine except what is subtle, neither thickening nor muddying it. Because of this, a virgin urinates more delicately and for a longer period of time than does a woman who has been corrupted.

We understand this text to mean that Nicholus believed that in the female the urinary passage and the vagina were one and the same. Before defloration, the passageway is narrow, and so it takes longer for urine to be evacuated, and only the thinnest part is able to fit through. Afterward, the opening is larger, and urine passes more quickly with grosser matter contained in it.

This misconception about female anatomy is not unique to Nicholus. A pelvic structure in which the urethra and vagina are identical or connected seems to be assumed by virginity tests requiring suffumigation such as those by Gilbertus Anglicus set down below by Nicholus in Section V of this text. If introduction of particular odors into the vagina causes urination, presumably the odoriferous substance passes directly into the bladder, leading the woman to void. The early medieval *Liber matricis* prescribes a test of this type,[44] as does William of Saliceto, whose *Summa conservationis*, published in 1285,[45] post-dates Gilbert's death in 1250.

William was an eminent professor and surgeon at the medical school of Bologna during the thirteenth-century "anatomical Renaissance" when dissection began in the Latin west, and it would seem that his anatomical and surgical background would have been enough to have prevented him from construing the female pelvis in this manner. If we read further in his text, however, we find additional evidence of his confusion between the urethra and the vagina. William tells us that a virgin urinates with a more subtle hiss than a non-virgin, and it takes her longer to finish than it does a small boy.[46] Presumably, this is because the passageway is still narrow, for male penetration has not yet taken place. We have other examples of this misunderstanding in texts cited by Danielle Jacquart and Claude Thomasset. In the *Anatomia vivorum*, composed ca. 1225 and sometimes ascribed to Galen, the author states that "the opening of the cervix is so narrow that only urine can pass through." Similarly, the fourteenth-century surgeon Henry of Mondeville states that the "vulva or cunt" has a brown membrane hanging out somewhat because it is meant to act as a passage for urine so that it does not spill out into the whole vulva.[47] Clearly surgical training and the practice of dissection did not prevent medieval doctors from believing that urine passes through the vaginal opening.

Jacquart and Thomasset explain this confusion in part by pointing out the inaccuracy of the sources: these authors did not have access to Galen's *De usu partium*, where the urethra is described correctly, and the Arabic texts are not very clear on this subject.[48] We have evidence of this confusion in the *Canon of Medicine*, where Avicenna seems to indicate that the passage of urine begins in a different place, near to the mouth of the womb, but does not acknowledge that the two passageways have different openings.[49] More to the point is the fact that simple observation leads to the opposite conclusion; even a naive woman would be able to observe the difference between her vagina and urethra, and it would seem that a learned physician would surely be able to ascertain such a simple fact.

The French scholars argue that for the medieval mentality the external appearance of the organs was unimportant; what mattered was presenting a clear explanation for the mechanism of reproduction. Thus, the doctors and anatomists, both Arab and Latin, confuse the clitoris with the labia, and the author of the *Anatomia vivorum*, along with other Salernitan anatomists, refuses entirely to describe the external female organs, halting "at the place the cervix of the womb ends on the outside." In line with this approach, iconographical representation in the few manuscripts that illustrate reproduction is far from realistic; Jacquart and Thomasset refer to one codex that has captions proper to the female sex attached to a distorted diagram of the male apparatus.[50]

A second important reason for this error is the adoption of the Galenic idea that male and female sexual organs were analogous; as the ancient physician states in his *De usu partium*, the parts that are in the female on the inside are outside in the male; they were formed identically during the fetal stage, but because of the defect of the heat in females they did not emerge on the outside.[51] At the end of the twelfth century, this idea was taken over forcefully in the west by Toledan translations from the Arabic, and from this point on woman was described with reference to man.[52] Certainly if we look at Rhazes's *Liber continens*, one of Nicholus's sources, this is true: the Arab physician speaks, for example, of the woman's "testicles" which are smaller, wider versions of the man's.[53] Avicenna begins his description of the anatomy of the womb with a direct statement that the womb derives from the same root of creation as do the instruments of generation in the male (the penis and the rest of the apparatus), but his is completed and proceeds to the outside, while hers is diminished and retained within, and therefore can be considered the converse to the male instrument.[54] The thirteenth-century Salernitan *Anatomia Richardi Anglici* uses the analogy of a seal and its imprint on wax.[55]

Given this framework in which the male model determined female structure, we are provided with a partial explanation why Nicholus and his

Latin predecessors would assume that because the male voids his urine through the penis, a female would do so through her vagina. Just as medieval anatomists were unable to cope with the existence of the clitoris because it upset the neat system of inverse symmetry of organs,[56] so they could not see that the female urethra and vagina have two separate openings. What must have been obvious to all women and to most men was too difficult for learned physicians to accept. Galenic theory was more important than what they could see and touch.

V. Gilbert said that if a woman is covered with a piece of cloth and fumigated with the best coal,[57] if she is a virgin she does not perceive its odor through her mouth and nose; if she smells it, she is not a virgin. If she takes it in a drink, she immediately voids urine if she is not a virgin. A corrupt woman will also urinate immediately if a fumigation is prepared with cockle. Upon fumigation with dock flowers, if she is a virgin she immediately becomes pale, and, if not, her humor falls on the fire and other things are said about her.

Fumigation, as noted above, is used here to determine if the passageways are blocked. A similar use of this procedure is found in one of Hippocrates's fertility tests, quoted by the physician Bernard de Gordon (fl. 1283–4408), who comments that the experiment is valid only in virgins.[58] Fumigation is also used in medieval medicine to introduce healing substances into the interior of the body.

Another basis of medieval medical practice is diagnosis by urine. As explained by a commentator on the De secretis mulierum, a thirteenth-century treatise on the female reproductive system and astrology, the urine is divided into three regions. The upper region is examined for the superior members, such as the cerebrum and the head. The middle region is where the central members such as the kidneys and heart are considered. In the lower region, the testicles, loins and womb are inspected.[59] Thus, virginity would be judged by this third area.

The commentator provides us with some additional details on the urine of a maiden. This substance is clear, because virgins are hot and digest well (youth being one of the hotter stages of life), and urine takes on its color while crossing through the place of digestion, so it is colored in the kidneys. The experimenter who is testing the girl should take the urine after the first sleep because then digestion has been accomplished, and he should take care that it is not variegated with disease and thick nutriment. This text provides us with some of the rationale and more specific directions for the urine tests which are fairly standard in the texts we have examined: the urine of virgins is clear; it can also be golden but that indicates appetite for pleasure; if it is muddy the woman is corrupt.

As noted earlier, virginity tests are hardly the rule in medieval treatises on gynecology,[60] and they are even less common in general medical writings and in tracts on uroscopy. Rhazes, for example, writes an entire chapter on difficulty of urination and does not mention a difference between virgins and non-virgins. Indeed, to underline the point made above on the importance of the male model, Rhazes's entire discussion of urinary disorders—retention, burning, inability to retain—centers around problems with the penis, and does not mention women at all.[61]

If we look at some of the texts on uroscopy in the *Collectio Salernitana*, we see that urine is observed to change during different stages of life, but defloration is not one of these stages. Thus, in youth which is hot and dry urine should be red and thin: red because of the dominant heat, and thin because of the intensity of dryness.[62] Urine is used to diagnose disorders of the womb, retention of menses or emission of seed, but difficulties caused by losing one's maidenhead are not part of these problems.[63] Although occasionally a treatise on urines will mention differences between the urine of virgins and non-virgins,[64] virginity tests are not normally found in these writings.

VI. It sometimes happens that when a virgin is deflowered her vulva becomes blown up and swollen. This is cured by sitting in water in which mallows and pennyroyal have been cooked, and by an external application of rose oil as an aromatic.

Avicenna said that virgins suffer pain when they are violated, especially when the neck of the womb is narrow and the membranes on its surface are weak and of a thin texture so that they break easily. This occurs when the male organ is thick, which results in their rupture. Defloration in this fashion leads to a flow of blood and pain. For a cure, the woman must sit in styptic waters such as a decoction of rose and myrtle in order to heal and to prevent the flow of menses to that place. She should sit in cooked wine and oil, as Musahan said in the commentary on the *Continens,* in order to ease the pain.

Then when the pain has diminished and the flow of blood has stopped, Avicenna said that a wax plaster wrapped in wool on a reed should be administered, not in order to heal the broken follicles which are not meant to be knit together, but to prevent the lips of the neck of the womb from adhering to one another and causing a closure of the cervix. This reed or something similar will prevent a blockage, and sexual intercourse should be performed lightly or even prohibited entirely until healing is accomplished.

Once the area has been washed and cleaned of all dirt if there was any, a consolidating ointment should be applied from the substances mentioned in the preceding chapter, in order to knit together the parts that have been broken. Sometimes, states Avicenna, pottery shards[65] and similar substances such as Armenian clay, gum arabic, and things of this type should be administered with this ointment.

Also, concerning things helpful in this condition, cooked milk should be given. Galen said in his book *On Simple Medicine* that milk cooked with stones or iron and other substances helps to heal an ulcerated womb.

The assumption in this passage is that defloration is a medical event, normally causing injury to the woman that requires professional care. Nicholus's main source here is Avicenna, and the Islamic physician has worked out an elaborate treatment for this "disorder." Just as today normal stages in the female life course such as childbirth and menopause have been medicalized, so according to Avicenna and his followers a woman's first sexual encounter was an occasion for medical treatment.

If we look at the Salernitan texts, we see that this attitude was by no means universal. Roger of Salerno, for example, deals in his *Liber de chirurgia* with a corrosion of the vulva or the male penis, and instructs his reader in the preparation of a plaster to treat this problem.[66] In none of the cases is the corrosion caused by the act of defloration.

Avicenna and Nicholus, on the other hand, assume that the male will possess the woman roughly enough to cause physical damage. The text describes how a thick male organ breaks the membranes, resulting in bleeding and pain, but accepts the fact that these are not meant to be healed. The fifteenth-century physician Anthonius Guainerius also acknowledges that a man injures his partner during the sex act. His *Treatise on the Womb* describes how a "raging male penis entering her and disrupting the vein because of its magnitude" can lead to excess menstrual bleeding.[67]

Although defloration may not have been universally recognized as having physical consequences to the woman, one theme that does run through ancient and medieval gynecological texts is "sophistication," or apparent restoration of lost virginity. Giulia Sissa notes that Galen recommends inserting perfumed pessaries into the vagina to alter and revitalize its appearance.[68] The early medieval gynecological writer Theodorus Priscianus, who relied heavily on Soranus,[69] includes in his work a chapter entitled "For the violated woman, that this be kept secret,"[70] and the Trota text presents complicated recipes for this purpose.[71] The author prefaces his remarks with an apology, stating that he would never treat such a subject unless there were an honorable reason, but a too-flaccid vulva sometimes hinders conception.[72] Joan Cadden has demonstrated that this passage was problematic in later versions of the text; not all compilers and copyists included directions for counterfeiting virginity, and some censure it directly.[73]

Trota's concern with morality is not typical of medieval discussions of sophistication. Rhazes, for example, inserts in the *Continens* a chapter on substances which constrict the vulva, and he is very forthright about the purpose for this procedure, suggesting as well that the woman fill a dove's intestine with blood and insert it into the vagina so that she will bleed as if it were her first sexual experience.[74] These directions are repeated by William of Saliceto, who is not always so frank about sexual matters;[75] and Gilbertus Anglicus, too, makes available to his readers recipes for "sophistication."[76]

Gilbert is extremely cognizant of the social and psychological consequences of defloration, and sets them down in a passage that is unusual for medieval medical writing. The thirteenth-century physician begins his chapter "On the Sophistication of the Vulva" by stating that virgins are sometimes corrupted so that their passage is widened and the corruption becomes obvious to whoever touches this bodily part. Deservedly they suffer repudiation, and both men and women who participate in this corruption risk unending shame and divorce. Thus, continues Gilbert, it is necessary to constrict this defective enlargement, and it is the woman's task to cover it up by her effort.[77]

Although we do not normally find such overt censure in a medical text, some of Gilbert's milder remarks are repeated in other writings. The English physician states that the signs of virginity are modesty, a faultless gait and speech, approaching men with eyes cast to the side.[78] The *De secretis mulierum* begins the chapter "On the Signs of Chastity" with an almost identical statement, however, the author follows it with the remark that "some women are so clever that they know how to resist detection by these signs and in this case a man should turn to their urine."[79] Clearly modesty and virginity are linked by some medieval scientists.

Another medieval text on sophistication acknowledges the passion that makes the procedure necessary. A thirteenth-century Latin poem, *De secretis mulierum*, based on Chapter 35 of the Trota text and attributed to Roger of Salerno[80] devotes the last two verses to restoring virginity and alleviating the swelling of the vulva after coitus. The poem begins by stating that the woman who needs the medicament described in the book is the one whose vaginal passage became extremely large by opening her thighs to friends, loaded with desire, to be deprived of her virginity. When it is time to get married, it will be necessary to blind her husband to the truth.[81] The almost pornographic character of the introduction reminds us of some of the Arabic medical material on sexual intercourse,[82] and also presents a tone rarely found in Western medieval medical writings.

A final noteworthy point about this passage is Avicenna's recommendation that a solid object be inserted into the vagina in order to "prevent the lips of the neck of the womb from healing together and causing a closure of the cervix." This procedure reminds us of some of the practices associated with clitoridectomy,[83] which was practiced in the medieval Arab world; when a large portion of the labia has been removed, a stick is often inserted during the healing period. Avicenna's prescription of a wax plaster wrapped in wool on a reed may have nothing to do with practices of sexual mutilation, but may simply be a common sense approach to a medical situation. In order to necessitate the plaster, however, injury to the vagina would have had to have been severe.

Thus Nicholus's directions in this last section of the chapter are designed to aid the deflowered virgin in overcoming the effects of vaginal and cervical injury, which are regarded as inevitable. Unlike some other writings on this subject, his discussion is non-judgmental and matter-of-fact. Neither the moral aspects, nor the social consequences of premarital sex are addressed by our author. He relies heavily on Avicenna in instructing the physician to provide thorough medicinal treatment for what to him is clearly a medical condition.

Virginity: Historical Perspectives

The defloration of a virgin, although discussed here by Nicholus within a medical context, has larger significance within a society. Whether female virginity is prized, and under what circumstances, reflects society's valuation of women, and affects their lifestyles and life choices. The evolution of the concept that a woman possesses a membrane within the vagina that guards her purity for her husband or for God goes hand in hand with an increasing control over her life by men.

In primitive matrilineal societies, female sexuality was free and unhindered and virginity was worshipped. Virgins, surrounded by mystical powers, sometimes experienced ritual defloration before the wedding night. Some tribes imagined that a serpent lay in the maiden's vagina, waiting to bite the husband's penis just as penetration occurred, and frightful powers were also ascribed to virginal blood. To counteract this evil, villagers would form a circle, rendering the male invulnerable, and he would break the hymen with a stick or a bone. In Samoa, he used his fingers wrapped in a white cloth, which was torn into bloody bits and distributed to persons present.[84]

The awe and power that encircled virgins can be traced back to religious beliefs in a Great Goddess. Egyptian, Sumerian, Babylonian, Greek and Assyrian mythology all recount creation at the hands of a Mother-Goddess. The Greek Earth-Goddess Gaia, for example, created the sky Uranos in a virgin birth and fashioned humankind as well. We learn from archaeological data that the principal deity in the Neolithic and Chalcolithic periods was the Mother Goddess: female Goddess figures, represented by pregnant women, are surrounded by eggs and forms of vegetation, symbolizing fertility of humans, animals and plants. This feminine divinity had power over nature and the seasons, as we see by her frequent association with the moon. Goddesses, like Ishtar and Aphrodite, were revered for their sacred sexuality and their power to give life, which included the ability to heal. Sexuality of the goddess, regardless of the name she was called, conferred the blessings of fertility to the earth and to the people who used rituals and offerings to please her.[85] In Rome, Vestal Virgins played a role in agricultural and fertility rites, demonstrating further that purity and intactness can be viewed as stored up fertility.[86]

The worship of female virginity did not end with these ancient civilizations. Many people held on to their faith in the powers of virgins; a particularly interesting example is found in Galicia, the northwest province of late Roman and Visigothic Spain, studied by Joyce Salisbury. The excessively infertile quality of Galician soil led the inhabitants to devise rituals to inspire the land to produce a sufficient harvest, and at the base of these practices was the belief that sacrificing procreation in one area would guarantee it in another. Virgins became an important focus of this ritual; some women gave up personal procreativity to become a town's lucky charm. They believed that retaining physical virginity was the biggest human sacrifice a woman could offer, and hoped that, in return, fertility would be bestowed on the rest of the community.[87]

The power of virgins to cause others to bear fruit was a passive form of control; they were associated with light, or the moon, which dominated water, a source of fertility. Similarly, the menstrual blood of virgins was passively regulated, and constituted the "magic, fertile water" directed by the moon. This sexual symbolism was a part of the earlier Iberian Celtic mythical structure, and became subsumed into a Christian framework from the late fourth century on. Virgin martyrs replaced pagan goddesses and Gallegan female saints expressed their mystical ideas in sexual imagery: Iberian virgins were brides of Christ who possessed knowledge, and this knowledge was referred to as a child carried in their womb.[88]

Women had good reason to choose virginity as a way of life during this period. Virgins had great freedom and independence to come and go as they pleased, as well as a community of women to depend upon. We see them making pilgrimages to the Holy Land, visiting friends, living alone on occasion, and moving frequently. Further, their independence was spiritual as well: their vows of celibacy took place in a private discussion with God, without the aid or constriction of the church. These vows made the virgins closer to God, and raised their standing in the eyes of villagers, who regarded these blessed women with awe.[89]

Pre-Christian patriarchal religions viewed virginity differently from matriarchal ones. To guarantee legitimate heirs, men demanded virginity before marriage and fidelity afterward. Under Levite law of the Hebrew texts, fear of God controlled female sexuality, and loss of virginity before marriage would cause a woman to be stoned or burned to death.[90] In Hinduism, a preoccupation with the protection of women's bodily orifices continues to the present day. Because children take the caste of the mother, physical purity of unmarried female children is of utmost importance. Girls are married before menarche to increase the likelihood that they will be maidens. The pressure is highest for Brahman (upper-caste) girls, since their pollution would have the gravest consequences.[91]

The testing of a woman's chastity became a major preoccupation of patriarchal civilizations. It is worthy of note that the variety of "purity tests" used many symbols that had been associated with female magic and strength to betray the maiden in question. In ancient Greece, gods and goddesses were invoked through divinatory ritual to reveal the truth. Remember that it was the same set of goddesses who represented fertility, sexuality and female power that were called upon to judge young girls.[92] The moon, an important female symbol, was also used to determine if a woman was virginal. In the medieval Arab and Latin worlds, astrologers investigated the positions of the moon and the stars when questioned about a woman's purity: Zahel in the ninth century used stellar constellations, and Abenragel in the eleventh century used the phases of the moon in conjunction with the stars. The most extensive treatment was by the Latin Guido Bonatti, in the thirteenth century, who used astrology to interpret different sexual situations and determine whether or not a woman gave into her desire.[93] The credibility of these tests was strengthened by beliefs in women's mystical powers as connected to the moon, the menstrual cycle and fertility.

Within the patriarchal Christian church, female virginity took on an entirely new meaning. Whereas matriarchal religions had celebrated female sexuality and the mystical powers of virgins, Christianity denounced carnality, and used virginity as the only way to improve women's status in society and in the eyes of God. According to the Church, the valuation of women was directly dependent on whether they were virgins under ecclesiastical supervision. St. Jerome made it popular to remain virginal instead of marrying,[94] and Saint Paul, Cyprian, John Chrysostom and Fortunatus also stated that virginity is the chosen way.[95] This advocacy of consecrated virginity continued into the high Middle Ages. Aelred of Rievaulx believed that virgins were closer to Christ than non-virgin women, and Thomas Aquinas put virginity above marriage.[96] In the Augustinian tradition, the ecclesiastical *Hali Meidenhad* praised virginity as a supernatural gift from God, which, once lost, can never be restored.[97] The thirteenth-century moralist Philippe de Navarre wrote that if a woman's body was intact, all other defects would be hidden, while all good qualities would be obscured if a woman sinned.[98] The redefinition of virginity as a controlled way of life greatly restricted the independence and freedom that these women had previously enjoyed. Virginity became a means to an end, smoothing a woman's way to salvation, instead of a free and celebrated lifestyle.[99]

Surprisingly, if we look more closely at the concept of virginity in the earlier patriarchal societies, we see that the term "virgin" does not always signify a woman who has been untouched by a man. With the introduction of male control came an interpretation of virginity that places restrictions on sexual freedom, but these boundaries were not defined by physical violation. In the Hebrew texts, the word for virgin means "young woman," not "chaste woman." The most significant usage of the word "virgin" was in contrast to the word "married." It was also the same term used for a prostitute. Ishtar, the Mesopotamian Mother Goddess of the Semitic peoples, wore a veil, or *posin,* as did both prostitutes and virgins in Judaism, and the sacred prostitutes of her temples were called "holy virgins." The progeny of these priestesses were called "virgin-born."[100]

In Greece, the *parthenia* were unmarried moral maidens who were to be chaste until marriage. In spite of this, these women could lead secret lives of sexual activity as long as they were never discovered. The word for bastard (or virgin born) in Greek is derived from *parthenos* (virgin), so it is clear that the *parthenia* were not expected to hold absolute unwavering chastity, although they were required to remain childless. Since a child was usually the one proof of a woman's sexual transgression, punishment for her now public violation was heavy, and her status was lowered to that of a slave.[101]

An important part of the ancient Greeks' unusual definition of virginity is their conception of female physiology. According to a recent work by Giulia Sissa, the Greek medical community did not believe that young virgins possessed a membrane blocking the virginal pathway. Without a hymen, the purity of a woman was a judgment to be made by the gods, not the doctors. When the gods held a woman under suspicion, her whole life was examined, including her moral conduct. Her body's intactness was never the focal point of the discussion.[102]

A "hymen," in the terms of Greek physiology, was defined by Aristotle as a membrane that wrapped all parts of the body and was indispensable to each organ's function and conservation.[103] There is no reference to a specific membrane that blocks the vagina of a virgin. The Hippocratic tradition that this concept reflects makes it clear that virgins were not thought of as having a different anatomy from non-virgin women. By the time of the Romans, Soranus, a Greek physician of the second century A.D., found it necessary to dispute a new belief that such a virginal hymen existed.

> In virgins the vagina is depressed and narrower [than in other women] because it contains ridges that are held down by vessels originating in the uterus; when defloration occurs, these ridges unfold, causing pain; they burst [the vessels], resulting in the excretion of blood that ordinarily flows. . . . In fact, belief that a thin membrane grows in the middle of the vagina, and that it is this membrane that tears in defloration or when menstruation comes on too quickly and that this same membrane, by persisting and becoming thicker, causes the malady known as 'imperforation,' is an error.[104]

According to Sissa, this is the first Greek medical text that mentions a virginal hymen.

Soranus went even further in his argument against the possibility of a hymen by stating that any membranous blockage of the vagina could interfere with either coitus, conception, or childbirth. His prescription was a speedy removal of the impediment, in order to restore the patient's body to proper female anatomy. Soranus had explained the pain of defloration by the unfolding of ridges, so there was no need in this anatomical framework for a hymen. Thus, the *parthenia* of Greece could remain virginal or enjoy secret rendezvous with lovers and still retain her status, because no irreparable damage had taken place.[105]

Galen, who practiced in Rome about 75 years after Soranus, also believed that defloration did not involve the rupture of a membrane. Although he discusses the body parts thoroughly, and declares that there is nothing about which he has not spoken in detail, he makes no mention of a genital hymen. For Galen there is but one hymen: the membranous covering of the inner parts of the body described by Aristotle, which ties all organs together. In the fourth century Oribasius, the Emperor Julian's personal physician, also took Soranus's point of view and denied the existence of a virginal hymen.[106]

The Christians did not adopt this conception of female physiology, but instead resurrected the earlier belief in the significance of defloration. Within Christianity, virginity is once again defined strictly, but this definition has its place in a religion in which women are regarded as ritually impure.[107] Unlike the matriarchal societies we examined earlier, where physical virginity represented power, or ancient Greece where virginal intactness did not exist as a concept, in Christianity bodily purity is demanded in a context where women are conceived of as tainted beings. A virgin becomes defined as *virgo intacta,* a woman who has never experienced sexual intercourse, and this purity of body is to be combined with a purity of mind for God. Although men, too, are supposed to retain physical integrity, they can be rewarded with the priesthood and thus the ultimate closeness to the Lord. Women must settle for lesser status, and their physical virginity is given much greater emphasis.

Conclusion

Chapter 30 of Nicholus's fifteenth-century book *Diseases of Women,* "On the Defloration or Violation of a Virgin," raises a number of significant issues. Although virginity was prized and connected with female sexual power in matriarchal societies, patriarchal religions like Judaism, Hinduism and Christianity demanded woman's physical intactness in order to control her. The ancient Hebrews and Greeks, however, did not define female virginity as a state in which the woman had never been penetrated by a man, but rather a condition of moral purity and childlessness. Greek medicine did not accept the existence of a vaginal hymen.

The Christian tradition, which Nicholus's text reflects, placed great store in bodily intactness, and medieval doctors become concerned with physical maidenhood. They devised urine tests to determine if a girl had been deflowered, based on the mistaken notion that women, like men, void through their genital opening. Defloration, according to Nicholus, was a traumatic event, usually involving injury to the woman which required medical intervention. He did not include in his prescribed treatments the recommendation by some other physicians that the violation be camouflaged, nor did he concentrate on the social consequences of the sex act. Nicholus's main concern in this chapter is with diagnosing and treating a medical condition.

Appendix

Nicholus, de Passionibus Mulierum

Cap. xxx: De defloratione[108] seu violatione virginis[109]

I. Mulier que virgo est discernitur violata et corrupta per visum et tactum obstetricis.

II. Quoniam ante deflorationem ut in precedentibus est dictum os matricis est velatum panniculo contexto venis arteriis qui cum defloratur rumpitur et inde sanguis emittitur.

III. Et discernitur iste sanguis a sanguine menstruo quia est clarus non turbidus et quia est paucus. Et quia solum tunc emittitur et non ante neque post.[110]

IV. Et urina quidem virginis est subtilis et limpida quia via matricis eius et vulve stricte sunt quia non descendit in urina eius nisi quid subtile non ingrossans neque turbificans eam. Et cum hoc virgo mingit subtilius et ad longius quam corrupta.

V. Dixit Guillibertus si fumigetur mulier gate optime pannis tecta si virgo est non sentitur fumum eius per os et nares. Nam si senserit ipsum virgo non est. Et si sumpserit eum in potu si virgo non est statim minget. Item si fiat fumigatio cum ghet si virgo non est statim minget. Item si fumigetur floribus ramicis si virgo est statim palefiet et si non humor eius cadat super ignem ipsius et dicuntur etiam alia.[111]

VI. Contingit tamen aliquando in defloratione virginis quod vulva eius inflatur et tumescit. Et curatur cum sessione in aqua decoctionis malve et pulegii et inunctione facta ab extra cum oleo rosato retenti vel olfactionis. Dixit Avicenna[112] de mulieribus scilicet virginibus est cui accidunt dolores magis cum violantur praecipue cum collum matricis eius est strictum et panniculi scilicet superficiei colli eius sunt debiles id est et rare texture facile frangibiles et proprie cum virga devirginans est grossa dirrumpens eos ad quorum disruptionem sequitur sanguinis fluxus et dolor. Et necesse est ad curam ut sedeat in aquis stipticis ut decoctionis rosarum et mirtillorum ad consolidationem et prohibitionem fluxus menstruorum ad locum ut sedeat in vino scilicet decocto vel sappa et oleo ut dixit Musahan commento Continentis et hoc ut sedetur dolor. Deinde sedato dolore et prohibito fluxu dixit Avicenna administretur ad eam cerotaria in lana involuta super cannam prohibentem a consolidatione non quidem panniculorum eruptorum quia tales non dicuntur consolidari sed labiorum colli matricis ne adhereant et invicem consolidentur et fiat inde clausura colli eius. Prohibentur autem adhaerere per cannam intromissam super vel aliud simile et allevietur super eam concubitus ymmo prohibeatur omnino donec consolidatio facta fuerit. Et deinde intendendum est ad consolidationem partium solutarum et praemissa ablutione loci et mundificatione eius ab omni sorde si aderit[113] supponatur unguentum consolidativum ex hiis que dicta sunt in capitulo precedenti. Et quandoque cum illo unguento dixit Avicenna administretur terra sigillata et similia et ut bolus ar. gummi arabici et huiusmodi. Et de conferentibus utiliter est ut administretur lac decoctum. Dixit enim Galenus in De simplici medicina multotiens confert matricibus ulceratis crescere ex lacte decocto cum lapidibus vel ferro igni et cetera.[114]

Notes

1 On f. 5 of Lille ms. 334 Nicholus comments that the celestial bodies exert an influence upon different regions, causing the populations of some to be infertile, and the inhabitants of others to be prolific, "which can be seen in my own city of Florence" (quod monstrari potest in mea propria civitate Florentina).

2 Following "De passionibus mulierum," there are two words that are very light and difficult to decipher in the microfilm. According to the catalog of the Lille library, the full title is "De passionibus mulierum in partu." See M. Le Glay, *Catalogue descriptif des manuscrits de la Bibliotheque de Lille* (Lille: Vanackere Librairie, 1848), 285.

3 M. Le Glay, 285.

4 *Catalogue General des Manuscrits des Bibliotheques Publiques de France, Departements*, (Paris: Plon, Nourrit et cie., 1897), vol. xvi, 239. Ms. Lille 335 states on fol. 19v: Michi Guillermo de Naste, medico, pertinet vere liber iste. *Catalogue*, 240.

5 The name "Haly" is used to refer to a number of different medieval writers. Constantine's *Pantegni* is a translation of Ali ibn Abbas al-Majusi's medical treatise; Ahmad ibn Yusuf, the author and commentator of the *Centiloquium*, named in medieval manuscripts as "medicus et astrologus" is also known as "Haly." See Richard Lemay, edition of Abu Ma'shar's *Introductorium in astrologiam*, tr. Hermann of Carinthia, Introduction, 59–60, to appear Naples, 1991.

6 e.g., f. 81, 87v, 91, 92, etc.

7 Monica Helen Green, *The Transmission of Ancient Theories of Female Physiology and Disease Through the Early Middle Ages* (Princeton University Dissertation, 1985), 75–77.

8 Gallie drachma iii gariofili drachma i musci drachma sexta pars sumantur et trita omnia in unam vini unciam mittant in quo pannus made factus in vulva mittatur. Rhazes, *Liber ad Almansorem decem tractatus continens cum nonnullis additionibus interlinearibus Gerardi Cremonensis nusquam antea impressis in Opera parva* (Lugduni: Gilbert de Villiers, 1511), f. cxliii.

9 Sumatur etiam galle balaustie, cupulie glandium, folia mirti et coquantur in aqua donec rubea fiat, et sedeat in ea et lavetur ex ea. Rhazes, *Liber ad Almansorem . . . continens*, Book ix, cap. 81: De exitu matricis et ani, fol. 177–177v.

10 Danielle Jacquart, *Le milieu medical en France du XIIe au XVe siècle* (Geneva: Droz, 1981), 208 and note 2; Luke Demaitre, *Doctor Bernard de Gordon: Professor and Practitioner*, (Toronto: Pontifical Institute of Mediaeval Studies, 1980), 110.

11 Sagathe mulier subfumigetur et optime cooperiatur et si per os et nares fumum senserit virgo non est. Item detur in potu si virgo non est statim comminget se. Similiter fiat ex gith fumigatio si non est virgo minget. Item fumigetur floribus reumicis, si virgo est pallescet, si non humor ipsius cadet supra ignem. Gilbertus Anglicus, *Compedium medicinae* (Lyons: Mercuriali, 1510), Liber septimus, Cap. "De sophisticatione vulve," fol. cccv ra. On Gilbertus Anglicus see Henry E. Handerson, *Gilbertus Anglicus: Medicine of the Thirteenth Century*, (Cleveland, Ohio: Cleveland Medical Library Association, 1918).

12 Monica Green, 455.

13 Danielle Jacquart, *Le milieu medical*, 50–51.

14 Quidam vero volunt notare super virginitatem per aspectum in ore vulve, et hoc est officium obstetricis que consueta est in hoc et docta fuit a medico secundum

viam anothomie illius loci . . . Guilielmus de Saliceto, *Summa conservationis et curationis* (Venice, 1489), f. i 3 ra.

15   Marina Warner, *Joan of Arc: The Image of Female Heroism* (New York: Vintage, 1982), 16. Thomas Benedek has suggested that the midwives who examined Joan were selected on the basis of their political rather than their medical reliability. See, Thomas G. Benedek, "The Changing Relationship Between Midwives and Physicians During the Renaissance," *Bulletin of the History of Medicine* 51 (1977), 561.

16   Benedek, "Changing Relationship," 560.

17   Giulia Sissa, *Greek Virginity*, tr. Arthur Goldhammer (Cambridge, Mass., and London: Harvard University Press, 1990), 115.

18   Renate Blumenfeld-Kosinski, *Not of Woman Born: Representations of Caesarean Birth in Medieval and Renaissance Culture* (Ithaca and London: Cornell University Press, 1990), 94–95.

19   Renate Blumenfeld-Kosinski, Chapter III: "The Marginalization of Women in Obstetrics."

20   De strictura vero nimia sive amplitudine aut oris tortuositate ubi certificare cupias tu ipse ubi phas sit experire. . . ." Anthonius Guainerius, "Tractatus de matricibus" in *Opera Omnia* (Pavia, 1481), f. 2z1ra. See Helen Rodnite Lemay, "Anthonius Guainerius and Medieval Gynecology," in *Women of the Medieval World*, ed Julius Kirshner and Suzanne F. Wemple (Oxford and New York: Basil Blackwell, 1985), 322.

21   R.E. Latham, *Revised Medieval Latin Word List*, (London: Oxford University Press, 1965), 330.

22   Giulia Sissa, 214 n. 49.

23   Rhazes, *Liber ad Almansorem . . . continens,* Tractatus Primus, Cap xxxvi: Matricis preterea collum ad mulieris porrigitur vulvam, quod in muliere est sicut in viro virga. Vulve autem orificium in virgine constrictum est et rugosum. In rugis autem ipsius colli virginalis quinque vene contexuntur subtiles, que quando corrumpitur virgo abrumpuntur, et predicte dilatantur ruge.

24   Et ante violationem puelle virginis sunt in ore matricis panniculi contexti ex venis et ligamentis subtilibus valde ortis ex omni membro eius quod destruit violator et currit quod in eis ex san. est. Avicenna, *Liber canonis* (1507 reprint Hildesheim, 1964), Liber III, fen xxi, cap i, f. 360v.

25   Averroes, *Colliget* (Venice, 1549), f. 49v.

26   Manfred Ullman, *Islamic Medicine* (Edinburgh: Edinburgh University Press, 1978), 54.

27   On this text see Monica Green, 446.

28   Quale ergo est orificium matricis? Apud virgines, quae nondum devirginatae sunt, pulposum et molle. . . . Muscio, "De matrice sive utero Cap. II, prior" in *Harmoniae gynaeciorum sive de morbis muliebribus liber ex Prisciano Cleopatra Moschione libro Matricis dicto et Theodoro Prisciano collectus* (Argentinae: Zetzner, 1597), 1. For a modern edition, See Rino Radicchi, ed., *La 'Synaecia' di Muscione: Manuale per le Ostetriche e le mamme del VI sec. d. c.* (Pisa: Editrica Giardini, 1972), 42.

29   The translations were prepared in the twelfth century, but not really used by scholars until the thirteenth. See Nancy G. Siraisi, "The Medical Learning of Albertus Magnus," in *Albertus Magnus and the Sciences: Commemorative Essays 1980*, ed. James A. Weisheipl (Toronto: Pontifical Institute of Mediaeval Studies, 1980), 392, and Luke Demaitre, *Doctor Bernard de Gordon: Professor and Practitioner* (Toronto: Pontifical Institute of Mediaeval Studies, 1980), 110, 112.

30 Claude Thomasset, "La représentation de la sexualité et de la génération dans la pensée scientifique médiévale," in *Love and Marriage in the Twelfth Century* (Louvain: Leuven University Press, 1981), 4.

31 Nancy G. Siraisi, "The Medical Learning of Albertus Magnus," 389.

32 Albertus Magnus, *De animalibus* (Stadler tr. 2, ch. 24, 164, #458) cited by Danielle Jacquart and Claude Thomasset, *Sexuality and Medicine in the Middle Ages*, tr. Matthew Adamson (Princeton: Princeton University Press, 1988), 44.

33 It is interesting to note that in his *De mineralibus* Albertus Magnus includes a virginity test that utilizes the power of stones. See John M. Riddle and James A. Mulholland, "Albert on Stones and Minerals," in *Albertus Magnus and the Sciences*, 208.

34 Helen Rodnite Lemay, "William of Saliceto on Human Sexuality," *Viator* 12 (1981), 165–181.

35 . . . nam foramen vel os vulve per quam virga hominis ad matricem ingreditur ante quam corrumpatur nodus virginitatis est strictum contextum venis et artariis [sic] manifestis rugatum in cuius textura et rugatione sunt eminentie parve ad modum acuitatis ciceris. Guilielmus de Saliceto, *Summa conservationis et curationis* (Venice 1489), f. i3 ra.

36 Danielle Jacquart and Claude Thomasset, *Sexuality and Medicine in the Middle Ages*, 44.

37 . . . et differentia inter illum sanguinem qui exit hora illa a vulva et sanguinem menstruum in tempore quantitate et colore tempus enim exitus sanguinis corruptionis virginitatis minimum est comperatione temporis menstruorum et quantitatis minima etiam; color vero sanguinis qui exit hora corruptionis virginitatis clarus et non fuscus est, eo quod a venis et arteriis per violentiam et non in modum superfluitatis exit. Color vero menstruorum ex causis contrariis fuscus et turbidus reperitur et apparet. Guilielmus de Saliceto, f. i3 rb.

38 Trotula of Salerno, *The Diseases of Women*, tr. Elizabeth Mason-Hohl (Los Angeles, 1940), 1–2. For the Latin text see "Erotis medici liberti Iuliae quem aliqui Trotulam inepte nominant muliebrium liber. . ." in *Harmoniae Gynaeciorum*, 42.

39 Pseudo-Albertus Magnus, *De secretis mulierum* (Lyons, 1580), 19ff.

40 Pseudo-Albertus Magnus, *De secretis mulierum*, Chapter I.

41 Pseudo-Albertus Magnus, *De secretis mulierum*, Chapters I, II, IV.

42 Item ad magnitudinem instrumenti et gravem eius odorem ne inepte et fastidio se viris appareant et non contemnantur et ut moderetur natura artificio . . . fiat aqua constrictiva et aromatica, Gilbertus Anglicus, f. cccv rb.

43 Ut redolere queat melius, foveatur et istis. *De virginitate restituenda sophistice*, cap. 45, in Salvatore de Renzi, iv, 23.

44 *Liber matricis* in *Harmoniae Gynaeciorum*, 2.

45 On this text see Helen Rodnite Lemay, "William of Saliceto on Human Sexuality," 165–81.

46 Guilielmus de Saliceto, *Summa conservationis et curationis* (Venice, 1489), fol. i3ra.

47 Danielle Jacquart and Claude Thomasset, *Sexuality and Medicine in the Middle Ages*, 37, 45.

48 Danielle Jacquart and Claude Thomasset, *Sexuality and Medicine in the Middle Ages*, 45.

49 Meatui autem urine in ea est locus alius et est propinquior ori matricis ab eo quod sequitur supremum eius. Avicenna, *Liber canonis*, Liber III, fen xxi, f. 360vb.

50   Danielle Jacquart and Claude Thomasset, *Sexuality and Medicine in the Middle Ages*, 11, 25, 35, 38.

51   Galen, *De usu partium* xiv, 6. See *Galen on the Usefulness of the Parts of the Body* tr. Margaret Tallmadge May (Ithaca, NY: Cornell University Press, 1968), 628–29.

52   Danielle Jacquart and Claude Thomasset, *Sexuality and Medicine in the Middle Ages*, 36.

53   Post autem ista dua additamenta mulieris locantur testiculi, qui virorum testiculis minores sunt et latiores, a quibus muliebre sperma ad concavitatem descendit matricis. Rhazes, *Liber ad Almansorem . . . continens*, tract. I, cap. xxxvi "De forma matricis," f. xx verso.

54   Dico quod instrumentum generationis mulieris est matrix et est in radice creationis similis instrumento generationis quod est in viris et est virga et que cum ea sunt. Sed unum eorum est completum procedens ad exteriora et alterum est diminutum retentum in interioribus et est quasi conversum instrumentum virorum. Avicenna, *Liber canonis*, Liber III, Fen xx, tract. II cap 1, f. 356rb.

55   C. Thomasset, "Representation," 7.

56   Danielle Jacquart and Claude Thomasset, *Sexuality and Medicine in the Middle Ages*, 46.

57   The term used here, *gate*, reads *ggthe* in the Gilbertus Anglicus edition. Professor John Riddle has kindly informed us that a similar passage exists in Albertus Magnus's *Book of Minerals* (2.2.7, p. 93, Dorothy Wycoff edition): "They say, too, that experience shows that if water in which it has been washed is strained and given with some scrapings [of the stone/mineral] to a virgin, after drinking it, she retains it and does not urinate; but if she is not a virgin, she urinates at once. And this is the way virginity should be tested."

58   Luke Demaitre, *Doctor Bernard de Gordon*, 129.

59   Pseudo-Albertus Magnus, *De secretis Mulierum*, "De signis castitatis," Commentary A (Lyons, 1580), 120: Nota, quod in urina sunt tres regiones, scilicet superior, ubi considerantur membra superiora, scilicet cerebrum, et caput. Secundo in medio, ubi considerantur membra media, scilicet renes et cor. Sed tertia est inferior, ubi considerantur testiculi, lumbi et matrix.

60   Nancy Siraisi has discovered two tests for virginity in one of the *consilia* of the thirteenth-century papal physician Guglielmo, both, as she comments "(wisely) hard to fail." See Nancy G. Siraisi, *Taddeo Alderotte and His Pupils: Two Generations of Italian Medical Learning* (Princeton: Princeton University Press, 1980), 280.

61   Rhazes, *Liber ad Almansorem . . . continens*, Tractatus Nonus, cap. lxxiii: "De difficultate mingendi," cap. lxxvi: "De ardore que fit in mictu," cap. lxxviii: "De his que non possunt retinere urinam," fol. clxxii verso–clxxv.

62   "De urinis et earundem significationibus liber," in Salvatore de Renzi, ed., *Collectio Salernitana* (Naples: 1852–1856), vol. II, 415: In juventute vero quae calida est et sicca, urina debet esse rubea et tenuis, rubea pro calore dominante, tenuis pro siccitatis intensione.

63   "De urinis et earundem significationibus liber," in de Renzi, volume II, 417; Maurus, "Regulae Urinarum," in de Renzi, volume III, 6–9; Joannes Platearii Salernitani, "Regulae urinae," in de Renzi, vol. IV, 410–411.

64   Joan Cadden of Kenyon College has kindly informed me that the "De urinis" in British Library Sloane manuscript 431, f. 42 contains the urine test for virginity.

65   John Riddle has kindly informed us in a private communication (2/27/91) that the term *terra sigillata* is pottery, probably broken shards with painting. Professor Riddle notes that in Gerard of Cremona's translation of Avicenna it is called *lotum sigillata*, that is "earth/dirt" (*Canon* Bk.2, tract. 2, chapter 421, fol. 126v of Venice ed., 1507, rpt. Hildesheim 1964). The use of broken pottery goes back to Egyptian medical papyri. In her translation of an early fifteenth-century *Medieval Woman's Guide to Health* (Kent State University Press, 1981), Beryl Rowland translates this term as "Lemnian earth" (115).

66   Roger of Salerno, *Liber de chirurgia*, Book III, cap. 52: "De corrosione in virga virili vel vulva" in de Renzi, vol. IV, 119.

67   Anthonius Guainerius, f. y3vb; See Helen Rodnite Lemay, "Anthonius Guainerius," 335.

68   Giulia Sissa, 121, and n. 64, citing Galen, "De remediis parabilibus," xiv, 478, in Kuhn, 486.

69   Monica Green, 135.

70   Ad violatam, ut non cognoscatur. Priscianus in *Harmoniae gynaeciorum*, 2.

71   On the authorship of this text see John Benton, "Trotula, Women's Problems and the Professionalization of Medicine in the Middle Ages," *Bulletin of the History of Medicine* 59 (1985), 30–53.

72   Nisi de restrictione amplitudinis vulvae propter honestam causam liceret tractare, nullam de ea mentionem faceremus: sed cum per hanc impediatur aliquando conceptio, necesse est tali impedimento sic subvenire. "Erotis Medici Liberti Iuliae quam aliqui Trotulam inepte nominant Muliebrium Liber," in *Harmoniae Gynaeciorum*, 53.

73   Joan Cadden, "Medieval Scientific and Medical Views of Sexuality: Questions of Propriety," *Mediaevalia et Humanistica*, n.s. 14 (1986), 164.

74   Cum autem vulva multum stricta fuerit atque vir ut coeat ad mulierem accesserit parva pars intestini sanguine columbe impleatur et vulve antequam vir ad eam accedat immittatur. Postquam enim ad eam accesserit, et cum ea coire ceperit scindetur intestinum et sanguis fluere incipiet. Rhazes, *Liber ad Almansorem . . . continens,* Tractatus Quintus, cap. lxix: "De his que constringunt vulvam," fol. xcvi.

75   See Helen Rodnite Lemay, "William of Saliceto," 176.

76   Ad sophisticandam ianuam ut virginis appareat fiat proclisma. Recipe aluminis pulveris. . . . Gilbertus Anglicus, "Liber Septimus, Cap. de sophisticatione vulve," f. cccv ra.

77   Corrumpuntur quandoque virgines unde et ianua ampliatur ita ut corruptela pateat contigenti et merito repudium patiuntur et in sempiternum dedecus vel divortium in utriusque periculum tam viri quam mulieres sortiuntur. Igitur hoc elargatum oportet restringere vitium et est ipsius mulieris conamine sophisticatum palliare. Gilbertus Anglicus, f. cccv.

78   Virginitatis autem signa sunt pudor et verecundia cum casto incessu loquele gestus, gressus cum despectu applicationis ad virum quodam torvo aspectu. Gilbertus Anglicus, f. cccv ra.

79   Signa castitatis sunt haec, pudor, verecundia, timor, cum casto incessu, et loquela, cum despectu applicans se viris et virorum actibus: sed quaedam ita astutae inveniuntur, quod omnibus istis obviare sciunt, et tunc homo covertat se ad urinam. Pseudo-Albertus Magnus, *De secretis mulierum*, 119.

80   See Charles Daremberg, "Sul poema medicum lettera. . . ." in de Renzi, vol. iv, 177–184.

81   Cap. 45: "De virginitate restituenda sophistice"

Indiget istius etiam medicamine libri
Quam secretus amor veneris furibunda voluptas
Perlargam dederant ut amicis crura relaxans
Voto freta suo privetur virginitate
Nubere cum sit opus, ignoret ut ista vir ejus
Excecabit eum sic virgo sophistica caute
Pulvere contritum zucarinum sumat. . . (de Renzi, vol. IV, 23).

82   See Franz Rosenthal, "Sources for the Role of Sex in Medieval Muslim
Society," in *Society and the Sexes in Medieval Islam, Sixth Giorgia Levi Della Vida
Biennial Conference,* ed. Afaf Lutfi Al-Sayyid-Marsot (Malibu, California, 1979). See
also Martin Levey and Safwat S. Souryal, "Galen's On the Secrets of Women and On
the Secrets of Men: A Contribution to the History of Arabic Pharmacology," *Janus* 55
(1968), 208–19. This article provides a description of an Arabic manuscript from the
ninth century or earlier containing sexual recipes such as "Drugs that make
lesbianism so desirable to women that they would keep busy with it and passionately
lust for it forgetting all about their work," or "Drugs which excite the desire of women
so that they go wandering around, leaving their homes, looking for sexual
satisfaction, throwing themselves before men and searching for a good time." Two of
its recipes pertain to virginity: one hardens the hymen of virgin girls so that it is
impossible to break it, and another softens the hymen so that it breaks without
contact with a man.

83   See Fran P. Hosken, *The Hosken Report, Genital and Sexual Mutilation of
Females* (Lexington, Mass.: Women's International Network News, 1979).

84   Simone de Beauvoir, *Second Sex* (New York: Vintage Books, 1952), 172–
173.

85   Gerda Lerner, *The Creation of Patriarchy* (New York and Oxford: Oxford
University Press, 1986), 146–50.

86   Sarah B. Pomeroy, *Goddesses, Whores, Wives and Slaves: Women in
Classical Antiquity* (New York: Schocken Books, 1975), 211.

87   Joyce E. Salisbury, "Fruitful in Singleness," *Journal of Medieval History* 8
(1982), 98.

88   Joyce E. Salisbury, 98–101.

89   Joyce E. Salisbury, 100, 103.

90   Deuteronomy 22: 20–22; Merlin Stone, *When God Was a Woman* (San
Diego, New York and London: Harcourt, Brace, Jovanovich, 1976), 182, 156, 190.

91   Martha J. Reineke, "Out of Order," in *Women: A Feminist Perspective,* ed.
Jo Freeman (Mountain View, Calif.: Mayfield Publishing Co., 1989), 398.

92   Giulia Sissa, 86.

93   Helen Rodnite Lemay, "The Stars and Human Sexuality: Some Medieval
Scientific Views," *Isis* 71 (March 1980), 130–31.

94   Pierre Payer, "Early Medieval Regulations Concerning Marital Sexual
Relations," *Journal of Medieval History* 6 (1980), 354.

95   Pierre Payer, p. 354; Julia O'Faolain and Lauro Martines, *Not in God's
Image* (New York and London: Harper and Row, 1973), 137–39.

96   Clarissa W. Atkinson, "Precious Balsam in a Fragile Glass: The Ideology
of Virginity in the Later Middle Ages," *Journal of Family History* 8,2 (Summer
1983), 136; Julia O'Faolain, *et al.,* 139.

97   For an in-depth discussion of virginity in the monastic tradition, see John
Bugge, *Virginitas: An Essay in the History of a Medieval Ideal* (The Hague: Martinus
Nijhoff, 1975), 116. On the *Hali Meidenhad* see also Clarissa Atkinson, 138.

98   Julia O'Faolain, *et al.*, 141. On Philippe de Navarre see Ulysse Chevalier, *Repertoire des Sources Historiques du Moyen-Age; Bio-bibliographie* (New York: Kraus reprint, 1960), vol. II, 3638.

99   Joyce E. Salisbury, 104.

100   Robert Briffault, *The Mothers* (New York and London, 1927), III, 169–170.

101   Giulia Sissa, 78, 83, 88–99. The falling of a woman's status is referred to in Plutarch, *Concerning the Laws of Solon*, 23. See Giulia Sissa, 87, who cites as well A.R.W. Harrison, *The Law of Athens*, vol. 1 (Oxford, 1968), 73, n. 2.

102   Giulia Sissa, 106.

103   Giulia Sissa, 110.

104   Soranus, *Gynaikeia*, Book I, chapters 16–17 cited by Giulia Sissa, 113.

105   Giulia Sissa, 112–16.

106   Giulia Sissa, 111–13.

107   On female ritual impurity see Suzanne Fonay Wemple, *Women in Frankish Society: Marriage and the Cloister 500–900* (Philadelphia: University of Pennsylvania Press, 1981), 139 ff.

108   et *add. ms*

109   Divisions of the text by Roman numerals have been made by the editors for convenience of reference. They do not exist in the manuscript.

110   In margin: Nota de urina virginis.

111   Gilbertus Anglicus, fol. cccv ra.

112   Avicenna, *Liber canonis* (1507, rpt Hildesheim, 1964), Liber 3, fen 21, cap. 11, f. 372va.

113   ms: adderit.

114   Galenus, *De simplicium medicamentorum temperamentis ac facultatibus*, Liber x, cap. II, 8: De sero lactis, in *Opera*, ed. Kuhn (Leipzig, 1826), vol. XII, 266–268.

Disclosure

TEXTS, NAKED AND THINLY VEILED: EROTIC ELEMENTS IN MEDIEVAL ITALIAN LITERATURE

Christopher Kleinhenz

The one hundred cantos of Dante's sublime *Divine Comedy*, which celebrates the transcendental nature and power of love, are matched, at least in number, by the one hundred tales in Boccaccio's "human comedy," the *Decameron*. In these two works, separated by a mere three decades, we note the two extremes of medieval Italian literature—the *Divine Comedy* representing all creation as seen *sub specie aeternitatis*, and the *Decameron* depicting the multiplicity of the human condition as seen *sub specie humanitatis*. For Dante the end of human activity lay either in the rewards or in the punishments allotted in the afterlife,[1] while for Boccaccio the end of human endeavors remained on earth. The divine teleology of the *Comedy* is countered by the invariably secular goals of Boccaccio's characters who act in a variety of ways to obtain their worldly reward, be it riches, political power, sensual pleasures, or fame and glory. While Boccaccio gained early on a certain notoriety for his often irreverent and salacious tales, Dante became associated with a severe sense of morality that made him appear prudish to some of his readers, or that at least made some of his readers adopt a more prudish tone when dealing with the *Comedy*.[2] In consequence, critics rarely discuss sexual matters in the *Divine Comedy*.[3] These popular views of the two authors are, at best, incorrect and, at worst, misleading, for they more likely reflect the moral preoccupations, sexual inhibitions, and cultural attitudes of the reader's age, rather than those of thirteenth- and fourteenth-century Italy.

While much has been written about sexual practices in medieval Europe,[4] relatively little research has been conducted on the "evidence" of sexual activity found in medieval Italian literature.[5] In this essay I hope to provide a number of examples of what could be termed erotic and sexual activity in order to suggest that these topics were very much a part of the literary tradition. Nevertheless, the ambivalence concerning these practices among medieval authors and scribes and subsequent generations of readers produced several results. Authors would often conceal their erotic subject matter under thinly veiled wraps, employing euphemisms and *double-entendres* to produce a culturally acceptable version. Sometimes the editors or the readers themselves—through piety or moral conservatism—would excise the morally "offensive" passages to protect themselves and posterity from these corrupting elements.

It is far easier to say what this essay is not: it does not provide a theoretical discussion of the phenomenology of love or the psychology of desire, nor does it attempt to define the often hazy borders between "courtly" love and eros, between eros and pornography, or between pornography and the obscene. It does not investigate, nor does it question, the relationship between certain sexual attitudes and practices described in literary texts and their possible real counterparts in the historical social milieu of the Middle Ages. Rather, it accepts the textual "evidence" at face value and attempts to render an accounting of the variety of heterosexual erotic elements in medieval Italian literature.[6] Within its limited scope this essay cannot make any claims at exhaustive—or even minimal—coverage of the subject. It does, however, aim to provide—perhaps for the first time—in summary fashion some sense of the number and variety of erotic/sexual elements in medieval Italian lyric poetry and prose. To accomplish this limited goal within the allotted space this essay will remain primarily descriptive; however, I hope that these few materials may be sufficient to encourage interest and to stimulate research in the area.

Poetry

Given the large body of existing scholarship, it would be redundant to rehearse here the entire history of Italian literature in the thirteenth and fourteenth centuries.[7] However, some historical background is necessary if only to establish the general frame of reference, to call attention to the different schools of poetry and to remark the various stylistic levels, which range from the refined and courtly to the crude and popular. After this brief excursus on the development of lyric poetry in medieval Italy we will examine a number of poems chosen from various moments and schools in this historical period that disclose erotic or sexual elements in varying degrees of clarity.

The Italian lyric tradition began with the group of poets gathered at the Imperial court of Frederick II of Hohenstaufen in Sicily during the period 1220–1250. Most of these poets, usually referred to as the *poeti siciliani* ("sicilian poets") or as the members of the *scuola siciliana* ("Sicilian school"), were professionals (physicians, notaries, jurists, lawyers) attached to Frederick's court in some official capacity: Giacomo da Lentini, the most prolific poet and presumed inventor of the sonnet, was a notary at court and refers to himself in his lyrics by this official title, "il Notaro." Pier della Vigna was Frederick's secretary and longtime counselor, until his fall from grace, imprisonment, and subsequent suicide—well known through the episode in canto 13 of Dante's *Inferno*. Noted primarily for the poem "Già mai non mi conforto," in which the woman laments the departure of her beloved on the Crusades, Rinaldo d'Aquino may have been the falconer at court. By and large, the Sicilian poets adopted many of the metrical forms and much of the content of the Provençal troubadour love lyrics. They sang in their native idiom to complain about the tyranny of the God of Love and their lady's cruelty, to lament their generally unrequited carnal passion, to praise the worth of their lady and to pledge themselves to selfless devotion and endless service to her. The concept of *Frauendienst*, which informs occitanic poetry, is central to the Sicilian literary corpus, even though the social and political conditions which fostered it in the rigidly hierarchical feudal baronries of Provence, northern France, and Germany were not present at the imperial court, with its centralized, bureaucratic organization, cosmopolitanism, and openness to science, learning, and the arts. In the transplantation of this tradition to Sicily some of its identifying characteristics were lost or changed radically (e.g., feudal terminology was, for the most part, abandoned), while others were retained (the concept of beauty, embodied in the blond-haired woman, was a commonplace). As was the case in troubadour poetry, the *persona* of the Sicilian lyrics dedicates his life to serving his lady, haughty though she may be. This is the lover who ardently seeks and patiently pursues his elusive goal or reward (*guiderdone*), which is the obtaining of "joy" (i.e., the gift of love), and moral or social betterment.

Much of the Sicilian manner was continued on the peninsula by the Tuscan imitators of the Sicilian School (the *poeti siculo-toscani*, "Sicilian-Tuscan poets")—Bonagiunta da Lucca, Bondie Dietaiuti, Maestro Francesco, Pucciandone Martelli, et al.)—who, geographically removed from Sicily, lived and wrote in a greatly different cultural milieu, primarily in the mercantile centers of Tuscany, Umbria, and Emilia-Romagna. However, Guittone d'Arezzo reacted against what he viewed as the *démodé* poetic manner of the Sicilians and their followers and attempted to change the course of the lyric tradition through a renewal of its language, themes, and forms. In addition to amorous topics, he expanded his poetic repertory to include moral, religious, and political subjects. Thus, around the middle of the thirteenth century, while some poets followed the general outlines of the *scuola siciliana*, others—the "Guittonians"—wrote verses in the style of Guittone. Most of these latter poets (Panuccio del Bagno, Monte Andrea, Chiaro Davanzati, Meo Abbracciavacca, et al.) came from the nearby urban centers in Tuscany and shared, to some extent, the same political, ethical, and moral concerns as their mentor; moreover, the distinctive style of their poetry—highly artificial, elaborate use of rhetorical devices, *recherché* idiom—demonstrates their allegiance to Guittone.

Dissatisfaction with one literary movement or attitude usually results in the emergence of another, which opposes it in some way; thus, through the never-ending process of reaction and action, the literary tradition continually renews and recreates itself. As with Guittone d'Arezzo and his followers, so was the case with Guido Guinizzelli and the advent of the Dolce Stil Nuovo ("Sweet New Style"). For his role in the transformation and renewal of the lyric tradition, Guinizzelli has generally been recognized as the father of the Dolce Stil Nuovo, whose "members" included, among others, Guido Cavalcanti, Dino Frescobaldi, Cino da Pistoia, and Dante. In his doctrinal *canzone* "Al cor gentil rempaira sempre Amore" Guinizzelli addresses certain fundamental problems regarding the definition of human nobility, the nature of the beloved, and the value of earthly love. The worth of an individual does not depend on wealth, lineage, and other external circumstances, but rather upon one's natural disposition; thus, the capacity to love with pure and noble sentiments is reserved for those to whom nature has given the "noble heart" (*cor gentil*). Unlike her generally passive predecessors in the lyric tradition, Guinizzelli's lady assumes in the elaborate analogies of the poem a power and status equal to that of God and is responsible for activating in her admirer that innate potentiality to love; she becomes a true "donna angelicata" ("angelicized woman") comparable to the angelic intelligences that move the eternal spheres. Given the philosophical pretensions and the numerous metaphysical parallels and analogies of this *canzone*, Guinizzelli obviously had in mind to ennoble human love by transforming it into a sort of secular *caritas*. Although unsuccessful in accomplishing this great goal of reconciling human affection for woman and divine love for God, Guinizzelli at least indicated the new direction for poets to follow in their amorous poetry. It is to this model that Dante turns in his own amorous and poetic experiences recounted in the *Vita Nuova* ("New Life"). The praise accorded Beatrice there and in the *Divine Comedy* and her role in the latter work as Dante's personal bearer of spiritual salvation represent the supreme achievement of the Dolce Stil Nuovo.

In the fourteenth century imitators of the Dolce Stil Nuovo were legion throughout Italy and include Fazio degli Uberti, Niccolò de' Rossi, Sennuccio del Bene, and Giovanni Boccaccio. Although he used many of the themes and images of the earlier lyric tradition, Francesco Petrarch was able to infuse poetry with a new life and meaning. His poetry may be characterized by his concentration on the inner workings of the human psyche, by his intense concern for the individual, by his incorporation of themes and images from classical antiquity, and by his ability to achieve a balance and sense of proportion in each verse of each poem. In the *Canzoniere* Petrarch captured the lyrical quality of his desires and aspirations, expressed his internal conflict between love and reason and his simultaneous quest for earthly glory and spiritual salvation, and demonstrated his rhetorical skill in moral and political invective. Petrarch's themes and style established the model which was imitated by countless poets throughout Europe in the Renaissance (Petrarchism).

Alongside these refined "courtly" poets from the Sicilian School through Petrarch there were, in late-thirteenth- and fourteenth-century Italy, a number of burlesque poets who composed lyrics in a decidedly lower stylistic register: Rustico di Filippo, Cecco Angiolieri, Meo dei Tolomei, and others. The language of their compositions is generally less refined, more coarse, the diction dialectal and more colloquial; hyperboles abound, and the images often reflect an ordinary or homey environment, while the rhetorical flourishes and adornments have much in common with those of the courtly tradition.[8] The subject matter consists largely of commentaries on daily events and of virulent attacks on individuals, at the heart of which lie materialistic interests (money), sexual practices and abnormalities, physical weaknesses and defects, petty jealousies, antifeminism, and the like. These topics are, of course, standard features of comic poetry in Western Europe. The simultaneous presence of these several stylistic registers throughout these centuries—and sometimes within the poetic corpus of a single author (e.g., Dante, Rustico di Filippo, Guido Cavalcanti, et al.)—demonstrates the impressive richness and diversity of the medieval Italian lyric tradition.

The goals of any love lyric are several: to praise the beauty and excellent qualities of the object of desire, to celebrate the sentiment both as an abstract quality and as a very real and powerful personal emotion, to describe the effects of this passion on the individual, to convince the beloved through rhetorical means to reciprocate the affection of and bestow favors on the lover—in short, to persuade and move the recipient of the poem to fulfill the desire and intention of the author. The formulae of the love lyric are numerous, and the style may vary greatly—from lofty sentiments and refined phrases to base desires and coarse terminology—but the end, the reward (the *guiderdone*) is generally the same: erotic satisfaction. The erotic, then, lies at the root of the poem and is its main inspiration. The following discussion treats four types of texts which may be distinguished, one from the other, by their degree of explicit sexuality, by the presence or absence of erotic elements.

Texts Elegant and Sublime

In most lyrics of this period sexual desire is sublimated, to the degree that there are very few overt references to sexuality. Thus, while the ultimate goal of the lover—coitus—was always understood, it was rarely stated, remaining constantly hidden behind the amorous and joyful, but erotically neutral language of the text. In the following sonnet by Giacomo da Lentini we may perceive the delicate balance or, perhaps better put, the state of tension that exists in the early Italian lyric between sublimated desire and sexual passion:[9]

Io m'agio posto in core a Dio servire,
com'io potesse gire in paradiso,
al santo loco, ch'agio audito dire
si mantien sollazo, gioco e riso;

sanza mia donna non vi vorria gire,
quella c'à blonda testa e claro viso,
chè sanza lei non poteria gaudire
estando da la mia donna diviso.

Ma no lo dico a tale intendimento
perch'io peccato ci volesse fare,
se non veder lo suo bel portamento,

lo bel viso e lo morbido sguardare,
chè lo mi terria in gran consolamento,
vegendo la mia donna in gloria stare.

[I have set my heart to serving God so that I may go to Paradise, to the holy place, where I've heard there is always pleasure, joy, and laughter. I would not wish to go there without my lady, that one with the blond hair and the clear face, for without her I would not be able to have joy, since I would be separated from my lady. But I do not say this to mean that I would wish to commit a sin there, but only to see her lovely bearing and her lovely face and her soft glance; for I would consider it a great pleasure to see my lady there in glory.]

Here, sensual desire prompts the poet to serve God, for in this way he may be admitted to Paradise, which he describes as the abode of all earthly delights ("sollazzo, gioco e riso"). His desire is further clarified in the second quatrain, where he declares that, if his lady is not there, then he, too, does not wish to be, for, in his words, he would not be able to enjoy himself ("ché sanza lei non poteria gaudere"). The tercets begin by negating the inference of the quatrains. The poet says that he does not really expect to enjoy carnal pleasure with his lady in Heaven, but only to gaze upon her corporeal perfection. However, given that this celebration of earthly beauty will occur in Paradise, in the presence of God, we sense in the poet's attitude of worshipful adoration the beginnings of that upward movement in love, that transfiguration of the lady into the transcendental being, the true "donna angelicata" ("angelicized lady") of the Dolce Stil Nuovo through whom the poet-lover may rise to the Divine. This one poem may serve to represent the great majority of love lyrics in the thirteenth and fourteenth centuries that celebrate the joys of carnal passion and sexuality, but in a sanitized manner.

Texts Reasonably Refined but Ambiguous

Poetry in this category is basically no different from that in the first division in terms of language, theme, and style; however, the presence of certain words and images make these lyrics susceptible to other, more erotic interpretations.[10] For example, in the following sonnet Bonagiunta Orbicciani da Lucca discloses his indebtedness to the Sicilians in his play on the polyvalent word "fiore":[11]

Tutto lo mondo si mantien per fiore:
se fior non fosse, frutto non seria;
e per lo fiore si mantene amore,
gioie e alegrezze, ch'è gran signoria.

E de la fior son fatto servidore
sì di bon core che più non poria:
in fiore ho messo tutto 'l meo valore;
si fiore mi falisse, ben moria.

Eo son fiorito e vado più fiorendo;
in fiore ho posto tutto il mi' diporto;
per fiore aggio la vita certamente.

Com' più fiorisco, più in fior m'intendo;
se fior mi falla, ben serïa morto,
vostra mercé, madonna, fior aulente.

[The entire world is maintained by the flower. If there were no flower, there would be no fruit; and because of the flower love, joy and happiness are maintained, which is a great dominion. And I have become the servant of the flower so willingly that I could do no more: I have placed all my worth into the flower; if it (she) were to fail me even a little, I would indeed die. I am all aflower, and I continue to flourish more and more; I have put all my pleasure in the flower; I most certainly possess life because of the flower. The more I flourish, the more I love the flower; if the flower fails me, I would certainly die, be merciful, my lady, sweet-smelling flower.]

In the first verse the dependency of all earthly things rests on the concept of *fiore*, a metaphor for that "love" which binds the universe together. It is appropriate that this all pervasive force be presented at the beginning of the poem, in rhyme position, and in its abstract substantive form, for in the second verse it assumes a more precise horticultural meaning: the "flower" that precedes the fruit. Similarly, in vv. 3–4 we observe the social effects of such an image. The masculine and abstract form ("lo fiore") used in the first quatrain metamorphoses in gender in the second to become the symbol for the lady ("la fior") in whom ("in fiore") the poet has placed all his "valore" (i.e., his vital energy and power). The final "fiore" (v. 8) in the quatrains is adverbial, thus assisting in its transition from a non-active usage (as nouns) to a dynamically active one (as verbs), which the first verse of the tercets announces: "Eo son *fiorito* e vado più *fiorendo*." On one level, this sonnet is a hymn of praise to the perfection of the flower and its regenerative power. On another level, it is a very bold and highly erotic statement of the life-giving, recreative power of sexual intercourse. The lover on two occasions speaks in very physical and spatial terms of "placing" ("ho messo") or "putting" ("ho posto") his penis—metaphorically defined as his "valore" and "diporto"—into the woman, the fragrant flower ("in fiore").[12]

The double meaning which is found in Bonagiunta's sonnet is present in many other poetic compositions from the last half of the thirteenth century, those by the lofty-minded poets of the Dolce Stil Nuovo included. In the so-called *rime petrose* Dante presents the desperate quality of his love for the woman usually referred to as Donna Petra (the "Stone Lady"). In particular, two strophes of his *sestina* "Al poco giorno e al gran cerchio d'ombra" contain language that suggests the subtle play of double meanings and lend themselves to an erotic interpretation:[13]

Io l'ho veduta già vestita a verde,
sì fatta ch'ella avrebbe messo in petra
l'amor ch'io porto pur a la sua ombra:
ond'io l'ho chesta in un bel prato d'erba,
innamorata com'anco fu donna,
e chiuso intorno d'altissimi colli.

> Ma ben ritorneranno i fiumi a' colli
> prima che questo legno molle e verde
> s'infiammi, come suol far bella donna,
> di me; che mi torrei dormire in petra
> tutto il mio tempo e gir pascendo l'erba,
> sol per veder do' suoi panni fanno ombra. (25–36)

[I once saw her clothed in green and such that she would have imparted to stone the love that I bear to her mere shadow; hence I have desired her in a fair grass field—as much in love as ever a woman was—enclosed by great hills.

But surely rivers will return to the hills before this wet green wood catches fire, as is the way of fair woman, for me—who would consent to sleep on stone all my days and go about eating grass, only to see where her dress casts a shadow.]

While the translation provides a traditional, non-sexual interpretation of these stanzas, other meanings are possible. The lover claims to have once seen the woman "vestita a verde," which could mean "naked," and such that she would have caused his love for her to become petrified (i.e., for him to have an erection); he further states that he desired her ("l'ho chesta") in this secluded *locus amoenus*, and the verb has distinct erotic overtones. The impossibility topos (*adynaton*) that begins the next strophe set the temporal stage (i.e., never) for his complaint about the woman's "greenness," that is, her inability to be kindled with love for him. Thus, the lover notes, he would gladly sleep in/on stone (i.e., have intercourse with Donna Petra) and feed on "erba" (i.e., the "erba" that is intertwined with her bodily parts as related earlier in the poem) if only to be able to see where her clothes cast a shadow, which is, of course, always *under* her clothes!

The following madrigal presents a situation replete with sexual *double-entendres*. Here the Florentine poet Niccolò Soldanieri imagines himself to be a bat, whose call, the onomatopoeic *zi zi*, represents both the animal's cry and the name of the woman, Zita:[14]

> I' sono un pipistrel che vo gridando
> *zi zi* di notte intorno a una tana,
> aspettando *zi zi* con voce piana.
>
> *Zi zi* non viene e io non so che farmi
> e volo in giú e 'n su *zi zi* chiamando,
> tanto che l'alba si viene appressando.
>
> Omè, omè!, sogn'io o vo sognando?
> *Zi zi* rispuose: "Entra." e fe' entrarmi
> ov'io piú amo e sto fra dolce lana.

[I am a bat that goes crying *zi zi* at night around a hollow, waiting for *zi zi* with a quiet voice. *Zi zi* does not come, and I don't know that to do, and I fly up and down calling *zi zi*, until dawn nears. Oh me, oh my! Do I dream or am I dreaming? *Zi zi* replies: "Come in." And she lets me enter there when I most love to be and where I remain in great comfort.]

Through the repetition of *zi zi*, the many verbs, and the rapid, short phrases Soldanieri succeeds in representing the highly excited state of the lover who in the guise of a bat constantly flutters around a *tana*, the woman's "cavity" to which he is temporarily denied access. After much pleading, the "bat" (penis) is finally permitted to enter the "cavity" (vagina) where it is content to remain.

Texts Playful and Direct

Poems in this category are generally less refined than those in the first two divisions and are characterized by their open expression of erotic elements and sexual activity. Instead of the standard, rarefied setting and often idealized relationship between the sexes we find scattered but clear references to the pleasures and power of sensual passion. In his *canzonetta* "Dolce cominciamento," Giacomo da Lentini presents a dialogue between the lover and his lady: In the following strophe the woman asks the man to remember the origin of their love and specifically the moment of its consummation:[15]

> Dolce meo sir, se 'ncendi,
> or io che degio fari?
> Tu stesso ti riprendi
> se mi ve' favellari
> ca tu m'ài namorata;
> a lo cor m'ài lanzata,
> sì ca di for non pari.
> Rimembriti, a la fiata
> quand'io, tebi abrazzata. . . .
> A! li dolzi basciari! (11–20)

[My sweet lord, if you burn, what must I do? You blame yourself if you see me burn, for you have made me fall in love; you have pierced my heart in such a way that it does not appear externally. Remember that time when I, locked in your embrace. . . . Ah, the sweet kisses!]

The specific reference to the amorous embrace and the "dolzi basciari" ("sweet kisses") in this earlier time provides the point of departure for the third strophe in which the lover recalls more details of that blissful encounter:[16]

> Ed io basciando stava
> in gran dilettamento
> con quella che m'amava,
> bionda, viso d'argento;
> presente mi contava,
> e non mi si celava
> tutto suo convenente.
> E disse: "Io t'ameragio
> e non ti falleragio
> a tutto 'l mio vivente." (21–30)

[And with great pleasure I was kissing the one who loved me, the one with blond hair and silver face. Presently she told me everything, hiding nothing and said: "I will love you and will not betray you for my entire life."]

While the description of the woman—blond, fair complexion—is stereotypical, the mutual, reciprocal nature of the love, and its expression in terms of erotic passion, are unusual in the Italian lyric tradition.

Some poets roughly contemporaneous to the Sicilian School—and generally classed as "members" of it—are more popular in their style and lyrical forms which disclose unmistakable erotic elements. Sexual desire and poetic composition are linked by Giacomino Pugliese, who notes in his *discordo* "Donna, per vostro amore" that he "has pleasure" ("ò sollazo") and "makes verses" ("versi fazo") because of his lady ("per voi") and continues by commanding her to embrace him:[17]

> or m'abraza
> a tuo' braza,
> amorosa
> dubitosa. (33–36)

[now embrace me, hold me in your arms, my shy love].

Giacomino presents these overt references to erotic passion together with more more conventional phrases in which he proclaims himself to be her servant:

> Co lo dolze riso
>
> conquiso—voi m'avete, fin amore:
> vostro sono leale servidore. (37–39)

[you have conquered me with your sweet smile, my true love: I am your loyal servant].

In his lyrics Giacomino frequently introduces the concept and function of *rimembranza* ("memory"), which generally evokes a scene or moment of sexual passion, as, for example, in the *canzonetta* "Isplendïente," where the lover asks the lady to recall the day they consummated their love:[18]

> or ti rimembri, bella, la dia
> che noi fermammo la dolze amanza.
>
> Bella, or ti sia
> a rimembranza
> la dolze dia
> e l'alegranza
> quando in diporto istava con vui,
> basciando dicìa: "Anima mia,
> lo dolze amore, ch'è 'ntra noi dui,
> non falsasse per cosa che sia." (7–16)

[now, beautiful one, remember the day that we consummated our love.

Beautiful one, may you remember the sweet day and the happiness when I was blissfully with you, and said: "My soul, may the sweet love that is ours not be betrayed by anything."]

In the fourth and fifth strophes of this poem he recalls the time she came down to him from her room in the castle and lost her virginity:

membrando ch'èite a lo mio brazo,
quando scendesti a me in diporto
per la finestra de lo palazo.

    Allor t'èi, bella,
    in mia balìa,
    rosa novella,
    per me temìa.
Di voi presi amorosa vengianza;
oi 'n fide rosa, fosti patuta! (30–38)

[remembering that I held you in my arms when you descended to me in pleasure from the window in the palace.

Then I had you, beautiful one, in my power, fresh rose, because of me you were fearful. I took amorous vengeance on you; o true rose, you were plucked!]

Giacomino also alludes to this decisive moment in their relationship in the *contrasto* "Donna, di voi mi lamento,"[19] where the man refers to the "la sera che mi serraste / in vostra dolze pregione" (25–26, "the night you closed me in your sweet prison"). The sexual overtones of the image of the "sweet prison" (the woman's vagina) are unmistakable.

In another *canzonetta*, which has been attributed to Giacomino Pugliese by one authoritative manuscript,[20] we find a much more graphic account of a past amorous interlude:[21]

La dolce ciera piagente
e li amorosi sembianti
lo cor m'allegra e la mente
quando mi pare davanti,
sì volontieri la vio
quella cui eo amai;
la bocca ch'eo basai
ancor l'astetto e disio!

L'aulente bocca e le menne
de lo petto le cercai,
fra le mie braza la tenne;
basando m'adomandai:
"Messer, se ve n'ate a gire,
non facciate adimoranza,
chè non esti bona usanza
lassar l'amore e partire." (1–16)

[The sweet and pleasing face and amorous looks gladden my heart and mind, when it appears before me, so willingly I look at it, for she is the one I love; I can still taste and desire the mouth I kissed.

I sought her fragrant mouth and the nipples of her breast as I held her in my arms; as we were kissing, she asked me: "My lord, if you must leave, don't stay away too long, for it is not good manners to leave your love and go away."]

The explicit reference to specific parts of the female anatomy is uncommon in the Italian love lyric. On the other hand, the central importance of the mouth and the kiss as the object of desire in the amorous relationship is such that, in addition to its metaphysical significance (i.e., the bestowing of grace, the ennoblement of the lover), the kiss itself has a very sensual dimension and can even serve as a euphemism for coitus.[22] The woman's words in this passage sum up in a very practical way the fact that it is not good amorous practice to make love and then leave!

The two extant lyrics by Compagnetto da Prato are charged with sensuous overtones.[23] In one ("Per lo marito c'ò rio") we have the lament of the *malmaritata* who is able to obtain happiness with a perfect lover ("fin'amante"), and in the other ("L'amor fa una donna amare") we see the gradual development of the female protagonist who breaks all the "rules" to act on her own in order to achieve sexual fulfillment. The final stanza of the latter poem presents the dialogue between the lover and the lady:[24]

> "Dimmi, s'è ver l'abrazzare
> che mi fai, donna avenente,
> chè sì gran cosa mi pare,
> creder no 'l posso neiente."
> "Drudo mio, se Dio mi vaglia
> ch'io del tuo amor mi disfaccio,
> merzè, non mi dar travaglia!
> Poi che m'ài ignuda in braccio,
> meo sir, tenemi in tua baglia!" (46–54)

["Tell me if the embrace you are giving me is real, beautiful lady, for it seems to me to be such a grand thing that I cannot believe it." "My love, may God help me, for I am dying for love of you; please, don't give me trouble! Since you have me naked in your arms, my lord, hold me in your power."]

The amazement and resulting hesitancy of the male figure in the face of the rapidity and dramatic quality of the sexual embrace is countered by the reassurances of the woman who yields to him completely.

One of the best known lyrics from the first decades of the Italian poetic tradition is Cielo d'Alcamo's *contrasto* "Rosa fresca aulentissima,—c'apari inver la state," which presents an amorous debate between an itinerant *jongleur* and a woman of the bourgeoisie. In short, the man desires to have sexual intercourse with the woman and uses every means possible to counter her arguments and break down her resistance. The entire poem is suffused with erotic innuendoes and sexually oriented *double-entendres*, which gradually build to a dramatic conclusion. We shall discuss in some detail the various stages in this lengthy poem (160 verses). The opening verses praise the beauty and desirability of the woman:[25]

> Rosa fresca aulentissima,—c'apari inver la state,
>   le donne ti disïano—pulzell' e maritate

[Fresh, most fragrant rose, that appear in the summer, the ladies—married and unmarried—desire you.]

and the next three verses describe the man's desperate state because of love:

> trajimi de ste focora—se t'este a bolontate;
>   per te non aio abento notte e dia,
>   penzando pur di voi, madonna mia. (3–5)

[remove me from these fires if it pleases you; for you I have no rest night and day, thinking only of you, my lady.]

As early as the third strophe, the woman is reduced from the sweet-smelling, aesthetically pleasing rose of the first line—one to be admired and desired, but not touched—to a commercial, garden variety rose to be plucked and enjoyed—"rosa fresca de l'orto" (13, "fresh rose of the orchard")—and the poet states his objective by proposing that they make love: "poniamo che s'aiunga il nostro amore" (15, "let's suppose that our love is consummated").

Roughly half-way through the *contrasto* (in the fourteenth strophe) and after much verbal dueling, the woman states her conditions to their sexual union:

"Poi tanto trabagliastiti,—faccioti meo pregheri
che tu vadi adomannimi—a mia mare e a mon peri.
Se dare mi ti degnano,—menami a lo mosteri
  e sposami davanti da la jenti;
  e poi faro li tuo' comannamenti." (66–70)

["Since you have worked so hard, I'll say that you should go to my mother and father and ask for me. If they deign to give me to you, take me to the church and marry me in front of the people, and then I'll do what you command."]

To accomplish his desire he must ask her parents' consent and marry her "davanti da la jenti." The man is not interested in such an arrangement and begins a new tack:

"Di ciò che dici, vitama,—neiente non ti bale,
ca de le tuo parabole—fatto n'ò ponti e scale.
Penne penzasti mettere,—sonti cadute l'ale,
  e dato t'aio la botta sottana;
  dunque, se poti, teniti, villana." (71–75)

["My life, nothing you say will help you, for I have made bridges and ladders out of your words. You thought to put on feathers, your wings have fallen off, and I have given you the fatal blow; therefore, if you can, defend yourself, peasant."]

The man cleverly forecasts his victory by declaring that he has used her own words to win her love. His reference to the military assault—the "botta sottana"—that he has given her introduces war imagery to the poem. Her response continues along these lines:

"En paura non mettermi—di nullo manganiello:
istomi 'n esta grorïa—de sto forte castiello." (76–77)

["Don't threaten me with any war club: I am here in glory within this strong castle."]

The woman describes herself as a fortified castle and refers precisely to the instrument of war, the "manganiello," which also signifies the male sex organ. Later in the *contrasto* we will find the delicious play on the double meaning of "arma" ("soul" ["anima"] and "weapon").

Having been ordered to leave, the man states very clearly that he will never go away until he enjoys her sexual favors:

"Di quaci non mi mosera—se no aio de lo frutto,
  lo quale staci ne lo tuo jardino:
  disïolo la sera e lo matino." (83–85)

["I'll not move from here unless I have some of the fruit that is in your garden: I desire it night and day."]

The fragrant rose of the first verse which became the rose of the orchard has now been transformed into the "fruit" that is found in the woman's "garden." Ever weakening, the woman again raises in a negative sense the prospect of marriage:

> "S'a le Vangele iurimi—che mi sia a marito,
>   avereme no poter' a sto monno,
>   avanti in mare jittomi al perfonno." (118–120)

["Unless you swear to me on the Gospels that you will be my husband, you will not have me in this world; before [that would happen] I will throw myself into the depths of the sea."]

To the woman's threat to commit suicide by drowning, the man says that he would follow her into the sea and, upon finding her lifeless body on the beach, would "join [himself] to [her] in sin":

> "Se tu nel mare gittiti,—donna cortese e fina,
> dereto mi ti misera—per tutta la marina,
> e, da poi ca 'nnegasseti,—trobareti a la rina,
>   solo per questa cosa ad impretare:
>   con teco m'aio agiungere a peccare." (121–125)

["If you throw yourself into the sea, lady courtly and refined, I would follow you in, and, after you have drowned, I would find you on the sand, only to carry out this act: to join myself to you in sin."]

Although some critics explain these verses as a reference to suicide as a sin (i.e., the man will commit suicide, as the woman has done), it seems obvious that he will join himself to her by a desperate act of necrophilia. This reading of the verse is supported by the woman herself in the next strophe, where she discloses her acute understanding of his not too obscure words by noting that once a woman is dead there is no pleasure left:

> "Morta si è la femmina a lo 'ntutto,
> perdeci lo saboro e lo disdutto." (129–130)

["Once a woman is completely dead, she loses her flavor and pleasure."]

The war imagery continues with the man's request to the woman to kill him with "esto cortel novo" (142, "this new [or strange] knife"), for his soul / penis ("arma") is becoming sad together with his heart (145, "che l'arma co l core mi si 'nfella"). Recognizing his *arma*'s distress—"Ben sazzo l'arma doleti—com'omo c'ave arsura" (146, "Indeed I know your soul/weapon grieves you, like a man who is burning")—the woman, departing from her earlier demands of marriage, now asks only that the man swear on the gospels in order to have her:

> "Sto fatto far non potesi—per null'altra misura
> se non a le Vangelïe—che mo ti dico iura,
>   avereme non puoi in tua podesta." (147–149)

["The only way that this can be done is for you to swear on the Gospels; otherwise you cannot have me in your power."]

The final two strophes present a rapid and sexually satisfying conclusion to the events:

"Le Vangelïe, carama?—ch'io le porto in sino!
A lo mostero presile,—non ci era lo patrino.
Sovr'esto libro iuroti—mai non ti vegno mino.
    Arcompli mi' talento in caritate,
    che l'arma me ne sta in suttilitate."

"Meo sire, poi iurastimi,—eo tutta quanta incenno;
sono a la tua presenzïa,—da voi non mi difenno.
S'eo minespriso aioti,—merzè, a voi m'arenno.
    A lo letto ne gimo a la bon'ura,
    chè chissa cosa n'è data in ventura." (151–160)

["The Gospels, my dear? I have them inside my shirt! I took them from the monastery when the priest wasn't there. Upon this book I swear to you that I will never disappoint you. Fulfill my desire charitably for my soul/weapon is in a desperate state."

"My lord, since you have sworn to me, I am burning all over; I am yours; from you I give myself to you. If I have underestimated you, please forgive me, I yield myself to you. Let's go to bed quickly for this pleasure is given to us by good fortune."]

The man swears over the stolen gospels he *claims* to have hidden inside his shirt, and the woman suggests that they go to bed immediately in consequence to the "swearing ceremony." The elaborate structure of the *contrasto*, together with its highly nuanced language and vibrant sexual images, make it one of the most developed and sustained poems of seduction and sexuality in early Italian poetry.

In the following madrigal by the fourteenth-century Florentine poet Alesso di Guido Donati, we note another, similar description of thinly veiled sexual activity:[26]

Ellera non s'avvitola
più stretta verzicando ad alcun albero,
ch'a me tremando fe' la bella zitola,
pian, pian: "Che fo?" dicendomi
"i' sento sbadigliar la madre vetula:
fo vista di dormire e teco stendomi."

"Abracciami," risposile,
"e, s'ella ci ode e grida, fuor cacciamola."
E ciò dicendo volto a volto puosile

e colsi frutto del suo orto giovine.

[Ivy does not wrap its green runners more tightly around any tree than the lovely girl who wraps her arms around my trembling body and asks softly, "Guess what I'm doing? I hear my old mother yawning: I'll pretend to sleep and then come to lie with you." "Embrace me," I answered her, "and if she hears us and complains, we'll chase her out of here!" And saying this, I lay down with her face to face and plucked the fruit of her young garden.]

The humorous, realistically inspired scene is populated with stereotypical characters, such as the impatient young lovers and the querelous and watchful old woman (here the mother). As the man in Cielo d'Alcamo's *contrasto* expressed the desire to have the "fruit" in the woman's garden, so here we see the same image used to denote sexual intercourse.

In one of his more popular *ballate* Guido Cavalcanti follows the model of the Old French / Provençal *pastourelle* by describing the encounter of a man and a shepherdess in a wood ("In un boschetto trova' pasturella"). The last three stanzas describe delicately, joyfully, and directly the consummation of their love:[27]

> D'amor la saluta' imantenente
> e domandai s'avesse compagnia;
> ed ella mi rispose dolzemente
> che sola sola per lo bosco gia,
> e disse: "Sacci, quando l'augel pia,
> allor disïa—'l me' cor drudo avere."
>
> Po' che mi disse di sua condizione
> e per lo bosco augelli audìo cantare,
> fra me stesso diss'i': "Or è stagione
> di questa pasturella gio' pigliare."
> Merzé le chiesi sol che di basciare
> ed abracciar,—se le fosse 'n volere.
>
> Per man mi prese, d'amorosa voglia,
> e disse che donato m'avea 'l core;
> menòmmi sott'una freschetta foglia,
> là dov'i' vidi fior' d'ogni colore;
> e tanto vi sentìo gioia e dolzore,
> che 'l die d'amore—mi parea vedere. (9-26)

[I immediately greeted her with love and asked if she had a companion; and she replied sweetly to me that she was going all alone through the forest, and said: "You should know that when the bird sings, then my heart desires to have a lover."

After she told me of her condition and I heard birds singing in the forest, I said to myself: "Now is the time to have joy from this shepherdess." I asked her permission only to kiss and embrace her, if she would like to.

By the hand she took me, with loving desire, and said that she had given me her heart. She led me under a newly flowered bower, there where I saw flowers of every color; and I felt so much joy and sweetness there that I think I saw the god of love.]

The description of the progressive stages in lovemaking is both open and logical; indeed, it would appear that the woman takes the initiative when she explains how she decides when to love: "when the bird sings," i.e., when it is spring and all thoughts turn to love. On hearing the birds sing, the man responds appropriately, but with some restraint; the woman then leads him by the hand to the lovers' bower where they consummate their passion, the orgasmic moment being described as a sort of metaphysical vision of the god of love.

Texts Coarse and Crude

Poems in this final category reflect a much lower stylistic register, use popular language, and contain unadorned descriptions of sexual activity.

Most lyrics of this sort belong to the comic or burlesque poetry of the time and take the form of accusations or the exchange of insults. For example, in his *tenzone* (poetic "duel" or correspondence, usually an exchange of sonnets) with Forese Donati, Dante accused his friend of neglecting his wife:[28]

> Chi udisse tossir la malfatata
> moglie di Bicci vocato Forese,
> potrebbe dir ch'ell'ha forse vernata
> ove si fa 'l cristallo in quel paese.
>
> Di mezzo agosto la truove infreddata:
> or sappi che de' far d'ogni altro mese!
> e non le val perché dorma calzata,
> merzé del copertoio c'ha cortonese. . . .
>
> La tosse, 'l freddo e l'altra mala voglia
> non l'addovien per omor' ch'abbia vecchi,
> ma per difetto ch'ella sente al nido. (1–11)

[Anyone who heard the coughing of the luckless wife of Bicci (called Forese) might say that maybe she'd passed the winter in the land where crystal is made. You'll find her frozen in mid August—so guess how she must fare in any other month! And it's no use her keeping her stockings on—the bedclothes are too short. . . . The coughing and cold and other troubles—these don't come to her from aging humours, but from the gap she feels in the nest.]

The sexual innuendoes are readily apparent: by failing to provide his wife with a proper coverlet—one too short ("cortonese" = "corto")—Forese discloses his sexual inadequacy; the woman suffers not so much from the humors relating to her age but from the absence ("difetto") of sexual intercourse in the conjugal bed ("nido"). Indeed, according to the medical lore of the time, "sexual intercourse is necessary for good health in women, as it seems to eliminate or purge the excessive 'humours.'"[29] The entire *tenzone* between Dante and Forese is characterized by the exchange of insults and thinly veiled references to sexual matters and belongs to a decidedly lower poetic style.[30]

One of the few Florentine rhymers in the burlesque tradition is Rustico di Filippo, whose poetic corpus (some 58 sonnets) is evenly divided between those which follow the refined "courtly" tradition and those which belong to the comic-realistic *filone*. In these latter compositions Rustico's language is local and colorful, the sentiments seemingly immediate and spontaneous. The situations and related events are described with an extreme frankness which often borders on vulgarity; obscene allusions are sometimes very thinly veiled, and *double-entendres* abound. Among the subjects that Rustico treats with gusto are sexual proclivities and appetites. The following sonnet, for example, presents the attempt by Aldobrandino's wife to exculpate herself from suspicion of adultery with Pilletto:[31]

> Oi dolce mio marito Aldobrandino,
> rimanda ormai il farso suo a Pilletto,
> ch'egli è tanto cortese fante e fino
> che creder non déi ciò che te n'è detto.

E no star tra la gente a capo chino,
ché non se' bozza, e fòtine disdetto;
ma sí come amorevole vicino
co.noi venne a dormir nel nostro letto.

Rimanda il farso ormai, piú no il tenere,
ch'e' mai no ci verrà oltre tua voglia,
poi che n'ha conosciuto il tuo volere.

Nel nostro letto già mai non si spoglia.
Tu non dovéi gridare, anzi tacere:
ch'a me non fece cosa ond'io mi doglia.

[O my sweet husband Aldobrandino, send the jacket back to Pilletto, for he is such a polite and refined young man that you should not believe what you've been told. And you should not go around with your head bowed down, for you have not been cuckolded, and I swear that to you; but he came as a friendly neighbor to sleep in our bed. Send his jacket back to him and do not keep it any longer, for he will never come here against your wishes, since he has understood your will. In our bed he will never again undress. You should not have complained, but remained silent, for he did nothing to me for which I am sorry.]

In addition to its wonderful mixture of common and courtly language, the beauty of this sonnet comes from its ironic stance: the "sincere, heartfelt plea" of the woman is nothing but a hypocritical utterance intended to deceive the husband about her infidelity. Her ploy is to profess innocence, whereas in reality she has enjoyed the sexual favors provided by Pilletto much more than those proffered by her husband Aldobrandino. The final verse puts the entire sonnet into the proper perspective: Pilletto has done nothing to cause her sorrow . . . quite to the contrary! The wife's characterization of the stupidity of the husband is heightened by the fact that Pilletto seems to have joined the two in bed and there had intercourse with the wife, as the gullible lout of her husband slept on!

In other sonnets Rustico speaks of sexual intercourse in rather explicit terms, as, for example, in "El Muscia sí fa dicere e bandire," where the extraordinary size of El Muscia's penis ("sedici once," "sixteen inches") is discussed,[32] or in "A voi, Chierma, so dire una novella," where the male sex organ is compared with that of a donkey ("somaio") and intercourse (anal? vaginal?) is described in very graphic images:[33]

A voi, Chierma, so dire una novella:
se voi porrete il culo al colombaio,
cad io vi porgerò tal manovella,
se non vi piace, io non ne vo' danaio.

Ma tornerete volontier per ella,
ch'ella par drittamente d'un somaio:
con tutto che non siate sí zitella
che troppo colmo paiavi lo staio.

Adunque, Chierma, non ci date indugio,
che pedir vi farabbo come vacca
se porrete le natiche al pertugio.

Tutte l'altre torrete poi per acca:
sí vi rinzafferò col mio segugio
ch'e' parrà ch'Arno v'esca de la tacca.

[Chierma, I'll tell you something: if you put your ass up in the air, then I'll place such a great rod there that if you don't like it, I won't want any money for it. But you will return willingly for it (the rod), for it is just like that of a donkey: although you aren't such a virgin that your bushel might appear too stuffed. Therefore, Chierma, don't make us wait, for I'll make you fart like a cow if you place your buttocks hole up. All the other rods you'll then think are nothing in comparison: for I'll plug your hole so much with my "big dog" that it'll seem that the Arno is flowing out of your crack.]

Prose

Within the restricted scope of this essay it would be impossible to discuss the entire medieval Italian prose tradition. Nevertheless, the presentation of a few *novelle* (short stories) from the *Novellino*, a collection of one hundred anonymous tales, and from Boccaccio's *Decameron* should give some indication of the sorts of sexual activity they describe. By and large, we could adopt the same divisions for the prose that we used for poetry, but in the interest of concision we will discuss our prose texts under the following single rubric.

Texts Ambiguous, Censored, and Defended

Rustico di Filippo's attention to the dimensions of El Muscia's penis in the sonnet mentioned above is echoed in one story (No. 86) of the *Novellino*, where the obviously salacious punch line is omitted:[34]

Fu uno c'avea sì grande naturale, che non trovava neuno che fosse sì grande ad assai. Or avenne c'un giorno si trovò con una putta che non era molto giovane e, avegna che molto fosse orrevole e ricca, molti n'avea veduti e provati. Quando furo in camera, et elli lo mostrò; e per grande letizia la donna rise. Que' disse: "Che ve ne pare?" E.lla donna rispose:

[There was a man who had such a large penis that no one could be found who had one so big. Now it happened one day that this man was with a whore who was not very young and, although she was very honorable and rich, she had seen and tried out many penises. When they were in the bedroom, and he showed it to her, the woman laughed with great joy. The man said: "What do you think about that?" And the woman replied: (text missing)]

The missing conclusion or "punch line" represents what appears to be a clear case of censorship, but we cannot determine when in transmission of the text the suppression may have occurred.

The following story (No. 87) in the collection concerns the ambiguous advice a priest gives to a man who, in confession, complains that his sister-in-law persists in making amorous advances toward him:[35]

Uno s'andò a confessare al prete suo, et intra l'altre cose li disse: "I'ho una mia cognata, e 'l mio fratello è lontano; e, quando io torno in casa, ella,

per grande dimestichezza, mi si pur pone a sedere in grembo. Come debbo
fare?" Rispuose il prete: "A me il si facesse ella! Ch'io la ne pagherei
bene!"

[A man went to confess to his priest, and among other things, he said to him: "I have
a sister-in-law, and my brother is far away; and, when I come home, she with great
familiarity comes to sit in my lap. What should I do?" The priest replied: "Would that
she would do it with me! For I would pay her back well for it!"]

The words of the priest—"A me il si facesse ella! Ch'io la ne pagherei
bene!"—can be understood in two very different ways: either as a firm
statement of the proper punishment that the woman should receive for her
offense against morality, or as a humorous ejaculation by the confessor on
the manner—obviously sexual—in which he would act/respond, should he
find himself in a similar situation.

The sexual proclivities of the clergy were, of course, a common theme
in medieval literature and provided the subject for many a *novella* in
fourteenth-century Italy. Clerical licentiousness was certainly criticized by
many as hypocrisy and as one of the reasons for the degeneracy of the
Church. While held up as negative *exempla* by moralistically inclined
authors, the erotic escapades of the clergy were treated by Boccaccio in a
remarkably non-judgmental way. Indeed, the author of the *Decameron*
presents numerous stories in which monks and nuns actively engage in
sexual adventures; however, Boccaccio does not present these tales as part
of any anti-clerical stance, but rather to underline his basic point, expressed
throughout the collection of one hundred *novelle*, that all human beings act
naturally and follow their natural desires, inclinations, and instincts to
fulfillment. This point is concisely made by the abbess in the second story
of the ninth day. The abbess must punish one of her nuns who has been
caught with her lover; however, the abbess also has a lover—a priest—with
whom she had just been dallying. In her haste to confront the wayward nun,
the abbess mistakenly puts the priest's trousers on her head instead of her
wimple. Being made aware of her own error in the presence of all the nuns,
the abbess notes that "impossibile essere il potersi dagli stimoli della carne
difendere; e per ciò chetamente, come infino a quel dì fatto s'era, disse che
ciascuna si desse buon tempo quando potesse" ["it was impossible to defend
oneself from the goadings of the flesh. And she told them that provided the
thing was discreetly arranged, as it had been in the past, they were all at
liberty to enjoy themselves whenever they pleased."].[36] The defense is
essentially that one cannot deny one's natural instincts, one's humanity,
and that to act in any other way would be hypocritical.

The description of amorous adventures in the *Decameron*—illicit or
not, with or without erotic elements—takes a variety of forms. We have the
elegant and refined account of the numerous adventures of Alatiel (II, 7), the
Sultan's daughter, who is kidnapped on the way to her wedding and passes
from man to man until she is restored "in a virgin state" to her father! We
have the tale of the young lovers Ricciardo Manardi and Caterina, the
daughter of Messer Lizio da Valbona (V, 4), whose lovemaking is

euphemistically described as "caging nightingales" ("e poi con lei lungamente in pace e in consolazione uccellò agli usignuoli e di dì e di notte quanto gli piacque": "and for many years thereafter he lived with her in peace and happiness, caging nightingales by the score, day and night, to his heart's content"]. Another tale that uses sexually oriented *double-entendres* to convey erotic elements is that of Peronella (VII, 2) who continues having intercourse with her lover on top of the tub her husband is cleaning.

One of the most celebrated *novelle* (III, 10) of the *Decameron* concerns the quest for holiness undertaken by Alibech who, having gone into the desert, meets the monk Rustico and begins under his guidance her particular service to God, which, simply put, is to assist Rustico in putting the devil back into hell ("rimettere il diavolo in Inferno"). Whenever the devil (Rustico's penis) would rear its ugly head, hell (Alibech's vagina) would receive it willingly and conquer its pride. Alibech's innocent zeal in serving the Lord quickly outstripped Rustico's ability to conjure the devil. The wonderfully humorous play on words and sacrilege of Christian beliefs[37] so scandalized readers of the *Decameron* that the story was replaced by others in editions and translations of the work from the Renaissance through the nineteenth century; indeed, some translations from the last century present the tale, but switch to the Italian text (with a French version in the notes!) precisely when the erotic elements appear.[38]

Boccaccio was obviously well aware of the criticism lodged against his work, and particularly against the tale of Alibech and Rustico, for he prefaces the fourth day with a defense of his literary work. He responds to criticism by telling a story—of Filippo Balducci and his son—which demonstrates the inability to overcome natural instincts by isolation, linguistic means, or appeals to some external moral code. Concerned with the question of language and its expressive power, Boccaccio argues forcefully in the conclusion to the *Decameron* that writers should be accorded the same privileges that artists enjoy:

> Sanza che alla mia penna non dee essere meno d'auttorità conceduta che sia al pennello del dipintore, il quale senza alcuna riprensione, o almeno giusta, lasciamo stare che egli faccia a san Michele ferire il serpente con la spada o con la lancia e a san Giorgio il dragone dove gli piace, ma egli fa Cristo maschio e Eva femina, e a Lui medesimo, che volle per la salute della umana generazione sopra la croce morire, quando con un chiovo e quando con due i piè gli conficca in quella.

[Besides, no less latitude should be granted to my pen than to the brush of the painter, who without incurring censure, of a justified kind at least, depicts St. Michael striking the serpent with his sword or lance, and St. George transfixing the dragon wherever he pleases; but that is not all, for he makes Christ male and Eve female, and fixes to the cross, sometimes with a single nail, sometimes with two, the feet of Him who resolved to die thereon for the salvation of mankind.]

Just as an artist has the license to depict things the way they are and particularly to represent the sexual differences of male and female,[39] so writers should be able to "call a spade a spade" and to use language and terminology that corresponds to the reality being presented. In his final response to his critics, Boccaccio concentrates on two points: content and language. He says:

> Primieramente se alcuna cosa in alcuna n'è, la qualità delle novelle l'hanno richesta, le quali se con ragionevole occhio da intendente persona fian riguardate, assai aperto sarà conosciuto, se io quelle della lor forma trar non avessi voluto, altramenti raccontar non poterlo. E se forse pure alcuna particella è in quella, alcuna paroletta più liberale che forse a spigolistra donna non si conviene, le quali più le parole pesan che' fatti e più non si dee a me esser disdetto d'averle scritte che generalmente si disdica agli uomini e alle donne di dir tutto dì "foro" e "caviglia" e "mortaio" e "pestello" e "salsiccia" e "mortadello", e tutto pien di simiglianti cose.

[In the first place, if any of the stories is lacking in restraint, this is because of the nature of the story itself, which, as any well-informed and dispassionate observer will readily acknowledge, I could not have related in any other way without distorting it out of all recognition. And even if the stories do, perhaps, contain one or two trifling expressions that are too unbridled for the liking of those prudish ladies who attach more weight to words than to deeds, and are more anxious to seem virtuous than to be virtuous, I assert that it was no more improper for me to have written them than for men and women at large, in their everyday speech, to use such words as *hole*, and *rod*, and *mortar*, and *pestle*, and *crumpet*, and *stuffing*, and any number of others.]

We note in Boccaccio's words an impassioned, but eminently reasonable plea for freedom of expression, for a concept and acceptance of literature free of didactic and moralistic constraints and directed toward the amusement, pleasure, and consolation of the reader. Boccaccio's defense of his craft appropriately concludes this relatively short presentation of erotic and sexual elements in medieval Italian literature. For today, almost six and one-half centuries after Boccaccio wrote the *Decameron*, we are still engaged in controversy regarding the limits of art and freedom of expression in the representation of erotic elements in literature and art.

Notes

1   The allegorical meaning of the *Divine Comedy* is presented in the *Letter to Can Grande* (in Paget Toynbee, *Dantis Alagherii Epistolae: The Letters of Dante*, 2nd ed. [Oxford: Clarendon Press, 1966], 177, 201) as follows:

> Et si totius operis allegorice sumpti subiectum est homo prout merendo et demerendo per arbitrii libertatem est iustitiae praemiandi et puniendi obnoxius, manifestum est in hac parte hoc subiectum contrahi, et est homo prout merendo obnoxius est iustitiae praemiandi.

> [And if the subject of the whole work from the allegorical point of view is man according as by his merits or demerits in the exercise of his free will he is deserving of reward or punishment by justice, it is evident that in this part this subject has a limitation, and that it is man according as by his merits he is deserving of reward by justice.].

2   This, of course, should not be the case, for in the *Divine Comedy* there are numerous references to the erotic, though almost always for the purpose of highlighting the dangers that are inherent in lust which, rampant, conquers reason. For example, Virgil, Dante's guide through Hell, describes the lustful sinners as those

who "la ragion sommettono al talento" ["subjected reason to desire," 5:39]. The tale of the end to which sexual desire brought Paolo and Francesca (*Inferno* 5) is well known.

While the *Vita Nuova* ("New Life") generally lacks any erotic elements or innuendoes, the episode concerning Dante's dream of the God of Love who comes bearing in his arms the almost naked and sleeping Beatrice is highly charged with sexuality (the text follows Dante Alighieri, *Vita Nuova—Rime*, ed. Fredi Chiappelli [Milano: Mursia, 1965], 22):

> Ne le sue braccia mi parea vedere una persona dormire nuda, salvo che involta mi parea in uno drappo sanguigno leggeramente; la quale io riguardando molto intentivamente, conobbi ch'era la donna de la salute, la quale m'avea lo giorno dinanzi degnato di salutare. E ne l'una de le mani mi parea che questi tenesse una cosa la quale ardesse tutta, e pareami che mi dicesse queste parole: *Vide cor tuum.* E quando elli era stato alquanto, pareami che disvegliasse questa che dormia; e tanto si sforzava per suo ingegno, che le facea mangiare questa cosa che in mano li ardea, la quale ella mangiava dubitosamente.

> [I seemed to see in his arms a sleeping figure, naked but lightly wrapped in a crimson cloth; looking intently at this figure, I recognized the lady of the greeting, the lady who earlier in the day had deigned to greet me. In one hand he seemed to be holding something that was all in flames, and it seemed to me that he said these words: "Behold thy heart." And after some time had passed, he seemed to awaken the one who slept, and he forced her cunningly to eat of that burning object in his hand; she ate of it timidly. Tr. Mark Musa, *Dante's "Vita Nuova"* (Bloomington: Indiana University Press, 1973), 5]

On this occasion Dante says that he wrote a sonnet—"A ciascun'alma presa e gentil core"—which he sent to various poets for clarification. Of the several responses extant, the one by Dante da Maiano ("Di ciò che stato sei dimandatore") provides a quasi-medical analysis; in it Dante is advised to wash his testicles well so as to expel the noxious vapors that have caused him to have such wildly erotic dreams and to have spoken in such a raving manner. For the text of and commentary on Dante da Maiano's sonnet see *Dante's Lyric Poetry,* ed. and tr. K. Foster and P. Boyde, 2 vols. (Oxford: Clarendon Press, 1967), I:16–17 and II:29–31.

 3   Some recent exceptions to this are Douglas Radcliff-Umstead, "Erotic Sin in the *Divine Comedy*," in *Human Sexuality in the Middle Ages and Renaissance,* ed. Douglas Radcliff-Umstead (Pittsburgh: University of Pittsburgh Center for Medieval and Renaissance Studies, 1978), 41–96.

 4   For an excellent annotated reference work to writings on this subject, see Joyce E. Salisbury, *Medieval Sexuality: A Research Guide* (New York: Garland, 1990).

 5   See, however, the study by Luigi Romeo, "A Sociolinguistic View of Medieval Romance Erotic Poetry," *Forum Italicum,* 7 (1973), 81–101, and the anthology, *L'altra faccia della poesia italiana,* ed. Riccardo Reim and Antonio Veneziani (Milano: Savelli, 1982).

 6   There are some references to homosexual activities in medieval Italian literature. Dante's discussion of sodomy both in the *Inferno* and in the *Purgatorio* contains clearly erotic elements. Among the sodomites in Hell we find Brunetto Latini, Guido Guerra, Jacopo Rusticucci, and others. While Dante never describes the sin explicitly, he leaves no doubt about its sexual nature when he notes that the bishop Andrea di Mozzi was transferred from Florence to Vicenza "dove lasciò li mal

protesi nervi" ("there he left his tendons strained by sin," *Inf.* 15:114). While, on one level, this statement is a periphrasis for "he died," on another level, it relates the fact that it was there "where he died, leaving the body whose muscles had been 'ill-stretched' in the sinful act of sodomy" (Dante Aligheri, *The Divine Comedy, Inferno: 2. Commentary*, tr., with a commentary, by Charles S. Singleton [Princeton: Princeton University Press, 1970], 272).

Other lyrics by Cecco Angiolieri and the so-called *poeti perugini* ("Perugian poets")—Cecco Nuccoli, Neri Moscoli, Marino Ceccoli—contain erotic elements of a homosexual nature. For further information, see, among others, Achille Tartaro, *Forme Poetiche del Trecento* (Bari: Laterza, 1971) and Renzo Paris and Antonio Veneziani, eds., *L'amicizia amorosa: Antologia della poesia omosessuale italiana dal XIII secolo a oggi* (Milano: Gammalibri, 1982).

7   On this point, the reader might wish to consult any of the following works: Mario Apollonio, *Uomini e forme nella cultura italiana delle origini* (Firenze: Sansoni, 1934); Giulio Bertoni, *Il Duecento*, 3rd ed. (Milano: Vallardi, 1939); Peter Dronke, *The Medieval Lyric* (New York: Harper and Row, 1969); *Le origini e il Duecento*, Vol. I, *Storia della letteratura italiana*, ed. Emilio Cecchi and Natalino Sapegno (Milano: Garzanti, 1965); Emilio Pasquini, *La letteratura didattica e la poesia popolare del Duecento* (Bari: Laterza, 1971); Emilio Pasquini and Antonio Enzo Quaglio, *Le origini e la scuola siciliana* (Bari: Laterza, 1971) and *Lo stilnovo e la poesia religiosa* (Bari: Laterza, 1971); Antonio Enzo Quaglio, *La poesia realistica e la prosa del Duecento* (Bari: Laterza, 1971); Natalino Sapegno, *Storia Letteraria del Trecento* (Milano: Ricciardi, 1963) and *Il Trecento* (Milano: Vallardi, 1933); Achille Tartaro, *Forme Poetiche del Trecento* (Bari: Laterza, 1971); *Il Trecento*, Vol. II, *Storia della letteratura italiana*, ed. Emilio Cecchi and Natalino Sapegno (Milano: Garzanti, 1965); and Maurice Valency, *In Praise of Love: An Introduction to the Love-Poetry of the Renaissance* (New York: Schocken Books, 1982).

8   There is a body of anonymous poems in a popular vein contained in the Bolognese notarial acts—the "Memoriali Bolognesi"—which present everyday events, occasionally with erotic elements. For example, in the *ballata* "Mamma, lo temp' è venuto" a young woman wants to marry at all costs and argues with her mother who is opposed to the idea. The following verses display the sexual intentions of the daughter (the text of the poem follows Gianfranco Contini, ed., *Poeti del Duecento* (Milano: Ricciardi, 1960), I, 771–772):

> Matre, tant ò 'l cor açunto,
> la vogl[i]a amorosa e conquisa,
> ch'aver voria lo meo drudo
> vixin plu che non è la camixa.
> Cun lui me staria tutta nuda
> né mai non voria far devisa:
> eo l'abraçaria en tal guisa
> che 'l cor me faria allegrare. (37–44)

[Mother, my heart is so taken with overwhelming amorous desire that I would like to have my lover closer to me than my dress. With him I would be completely naked and would never have to separate myself from him. I would embrace him in such a way that my heart would rejoice.]

9   The text follows Bruno Panvini, ed., *Le rime della scuola siciliana*, Biblioteca dell "Archivum Romanicum," Ser. I, 65 (Firenze: Olschki, 1962), 49.

10   The hermetic quality of some of Guittone d'Arezzo's poetry has obscured certain erotic elements. For the sexual imagery in the sonnet "A fare meo portto, c'à

'n te, partt'e' cheo" see D'Arco Silvio Avalle, "Un 'vanto' di Guittone," *Cultura Neolatina*, 37 (1977), 161–66. Other, more obvious erotic elements are also present in Guittone's poetry, as, for example, in the following verses from his distinctly anti-courtly sonnet "Villana donna, non mi ti disdire" (Contini, *Poeti del Duecento*, I, 250):

Ca, per averti a tutto meo desire,
eo non t'amara un giorno per amore,
ma chesta t'ho volendoti covrire.

[For, in order to have from you all that I desire, I would not love you one day for love, but I wooed you because I wanted to screw you.]

11   The text of the poem follows Contini, *Poeti del Duecento*, I, 271.

12   Cf. the highly erotic conclusion of the Old French *Roman de la Rose*. In *Il Fiore*, the Italian redaction (perhaps by Dante) of the *Rose* (in 232 sonnets), we find similarly erotic elements. For example, in sonnet CCXXX we find the graphic description of coitus, which combines the metaphors of deflowering and sowing (text from Gianfranco Contini, ed., *Il Fiore e il Detto d'Amore attribuibili a Dante Alighieri* [Milano: Mondadori, 1984], 462]:

Sì ch'io allora il fior tutto sfogliai,
e la semenza ch'i' avea portata,
quand'ebbi arato, sì.lla seminai.

[Thus, I then completely deflowered the flower, and the seed that I had brought, after I had plowed, so I sowed it.]

For a recent study on the relationship between the *Rose* and the *Divine Comedy*, see Aldo S. Bernardo, "Sex and Salvation in the Middle Ages: From the *Romance of the Rose* to the *Divine Comedy*," *Italica*, 67 (1990), 305–18.

13   The *sestina* is modeled on Arnaut Daniel's equally playful and ambiguously erotic "Lo ferm voler q'el cor m'intra" ["The firm will that enters into my heart"]. For a discussion of its sexual overtones, see Charles Jernigan, "The Song of Nail and Uncle: Arnaut Daniel's Sestina 'Lo ferm voler q'el cor m'intra,'" *Studies in Philology*, 71 (1974), 127–151. The text of the poem follows Dante, *Rime*, ed. Gianfranco Contini (Torino: Einaudi, 1965), 159; the translation follows *Date's Lyric Poetry*, ed. and tr. K. Foster and P. Boyde, 2 vols. (Oxford: Clarendon Press, 1967), I, 165. For the erotic interpretation of Dante's *sestina* see, among others, Robert M. Durling and Ronald L. Martinez, *Time and the Crystal: Studies in Dante's "Rime Petrose"* (Berkeley: University of California Press, 1990), esp. 126–27.

14   Some manuscripts have *ci ci*, which would suggest that the woman's name is Cecilia. The text follows that in *Rimatori del Trecento*, ed. Giuseppe Corsi (Torino: Unione Tipografico Editrice Torinese, 1972), 742.

15   The text follows Panvini, *Le rime della scuola siciliana*, 33–35.

16   The kiss is one of the most important erotic elements in medieval literature and has been the subject of an excellent investigation by Nicolas James Perella, *The Kiss Sacred and Profane: An Interpretative History of Kiss Symbolism and Related Religio-Erotic Themes* (Berkeley: University of California Press, 1969). One of the most famous kisses in Western literature is that shared by Paolo and Francesca in Dante's *Divine Comedy* (*Inferno* 5). In this episode Francesca describes the successive stages of their love as follows (the text follows *La commedia secondo l'antica vulgata: Inferno*, a cura di Giorgio Petrocchi, Società Dantesca Italiana, Edizione Nazionale [Milano: Mondadori, 1966]):

Ma s'a conoscer la prima radice
del nostro amor tu hai cotanto affetto,
dirò come colui che piange e dice.
Noi leggiavamo un giorno per diletto
di Lancialotto come amor lo strinse;
soli eravamo e sanza alcun sospetto.
Per più fïate li occhi ci sospinse
quella lettura, e scolorocci il viso;
ma solo un punto fu quel che ci vinse.
Quando leggemmo il disïato riso
esser basciato da cotanto amante,
questi, che mai da me non fia diviso,
La bocca mi basciò tutto tremante.
Galeotto fu 'l libro e chi lo scrisse:
quel giorno più non vi leggemmo avante." (*Inf* 5:124–138)

[Yet if you long so much to understand / the first root of our love, then I shall tell / my tale to you as one who weeps and speaks. / One day, to pass the time away, we read / of Lancelot—how love had overcome him. / We were alone, and we suspected nothing. / And time and time again that reading led / our eyes to meet, and made our faces pale, / and yet one point alone defeated us. / When we had read how the desired smile / was kissed my one who was so true a lover, / this one, who never shall be parted from me, / while all his body trembled, kissed my mouth. / A Gallehault indeed, that book and he / who wrote it, too; that day we read no more. Tr. Allen Mandelbaum: Dante Alighieri, *Inferno* (New York: Bantam, 1982).

17   The text follows Panvini, *Le rime della scuola siciliana*, 183–87.

18   The text follows Panvini, *Le rime della scuola siciliana*, 193–95.

19   The text follows Panvini, *Le rime della scuola siciliana*, 189–91.

20   The poem is attributed to Giacomino Pugliese in Vatican manuscript Lat. 3793, and to Pier della Vigna in two other manuscripts: Banco Rari 217 (formerly Palatino 418, Biblioteca Nazionale Centrale, Florence) and in Vatican codex Chigiano L.VIII.305.

21   The text follows Panvini, *Le rime della scuola siciliana*, 426–28.

22   See Perella, *The Kiss Sacred and Profane*, especially the section on "The Medieval Love Lyric," pp. 84–123.

23   See the fine study by Anna Granville Hatcher, "Compagnetto da Prato: A Sophisticated Jongleur," *Cultura Neolatina*, 19 (1959), 35–45.

24   The text follows Panvini, *Le rime della scuola siciliana*, 231–32.

25   The text follows Panvini, *Le rime della scuola siciliana*, 169–76.

26   The text follows that in *Rimatori del Trecento*, ed. G. Corsi, 540.

27   The text follows Contini, *Poeti del Duecento*, II, 555–56.

28   The text and translation follow Foster and Boyde, *Dante's Lyric Poetry*, I, 148–49.

29   Foster and Boyde, *Dante's Lyric Poetry*, II, 246.

30   Dante's descent into the comic style was not the only departure by the *stilnovisti* into this other realm of poetry; indeed, Guido Guinizzelli and Guido Cavalcanti also adopted the comic style for some of their compositions (e.g., Guinizzelli's "Chi vedesse Lucia un var capuzzo" and "Volvol te levi, vecchia rabbiosa" and Cavalcanti's "Guata, Manetto, quella scrignutuzza"), some of which have erotic elements. For example, Guinizzelli's sonnet "Chi vedesse a Lucia" contains a very explosive declaration of sensual desire (text from Contini, *Poeti del Duecento*, II, 479):

Ah, prender lei a forza, ultra su' grato,
e bagiarli la bocca e 'l bel visaggio
e li occhi suoi, ch'èn due fiamme de foco!

[Ah! to take her by force, against her will, and to kiss her mouth and lovely face and eyes, that are two flames of fire!]

31   The text follows Rustico Filippi, *Sonetti*, ed. Pier Vincenzo Mengaldo (Torino: Einaudi, 1971), 43.

32   The text follows Rustico Filippi, *Sonetti*, ed. Mengaldo, 79.

33   The text follows Rustico Filippi, *Sonetti*, ed. Mengaldo, 75.

34   The text follows Guido Favati, ed., *Il Novellino* (Genova: Fratelli Bozzi, 1970), 328.

35   The text follows Favati, *Il Novellino*, 329.

36   All passages from the *Decameron* follow Vittore Branca's edition, Vol. IV of *Tutte le Opere* (Milano: Mondadori, 1976). The translations follow that of G.H. McWilliam: Giovanni Boccaccio, *The Decameron* (Middlesex: Penguin Books, 1972).

37   See, for example, the famous phrase used to describe Rustico's erection: "E così stando, essendo Rustico più che mai nel suo disidero acceso per lo vederla così bella, venne la resurrezion della carne" ["In this posture, the girl's beauty was displayed to Rustico in all its glory, and his longings blazed more fiercely than ever, bringing about the resurrection of the flesh"].

38   See G.H. McWilliam's "Translator's Introduction" to the *Decameron*, especially pp. 31–34.

39   It should not go unnoticed that the mention of Saints Michael and George with their sword and lance also have highly charged sexual overtones. While it may be surprising to find the reference to Christ, where Adam might be expected, the sexuality of Christ was appearing more frequently in art of this period; see Leo Steinberg, *The Sexuality of Christ in Renaissance Art and in Modern Oblivion* (New York: Pantheon, 1983).

A FIFTEENTH-CENTURY PHYSICIAN'S ATTITUDE TOWARD SEXUALITY: DR. JOHANN HARTLIEB'S *SECRETA MULIERUM* TRANSLATION

Margaret Schleissner

With nearly one hundred Latin manuscripts, fifty-five Latin incunable editions, vernacular translations from as early as the fourteenth century, and printed editions until well into the eighteenth century, the late thirteenth-century *Secreta mulierum*, spuriously attributed to Albertus Magnus, constitutes one of the most widespread examples of medieval gynecological literature. Its dedication to a "most dearly beloved friend and associate in Christ" (*dilectissimo sibi socio et amico in cristo*) suggests that it was written in the context of the university or cloister, possibly by a student of Albert's, and introduces the male-to-male discourse about women which is the most characteristic feature of this text. Despite its titillating title, it is not about female "secrets" (sexuality) or women's medicine *per se*. Rather, its twelve chapters, with alternating text and commentary, contain theoretical notions about female nature and human reproduction: theory of conception, embryology, especially in its astrological aspects, spontaneous generation, heredity and abnormal births, signs of pregnancy, fetal sex determination, signs of virginity, infertility and the nature of the male sperm.

Of the vernacular translations, none, to judge by the number of extant manuscripts, proved so popular as two, independent South German versions which arose practically simultaneously in the third quarter of the fifteenth century. One, written between 1460 and 1465 by Dr. Johann Hartlieb, was an original compilation drawn from several gynecological sources. Together with his adaptation of the gynecological treatises attributed to Trotula of Salerno, it was dedicated to Duke Siegmund of Bavaria-Munich, whom Hartlieb served as court physician.[1] The other, an anonymous translation, which follows the Latin original on the whole (the German gloss paraphrases and elaborates at certain points), circulated primarily among the Nürnberg patriciate.[2] Perhaps even as a reaction to Hartlieb's version for the high nobility, the anonymous German translation represents an act of cultural appropriation, an effort to appropriate the contents of Latin learning, for the educated urban bourgeoisie, and, to a lesser extent, the minor nobility in the country.[3]

Johann Hartlieb's *Secreta mulierum* translation affords a perfect opportunity to examine the context of vernacular gynecological literature, since both the translator, Hartlieb, and the immediate recipient, Duke Siegmund, who commissioned the translation for his personal use, are well-known historical figures. The almost immediate influence of Hartlieb's *Secreta* translation beyond the Munich court, moreover, is attested by a copy commissioned by Emperor Frederich III following Siegmund's visit to the imperial court in 1465.[4]

There are at least four ways of gauging a text's function, its status in everyday life or "Sitz im Leben," as Hugo Kuhn called it.[5] The first is codicological: what can the manuscripts themselves (provenance, history of ownership, principles of collection within manuscripts, format, marginal annotations and the like) tell us about their actual use? The second is literary: the privileged (because often very rare) route of references to the text in literature. The third is rhetorical: what does the text itself express about authorial intention and (intended) reader reception? (In the case of the *Secreta*, the various translations and commentaries themselves, insofar as they manipulate the tradition, offer specific examples of text reception.) A fourth line of inquiry has been suggested recently by Bernhard Schnell, who demonstrates the value of examining principles of collection within libraries, to the extent that these are historically accessible, in order to arrive at a notion of the literary interests of book owners.[6]

Hartlieb's text is marked not just by important deviations from the original arising from the technique of compilation but by a great number of authorial interpolations which constitute personal commentaries on the material. It is the purpose of this essay to analyze those passages in which Hartlieb addresses the reader directly or comments upon the material, those author-audience transactions which, in effect, offer instructions for reading and hence reveal something about the translator's intention and attitude toward his subject. Other criteria, codicological, literary and bibliophilic (for lack of a better term to describe the activity of book collectors), will be used to corroborate this information.

A consideration of Hartlieb's *Secreta mulierum* in the context of his life and oeuvre provides a first indication of authorial self-consciousness.[7] Born ca. 1400, probably in Möglingen in Württemberg, Johann Hartlieb was associated early in life with Duke Ludwig VII of Bavaria-Ingolstadt.[8] He studied medicine in Padua, where he received the title of master in 1437 and doctor in 1439.[9] He spent some time in Vienna, where he was associated with the court of Duke Albrecht VI of Austria, for whom he translated Andreas Capellanus' *De amore* in 1440. From 1440 on, he served the Dukes of Bavaria-Munich as court physician, first Albrecht III (d. 1460) and later his son Siegmund. His adaptations of the romance of Alexander shortly after 1450 and the legend of St. Brandan (before 1457) are dedicated to Albrecht III and his wife Anna of Braunschweig, the latter to Anna only. He also

undertook diplomatic missions for the Munich court, for example, in 1455
or 1456 to Markgrave Johann of Brandenburg to sue for the hand of his
niece, Margareta, daughter of Friedrich II, Elector of Brandenburg, on behalf
of Siegmund. Upon his return, he wrote at the request of Markgrave Johann
"the Alchemist" his *buch aller verpoten kunst*, a detailed description and
repudiation (!) of all forms of necromancy. Before 1467 he translated Book
II of Caesarius of Heisterbach's *Dialogus miraculorum*, a collection of
morally edifying saints' lives and *exempla*, for the Munich patrician Hans
Pterich. His scientific and medical works include an herbal (date
unknown),[10] a list of prices of medicines for the city of Munich from
1453,[11] and, finally, the *Secreta mulierum* and *Trotula* translations for Duke
Siegmund (1460–65).[12]

New biographical information about Hartlieb has come to light,
establishing the inauthenticity of several works traditionally attributed to
him: a book on mnemonics, four works on magic (lunar prognosis,
onomatomancy, geomancy, and chiromancy) and a book on hot baths.[13]
This would resolve the apparent contradiction within Hartlieb's oeuvre
between works of black magic and those with an overtly Christian focus
(*Brandan, Dialogus* and, especially, *puch aller verpoten kunst*, which
exhorts its patron, Markgrave Johannes, as moral exemplar, to reject and
ban magic in his realm). It strengthens Bosselmann-Cyran's assertion that
with his *Secreta mulierum* and *Trotula* translations Hartlieb is concerned not
just with Siegmund's sexual conduct but with his moral conduct as well.[14] As
Bosselmann-Cyran points out, it is important to distinguish between
Siegmund's historically attested indolent and profligate character and
Hartlieb's role as personal physician. These treatises, then, would conform
to a more general didactic tendency (moral guidance and enlightenment)
within Hartlieb's work overall. Just as Hartlieb's *Secreta mulierum* prologue
addressed to Emperor Friedrich praises this (older) monarch's thirst for
knowledge, so his *Alexander,* intended as a mirror of princes, seeks to
delight and instruct.[15] Through his literary oeuvre, Johann Hartlieb emerges
first and foremost as a *litteratus,* a member of a class of university-trained
professionals (many of whom rose from the ranks of the bourgeoisie to a
court position), engaged in transmitting Latin learning to a scientifically
interested lay audience.[16]

Another way of understanding Hartlieb's perspective is to consider the
rhetorical situation of the Latin *Secreta mulierum* as well as that of other
German translations. The two-fold function of the text (medical and
confessional) as stated in the most widespread version of the Latin
commentary, *ut ipsis infirmantibus possumus dare remedia et ipsis
confitentibus scire dare poenitentias debitas ad delictum,*[17] has nothing to
do with the actual material. Rather, like the prologue's familiar topos of the
unwilling author whose associates prevail upon him to share his
knowledge, in this case, to enlighten men about the hidden nature of women
(*ut quaedam nobis, quae apud mulierum naturam et conditionem sunt occulta
et secreta, lucidius manifestarem*),[18] it transforms the *I-thou* of the

epistolary dedication into a *we-them* configuration. The commentary amplifies: the text was written specifically to warn men against the dangers of menstruating women who poison animals, taint mirrors and infect little children and men who have intercourse with them with leprosy and cancer. Evil can only be avoided through knowledge (*quia malum non evitatur nisi cognitum*).[19]

An atmosphere of intimacy in which secrets can be divulged is created, first, through the privileging of the audience (most dearly beloved friends and associates in Christ) and, secondly, through the prohibition against allowing children, be they children by virtue of age or behavior, access to the book. Appealing to constancy and discretion (*constans ac celans*), the author establishes an elite audience primed to receive secrets in the proper frame of mind.[20]

What is at work here is precisely the connection Foucault identifies between the tradition of the penitentials (the technique of confession) and the science of sexuality: both are mechanisms for the proliferation of discourse on sex.[21] The tension between openness and secrecy and the tone of complicity between author and audience created by the first-person/ second-person address forms of the prologue (*scribo vobis*) are echoed in the text, for instance in the passage beginning *Sciatis autem socii mei . . .*[22] warning men against evil women who wound men in the penis during coitus with an iron inserted in the vagina. Women, moreover, deceive men by concealing pregnancy, inducing abortion and counterfeiting virginity. Female strategies of concealment are counteracted by male disclosure (a gendered form of knowledge-power).

The intrinsic formulicity of the epistolary dedication is demonstrated by the fact that the names of the author and addressee in the Latin manuscripts are entirely variable.[23] Most often (fictional) initials are used to preserve anonymity and heighten the atmosphere of secrecy. The prologue's account of the circumstances of composition, audience prohibition and instructions for use are variously transformed in the vernacular versions. Thus the Old French and Flemish adaptations begin with the book-as-courtly-love-service topos: *Vne damoiselle me pria pour loyalle cortoysie/ Mijn lieve joncfrouwe heeft mi gebeden*, echoing the humility formula of the Latin text, *cum vestra favorabilis & gratuita . . . societas . . . me rogavit*.[24] To this, the Old French adds a fictional papal decretal against showing the work to women(!) on pain of excommunication: *. . . deffandus de reveler a fame par nostre sainct pere le pape sus paine descommuniement en la Decretal ad meam decretam*.[25]

A High German translation from shortly before 1400, on the other hand, warns against revealing the contents to imprudent people (those lacking sound judgment and discretion),[26] as does an East Middle German translation, adding that the text might be used to slander decent women.[27] An independent High German paraphrase warns readers to keep the book away from foolish and vulgar people (toren menschen/ etlicher grober mensch).[28] An Alemannic version, by citing the first sentence of

Aristotle's Metaphysics on the universal human desire for knowledge, gives the male-to-male transfer of knowledge about women a larger, cosmological or natural philosophical focus, in the tradition of question and problem literature.[29] Finally, a text entitled *"Secreta mulierum"* in a Prague manuscript, containing the most rudimentary instructions for conception (proper conduct during intercourse, causes of infertility, signs of pregnancy, sex prognostication, sterility tests and the like) expresses quite the opposite intention. The text is written for the benefit of ignorant men and women (specifically, married couples), so they might conduct themselves with greater understanding:

> Nach noczwerkeit der vnuerstendigen frauwen und der vnwisen mannen die keines dinges vnderscheit wisen wie sie sich halten sollen das sie das thun mit vnderscheit vnd mit verstendigen sinnen. Zu erkennen dies dinges vnderscheid her vmb so schriben ich den elich luten dorch nocze willen mancherley vnderscheid das sye sich vorsehen mogen der frauwen heymelichkeit vnd sich wisen dar nach zu richten vnd czu reygeren.

[For the benefit of injudicious women and unwise men who have no knowledge of how to conduct themselves sexually with good sense and discretion. For the purpose of enlightenment, I am writing down certain information for the utility of married people so that they should be mindful of women's secrets and be guided and governed by this knowledge].[30]

Reflecting the genre consciousness which had developed around the *Secreta mulierum* by this time, this text, which is in fact not the *Secreta mulierum*, still uses some elements of the prologue.

Hartlieb's *Secreta mulierum,* addressed to Siegmund, echoes many of these sentiments exactly. The prologue opens with a reference to Albumasor, Ptolemy and Averroes on the divine nature of human reason. Wisdom, as opposed to carnal lust, distinguishes humans from all other species. The anonymous (or variable) opening dedication takes on greater specificity in the form of a personal address from "me, Doctor Hartlieb" to Duke Siegmund or Emperor Friedrich respectively. Praise for the noble patron's thirst for knowledge is reminiscent of a mirror-of-princes: wisdom adorns the prince and is as beneficial to his subjects as the evening rain.[31] Hartlieb's treatment of the notion of secrecy encompasses his fears that the work will be misused for extramarital lust (*puelschafft aus der ee*) as well as his repeated admonitions against allowing "unworthy" persons access to the text.[32] Since nothing is unhealthier than animosity between married people, his translation is intended solely for them (*allein durch die eelewt*).[33] Secrecy, finally, implies "secrets of nature," heavenly secrets which may not be revealed publicly without divine punishment.[34] The irony in all of this is, of course, that although Hartlieb claims to address married people, he in fact addresses the bachelor, Siegmund. Does he envision another audience besides Siegmund? Are his reservations sincere or are they just a rhetorical strategy, a conscious ploy or formulaic device for the revelation of "forbidden" erotic material?

That sexual practices at the Munich court may have conflicted with Hartlieb's devout Christianity[35] is borne out by those passages in which he expresses fear of God. For example, Hartlieb recommends that Siegmund have recipes for contraceptives and abortifacients (chapter 19 of *Buch Trotula*) written in secret letters to avoid misuse by frivolous people:

> Aller gnadigster furst Jch pitt dein gnad dz du ditz capittl verhaltest oder aber mit verporgn puchstabn der ich ewm furstlichn gnadn vil gebn hab schreybn lasst wan soltn die stugk kumen vntter leychtfertig lewt so wurd gro sund dauon geschechn das ich euch vnd mir nit gunnen wolt.

[Most gracious lord, I beg your grace to suppress this chapter or else to have it written in secret letters with which I have provided your noble grace, for should this passage come into the hands of imprudent people, grave sins would result for which I would not wish you or me to bear responsibility.][36]

He expresses similar reservation with regard to the permanent sterilization of women who for medical reasons are unfit to bear children.

> Ich pesorg, solt die kunst aufkummen, so wurden etlich frauen und maid die treyben so ez nit not wer, und mocht vil vbels darauß kummen. Darvmb will ich es nit zu teutsch machen. Will aber ewr furstlich gnad das ye haben, so pin ich der ewr vnd han euch versprochen, das puch zu teutschen. So will ich es recht vnd wol teutschen vnd will das ton auf ewr sel, leyb, er vnd gut, vnd was vbels dauon geschech, da will ich nit tail an haben In dem namen Jesu Christi amen.

[I fear, should the technique come into use, some women and girls would practice it when it was not necessary and much evil would result. Therefore, I do not wish to translate it into German. But if your noble grace wishes to have it anyway, then I am yours and I have promised to translate this book into German. And so I will translate it accurately and will do so upon your soul, body, honor and property, and whatever evil results I will have no part in, in the name of Jesus Christ, Amen.][37]

He appeals to the loyal reader's sense of morality in guarding against possible non-medical uses:

> du trewr leser ditz puchs, sich an dein gbissn vnd die peynlich straff gotts vnd der natur vnd prauch dz capittl nit dan da ez not ist

[You, loyal reader of this book, consider your conscience and the excruciating punishment of God and nature and do not use this chapter except when necessary.][38]

Most scholars have seen in these passages a thinly veiled excuse for the presentation of erotica.[39] Yet Hartlieb expresses pride in his medical learning which allows him to synthesize a number of gynecological sources in order to present a comprehensive overview of the "state of the science" relating to women, insofar as such material would have been available to a fifteenth-century physician. He describes his method of compilation, stressing its utility for married people:

> auß iglichem, das dan in iglichs capittl gehort, getzogen nach dem bestn, als ich dan gethon hab . . . so glaub ich, das kain ainig puech in der natur von kunstlichn dingn, frauen antreffend, ye gemacht wurd, das puch sey lustiger, ntzer vnd pesser allen eelewten.

[. . . drawn from each the best material pertaining to each chapter, as I have done. . . . I believe that no single book was ever made about learned things concerning women that was more pleasing, useful and better for all married people].[40]

He distances himself from magic and astrology, insisting on a medical and Christian point of view, particularly in the prologue (*alles, das darin stet, das ist kain czawbrey vnd geet alles czw mit kreyttern, salben, wurtzen, greyffen* [nothing contained herein is magic, rather everything is effected through herbs, salves, plants and creams]) and in the introduction to the eighth (astrological) chapter.[41] As Klaus Grubmller and Kristian Bosselmann-Cyran argue, Hartlieb sees himself both as a moral preceptor (especially with regard to Siegmund) and as a transmitter of scientific information (especially with regard to Friedrich). In the *Secreta mulierum* he consciously instructs a lay audience in matters of general knowledge, much like a present-day "Konversationslexikon" (*das wayß dein furstlich gnad hinfur, ob es czw red kem, wol verantwurten* [this your noble grace will know how to answer if it arises in conversation]).[42] The *Buch Trotula*, with its innumerable recipes, represents much more of a "how-to" manual or self-help book.

In certain key passages, Hartlieb addresses not just Siegmund or Friedrich, but all men. These passages reveal something about Hartlieb's attitude toward women and female sexuality. The first, which concludes the chapter on the nature of the menses, enjoins men to help women during menstruation (which is absolutely crucial to their health and well-being) just as one would aid a patient following a botched venesection:

> Merck gueter man, so mon der menschen schonen vnd wol pflegen soll jn ainer schlechten aderlas, warvmb solt man dan nit der frawen czu der tzeit, da all jr hayl vnd gesunthait an leyt, schonen vnd yr mit speys vnd tranck wol pflegen.

[Take note, good men, just as one should take good care of and tend to a person during a bad bloodletting, why shouldn't one care for women and attend to them with food and drink during a time upon which their entire health and well-being depends].[43]

This tone is quite the opposite from that heard elsewhere, for example in the chapter on the malignity of the menses (chapter 61, *wie man sich hwtten soll vor frawben in jr wochen* [how one should avoid women during their menstrual periods])[44] which Hartlieb embellishes with the anecdote of the venomous maiden from the *Secret of Secrets*. The second, beginning "*O lieber gueter man*,"[45] calls upon men to recognize the symptoms of increased sexual desire in women's eyes and gestures following the first month of pregnancy. As in preceding passages on superfetation (multiple conceptions caused by women's excessive sexual appetite) Hartlieb, unlike his Latin source, seems extremely accepting of female eroticism: he simply refers the reader ahead to "secrets" (full instructions on how to arouse women) in other treatises, especially *Buch Trotula*.[46] The effect is to soften the misogynous tone of the original which leads, in other contexts (Latin commentaries and the contemporaneous anonymous German translation), to an entire series of invectives against women. While it is difficult to judge the semantic level of fifteenth-century German, the difference in tone between the two major versions seems to be reflected in the sexual vocabulary. Whereas Hartlieb consistently uses either the euphemism, *gulden porten*, or the Latin technical term, *vulva*, to refer to female genitalia, the anonymous German translation piles up abusive language referring to women and female sexual anatomy (for example, 1. 2301: *zers futt huren* with respect to those who feign virginity).

That patriarchal interests are ultimately served is demonstrated by the greatly expanded section on signs of virginity (chapter 62) in which tests are enumerated and more detail is added. In general, signs of virginity, together with signs of pregnancy, sex prognostication and infertility (causes, tests and cures) form the most prevalent and persistent type of gynecological literature.[47] This chapter ends with a pro-feminist apology (to men) about women who restore virginity by tightening the vulva with a salve. Hartlieb, referring to *Trotula*, defends such methods which may be used to protect women's honor and virtue. Alluding to Gilbertinus (Gilbertus Anglicus), he adds that tightening the vulva increases sexual attractiveness and promotes love within marriage.[48]

The *Buch Trotula* represents in many ways the practical application of theoretical notions first elaborated in the *Secreta mulierum*. Viewed as an ensemble or program, the relationship between the *Secreta mulierum* and *Buch Trotula* is one between diagnosis and therapy,[49] theory and practice, (male-centered) *wort* and (female-centered) *werck*,[50] natural philosophy (cosmology) and medicine. Thus chapter 63 of Hartlieb's *Secreta* relegates remedies for menstrual disorders to medical books (*es gehort jn dye ertzeney*), while the list of cures for scantiness and superabundance of the menses in *Buch Trotula* is so long as to require an apology:

> Hochgepomer furst ewr furstlich gnad solt nit achten das dicz capittel von der frawen plûmen tzelang wirt dan aller frawen gesunthayt vnd wolmugens ligt daran.

[Honorable lord, your noble grace should not pay any attention if this chapter on "women's flowers" is too long, for all women's health and well-being depend on it].[51]

Chapter 6 of *Buch Trotula* counsels tightening and drying the vulva to avoid male sexual displeasure. A long section on sexual hygiene addressed to women is intended to benefit both sexes: by ensuring male and female sexual pleasure, it aids procreative sex within marriage.[52] Addressing the male reader, Hartlieb writes:

> Glaub du mir gutter man dz kain ding den leyb vnd gemt schedlicher ist dan der mynn mit vnlust zu pflegen...

[Believe me, good men, that nothing is more harmful to body and soul than intercourse without pleasure].[53]

Recipes for simulating virginity in chapter 8 (addressed to women), including insertion of a fish bladder filled with bird's blood into the vagina, are defended as a means to preserve women's honor and enhance their social status. Hartlieb cites as an example women of Naples who must present proof of virginity on the wedding night in order to receive their *Morgengabe*.[54]

Hartlieb's gynecological compendium thus provides a perfect example of what Jacquart and Thomasset term "the eroticization of medical discourse" in the wake of the growing influence of Avicenna's *Canon*. Coitus was deemed necessary for psychological as well as physical health and emission of female sperm (linked with orgasm) was believed necessary for conception to occur. Thus doctors were "granted . . . freedom of expression with, in addition, a justification which could not be neglected in a society which made sexual intercourse serve the sole end of reproduction."[55]

Because of its historical specificity and authorial interpolations, Hartlieb's translation constitutes a uniquely important document in the fifteenth-century reception of gynecological literature. Literary evidence of its circulation at the Munich court is provided by an allusion to the *Secreta mulierum* in Ulrich Fuetrer's *Buch der Abenteuer* of 1473 (a "remake" of popular thirteenth-century courtly novels) in connection with Merlin's supernatural birth:

> Albertus Magnus schreibt das michel wunder/ inn dem secret der haimlicheit, Trotula und auch Gilbertus sunder.

[Albertus Magnus writes about this supernatural event in the Secret of Secrets [sic], Trotula and Gilbertus].[56]

As corroboration, codicological evidence suggests that the source of Hartlieb's *Trotula* translation, in all likelihood, is contained in a Wolfenbüttel medical manuscript owned by another one his associates, his fellow court physician (and city physician) who studied at about the same time in Padua, Sigismund Gotzkircher. Hartlieb is named twice (along with other Munich citizens from among Gotzkircher's acquaintances: Endelczhawser, Putreich, Pötschner, Ridler, Ligsalcz) in connection with monetary loans on several pages of personal notes at the back of the manuscript.[57] We know from other personal notes, that Gotzkircher borrowed medical books from Hartlieb to have them copied for his own library.[58] It is therefore entirely possible that this exchange of books took place in the opposite direction, that is, that Hartlieb borrowed books from Gotzkircher's personal library. If that is the case, then a copy of the *Secreta mulierum* owned by Gotzkircher is almost certainly the source of Hartlieb's *Secreta* translation.[59] Finally, no fewer than four Trotula manuscripts and several copies of the *Secreta mulierum* (including printed versions) were owned by the Nürnberg humanist-physician and translator Dr. Hartmann Schedel. Schedel himself lists these manuscripts under the rubric "*Libri medicinales et ad sacram medicinam utiles*."[60] The interest of these book collectors thus appears to be medical and learned.

With greater specificity of context comes greater emphasis on utility and, it seems, greater openness toward female sexuality. Hartlieb's *Secreta mulierum* and *Trotula* translations, for a variety of reasons, offer an *ars erotica* as well as a *scientia sexualis*. One can easily imagine how, in the sixteenth and seventeenth centuries and in a different class setting, such material becomes incorporated into so-called "housefather" books, guides for paternal management of the household. Hartlieb's insistence that his compilation is intended to aid married people (and to increase knowledge for its own sake) should be taken at face value.*

*This article was written during an academic research leave from Rider College. Research was conducted at the Institut für Geschichte der Medizin der Universität Würzburg with a grant from the Deutsche Forschungsgemeinschaft, Sonderforschungsbereich 226. I wish to thank Professor Gundolf Keil for his generous support.

Notes

1   See Kristian Bosselmann-Cyran, '*Secreta mulierum*' *mit Glosse in der deutschen Bearbeitung von Johann Hartlieb. Text und Untersuchungen*, Würzburger medizinhistorische Forschungen, vol. 36 (Pattensen/Hannover: Horst Wellm, 1985). An additional Hartlieb manuscript containing both the *Secreta mulierum* and *Buch Trotula* from 1480 can be found in Milan, Biblioteca Nazionale Ms 986. See Franco Bazzi, *Catalogo dei manoscritti e degli incunaboli di interesse medico-naturalistico dell' Ambrosiana e della Braidense*, Quaderni di "Castalia," 7 (Bergamo: Stamperia Editrice Commerciale, 1961), 133. My thanks to Monica Green for bringing this manuscript to my attention. This brings the total number of manuscripts to fourteen (nine with both the *Secreta mulierum* and *Buch Trotula* and five with the *Buch Trotula* only; of these, eight are either fragmentary or condensed). An edition of the most widespread Latin Trotula tradition together with a facing-page translation and commentary is forthcoming in Monica H. Green and John F. Benton, *The Gynecological and Cosmetic Treatises Attributed to "Trotula" of Salerno: Edition and Translation*, University of Toronto Press.

2   Margaret Schleissner, "Pseudo-Albertus Magnus, *Secreta mulierum cum commento*, Deutsch. Critical Text and Commentary" (Ph.D. diss., Princeton University, 1987), forthcoming in Würzburger medizinhistorische Forschungen. This version is contained in fifteen manuscripts, with the addition of Admont, Stiftsbibliothek, Ms 584. For other, relatively isolated German *Secreta mulierum* translations (eleven manuscripts total), see Bosselmann-Cyran, 17–19, and Schleissner, 47–48. In addition, Nürnberg, Germanisches Nationalmuseum, Ms 19723, written in Bavarian dialect (1482–84), with its dedication to *holandrino Ertzbischoffen studenten der vil wirdigen parisischen schule*, belongs within the East Middle German tradition. Paris, Bibliothèque Nationale, Ms. all. 163, it must be stressed, is an independent High German paraphrase with additions from Ortolf von Baierland's *Arzneibuch*. Translations into other languages including French, Italian, Catalan, Czech, Polish and English (the latter as late as the eighteenth century) are noted by Bosselmann-Cyran, 14–15, and Schleissner, 40.

3   One Frankfurt manuscript (Stadt- und Universitätsbibliothek, Ms. germ. oct. 60) transforms the opening dedication (*Dem allerliebsten* etc.) into *Dem Hochgebornen fürsten vnd herren etc.* See Schleissner, 72–73.

4   Codicological evidence suggests that Munich, Bayerische Staatsbibliothek, Cgm 261, and Berlin, Staatsbibliothek Preußischer Kulturbesitz, Ms. germ. fol. 928 were produced both in close proximity to the archetype and to each other in or around Munich between 1467 and 1471. Berlin, Ms. germ. fol. 928, furthermore, is believed to be the copy made for the emperor, possibly under Hartlieb's own supervision.

Since Hartlieb died in 1468, it would have been produced between late 1467 and early 1468. See Bosselmann-Cyran, 67–71 and 331–336.

5   Kuhn refers to the rise of a new literary culture in the fifteenth century, exemplified by literary production at certain centers: at courts, notably Munich, by court officials (Hartlieb as court physician and Ulrich Fuetrer as court painter) as well as within cities by city officials (city physicians and chancellory officials). See Hugo Kuhn, "Versuch über das 15. Jahrhundert in der deutschen Literatur," in *Entwürfe zu einer Literatursystematik des Spätmittelalters* (Tübingen: Niemeyer, 1980), 81–82.

6   Bernhard Schnell, "Zur Bedeutung der Bibliotheksgeschichte für eine Überlieferungs- und Wirkungsgeschichte," in Überlieferungsgeschichtliche Prosaforschung, ed. Kurt Ruh (Tübingen: Niemeyer, 1985), 221–230.

7   On Hartlieb's life and works, see Karl Drescher, "Johann Hartlieb. Über sein Leben und seine schriftstellerische Tätigkeit," *Euphorion* 25 (1924), 225–241, 354–370, 569–590 and Euphorion 26 (1925), 341–367, 481–564, Klaus Grubmüller, "Ein Arzt als Literat: Hans Hartlieb," in *Poesie und Gebrauchsliteratur im deutschen Mittelalter*, ed. Volker Honemann et al. (Tübingen: Niemeyer, 1979), 14–36, and Klaus Grubmüller, 'Hartlieb, Johannes' in *Deutsche Literatur des Mittelalters: Verfasserlexikon*, ed. Kurt Ruh et al., 2nd ed. (Berlin and New York: Walter de Gruyter, 1978ff.), vol. III (1981), col. 479–496. I have benefited from a pre-publication copy of Bernhard Schnell, "Arzt und Literat: Zum Anteil der Ärzte am spätmittelalterlichen Literaturbetrieb," *Sudhoffs Archiv*, 75, Heft 1 (1991).

8   See the author attribution in the pseudoepigraphic(?) *De mansionibus* (Freiburg, Universitätsbibliothek, cod. 458, 134v) and the records of the University of Padua cited by Bosselmann-Cyran, 20. In 1437 he was stripped of a position (granted him by Duke Ludwig) as rector of St. Moritz's church in Ingolstadt because of an absence exceeding one year as well as his failure to become ordained. See Drescher, *Euphorion* 25 (1924), 226–27.

9   Bosselmann-Cyran, 20–21.

10   Edition in progress (Bernhard Schnell and Gerold Hayer).

11   Ed. Werner Dressendörfer, *Spätmittelalterliche Arzneitaxen des Münchener Stadtarztes Sigmund Gotzkircher aus dem Grazer Codex 311*, Würzburger medizinhistorische Forschungen, vol. 15 (Pattensen/Hannover: Horst Wellm, 1979), 132–59. On authorship and date, see 64–67.

12   P.O. Kristeller, *Iter italicum*, vol. II (London, 1967) 237 lists Venezia, Biblioteca Nazionale Marciana, cod. 53 (2687), "s. XV Jo. Hartlieb, Practica medicinae" (= Latini, classe VII). Kristeller, *Iter italicum* III (London; Leiden, 1983) 640 lists an "Arzneybuch" from 1432 now in Munich, Staatliche Graphische Sammlung (formerly Munich, Bayerisches Nationalmuseum 1501). On the Latin Venice manuscript, see Bosselmann-Cyran, 21–22.

13   Based on work by Frank Fürbeth. See Schnell, "Ärzt und Literat." The authenticity of Hartlieb's "mantic works" (including the book on mnemonics) had already been called into question by Martin Wierschin, "Johannes Hartliebs 'Mantische Schriften,'" *Beiträge zur deutschen Sprache und Literatur* 90 (1968): 57–100. Although mnemonics technically does not belong among the sciences forbidden by the church, the emphasis on "secrecy" in this text relegates it to the realm of occult science (see Grubmüller, 2VL [1981] 485). The book of baths, written by Jordan Tömlinger, had been adduced as evidence of Hartlieb's questionable character, especially in his relationship with Duke Siegmund (see Drescher *Euphorion* 25 [1924], 239 and n. 3).

14   Siegmund, officially a bachelor, had at least three illegitimate children with his bourgeois mistress. See Bosselmann-Cyran, 26–28.

15   Hannes Kästner ("Der Arzt und die Kosmographie," in *Literatur und Laienbildung*, ed. Ludger Grenzmann and Karl Stackmann [Stuttgart: Metzler, 1984], 504–531) describes the role of university-educated physicians in the spread of geographical knowledge in Germany during the fifteenth and sixteenth centuries. He cites Hartlieb's *Alexander* adaptation, specifically (508), as an example of exotic cosmography (particularly about India). The most obvious example is Dr. Hartmann Schedel, author of the Nürnberg World Chronicle (1493).

16   See Klaus Grubmüller, "Der Hof als städtisches Literaturzentrum. Hinweise zur Rolle des Bürgertums am Beispiel der Literaturgesellschaft Münchens im 15. Jahrhundert," in *Befund und Deutung*, ed. Klaus Grubmüller et al. (Tübingen: Niemeyer, 1979), 405–427. Other humanistically oriented German physicians from around this time in cities such as Munich, Nürnberg, Augsburg, Ulm and Erfurt are listed by Kästner (505).

17   Ed. Amsterdam, 1740, 4–5.

18   Ed. Amsterdam, 1740, 5.

19   Ed. Amsterdam, 1740, 5.

20   Ed. Amsterdam, 1740, 6. A similar set of rhetorical devices (secrecy, enlightenment, constancy) can be found in the prologue of the Middle High German *Lucidarius*, an encyclopedia (*imago mundi*) based on several Latin sources in the form of a dialogue between master and disciple, probably commissioned ca. 1195 by Duke Henry the Lion of Braunschweig, with the largest concentration of manuscripts in the second half of the fifteenth century. According to the rhymed prologue, "Lucidarius" (the title) signifies an illuminator (*luchtere/irluchter*): it reveals secrets hidden in books (*manic tôge dinc die an den bûchen verborgen sint*), promising the extraordinary (*vremde mere/wunders vil*) to the reader ready to receive it *mit stetem sinne* (with an attitude of loyalty, constancy or steady concentration). Lucidarius aus der Berliner Handschrift, ed. Felix Heidlauf, *Deutsche Texte des Mittelalters*, vol. 28 (Berlin: Weidmannsche Buchhandlung, 1915), xii–xiii and 1.

21   Michel Foucault, *History of Sexuality*, vol. I, tr. Robert Hurley (New York: Vintage Books, 1980) 18, 33, 58.

22   Ed. Amsterdam, 1740, 45.

23   See Lynn Thorndike, "Further Consideration of the 'Experimenta, Speculum Astronomiae,' and 'De Secretis Mulierum' ascribed to Albertus Magnus," *Speculum* 30 (1955), 428–429 and n. 30, also Christoph Ferckel, "Die Secreta mulierum und ihr Verfasser," *Sudhoffs Archiv* 38 (1954), 267, n. 2.

24   The Old French text from the first half of the fifteenth century was edited from four manuscripts by Drs. Al. C[olson] and Ch.-Ed. C****, *Ce sont les Secrés des Dames Deffendus à révéler* (Paris: Rouveyre: 1880). The Flemish version, found in a unique manuscript from 1405, was edited by Ph. Blommaert, Maetschappy der vlaemsche bibliophilen, 2e Serie, No. 3 (Gent: C. Annoot-Braeckman, [1846]). Another Flemish verse translation from 1351 is found in Brussels, Bibliothèque Royale Albert I, Ms. 15624–41 (ed. Napoleon De Pauw, *Der Mannen en Vrouwen Heimelijcheit*, in *Middelnederlandse Gedichten en Fragmenten*, vol. I (1893), 121–90. Christoph Ferckel ("Zur Bibliographie der Secreta mulierum," *Archiv für Geschichte der Medizin* 7 [1914], 48) suggests that the French and Middle Netherlandic traditions had a common Latin source.

25   It is presumably this version (or a related Latin one) which Christine de Pisan rails against in the *Livre de la Cité des Dames* (c. 1405):

"Un autre petit livre en latin vi, dame, qui se nomme *Du secret des femmes* qui dit de la composicion de leur corps naturel, moult de grans deffaulx."

Responce: "Tu puez congnoistre par toy meismes sans nulle autre preuve, que celluy livre fu fait a voulenté et faintement coulouré: car ce tu l'as leu, ce te puet estre chose magnifeste que il est traittié tout de mençonges. . . . Mais ne te souvient il que il dit a son commancement que ne sçay quel pappe escommenia tout homme qui le liroit a femme ou a lire luy bailleroit?"

Maureen Cheney Lois Curnow, "The Livre de la Cité des Dames of Christine de Pisan: A Critical Edition," diss. Vanderbilt University, 1975, pt. 2, 649–650.

26   Vienna, Österrreichische Nationalbibliothek, Cod. germ. 2962 and 12490 (both fragmentary), Wolfenbüttel, Herzog-August Bibliothek, Cod. Guelf. 69.14 Aug., and Budapest, University Library Cod., germ. 5 (with slight variations): *Das puech sagt vns von der haimleichait der frauwen daz niemant lesen sol noch hören lesen Er sei dan vernufftig vnd verstanden* (Vienna, Cod. Vindob. Pal. 12490, 123ra). To this highly condensed version in Vienna, Cod. Vindob. Pal. 12490 are appended the gynecological-embryological sections of Lucidarius, (ed. Heidlauf, 28–30) in which the master states: *die rede ist von Gottes tougeni, die sol nieman hören wen die vil gewissen sint.* Here (124va) the *Lucidarius* excerpt is introduced with *Hie ist ain frag aines iungers,* only the master's admonition becomes *die red ist von gotez taugen vnd ist chainer frawen(!) guet zu horen dan die gar weiss vnd verstanden sind vnd vernufftig,* and the whole thing ends *Expliciunt secreta mulierum* (125rb). Copies of the Vienna fragments were kindly sent to me by the Hill Monastic Manuscript Library.

27   Gotha, Landesbibliothek, Chart. B 1505 (a. 1477), Nürnberg, Germanisches Nationalmuseum 19723 (Bavarian dialect, c. 1482–84), and Budapest, Sézchényi National Library, Cod. germ. 11.

28   Paris, Bibliothèque Nationale, Ms. all. 163, 82r.

29   Einsiedeln, Stiftsbibliothek, Ms. 297, 389. See description in Henry E. Sigerist, "Deutsche medizinische Handschriften in Schweizer Bibliotheken," *Archiv für Geschichte der Medizin* 17 (1925), 205–40. This medical-astrological compendium is one of approximately twenty manuscripts containing texts which comprise the so-called "iatromathematical housebook." A great many recipes as well as instructions for magical inscriptions and amulets suggest its practical use either by physicians or male heads of households. The first sentence of Aristotle's *Metaphysics* opens the thirteenth-century *Placides et Timéo ou Li secrés as philosophes,* a question book in the form of a dialogue between master and disciple which, like the *Lucidarius,* belongs to the body of *imago mundi* literature. Cosmological in focus, it features a lengthy discussion of human reproduction. See Claude Thomasset, *Placides et Timéo ou Li secrés as philosophes,* édition critique avec introduction et notes (Geneva: Librairie Droz, 1980).

On problem literature, see Brian Lawn, *The Salernitan Questions: An Introduction to the History of Medieval and Renaissance Problem Literature,* (Oxford: Clarendon Press, 1963) and *The Prose Salernitan Questions* (London: Oxford University Press, 1979). Another example of this genre is the *Problemata Varia Anatomica,* edited by L.R. Lind (Lawrence: University of Kansas Publications, 1968) which Lawn, *The Salernitan Questions,* 99–103, calls "Omnes homines" from the incipit, the first words of Aristotle's *Metaphysics.* These pseudo-Aristotelian anatomical problems from the fourteenth century circulate in German under the title *Problemata Aristoteles deutsch* in manuscripts (from Nürnberg, c. 1500) whose single other text is the anonymous South German *Secreta mulierum* translation as well as in two Hartlieb manuscripts from 1570. The gynecological sections of "Omnes homines" are found separately, as well, in the collection of medical treatises known as the *Fasciculus medicinae* of Johannes de Ketham (Johannes Kirchheimer), printed 1491 in Venice, where they are entitled: *probleumata de membris generationis de matrice et testiculis seu de secretis mulierum.*

30 Prag, Státní Knihovna, Ms. XXIII F 129, 486r (old foliation, 502r). I am indebted to Gundolf Keil for bringing this manuscript to my attention and to the late John F. Benton and, indirectly, the Hill Monastic Manuscript Library for the microfilm copy. This text is also found in Berlin, Staatsbibliothek Preußischer Kulturbesitz, Ms. germ. fol. 1069.

31 The prologue addressed to Siegmund contrasts the love of wisdom with youthful lust (Bosselmann-Cyran, 101f., ll. 22–24). Passages warning against sexual excesses of youth are absent from the emperor's version. Thus, while the text may have served the duke's sexual curiosity, the prologue's emphasis on Friedrich's thirst for knowledge suggests that it addressed the emperor's intellectual curiosity instead.

32 Bosselmann-Cyran, 108, ll. 93, 99f./ 109, ll. 83, 86f. and 112f., 156–79/113f., 129–50. The emperor's version (108, ll. 101f.) adds that women of all social classes may be subject to slander.

33 Bosselmann-Cyran, 106, l. 89/ 107, l. 80.

34 Related to the notion of *curiositas* (as a subcategory of *superbia*) as sin. For discussions of motifs of arcaneness (secrecy as a literary topos), see Gundolf Keil, "Die Frau als Ärztin und Patientin in der medizinischen Fachprosa des deutschen Mittelalters," in *Frau und spätmittelalterlicher Alltag: Internationaler Kongress Krems an der Donau, 2. bis 5. Oktober 1984* (Vienna: Österreichische Akademie der Wissenschaften, 1986), 190 and 211, and William Eamon, "Books of Secrets in Medieval and Early Modern Science," *Sudhoffs Archiv* 69 (1985), 26–49, esp. the prologue of the pseudo-Aristotelian *Secret of Secrets*, cited by Eamon, 30. Eamon (35–40) describes the "domestication of secrets," that is, he sees books of experiments (recipes for magic and formularies) being written less for academics and increasingly for the private sphere, particularly (in Italy during the sixteenth century) by scholars for princely patrons.

35 See n. 14 above.

36 (Cgm 261, 79v).

37 Cited in Bosselmann-Cyran, 25.

38 Cgm 261, 77r.

39 Modern historians have viewed Hartlieb's motives in the *Buch aller verbotenen Künste* in a similar vein, i.e., by offering detailed instructions for magical practices, he provides an incentive rather than a deterrent, as claimed. See, for example, Thomas Kramer, *Geschichte der deutschen Literatur im säpten Mittelalter* (Munich: Deutscher Taschenbuch Verlag, 1990), 129. Frank Frbeth, on the other hand, characterizes Hartlieb as walking a thin line between concealment and disclosure of morally reprehensible material (Johannes Hartlieb, *Das Buch aller verbotenen Künste*, ed. and tr. Frank Fürbeth [Frankfurt am Main: Insel Verlag, 1989], 14).

40 Bosselmann-Cyran, 110f., ll. 148–55.

41 Bosselmann-Cyran, 109, ll. 88–90 and 124, ll. 6–16.

42 Bosselmann-Cyran, 155, ll. 60–61.

43 Bosselmann-Cyran, 132, ll. 53–57.

44 Ed. Amsterdam, 1740, 101–03.

45 Bosselmann-Cyran, 139, ll. 15–19 and 140, ll. 44–47.

46 Bosselmann-Cyran, 129, ll. 14–20 and 138f., ll. 10–20, 35–43. Such instructions, it is worth noting, are not present in the original. In this context it is also important to point out that Hartlieb, like most of his contemporaries, believed

that the *Trotula* treatises were composed by a woman, by nature an "expert" on female sexuality. In the prologue to the Kaiser version, he calls her a "queen of Greece" (Bosselmann-Cyran, 108, 1. 109). According to ancient and medieval theories of conception, emission of female and male seed (both products of blood "concocted" in the testes) was necessary for conception. Thus, female sexual pleasure and orgasm acquired an entirely different order of importance. For Hartlieb's acceptance of Galenic concepts of female seed and female testes, see Bosselmann-Cyran, 236, 11. 62–70 and 247, 11. 70–79.

47   See, for instance, Konrad von Megenberg, *Das Buch der Natur*, ed. Franz Pfeiffer (Stuttgart, 1861, rpt. Hildesheim: Olms, 1962), 38–42, and Steven Ozment, *When Fathers Ruled. Family Life in Reformation Europe* (Cambridge, Mass., and London, England: Harvard University Press, 1983), 112–13.

48   Bosselmann-Cyran, 233f., 11. 44–61.

49   Bosselmann-Cyran (38) suggests this with respect to the treatment of virginity: the *Secreta* offers virginity tests, while *Buch Trotula* lists methods for counterfeiting virginity.

50   The *wort-werck* dichotomy with respect to women's health care appears in Pseudo-Ortolf von Baierland, *Frauenbüchlein*, facs. ed. Gustav Klein, Alte Meister der Medizin und Naturkunde, 1 (Munich: Carl Kuhn, 1910) aiijr. Cited in Keil, "Die Frau als Ärztin und Patientin," 202.

51   Cgm 261, 52v.

52   Cgm 261, 60v–62r. Chapter 7 recounts the myth of the blind seer Teiresias, who having been turned into a woman and back into a man gives firsthand testimony (to the medical community in Athens!) that females experience greater sexual pleasure.

53   Cgm 261, 61r.

54   Cgm 261, 63r.

55   Danielle Jacquart and Claude Thomasset, *Sexuality and Medicine in the Middle Ages*, te. Matthew Adamson (Princeton: Princeton University Press, 1988), 130–32.

56   See note 5 above. *Die Gralepen in Ulrich Füetrers Bearbeitung (Buch der Abenteuer)* (Deutsche Texte des Mittelalters), ed. Kurt Nyholm (Berlin: Akademie Verlag, 1964) 23, str. 152. I am indebted to Edward G. Fichtner for this reference.

57   Wolfenbüttel, Herzog-August-Bibliothek, Ms. 784 Helmst., 243r–244r. I am most grateful to John F. Benton for sending me photographs of the relevant folio pages. For information on Gotzkircher's life and works, see Werner Dressendörfer, *Spätmittelalterliche Arzneitaxen*, n. 11 above, 54–60 and Werner Dressendrfer, "Gotzkircher, Sigismund" in *Deutsche Literatur des Mittelalters: Verfasserlexikon*, 2nd ed., vol. III, col. 202–04.

58   On two loose leaves in the Munich University Library with the signature, Cod. lat. 29103a: *Rosa anglicana* (John of Gaddesden or Gilbertus Anglicus?), Serapion's *De simplicibus*, and Arnold of Villanova, *Antidotarium*. Another such notation (*usque hunc habet libellus Hartlipp*) with reference to the *Unguenta* of Dino del Garbo is found in Berlin, Ms. lat. fol. 88, 300r. Paul Lehmann, "Haushaltsaufzeichnungen und Handschriften eines Münchener Arztes aus dem 15. Jahrhundert," in *Erforschungen des Mittelalters*, vol. III (Stuttgart: Anton Hiersemann, 1960), 275.

59   Graz, Universittsbibliothek, cod. 594. This codex may be indicated by one of two entries (*Liber generacionis embrionis* or *Libellus meus de secretis*) in Gotzkircher's library inventory (Munich, Universitätsbibliothek, Ms. q. 810), Lehmann, 287. Recipes in Berlin, Ms. lat. fol. 88 (including *ad menstrua provocanda*

. . . *pro ligsalczin* and *contra ruborem faciei* . . . *pro uxore ducis Ludovici iunoris*, that is Margarete von Brandenburg, daughter of the first Hohenzollern elector, Friedrich I, and wife of Duke Ludwig the Younger of Bavaria-Ingolstadt from 1441– 1445) suggest something about the social class of his patients (noble, patrician and bourgeois) and his interest in women's medicine. A fertility regimen for Margarete (Wolfenbttel, Herzog-August-Bibliothek, Cod. 444 Helmst., 45r–45v from 1440) may well have been written by Gotzkircher, although he probably did not own the manuscript in which it is found (Lehmann, 263, n. 30). See Karl Sudhoff, "Ein Fruchtbarkeitsregimen für Margaretha, Markgräfin von Brandenburg," *Sudhoffs Archiv*, 9 (1916), 356–59. As Sudhoff points out, the instructions for intercourse and pregnancy tests (ll. 56–81) are addressed to men.

60   One manuscript, München, Bayerische Staatsbibliothek, Clm 444, contains both the *Secreta mulierum* and *De ornatu*, the third, cosmetic treatise attributed to Trotula of Salerno. This and two other *Trotula* manuscripts, Clm 381 and 660, were owned previously by Hartmann's older cousin, Dr. Hermann Schedel. Clm 660 was owned originally by Dr. Christopherus de Barziziis de Bergamo, professor of medicine at Padua. Both Schedels studied medicine in Padua, Hermann (the elder) at about the same time and with some of the same professors, Antonius de Cermisonus and Christopherus de Barziziis de Bergamo, as Gotzkircher and Hartlieb. See Richard Stauber, *Die Schedelsche Bibliothek*, Studien und Darstellungen aus dem Gebiete der Geschichte, VI, 2 and 3 (1908) 12, 34, 119, 121, 125, 149, 155 and 158 (Clm 570 is not listed there), Lehmann, 260 and 267 on Gotzkircher's possible relationship to Hermann Schedel and Benton/Green, Manuscripts, Editions and Translations of the Trotula Texts (n. 1 above).

SEX AND CONFESSION IN THE
THIRTEENTH CENTURY

Pierre J. Payer

[D]epuis la pénitence chrétienne jusqu'aujourd'hui, le sexe fut matière
privilégiée de confession.

(Michel Foucault)

Of its many reforming decrees the twenty-first canon of the Fourth
Lateran Council (1215) likely had the most effect on the lives of ordinary
people and on the parish clergy alike. That canon required of all who had
reached the age of reason to confess their sins at least once a year to their
own priest, and required of confessors a satisfactory degree of knowledge
and understanding to fulfill their duties.[1] Within a short time a heightened
awareness of this canon became widespread, diocesan statutes provided
instructions for confessors, and a torrent of writings was unleashed to meet
the needs both of confessors and of penitents. The writings for priests were
of two types, those with an academic focus to provide summaries of the
knowledge required of confessors, and those with the practical aim of
offering instruction in the actual administration of confession. For the sake
of consistency the former will be called summas for confessors (*summae
confessorum*), the latter will be referred to as manuals or handbooks.[2] My
principal aim is to explore the presentation of sex as it is reflected in
confessional manuals of the thirteenth century.

Confession

In talking about confession one should be clear what it is that is being
talked about. Private penance or confession was a liturgical ritual falling
into three distinct parts, the reception of the penitent, confession and
questioning, and the enjoining of penances and absolution.[3]

The beginning of the ritual was taken up with obtaining information
about the penitent (cleric or lay? married or unmarried?), determining
whether the priest had jurisdiction over this person, allaying any fears or
embarrassment the penitent might feel, and encouraging a complete and
proper confession. Here at the outset a note of caution with sexual
overtones is frequently sounded. The confession of women is to be in a
public place, visible to all but out of earshot. The confessor is not to look

at their faces and is to keep his eyes cast down with his head covered. Such a directive sets a tone and constitutes the encounter as one fraught with some degree of sexual peril.

Because of the need for a full and open confession of all serious sins, confessors were encouraged to supplement the penitent's spontaneous confession with appropriate questions in order to refresh the person's memory and to make sure that the sins were confessed under their proper descriptions. This last requirement is a consequence of the need for the confession to be true; that is, what was done was to be expressed according to its proper specific nature. For example, it would not be enough to say that one had stolen if one had stolen vessels from a church. The circumstances make of that theft a sacrilege. Similarly, it would not be sufficient for a man to say that he had had illicit sexual relations *tout court* if they had been with another man or with a married woman. The former would have been sodomy or vice against nature, the latter was adultery. Each was to be confessed as such.[4]

The need to be specific coupled with ignorance among ordinary people of specific differences required the priest to question penitents so as to ensure a true confession. This need itself created a danger which is often signalled at the beginning of the discussion of how the priest is to interrogate penitents. And again it is a danger of a sexual nature that is noted. Although priests are encouraged to ask questions, they are to begin with the common or usual sins. They are not to descend to the unusual such as sodomy or deviant sexual positions unless the context warrants. If their questions are met with denial or incomprehension they should drop the matter. They are to be like skilled midwives extracting the coiled serpent of sin from the pit.[5] A not atypical example:

> He can ask questions in this manner: "If a man has intercourse with a woman, the natural way is that he be on top with the woman lying underneath. Have you done otherwise? If you have, don't be ashamed to say so." If he says no, go on to other things.[6]

The usual reason given for exercising care in questioning is to avoid having penitents leave confession worse off than when they entered because of having learned novel ways of sinning. Contexts suggest the concern was with sexual novelties. There was also the straightforward desire to protect both confessors and penitents from unchaste thoughts and desires.[7]

The confession concluded with the imposition of penance or satisfaction and the granting of absolution. Satisfaction through the performance of acts of penance was required for sins which were confessed, otherwise the penitent would pay for those sins in the far more excruciating penitentiary of purgatory. The traditional forms of penance were prayers, fasting, almsgiving, and bodily afflictions (*disciplinae*). (Penancing of sexual offenses will be discussed later in the penultimate section.)

At each stage of the confession concerns were expressed about propriety, correct procedures, cautious approaches to be taken. More often than not some aspect of sex was the object of these concerns which lend a sexual tone and aura to the ritual. It might be objected that talk of tone and aura is an impressionistic reaction to what in reality is simply commonsense advice balanced by the overall thrust of the instructions. However, that is not the case; preoccupation with sex is endemic to confessional manuals.

Concerns with Sexual Sins

Alan of Lille's penitential (ca. 1191) has a section dealing with how the priest ought to question penitents. It begins with advice to approach the inquiry in a general manner, using the example of intercourse to illustrate how the priest is to unmask the specific sins that had been committed.[8] These general observations are followed by remarks about specific points of view to be used in questioning, thirty-two additional topics (chapters 5–36). To illustrate his points Alan frequently uses examples of sexual behavior. Twelve of the thirty-three chapters adduce sexual behavior as illustrations (36% of the chapters).[9] Some of the accounts are substantial; in one case Alan provides a summary treatment of the traditional teaching on legitimate and illegitimate reasons for marital intercourse.[10]

The practice of illustrating approaches to questioning with examples taken from sexual behavior is not peculiar to Alan of Lille. It is particularly apparent in the approach taken to the circumstances of sins. Throughout the thirteenth century confessors were encouraged to question penitents along the lines of the circumstances of sins, the standard rhetorical *topoi*: who (*quis*), what (*quid*), through whom (*per quos*), how often (*quotiens*), why (*cur*), how (*quomodo*), when (*quando*).[11] The most frequently encountered examples in the explanation and application of the teaching on circumstances are from the sexual domain. In the view of Robert Grosseteste the reason for this is because circumstances are most operative in increasing or diminishing the gravity of that type of sin.[12]

In response to the reforming intentions of the Fourth Lateran Council the diocese of Angers (1217 x 1219) issued a set of statutes governing the life and practices of the clergy.[13] The second part of this collection is a confessional manual which, one assumes, was meant to provide the requisite instructions to enable parish priests to implement the decree of Lateran IV, which demanded annual confession of all men and women who had reached the age of reason. In fact, the section dealing with confession begins with the first words of the Lateran decree, "omnis utriusque sexus."[14]

This is a significant treatment of penance presenting as it does an official diocesan conception of confession that ordinary priests would be able to read and were required to have in their possession.[15] The statutes of Angers more than any other document demonstrate the emphasis that was placed on sexual offenses. After some preliminary canons on confession in general the treatment is organized around questions regarding the traditional capital sins. There are forty-eight canons in all (75–122), ten of which deal with general questions about the administration of the sacrament. Of the remaining thirty-eight, which deal with specific sins fully, nineteen (canons 86–104) or 50% are about sins of lechery. It is difficult to avoid the impression of a preoccupation with sexual offenses in the face of such figures.[16]

Finally, note might be taken of several short confessional pieces among the works of William of Auvergne which, in the view of Pamelon Glorieux, are from the pen of Robert of Sorbonne.[17] They exemplify a pronounced preoccupation with sexual sins:

1. Incipit: "Si dicat peccator, domine vigilans naturam meam pollui": a short work apparently standing alone dealing exclusively with sins of lechery.[18]
2. Incipit: "Cum repetes a proximo . . . (Deut. 24.10-11). Ex hac authoritate. . . . si es Domine in corde confitentium tibi." After introductory remarks justifying the legitimacy of questioning penitents, the work deals with the capital sins. Seven of ten columns dealing with sin are concerned with sexual offenses.[19]
3. In the printed edition, "Cum repetes a proximo" concludes with remarks on sins against nature, (incipit) "Sic revertendum est ad peccatum contra naturam." Glorieux treats this concluding piece as a separate fragment by an unknown author.[20] In fact, it is a précis of a lengthy account of sodomy or vice against nature found in the confessional manual of Paul of Hungary. While it may be by an unknown author, it could as well have been composed by Robert of Sorbonne for his own purposes and used to conclude a handbook of penance that had begun with a substantial presentation of sexual sins.[21]

The percentages catalogued above to show the preoccupation in confessional manuals with sexual offenses in the thirteenth century are within the same range as figures which emerge from a similar analysis of earlier penitentials from the sixth century onward.[22] An extension of this analysis would, I believe, confirm the impression that confessional manuals of the thirteenth century are disproportionately concerned with sexual sins in comparison with other types of offense. The fact is readily demonstrable; how one might explain the fact is another matter. Some suggestions will be offered in our conclusion.

The Treatment of Sexual Sins

Diversity in literary presentation, the genius and educational background of authors, and their targetted audience make it hazardous to generalize about the contents of handbooks for confessors. One is better advised to examine individual works, but two generalizations can safely be made.

First, all authors share the overall sexual ethic of the period which was concisely enunciated by the Synod of Angers (ca. 1217):

> In regard to the sacrament of marriage it must be said that every voluntary emission of semen is a mortal sin in both males and females unless excused by legitimate marriage. But faith teaches that sexual intercourse between male and female is excused by legitimate marriage as long as the union is in the proper manner.[23]

Although not in the section on confession in the statutes of Angers, a similar principle is incorporated into that section in several English statutes which counsel the priest to inculcate it in confession and preaching.[24]

A second feature characterizing the treatment of sexual offences by confessional manuals of the thirteenth century is the organizing role played by the idea of the sin of lechery (*luxuria*), one of the seven capital sins.[25] From the time of the *Decretum* of Gratian there had been an evolution in theological accounts of the parts or species of lechery. No universally accepted division emerged but there was a core which is found in virtually all accounts: adultery, fornication, incest, violation of virgins (*stuprum*), rape/abduction (*raptus*), and the sodomitic vice or vice against nature.[26] Some such division of lechery provides the framework for questioning the penitent in an effort to elicit a full and true confession of sexual sins. Emphasis is usually placed on adultery, fornication, and vice against nature which embraced more than what would be understood as sodomy or homosexuality today. Confessional manuals, which are not overly concerned with the niceties of theological distinctions, often include marital sexual sins under the general rubric of lechery or under headings such as "The sins of the married."

Whatever the division employed, the manuals of the thirteenth century betray a wide variety of approaches to sexual sins. I would like to examine the treatment in two works, the section on confession in the statutes of Angers, and the *De confessione* of Paul of Hungary.[27] These works represent the two most common types of confessional manual. The synodal statutes are severely practical, emphasizing the questions to be asked of the penitent in an effort to elicit a correct confession. The section on confession belongs to the class of schematic manuals called 'formularies' by Michaud-Quantin.[28] Furthermore, these statutes in particular, as noted already, influenced virtually all subsequent diocesan statutes in the West.[29] While practical in character, Paul of Hungary's work is representative of the many confessional manuals which lie between academic summas for confessors and schematic questionnaires.

Synod of Angers

The treatment of sexual offences in the statutes of Angers is divided in a manner which roughly approximates widespread divisions of lechery:

prostitution and simple fornication, adultery, defloration of virgins (*stuprum*), intercourse with nuns, incest, sexual delicts in marriage, homosexuality, nocturnal pollution, *mollities*, and incidental matters related to sex such as looks, desires, touches, embraces, and kisses.[30]

Prostitution is of particular concern in these statutes which mention it on three occasions. The penitent is to be asked whether he approached prostitutes, along with relevant circumstances: the number of prostitutes (at least an estimate), frequency, the length of time he remained in the sin, and the place in which the sin was committed.[31] The confessor is to warn the penitent of the spiritual and physical dangers of prostitution. Spiritual dangers arise from the fact that one who visits prostitutes may not know the nature of the sin that was committed. The prostitute may actually be related to him (incest), or be married (adultery), or even be a nun (sacrilege). Faced with these possibilities and unable to verify the species of sin, the safe course for the confessor to follow is to impose the penance for adultery. In an obvious effort to dissuade the penitent, he is to be told of the physical danger of leprosy which is often caught from prostitutes.[32] Later the issue of pimping is raised, that is, any action which helps another find a prostitute. Pimps must realize that their guilt is no less than the guilt of those they help.[33]

The treatment of the defloration of virgins is more concerned about the future fate of the women than with the sinfulness of the sex act as such. In fact, its penance is assimilated to the relatively mild penance for simple fornication. However, in addition to the straightforward penance a kind of restitution is required of the offender. He is to attempt to arrange for the marriage of the virgins involved or for the marriage of other poor virgins in their place. He should at least provide for them if they are in need, or to arrange for their entry into religious life if that is their desire. Perhaps here we get a glimpse of the debilitating social consequences for women who had lost virginity before marriage. The section concludes with a warning that if those who had lost virginity are not cared for, those responsible for setting them on the course of sexual promiscuity will share in their future sins.[34]

The statutes continue with two classes of reserved sin whose perpetrators must be sent to the bishop for absolution—intercourse with nuns, and incest. Three types of incestuous relation are mentioned, spiritual incest (i.e., a priest having sexual relations with a woman he had baptized or whose confession he had heard), blood relations, and affinity relations through marriage.[35]

The subject of marital intercourse is then broached. The priest is to ask whether the man's wife was known in an undue manner (*indebito modo*). If the penitent asks how, the priest is not to reply (the assumption being that the question was not understood and nothing untoward done). If he answers in the affirmative, the priest is to ask for further details about the circumstances of the act.[36] The statutes do not say why this additional inquiry is required. It is likely because of the need to know whether the undue manner was a variation on the usual position but with vaginal intercourse, or was nonvaginal. The former case would not be as serious and could even be excused with cause (e.g., obesity, advanced stage of pregnancy). The latter case was considered unnatural vice and could never be excused under any circumstance.[37]

Three particular concerns with marital relations stemming from the the physical condition of the woman are taken up: (1) intercourse immediately after childbirth, since it is prohibited in the Law (based on the purification rules of Lev. 12.1-5); (2) intercourse during menstruation, since it poses dangers of contagion to the male seed which doctors say corrupts the fetus (fear of leprosy and of physical deformity);[38] (3) during pregnancy (since there is danger of abortion).[39]

Following the paragraph dealing with intercourse during pregnancy there is a short text whose meaning is not clear to me, "Again, ask if he sinned only with women; if he says he sinned with another, ask with what thing and in regard to other [matters] as above."[40] The synod seems to be following Peter of Poitiers here. I suspect that this cryptic statement is a clumsy and overly delicate attempt to telescope Peter's forthright treatment of homosexuality and bestiality.[41]

After directing the confessor to counsel the penitent to avoid the occasions of sin, the statutes of Angers return to the sins of lechery with the consideration of nocturnal pollution, the sin of *mollities*, and matters relating to modesty: looks, desires, advances, touches, and kisses.[42] The treatment of nocturnal pollution is quite traditional with the focus of the canon on determining the extent to which there was conscious and willing complicity in the occurrence.[43]

The account of the sin of *mollities* is unusual and needs to be interpreted against the background of Peter of Poitiers. By the thirteenth century the term 'mollities' meant masturbation and certainly did not mean pederasty (Pontal's translation). However, the seven-year penance enjoined by the statutes is unparalleled for masturbation in the penitential tradition. Perhaps the compiler of this directive, persuaded of the horror of masturbation as described by Peter of Poitiers, imposed the onerous penance of the discipline (self-flagellation) which was to be inflicted every week for seven years. Peter of Poitiers has a chapter entitled "On monstrous masturbation" (De monstruo mollitei) in which he makes a parallel with sodomy since both are against nature. Peter notes that in masturbation only one person is corrupted while two are corrupted in sodomy. However, masturbation is more monstrous, not in the sense of being a more serious sin but in the sense that the person practising it is a freak of nature. The same person is both agent and patient, as if he were man and woman, a hermaphrodite.[44]

The statutes of Angers take an eminently practical approach to the confession of sexual offences, warning, frightening, encouraging penitents to a true and full avowal of their sins. While in line with academic teaching of the day, they are neither weighted with the baggage of academe nor concerned with refined conceptual distinctions. They were written for pastors whose educational attainments were likely minimal at best. In this they differ from the next work to be examined.

Paul of Hungary

Paul of Hungary, a law professor at Bologna and an early recruit to the Dominican order, composed a manual for confessors about 1221.[45] The tract was compiled for the use of the brethren and the salvation of those who confess (p. 191b). The brethren here are, no doubt, the Dominican friars who received a basic education and who were destined for the mission of hearing confessions and preaching, not for university studies.[46]

The treatise of Paul of Hungary is an instructional manual aimed at providing a summary of the knowledge required of confessors. Whereas the Synod of Angers focuses on the actual administration of the sacrament by taking the priest through different sorts of sins, Paul's *De confessione* provides a systematic body of knowledge. While not an academic treatise, Paul's educational background is evident in the care he shows to provide references, usually to the *Decretum* of Gratian, for the positions that he proposes.

The treatment of sex in the *De confessione* is of two sorts. It offers the usual cautions about questioning and the need to approach unusual sexual behaviour in a roundabout manner, and it provides a common division of lechery into fornication, defloration of virgins, adultery, incest, rape/abduction, and vice against nature.[47] There is no detailed interrogatory for any sins.

In addition to this traditional approach the work of Paul of Hungary singles out three topics for special consideration: nocturnal pollution, marital intercourse, and vice against nature. The treatment of nocturnal pollution does not depart from the views of Gregory the Great whose account of the matter was accepted by everyone at this time. If the pollution occurs because of over-eating, it is a venial sin. A lay person may receive the eucharist afterwards but a priest cannot celebrate mass except in a necessity and if another priest is not available. If a natural buildup of semen caused the pollution, there is no sin. If previous shameful thoughts were the cause, then there is sin and the person ought to abstain from the eucharist. However, the sin is not to be considered mortal unless the preceding thoughts were accompanied by pleasure and feelings of lust (198b).

The discussion of marital intercourse ("De coitu coniugali") is cast in the form of a scholastic question, some version of which is found in every theological account of marriage in the thirteenth century, "Let us see whether a man in knowing his wife sins with her." In a few lines Paul summarizes the traditional theological teaching on the subject. He assesses the morality of marital relations from the point of view of the reasons (*causae*) motivating the sexual behaviour. By his day the reasons had been reduced to four: to procreate children, to pay the debt, to avoid incontinence, and to satisfy lust.

Since he does not enter into the complex casuistry of marital sex that was beginning to emerge, one must assume that Paul believed his account of the reasons would have been understood in their obvious sense. Intercourse with the intention of having children was blameless since that is what intercourse and marriage are for primarily. The idea behind the debt is that each spouse was believed to have power over the other's body where sex is concerned so that if asked each was to pay.[48] To pay the debt is not only sinless but may be meritorious.

Paul of Hungary seems to understand the third reason ("to avoid incontinence") in its obvious sense. That is, when in a state of sexual arousal one approaches one's spouse rather than seek an outlet through an adulterous liaison. This motivation, in the opinion of some, is a venial sin, but Paul considers it to be sinless, basing himself on the authority of St. Paul, "On account of fornication let each man have his own wife and each woman her own husband" (1 Cor. 7.2).[49]

The fourth reason for having sex is to satisfy lust or for the sake of pleasure. Paul does not pronounce on this in its bald formulation but qualifies it, "to satisfy lust when one uses hot [liquids] and incentives so as to be more potent in his duty or to make him do it even though he has no great desire for it." Under such conditions marital intercourse is a mortal sin. In support of his view Paul refers to a famous text in Gratian from Jerome. This text has a citation from a certain Sextus that had become a commonplace by the thirteenth century, "The too ardent lover of his own wife is an adulterer."[50]

A fifth point is raised having to do the manner of the sexual relations. One who knows his wife against nature (*contra naturam*) sins very mortally. I assume that this does not refer to deviations from the usual position but to intercourse which results in depositing semen outside the vagina. This assumption is supported by reference to Paul's own account of vice against nature, as we shall see. The discussion concludes with an admonition that the priest use his discretion in handing out penances to whose who sin in having marital sex (198b–199a).

The third section dealing with sex in the *De confessione* is a departure from the compact, summary approach of the work. The account of the vice of lechery, after some general remarks taken from Alan of Lille, consists in the traditional division accompanied by brief definitions of each species. The last in the enumeration is the vice or sin against nature (*vitium sive peccatum contra naturam*). After defining the idea, Paul of Hungary continues with a lengthy essay on the offence under four rubrics: (1) reasons for detesting the vice; (2) evils arising from it; (3) punishments inflicted on its perpetrators; (4) causes of the sodomitic vice.[51] In the confessional literature this essay of Paul of Hungary stands at the origin of a development which culminated in a penitential canon compiled by John of Freiburg out of elements from Raymond of Penafort, the gloss on Raymond by William of Rennes, and legal references in Hostiensis.[52] By the end of the thirteenth century, then, there was a sophisticated account of the vice against nature embedded in what was to become one of the most influential academic summas for confessors.[53]

Conceptually, Paul of Hungary writes about the vice against nature within the framework of a generic sense of *contra naturam*—a sexual act is a sin against nature "when one pours his seed outside the place assigned for that purpose" (207b). Any intentional emission of semen outside the vagina is to be considered an unnatural vice; those who do so are to be called sodomists. The view is reiterated in his conclusion, "So I say in brief that pollution outside the vessel of nature [i.e., the vagina] however it is done (although we have heard many ways in confession, we refuse and do not dare to make them public) is a vice against nature and all who are burdened in this way are deemed sodomists."[54] However, the purpose for writing the essay on the sin against nature does not seem to have been a desire to counter the vice in its generic sense but in the narrower sense of homosexuality. Paul is attacking a homosexual culture which does not consider the act a sin. In some regions, he tells us, men engage in this abuse as though in public; acting out of a certain courtliness, they call those with whom they sin "favoured ones" (*gratiosos*).[55] Space does not permit further discussion of this interesting treatment of homosexuality.

Penance and Satisfaction

The parts of penance were said to be interior sorrow (*contritio cordis*), oral confession (*confessio oris*), and satisfaction through deeds (*satisfactio operis*).[56] Satisfaction in the form of stipulated penances was needed to right the disorder caused by sins and to make up for the temporal punishment due the sins. Penitential handbooks before the thirteenth century provided definite penances for specific sorts of sin; lists of penanced sins are the hallmark of the ancient penitentials. Although such lists of tariffed offences did not disappear in the thirteenth century, their general use was replaced by two principles governing the imposition of penance: as a rule seven years penance was to be enjoined for serious sins, and in all cases the imposition of penance was to be subject to the discretion of the confessor.[57] There was a need to reconcile the old penitential canons with the new principles, a recognition that the canons had to be moderated but that their continued use served a purpose.

Robert Grosseteste attempted to chart a middle course between a literal application of the old canons (some of which were extremely harsh) and a purely *ad libitum* concocting of penances.[58] He shows how some can be moderated and from those examples expects that "the priest can more intelligently figure out how to temper other penances."[59] Aside from homicide and the accidental suffocation of children (*de puero oppresso*), the examples Grosseteste proposes are sexual: fornication, adultery, sacrilege, sodomitic vice, incest.[60] He then lists other traditional canons that the priest is supposed to know how to modify based on the extended examples he had elaborated. The discussion of tempering the canons occupies twenty-two sections in the edition, nineteen (or 86%) of those sections deal with sexual offences. Of the remaining 123 sections, forty-two (or 35%) are concerned with sexual delicts.

Since some serious sins are more serious than others, confessors had to be alerted to sins which required more than the regular seven-year penance. In this case sexual sins such as incest, sodomy, and bestiality suggested themselves as being particularly heinous.[61] A set of canons emerged called penitential canons which recorded noteworthy offences which were accompanied by older ecclesiastically stipulated penances. These canons, given their most traditional form by the canonist Hostiensis, cover the whole range of sins constituting, as it were, a mini-penitential in the midst of much broader treatments of confession. I have no idea how they were used, but they were recommended by not unimportant authorities at the end of the thirteenth century such as the Synod of Rodez and William Durandus.[62]

Hostiensis and later writers on confession present the penitential canons as examples of canons which prescribe determined penances which the priest is to know if he is to be worthy of being called a priest. They are bench marks to guide the confessor in his discretionary imposition of penance.[63] Some examples of canons dealing with sex:[64]

Canon 1: a detailed account of a ten-year penance for priests who fornicate.
Canon 2: a twelve-year penance for a priest who has sexual relations with a spiritual daughter, i.e., a woman he has baptized, confirmed, or whose confessor he had been.
Canon 3: for the vice against nature clerics are to be deposed; a layperson is to be excommunicated from the society of the faithful until adequate penance is done.
Canon 10: at least seven years (although it ought to be more) for incestuous relations with inlaws.
Canon 18: ten years penance for sexual relations with a nun.
Canon 23: five years for marrying a woman with whom one has had adulterous relations.
Canon 40: more than seven years for bestiality and incest.

It is unlikely that anyone in the thirteenth century applied these canons literally, but that is not to say that there were not taken seriously. In his account of the penance for priests who commit fornication (canon 1), Thomas of Chobham is probably representative of the approach that was taken. After citing the canon from Gratian he notes that the rigor of the canon is not observed in his day; the human body is unable to sustain such harshness. The prudent priest will make the penance bearable by relaxing it.[65]

Conclusion

With respect to the thirteenth century it would be difficult to gainsay Michel Foucault's claim noted at the beginning of this article. Sex was indeed privileged matter of confession to which particular consideration was given by writers of confessional manuals. Why this was the case cannot be easily answered but perhaps a few comments are not out of place.

In his instructions on how to temper penances Robert Grosseteste justifies his using canons on fornication and adultery with the claim that "knowledge of these is so much the more necessary because miserable mortals are more frequently wounded by these sins."[66] Perhaps that is the simple explanation for the concern with sexual offences. Christianity had been unsuccessful in realising its sexual ethic. When a renewed commitment to confession arose, attention was focused on the area of human behaviour which had always been resistant to the strictures of the orthodox morality.

The proceedings of a ruridecanal court (1300) is precious witness both to the failure of the ethic and to concerns with its enforcement. Fifty-five cases are dealt with by the court whose usual form of prescribed punishment was public whipping. Forty-seven cases concern fornication and six deal with adultery, sometimes noting that the parties were recidivists. How these cases moved from the private forum of confession to the public forum of an ecclesiastical court is not clear. Some mechanism must have been in place. However it occurred, the public record witnesses to a preoccupation that had its counterpart in the private forum of conscience.[67]

One must also look at the theological and spiritual anthropology of the time which saw in sex a particularly recalcitrant dimension of fallen human nature. Baptism was seen as the first plank of salvation after the shipwreck of the Fall; confession was the second plank offered to those who sinned after baptism.[68] While baptism re-establishes the possibility of gaining entry to the vision of God and offers strength to combat temptation, the powerful, unruly forces of lust (*libido*) and concupiscence remain after original sin has been washed away. These forces manifest themselves in sexual drives and urges which are particularly difficult to bridle. It is not that sexual sins are the worst sins, but they are the most overpowering and successful in controlling their victims. An institution such as confession which was to deal with the actual sins of people would understandably be pre-occupied with what was seen to be often a losing battle:

> Among all the struggles of Christians the greatest are the battles of chastity where fighting is frequent, victory rare. Continence is truly a great war.[69]

Notes

1   Lateran IV, c. 21 ("Omnis utriusque sexus"), in *Conciliorum oecumenicorum decreta*, ed. Joseph Alberigo et al., 3d ed. (Bologna, 1973), 245.

2   For questions of classification and terminology (with literature) see Leonard
E. Boyle, "Summae confessorum," in *Les genres littéraires dans les sources
théologiques et philosophiques médiévales. Définitions, critique et exploitation,*
Actes du Colloque internationale de Louvain-la-Neuve, 25–27 mai 1981 (Louvain-la-
Neuve, 1982), 227–37.

3   One of the clearest presentations of this structure is in a work entitled
Summa de penitentia fratrum predicatorum (incipit: "Cum ad sacerdotem") in (among
other manuscripts) Dublin, Trinity College MS 326, fols. 28ra–31ra. An edition has
been prepared by J. Goering and P. Payer. For a printed work in which the lines of the
structure of confession are discernible see, J. Goering and F.A.C. Mantello, "The
Early Penitential Writings of Robert Grosseteste," *Recherches de théologie ancienne
et médiévale* 54 (1987), 80–92.

4   See a sermon attributed to Robert Grosseteste, "Primum itaque confitendum
est quid egerit, ipsum videlicet factum non in genere set in *specie specialissima* ipsius
facti. Si enim fecerit adulterium non sufficit dicere quod lapsu carnis aut fornicando
peccaverit" (London, British Library, MS Royal 7.E.ii, fol., 315rb; my emphasis). I
am grateful to Prof. Goering for directing me to this manuscript. See Peter Quinel
(1287), *Summula,* 21, in F.M. Powicke and C. R. Cheney, eds., *Councils & Synods
with Other Documents Relating to the English Church. 2. A.D. 1205–1313. Part 2.
1265–1313* (Oxford, 1964), 1069.

5   See Job 26.13; Paul of Hungary, *De confessione,* Bibliotheca casinensis seu
codicum manuscriptorum, 4 (Monte Cassino, 1880), 195.

6   *Summa de penitentia fratrum predicatorum* (Dublin, Trinity College MS 326,
fol. 29va [collated]). When Albert the Great broached the theological discussion of
deviant sexual positions he excused himself on the grounds that he was compelled to
do so by the monstrosities heard in confession in his day, "Dicendum quod huiusmodi
turpes quaestiones numquam tractari debent nisi ad illa cogerent monstra quae his
temporibus in confessione audiuntur" (*In 4 Sent.,* D. 31, a. 24 [Borgnet ed., vol.
30.263]).

7   For the desire to safeguard both priest and penitent from sexual arousal see
Thomas Aquinas, *In 4 Sent.,* D. 19, expositio textus. Such concerns continued to be
expressed throughout the Middle Ages. One can only imagine what prompted Cajetan
(1519) to write his, *De pollutione ex auditione confessionis proveniente* (Lyons,
1581), Tract 22, 114–16.

8   Alan of Lille, *Liber Poenitentialis. 2. La tradition longue. Texte inédit
publié et annoté,* ed. J. Longère, Analecta mediaevalia Namurcensia, 18 (Louvain,
1965), 1.4, 26.

9   See chapters 4, 6, 7, 11, 12, 13, 26–31.

10   Alan of Lille, *Liber Poenitentialis* 1.26 (Longère, ed., 2.33–34).

11   This is the order of the terms in Raymond of Penafort whose work influenced
virtually all subsequent *summae confessorum* (*Summa* 3.34.29 [Rome, 1603], 463).
There are numerous variations in other authors. See Joannes Gründel, *Die Lehre von
den Umständen der menschlichen Handlung im Mittelalter,* Beiträge zur Geschichte
der Philosophie und Theologie des Mittelalters, 39.5 (Münster, Westf., 1963).

12   Robert Grosseteste, "Deus est" (Siegfried Wenzel, ed., "Robert Grosseteste's
Treatise on Confession 'Deus est,'" *Franciscan Studies* 30 [1970], 283). See *Summa
de penitentia fratrum predicatorum* (Dublin, Trinity College 326, fol., 30ra); Peter
Quinel, *Summula,* 20–28 (Powicke and Cheney, eds., *Councils & Synods,* Vol. 2, part
2, 1069–1072).

13   Odette Pontal, *Les status synodaux francais du XIIIe siècle précédés de
l'historique du synode diocésain depuis ses origines. 1. Les status de Paris et le*

Synodal de l'oeust (XIIIe siècle), Collections de documents inédits sur l'histoire de France. Section de philologie et d'histoire jusqu'à 1610. Serie 8, n. 9 (Paris, 1971). According to Pontal (136) these statutes were a prototype for virtually all statutes in the West up to the Council of Trent. An analysis of the sexual contents of these statutes is provided later.

14 Synod of Angers, 75 (Pontal, ed., 190).

15 "Seen as a whole the statutes of the thirteenth century present the most practical and most conscientious attempt by the ecclesiastical authorities of the time to acquaint a mainly plebian and ignorant parochial clergy with the rudiments of the Christian faith and the obligations which attached to the cure of souls. . . . The sacrament of confession and penance is in the foreground" (C. R. Cheney, "Some aspects of diocesan legislation in England during the thirteenth century," in C.R. Cheney, *Medieval Texts and Studies* [Oxford, 1973], 187).

16 This is a high proportion representing the upper limit encountered in handbooks of penance. In an English manual (after 1234) arranged around the capital sins the treatment of sins covers 787 lines, 277 lines of which are given over to the sin of lechery (35%) (see J. Goering, "The *Summa de penitentia* of Magister Serlo," *Mediaeval Studies* 38 [1976], 1–53). In a four-part work on penance (Prologue and four books) covering thirty-two folio pages the first book deals with sexual offences and covers 14 pages of the manuscript (44% of the whole) (see Cambridge, Trinity College MS 1109 [0.2.5], 108–39).

17 P. Glorieux, "Le Tractatus novus de Poenitentia de Guillaume d'Auvergne," in *Miscellanea moralia in honorem eximii domini Arthur Janssen*, Bibliotheca Ephemeridum theologicarum Lovaniensium, series 1, vol. 3 (Leuven-Louvain, 1948), 551–65.

18 Glorieux, "Le Tractatus novus," 565; William of Auvergne, *Opera omnia* 2, Supplement, 231–32.

19 Glorieux, "Le Tractatus novus," 565; William of Auvergne, *Opera omnia* 2, Supplement, 233–38a.

20 Glorieux, "Le Tractatus novus," 556–57, 565; William of Auvergne, *Opera omnia* 2, Supplement, 238a–b.

21 For the original see Paul of Hungary, *De confessione*, Bibliotheca casinensis 4.207–10. Paul's account is discussed below.

22 See Pierre J. Payer, *Sex and the Penitentials. The Development of a Sexual Code, 550–1150* (Toronto, 1984), 52–53.

23 Synod of Angers, 129 (Pontal, ed., 232–34).

24 Statutes of Salisbury I, 35 (1217 x 1219) (Powicke and Cheney, eds., *Councils & Synods*, vol. 2, part 1, 72); Statutes of Coventry (1224 x 1237) (Powicke and Cheney, eds., *Councils & Synods*, vol. 2, part 1, 222); Lambeth Council (1281), 9 (Powicke and Cheney, eds., *Councils & Synods*, vol. 2, part 2, 702–03). And see Robert Grosseteste, "Deus est," (Wenzel, ed., 246).

25 See Siegfried Wenzel, "The Seven Deadly Sins: Some Problems of Research," *Speculum* 43 (1968), 13.

26 Gratian's initial division (*Decretum* C. 36.1/2.2, dictum post) was taken up by Peter Lombard (*Sententiae in IV libris distinctae*, book 4.5–9.2 [Grottaferrata, 1981], 2.500). See the division written for ordinary priests in the course of an account of the sixth commandment, *Summa Fratris Alexandri* 3, n. 406 (Quaracchi, 1948), vol. 4.2, 595–56.

27 By far the most thorough treatment of sexual sins by any thirteenth-century writer is that provided by Thomas of Chobham (*Thomae de Chobham. Summa*

confessorum, ed. F. Broomfield, Analecta mediaevalia Namurcensia, 25 [Louvain, 1968], 330–404).

28   See Pierre Michaud-Quantin, "Deux formulaires pour la confession du milieu du XIIIe siècle," *RTAM* 31 (1964), 43–62.

29   See above, note 13.

30   I use the edition of Odette Pontal (see above, n. 13). One of the major sources for these statutes which is not sufficiently noted by Pontal is the summa of Peter of Poitiers, *Summa de confessione*. *"Compilatio praesens,"* ed. Jean Longère, CCCM 51 (Turnhout, 1980).

31   Synod of Angers, 86 (Pontal, ed., 198).

32   Synod of Angers, 88 (Pontal, ed., 200). See Danielle Jacquart and Claude Thomasset, *Sexuality and Medicine in the Middle Ages*, tr. Matthew Adamson (Cambridge, 1988), 183–88.

33   Synod of Angers, 104 (Pontal, ed., 210).

34   Synod of Angers, 90 (Pontal, ed., 201). See Peter of Poitiers (*Summa de confessione*, 12 [Longère, ed., 15]); Thomas of Chobham, *Summa confessorum* (Broomfield, ed., 384).

35   Synod of Angers, 91–94 (Pontal, ed., 202–04).

36   Synod of Angers, 95 (Pontal, ed., 204).

37   See Synod of Angers, 97 (Pontal, ed., 206).

38   See Lev. 15.24; 18.19; 20.18; Ezech. 18.6; Jerome, *Commentariorum in Hiezechielem, libri XIV*, 6, ed. F. Glorie, CCCM 75 (Turnhout, 1964), 235–36.

39   Synod of Angers, 96–98 (Pontal, ed., 204–06). See Peter of Poitiers, *Summa de confessione*, 12 (Longère, ed., 17).

40   "Item queratur si cum mulieribus tantum peccavit; si dicit cum alio se peccasse, queratur cum qua re et de aliis ut supra" (Synod of Angers, 98 [Pontal, ed., 206]).

41   See Peter of Poitiers, *Summa de confessione*, 12 (Longère, ed., 17, lines 57–69).

42   Synod of Angers, 99 (Pontal ed., 206); see Peter of Poitiers, *Summa de confessione*, 14 (Longère ed., 19). In Peter of Poitiers and in some manuscripts of the statutes the advice concludes with a vernacular proverb, "Que ayse fet larron."

43   Synod of Angers, 100 (Pontal, ed., 208); see Peter of Poitiers, *Summa de confessione*, 13–14 (Longère, ed., 17–19).

44   Peter of Poitiers, *Summa de confessione*, 14 (Longère, ed., 19). See the similar point made by Robert of Sorbonne, "Si dicat peccator" among the works of William of Auvergne, Opera omnia, 2, Supplement, p. 231b. Much later Jean Gerson will compose a special treatise on the confession of masturbation, *De confessione mollitiei*, ed. P. Glorieux, *Oeuvres complètes*, 8 (Paris, 1971), 71–74.

45   Paul of Hungary, *De confessione*, Bibliotheca casinensis seu codicum manuscriptorum, 4 (Monte Cassino, 1880), 195a. All references to Paul of Hungary are to the pages of this volume; *a* and *b* indicate left and right columns, respectively.

46   See Leonard E. Boyle, "Notes on the Education of the Fratres Communes in the Dominican Order in the Thirteenth Century," in *Xenia medii aevi historiam illustrantia oblata Thomae Kaeppeli O.P.*, ed. R. Creytens and P. Künzle (Rome, 1978), 1.249–67.

47   In the edition the advice not to descend "ad spiritualia peccata vel spiritualias circumstantias" should probably read "ad specialia peccata vel speciales circumstantias" (*De confessione*, 195a).

48   The scriptural warrant for this view is found in Saint Paul, 1 Cor. 7.3–5.

49   In the thirteenth century the liberal opinion of Paul of Hungary is not the more common view.

50   See Gratian, *Decretum* C. 32.4.5; Jerome, *Adversus Iovinianun* 1.49 (PL 23.293C). Paul's account of the four reasons is at 198b.

51   Paul of Hungary, *De confessione*, 207b–210b. The immediate background to the piece is a similar discussion by Peter the Chanter (*Verbum abbreviatum*, 138 [PL 205.333–335]), which is translated in John Boswell, *Christianity, Social Tolerance, and Homosexuality. Gay People in Western Europe from the Beginning of the Christian Era to the Fourteenth Century* (Chicago, 1980), 375–78. The account of William Peraldus, *De vitiis et virtutibus*, "De luxuria" (Schlägl, Stiftsbibliothek 12, fols., 8vb–9va) follows Paul of Hungary.

52   John of Freiburg, *Summa confessorum* 3.34, 124 (Rome, 1518), fols. 197vb–198ra, a composite from: Raymond of Penafort, *Summa* 3.34.42 (Rome, 1603), 474–75; William of Rennes, gloss on Raymond of Penafort, *Summa* 3.34.42, ad v., *ignominie* and ad v., *ordinate*; Hostiensis, *Summa, una cum summariis . . .* 5.60 (Lyons, 1537), fol. 283rb.

53   John Boswell seems not to have been familiar with this confessional tradition.

54   Paul of Hungary, *De confessione*, 210b. See the *exempla* concerning sins against nature gleaned from the confessional experience of Thomas of Chantimpré noted in A. Murray, "Confession as a Historical Source in the Thirteenth Century," in *The Writing of History in the Middle Ages. Essays Presented to Richard William Southern*, ed. R.H.C. Davis and J.M. Wallace-Hadrill (Oxford, 1981), 301–02.

55   Paul of Hungary, *De confessione*, 207b.

56   See Thomas Aquinas, *Summa theologiae* 3.90.2-3.

57   See Raymond of Penafort, *Summa* 3.34.41 (Rome, 1603), 472–474. For the rule of seven years see Gratian, *Decretum* C. 33.2.11 and dictum post.

58   This issue is part of the broader question of the meaning and implications of saying that penances were to be left to the discretion of the confessor (*penitentiae arbitrarie*). The majority position seems to have held that *prima facie* the old canons were to apply, but confessors could use their discretion in reducing or increasing them depending on their assessment of the situation. See Pierre J. Payer, "The Humanism of the Penitentials and the Continuity of the Penitential Tradition," *Mediaeval Studies* 46 (1984), 340–50.

59   Grosseteste, *De modo confitendi et paenitentias iniungendi* 2.36, in Goering and Mantello, eds., "The Early Penitential Writings," 99.

60   Grosseteste, *De modo confitendi et paenitentias iniungendi* 2.2–25, in Goering and Mantello, eds., "The Early Penitential Writings," 93–99.

61   William of Rennes, gloss on Raymond of Penafort, *Summa* 3.34.41, ad v., *hoc autem quamquam* (473).

62   See Payer, "The Humanism of the Penitentials," 350–54; Synod of Rodez, 15 (Mansi 24.992); William Durandus, *Instructions et constitutions de Guillaume Durand Le Spéculateur publiées d'après le manuscrit de Cessenon*, ed. J. Berthelé and M. Valmary (Monpellier, 1900), 20; *Repertorium sive Breviloquium aureum super corpus iuris canonici* (Rome, 1474), fols. cixra-cxrb. The recent edition of a work attributed to Conrad of Höxter notes a manuscript which adds to Conrad's work a chapter listing fifty-four penitential canons which likely antedate those of Hostiensis; see *Trois sommes de pénitence de la première moitié du XIIIe siècle. La 'Summula Magistri Conradi'. Les sommes 'Quia non pigris' et 'Decime dande sunt', 1. Prolégomènes et Notes complémentaires*, ed. Jean Pierre Renard, Lex spiritus vitae, 6 (Louvain-la-Neuve, 1989), 254–59. Contrary to Tentler's claim, the penitential

canons had a long history before the fourteenth-century Franciscan Astesanus of Ast incorporated them into his summa; see N.T. Tentler, *Sin and Confession on the Eve of the Reformation* (Princeton, N.J., 1977), 321.

63   See Hostiensis, Summa 5 (fol. 283rb). The reference to knowing the canons is based on Gratian, *Decretum* D. 38.5.

64   The numbers correspond to those assigned by Hostiensis.

65   Thomas of Chobham, *Summa confessorum* (Broomfield, ed., 382). See Robert Grosseteste, "Deus est" (Wenzel, ed., 293).

66   Grosseteste, *De modo confitendi et paenitentias iniungendi* 2.3, in Goering and Mantello, eds., "The Early Penitential Writings," 93.

67   F.S. Pearson, "Records of a Ruridecanal Court of 1300," in *Collectanea*, ed. S.G. Hamilton (London, 1912), 69–80. These records probably reflect an issue that has not been touched on in this article for lack of space, namely, the apparently widespread lack of belief in the sinfulness of what was called simple fornication (heterosexual intercourse between unmarried people). For public prosecution of fornication see James A. Brundage, *Law, Sex, and Christian Society in Medieval Europe* (Chicago, 1987), 459–61.

68   See Gratian, *Decretum, De penit.*, D. 1.72.

69   Peter the Chanter, *Verbum abbreviatum* quoted by M. Müller (*Die Lehre des hl. Augustinus von der Paradisesehe und ihre Auswirkung in der Sexualethik des 12. und 13. Jahrhunderts bis Thomas von Aquin* [Regensburg, 1954], 152, n. 79). Müller cites this passage from a manuscript of the *Verbum abbreviatum* reflecting a form which was revised with a view to its use as a work on penance. For the manuscript (Munich, Clm 17458) see J.W. Baldwin, *Masters, Princes and Merchants. The Social Views of Peter the Chanter and His Circle* (Princeton, N.J., 1970), 2.256. This text is based on Caesarius of Arles, Sermon 41 (*Sermones*, ed, G. Morin, CCSL 103 [Turnhout, 1953], 181) but was attributed to Augustine in the Middle Ages.

Diversity

A SMORGASBORD OF SEXUAL PRACTICES

Cathy Jorgensen Itnyre

An examination of medieval Icelandic sources reveals a smorgasbord of sexual practices known to these people. From seduction to genital size, from multiple sexual partners to adultery, the frankness of medieval Icelanders regarding these topics is rather surprising to a modern reader. Why were such practices so freely mentioned in the literature of 600–700 years ago, and what does the medieval Icelandic willingness to mention such acts signify? Much has been made of the late conversion of Icelanders to Christianity: can it be that the sexual habits of a pre-Christian era lingered on? Or does the lack of reticence signify instead something about the Icelandic character that has nothing to do with religious preference? This paper will first examine what the sources say about specific sexual practices, and then speculate on what this frankness may illustrate about the medieval Icelandic society.

Various categories of Old Norse sources treat sexual themes. While the family sagas are less explicit than certain legendary sagas, it is indeed the case that thirteenth- and fourteenth-century authors were not hesitant to refer to sexual habits in vivid language. Grethe Jacobsen has studied the Icelandic legal views on irregular sexual practices.[1] Divorce was permissible in medieval Icelandic society in cases of economic stress, bodily injury and, interestingly enough in terms of perceiving sexual attitudes, in cases of spousal refusal to have sexual relations.[2] This is in conformity with medieval European canonists' insistence on the mutual marital debt.[3]

What did *not* constitute grounds for divorce yields some fascinating insight into sexual attitudes of medieval Icelanders: adultery was not sufficient cause for divorce, although, as Jacobsen notes, this does not imply approval of the practice.[4] The family sagas reflect cases of adultery in which little or no negative action results from the offense. In *Eyrbyggja Saga*, an affair between Thurid and Bjorn results in some unhappiness on her husband's part, but the powerful chieftain Snorri persuades Bjorn to break off the relationship.[5] *Grettir's Saga* also contains an adulterous episode with no repercussions: Spes and Thorstein, Grettir's brother, conduct an extramarital affair despite the suspicions of Spes' husband. The couple is able to marry and achieve a long, happy life together, only to end up as hermits in a self-imposed punishment for their earlier adultery: "Our youth is well behind us, and we are getting on in years, but we have always lived more after our own desires than after Christian teaching or righteousness."[6] It is significant that the penance is self-imposed: it is a voluntary choice that leads the couple to undertake a pilgrimage and adopt an eremitic lifestyle.

Turning to male infidelity, an example from *Laxdoela Saga* indicates the non-serious nature of this practice: Jorunn says to her husband Hoskuld: "I'm not going to quarrel with this concubine you've brought home from Norway, however unpleasant her presence might be. . . ."[7] The often-cited example of Bergthora in *Njal's Saga* echoes this attitude: as Roberta Frank notes, Bergthora benignly ignores Hrodny, her husband Njal's mistress: when Hrodny commands Njal to "Stand up and get out of bed with my rival!,"[8] Bergthora fails to react with anger. To the contrary, she urges Njal to assist Hrodny.

There are many examples of fornication in the sagas. *Sturlunga Saga*, a thirteenth-century historical work, casually mentions that "þorstein was indoors [at Kamb in Kroksfjord]—he had a mistress there."[9] *Íslendinga Saga* describes an affair in nonpejorative terms: "þórð Sturluson and Helga, Ari's daughter, took up Ari's inheritance. þórd was not lucky enough to feel for Helga the love he should have, and in the end they were divorced. Then þórð took as mistress Hrodny, þórð's daughter, who was married to Bersi auðgi Vermundarson; they enjoyed a lasting love."[10] The family sagas also mention fornication; for example, in *Egil's Saga*, "Bjorgolf bought the girl for an ounce of gold and off they went to bed."[11]

Grethe Jacobsen has drawn attention to the penalties for fornication contained in the great Icelandic legal compilation *Grágás*.[12] Her assertion that economic considerations rather than moral concerns shaped the treatment of irregular sexual practices in *Grágás* is, I believe, correct. The references to sexual behavior in family, historical and legendary sagas are morally neutral: that is, the authors do not attempt to condemn the participants for their actions. As Jacobsen notes, "Fighting that results from these relationships is usually due to the lover's unwillingness to acknowledge paternity or to pay the *legoro rettr* but may be caused by the father's or law-warden's refusal to accept him as son-in-law."[13] It is not the practice *per se* that offends, but the complications that may arise from such affairs.

By now it is clear that Icelandic sources are not silent about sexual topics. It is time to turn to specific practices mentioned in the literature, for certain sagas yield remarkably detailed examples of sexual behavior. We find rape, seduction, genital size, castration, bestiality, and—for want of a better term—extra-human sex, involving giantesses and monsters. Clearly, it cannot be said that the latter occurred in actual medieval Icelandic society, but it is significant that the saga audience would appreciate hearing about such practices.

"Rape was in all [Scandinavian] laws considered a crime of violence, and the punishment was the same whether the victim was a virgin or not," writes Jacobsen.[14] According to *Grettir's Saga*, however, a great deal of shame on the part of the victim still ensued from this crime. After Grettir saves some women from being raped by beserkers, the mistress of the house thanks him with the words: "You have won great fame . . . and you have kept me and my household from a great disgrace—if you had not saved us, we would never have found any help."[15] The language here indicates more than just a crime of violence, for seldom is such vehement language attached to assault even when murder is involved. The *Kónungsbók* text of *Grágás* includes rape under the section on Treatment of Homicide.[16] Noting that "there are six women a man has the right to kill for,"[17] *Kónungsbók* goes on to specify what constitutes the act of rape:

> If a man arrives to find another man forcing a woman to lie with him there, a woman he has the right to kill for, and the man has forced her down and lowered himself down upon her, then he has the right to kill on her account there at that place; or likewise if he finds him in the same bed as the woman, so that they lie side by side, because it was his will to have wrongful intercourse with her; then a man has the right to kill on her account in both instances even if intercourse has not taken place.[18]

Further, intention alone provides grounds for legal action involving neighbors of the place of action; the neighbors must decide on the legality of the vengeance killing or injury of the would-be rapist.

In cases of seduction, the language used rarely elucidates specific practices. The family saga *Eyrbyggja Saga* depicts Snorri the chieftain whispering sweet words to his concubine,[19] but we do not know exactly what these words are. This saga later describes the thwarted attempts of the beserker Halli to court "a splendid-looking young woman . . . very proud and self-assured."[20] But when the girl's father learns of the beserker's interest in his daughter, he tells Halli "not to bring shame and disgrace on him by trying to seduce his daughter."[21] Although Halli is forbidden the pleasure of a normal courtship, he expresses the emotional sentiment that "I'm so much in love with her that I can't put her out of my mind."[22] Later in *Eyrbyggja Saga*, "a man named Thorleif had been found guilty of seduction and outlawed,"[23] although we are not told what methods he employed in his seduction. *Eyrbyggja Saga* also contains the adulterous case cited earlier in which the powerful Snorri requests Bjorn to "stop fooling around"[24] with his married sister Thurid. Bjorn, already by this time the author of a love-verse to Thurid,[25] responds to Snorri's request with the cautious statement, "I'll not promise you anything I can't carry out . . . and I'm not so sure that this is a promise I can honor while I'm living in the same neighborhood as Thurid."[26] His passion is such that he is unable to control it in her vicinity! Snorri wisely recommends that Bjorn move, thereby solving the problem.

Seduction is certainly a common theme in the great thirteenth-century *Njal's Saga*: for instance, Mord Valgerdsson advises Thorgeir Otkelsson to seduce Ormhild, in order to enrage her relative Gunnar.[27] Hrapp Orgumleidason "started making advances to Gudrun, and people said that he was seducing her."[28] Ursula Dronke, in her study *The Role of Sexual Themes in Njals Saga*, reminds us that Hrapp is also a rumored lover of Hallgerd.[29]

Several of the family sagas contain explicit references to genital size, as well as descriptive comments about the male organ's ability to function. In addition, the legendary sagas, originating in the twelfth century and committed to writing in the fourteenth century, according to Pálsson,[30] provide amusing speculation about a woman's ability to receive a large penis during intercourse.

The case of Hrutr and Unn is widely known by scholars: Dronke has written of "the cruel spell of sexual frustration"[31] that causes the couple to divorce. Hrutr, despite his engagement to Unn, has an affair with Queen Gunnhildr of Norway. When he decides to leave Norway, he lies to the Queen about his marital plans, claiming that he has no "girl back home" awaiting his return. "I believe you have, nevertheless,"[32] accuses the Queen. She then pronounces the curse: "If I have as great power over you as I think I have, then I lay this on you, that you may not have pleasure with the woman in Iceland that you intend to, but with other women you may have your will."[33] When Hrutr returns to Iceland and marries Unn, the specific nature of the royal curse is soon made clear: Unn implores her father Mord to help her divorce Hrutr, even though she cares about him. Pressed for details, she admits to her father: "He is unable to consummate our marriage and give me satisfaction, although in every other way he is as virile as the best of men."[34] Her father interrupts: "Be more specific!"[35] And Unn replies, "Whenever he touches me, he is so enlarged that he can't have enjoyment of me, although we both passionately desire to reach consummation. But we have never succeeded. And yet, before we draw apart, he proves that he is by nature as normal as other men."[36]

One consequence of Hrutr's impotence is that he temporarily becomes an object of ridicule: two small boys "play" Hrutr and Mord, one suggesting, "I'll be Mord and divorce you from your wife with the excuse that you couldn't screw her!"[37] Hrutr goes on to have many children, proving that Gunnhildr's curse, true to her word, applies only to his attempts with the unfortunate Unn. James A. Brundage discusses the issue of sexual incompatibility due to genital size in his book *Law, Sex and Christian Society in Medieval Europe.* The thirteenth-century canonist Tancred held that a marriage that could not be consummated due to genitals that were too large or too small could result in a divorce, with both sides able to remarry, but if the woman could accommodate her new husband's penis, she might be asked to try again with her previous husband. If the latter could now perform satisfactorily with her, then the first marriage should have precedence, and remain in effect.[38]

Too-small penises are also mentioned in Old Norse literature. Here the great *Grettir's Saga* provides the outstanding example: Grettir is a famous outlaw, widely admired for his strength and courage. One night he sleeps at a farm owned by a family with curious females. One of them boldly picks up the blanket covering the naked, sleeping Grettir; she is amazed that such a big man has such a small penis.[39] Grettir is naturally offended by this critical observation, and speaks two verses in his defense:

> The hussy is taking a risk.
> It's seldom one can get
> so close a look
> at a hair-girt sword.
> I bet that other men's testicles
> won't be bigger than mine,
> though their penises may be
> larger than this one.

and

> The wench has complained
> that my penis is small,
> and the boastful slut
> may well be right.
> But a small one can grow,
> and I'm still a young man,
> so wait until I get
> into action, my lass.[40]

After composing these verses, Grettir goes on to have sex with the curious "hussy."

Genital size also plays an interesting role in one of the legendary sagas, *Arrow-Odd*.[41] True to its genre, *Arrow-Odd* abounds with fantastic creatures: giants, ghosts, etc. One giantess, Hildigunn, is presented with the hero Arrow-Odd as a "pet"; she places him in a cradle with her new-born brother and then "She started caressing him, and when she thought he was becoming too restive in the cradle, she put him in her bed beside her and embraced him. Eventually Odd played all the games he felt like, and after that they got on very well together."[42] After some months, Hildigunn notices that she is pregnant: "I love you very dearly, small as you are, and I can't fool myself any longer that I'm not pregnant, though it must seem unbelievable that a useless little tot like you could manage to do so much."[43] The placing of Odd in a cradle next to a new-born giant prior to sexual play is one of two allusions to sexuality presented in the same context with children of which I am aware.[44] Of course, it is very clear to Hildigunn that Odd is indeed a full-grown man: "Then Odd told her that although he was so much smaller than the local people, he was no child."[45]

By far the most sexually explicit legendary saga is *Bosi and Herraud*. Bosi has several sexual encounters with farmers' daughters, and the size of his penis is alluded to in playful language. With one girl, he calls his penis his "warrior": "She asked him where the warrior was, and he told her to feel between his legs. But she pulled her hand back and asked why he was carrying a monster like that on him, as hard as a tree."[46] Despite his size, "he managed to complete his mission."[47]

With another partner, Bosi calls his penis his "stump," and his lady coquettishly fears that her "ring" may be too small to accommodate the "stump":

> Bosi went over to her bed and she asked what he wanted. He said he wanted
> her to put a ring on his stump. She said she wondered what ring he could be
> talking about, and he asked her didn't she have one? She answered that she

hadn't any ring that would fit him. "I can widen it if it's too narrow," he
said. "Where's that stump of yours? I've got a fair idea of what I can expect
from my narrow little ring."[48]

The last of Bosi's three partners seems more experienced and confident
than the two mentioned above; it is interesting that although the three
adventures are similar, the last girl fails to comment on Bosi's size,
concentrating instead on a playful criticism of his penis's shape. Here Bosi
is offering his organ as "a young colt" that needs to be watered: "'Do you
think you can manage it, my man?' she asked. 'He's hardly used to a well
like mine . . .' She took hold of the prick, and stroked it and said, 'He seems
a lively colt, though his neck is much too straight.' 'His head isn't all that
well set,' agreed Bosi, 'but he can curve his neck much better after he's had a
drink.'. . . Then he watered his colt generously, completely immersing him.
This pleased the girl immensely, and she was hardly able to speak."[49] Bosi
gives the rendered-speechless girl a ring after all sexual activity is finished;
with the other two, the gift of a ring comes early in the sex play: one
wonders if he felt they needed some extra persuasion!

There are several sexual innuendoes in Old Norse literature that deal
with women's stomachs. For example, in *Eyrbyggja Saga*, an old woman,
Katla, asks Gunnlaug if he is going to Geirrod's house "to stroke the old hag
up the belly."[50] In *Njal's Saga*, Hallgerd's foster-father Thjostolf is jealous
of her second husband Glum; in a calculated insult, "Thjostolf said that Glum
had not the strength for anything except romping on Hallgerd's belly."[51]
Further, in *Grettir's Saga*, the young hero is accused of laziness by his
shipmates: "You like it better to pat the belly of Bard the wife's mate than
to bear a hand in the ship."[52] The female abdomen is obviously a symbol of
fertility; yet it is interesting that it should be referred to in an insulting
context in these three instances. I have not found a reference in any positive
context.

The legendary sagas, with their penchant for supernatural beings,
provide us with further references to female body parts and sexual appetites.
The heroes in *Egil and Asmund* must rescue two kidnapped princesses in
Giantland. Egil and Asmund encounter giants along the way who make clear
how sexually active that race is. The first giantess they meet is Skin Beak,
who they greet with the words, "Who are you, O beautiful, bed-worthy
lady?"[53] When Asmund gives her a gold ring, she hesitates to accept it,
fearing that her mother, Queen Eagle-Beak of Jotunheim, will assume it is
"bed money."[54] The Queen asks the heroes to tell their life stories. Egil
relates that he once saw a giant fight with a giantess (who turns out to be the
Queen herself) over a golden ring: "She was wearing a very short dress, and
her genitalia were very conspicuous."[55] When Eagle-Beak reciprocates with
her own life story, her tremendous sexual appetite is freely admitted: ". . .
but ever since I've been driven by a sexual urge so strong that I don't seem
able to live without a man."[56] In her pursuit of "one of the men I had to
have,"[57] Eagle-Beak attacks the man's intended bride by changing herself
into a fly to crawl "under her clothes with the idea of ripping her belly open

at the groin."[58] Later, the giantess has sex with the god Odin but at a terrible cost: "First I slept with Odin, then I jumped over the fire and got the cloak, but ever since I've had no skin to my body."[59]

Preben Meulengracht Sørensen in his study of sexual defamation in Old Norse prose literature points out that "incest was an extremely serious crime, punished by outlawry."[60] Nevertheless, the practice appears in Old Norse literature, underscoring for the saga audience the extraordinary nature of this act. For instance, Meulengracht Sørensen notes that the use of incest in *Volsunga Saga*[61] is a device to "make possible the birth of the unique hero Sinfjotli."[62] He further states that "Breaking of taboos seems to characterise the hero, who lives and moves outside the norms of ordinary human beings."[63]

We find a humorously presented case of incest in one of the legendary tales, *Gautrek's Saga*. King Gauti of West Goteland impregnates a girl who lives in an isolated household of eccentric misers. The family is so anxious to leave large inheritances to its survivors that the elders commit suicide whenever their fortune is diminished even slightly. The pregnant girl and her siblings are warned not to increase the family's size:

> Now that the young people had taken over the property, they decided they'd better set things right. So they cut some wooden pegs and used them to pin pieces of cloth round their bodies so that they couldn't touch each other. They felt this was the safest method of controlling their numbers. When Snotra realized she was going to have a baby, she loosened the wooden pins that held her dress together, so that her body could be touched. She was pretending to be asleep when Gilling [her brother] woke or stirred in his sleep. He stretched out his hand and happened to touch her cheek.[64]

This inadvertent touch and the discovery that his sister is pregnant causes Gilling to assume that he is the father of the child:

> How stupid of me
> to move my hand
> and touch the woman's cheek.
> It doesn't take much
> to make a son
> if that's how Gautrek was got.[65]

Preben Meulengracht Sørensen deals extensively with sexual insults that involve sex with animals. We find an interesting example in *Njal's Saga*, where the laconic Skarphedinn accuses Thorkel of having had sex with a mare; he further insinuates that a shepherd observed and was disgusted by this act.[66] *Ale-Hood Saga* contains sexual insults in this vein. Thorkel Fringe is accused of being mated by Steingrim's stallion,[67] and it is suggested that Eyjolf Thordason changed himself into a mare in order to be mated.[68] *Hreidar the Fool* alludes to the unflattering nickname of King Harald Hardradi's father, Sigurd Sýr (sow): the fool Hreidar presents the king with a silver sow "with teats on it."[69] The king is enraged by this insulting gift. Thirteenth-century eddaic poetry refers to sexuality involving animals; for instance, in *Lokasenna* we are reminded that Loki fathered a wolf.[70]

The sexuality implicit in horses is affirmed in a number of Old Norse passages. I have already cited the amorous Bosi's reference to his penis as a "colt" that needs to be watered. His partner is delighted: "She said she'd never ridden a more slow-paced colt than this one."[71] Finn insults King Harald Hardradi in the latter's saga by referring to Harald's concubine Thora (Finn's own niece) as a mare: "No wonder you fought so lustily if the mare was with you!"[72] In *Islendinga Saga* we meet a woman named Hallfrið garðafylja (backyard filly), who warms Gizur between her thighs when the earl is frozen from hiding in a vat of whey.[73] The old woman Busla in *Bosi and Herraud* includes in her demonic prayer the following curse:

> . . . Frost giants shall fight you
> and stallions ride you . . .[74]

Castration, according to Preben Meulengracht Sørensen, ". . . served not only to punish adversaries or to render them harmless by making them physically non-combatant and unable to beget sons. . . . Mutilation also invalidated a man by humiliating him in an irremediable way. . . ."[75] He cites the gelding of Harald Gilli[76] and that of Orækja in Sturla þórðarson's *Islendinga Saga*.[77] Earlier in this saga, two priests are castrated.[78] Reference to this practice appears in the eddaic poem *Helgakvitha Hjorvarthssonar*: the hero Atli alternates verses with the giantess Hrimgerth, who says, "Thou wouldst neigh, Atli, but gelded thou art."[79]

Medieval Icelandic ecclesiastical literature also sheds light on irregular sexual practices. Jenny M. Jochen's "The Church and Sexuality in Medieval Iceland"[80] is a careful study of the church's attempts to influence native sexual morality. Just about the only celibate clergy in medieval Iceland appears to have been the bishops þorlákr þórhallsson and Guðmundr Arason—both venerated as saints partly for their forbearance in this regard. *þorlák's saga* tells of his attempts to impose conformity with church regulations on Icelandic marriages.[81] Most trying to the celibate þorlákr is his sister Ragnheið's status as concubine of the leading chieftain, Jón Loftsson. During þorlákr's episcopate, Archbishop Eysteinn of Níðaros wrote a letter condemning the immoral personal lives of the Icelandic chieftains.[82] We learn in *Hungrvaka*, an early thirteenth-century account of the first five bishops of Iceland, that the first bishop, Isleifr, faced severe problems. In addition to a generally low level of moral behavior (including disobedience, unspecified bad habits, and continued viking expeditions on the part of Icelanders), one particular scandal was that the lawspeaker had married both a mother and daughter![83]

It is time to address the questions asked earlier regarding the implications of such frank sexual references in medieval Icelandic sources. It is widely acknowledged that Iceland was in close contact with continental Europe during the medieval period; this contact had repercussions on both the cultural and political realms. Margaret Schlauch has pointed out that many foreign literary themes travelled far from their homelands to end up as topics in Icelandic tales.[84] Stephan Kuttner, by analyzing the hagiographical tradition of amending irregularities occurring in the saga of Bishop Jon Ögmundarson, demonstrates that "a certain amount of canonical learning had been carried to the remote North by the beginning of the thirteenth century."[85] Sveinbjörn Rafnsson has shown that the *Hauksbók* and *Sturlubók* redactions of *Landnámabák* both underwent revision in order to emphasize the Christian backgrounds of several Icelandic settlers.[86]

Clearly, Icelandic authors could choose to impress their views on any given native texts. Yet this option was not exercised when it came to excluding sexual references. Either the authors deliberately chose not to omit such references (if the oral-tradition proponents are correct in assuming the earlier origins of much of the literature), or they opted to use these references in their original composition of these sagas. In either case, where is the medieval Christian aversion to sexual matters? I believe that the inclusion of sexual practices underscores the secular outlook of the medieval Icelanders. Another example of weak Christian influence is the Icelandic refusal to espouse chastity for its clergy. I have cited only a few of the very many references to married priests, priests with concubines, and children of priests. The great celibate St. þorlákr þórhallsson himself was tempted to marry, and only resisted with the help of a supernatural vision.[87] Presumably, not many other clerics had such direct intervention to help preserve their chastity!

There is no easy way to gauge the persistence of pagan attitudes and influences on Christian Iceland.[88] The dating problems that surround the literary sources continue to engage the attention of specialists in this area. But the thirteenth- and fourteenth-century dates that scholars ascribe to the sagas are sufficiently late to allow for ecclesiastical tampering with the content and style of these works. Inclusion of sexual references in the sagas thus strongly indicates that Iceland did not share in the ethos which attempted to discourage or ignore sexual acts.

Notes

1 Grethe Jacobsen, "Sexual Irregularities in Medieval Scandinavia," in Vern L. Bullough and James Brundage, *Sexual Practices and the Medieval Church* (Buffalo, N.Y.: Prometheus Books), 1982, 72–88.

2 *Grágás*, 1852, chapters 149, 151.

3 Elizabeth Makowski, "The Conjugal Debt and Medieval Canon Law," *Journal of Medieval History* 3 (1977), 99–114.

4 Jacobsen, "Sexual Irregularities in Medieval Scandinavia," 73.

5 *Eyrbyggja Saga*, tr. Hermann Pálsson and Paul Edwards (Edinburgh: Southside, 1973), chap. 47, 154.

6 *Grettir's Saga*, tr. Denton Fox and Hermann Pálsson (Toronto: University of Toronto Press, 1974), chap. 91, 185.

7 *Laxdaela Saga*, tr. Magnus Magnusson and Hermann Pálsson (Baltimore, Md.: Penguin Books, 1969), chap. 13, 67.

8 *Brennu-Njáls Saga*, Einar dl. Sveinsson (Reykjavík: Hið Íslenzka Fornritafélag, 1954), 251: "Hróðny mælti: 'Statt þú upp ór binginum frá elju

minni. . . .'" See also Roberta Frank's article, "Marriage in Twelfth- and Thirteenth-Century Iceland," *Viator* 4 (1973), 473–84.

9 *Sturlu Saga,* in *Sturlunga Saga,* vol. I, Jón Jóhannesson, Magnús Finnbogason, and Kristján Eldjárn (Reykjavík: Sturlunguútgáfan, 1946), 71: "Ok var þorsteinn inni,—hann átti þar fylgjukonu,—"

10 *Íslendinga Saga,* in *Sturlunga Saga,* vol. I, 231: "þórðr Sturluson tók arf eftir Ara ok þau Helga, dóttir hans. þórðr bar eigi auðnu til at fella þvílíka ást til Helgu, sem vera átti, ok kom því svá, at skilnaðr þeira var gerr. En þórðr tókþá til sín Hróðnýju þórðardóttur, er átti Bersi in auðgi Vermundarson, ok helzt þeira vinátta lengi, . . ."

11 *Egils Saga,* tr. Hermann Pálsson and Paul Edwards (New York: Penguin Books, 1976), chap. 7, 30.

12 Jacobsen, "Sexual Irregularities in Medieval Scandinavia," 73–76.

13 Ibid., 76.

14 Ibid., 84.

15 *Grettir's Saga,* chap. 19, 43–44.

16 *Grágás* has been translated into English by Andrew Dennis, Peter Foote, and Richard Perkins, *Laws of Early Iceland, Grágás I* (Winnipeg, Canada: University of Manitoba Press), 1980. Here see chapter 90, page 154; in *Grágás* 1852, chap. 90, 164–65.

17 *Laws of Early Iceland, Grágás I,* chap. 90, 154.

18 Ibid.

19 *Eyrbyggja Saga,* chap. 19, 72.

20 Ibid., chap. 28, 95.

21 Ibid.

22 Ibid.

23 Ibid., chap. 36, 119.

24 Ibid., chap. 47, 154.

25 Ibid., chap. 29, 101–02.

26 Ibid., chap. 47, 154.

27 *Njal's Saga,* tr. Magnus Magnusson and Hermann Pálsson, Baltimore, Md.: Penguin Books, 1960, chap. 71, 161.

28 Ibid., chap. 87, 186.

29 Ursula Dronke, *The Role of Sexual Themes in Njáls Saga,* The Dorothea Coke Memorial Lecture in Northern Studies, University College, London, 27 May 1980 (London: Viking Society for Northern Research, 1980), 25.

30 *Gautrek's Saga and Other Medieval Tales,* tr. Hermann Pálsson and Paul Edwards (New York: New York University Press, 1968), 13, 19.

31 Dronke, *The Role of Sexual Themes in Njáls Saga,* 8.

32 *Njál's Saga,* chap. 6, 48. And in *Brennu-Njáls Saga,* p. 20: "þat hefi ek þó fyrir satt. . . ."

33 *Njál's Saga,* chap. 6, 49; and in *Brennu-Njáls Saga,* 21: "Ef ek á svá mikit vald á þér sem ek ætla, þá legg ek þat á við þik, at þú megir engri munúð fram koma við konu þá, er þú ætlar þér á Íslandi, en fremja skaltþþú mega vilja þinn við aðrar konur."

34 *Njál's Saga,* chap. 7, 52; and in *Brennu-Njáls Saga,* 24: "Hann má ekki hjúskaparfar eiga við mik, svá at ek mega njóta hans, en hann er at allri náttúru sinni annarri sem inir vǫskustu menn."

35 *Njál's Saga,* ibid., and in *Brennu-Njáls Saga,* ibid.: "Hversu má svá vera? . . . ok seg enn gørr."

A Smorgasbord of Sexual Practices

155

36 *Njál's Saga*, ibid., and in *Brennu-Njáls Saga*, ibid.: "þegar hann kemr við mik, þá er horund hans sva mikit, at hann má ekki eptirlæti hafa við mik, en pó hofum vit bæði breytni til þess á alla vega, at vit mættim njótask, en þat verðr ekki. En þó áðr vit skilim, sýnir hann þat af sér, at hann er í œði sínu rétt sem aðrir menn."

37 *Njál's Saga*, chap. 8, 55; and in *Brennu-Njáls Saga*, 29: "Ek skal þér M\O(o,ᵣrðr ok stefnaþér af konunni ok finna þat til foráttu, at þú hafir ekki sorþit hana." Ursula Dronke in her *Role of Sexual Themes in Njals Saga* uses the word "fuck" for the Old Norse *sorþit*.

38 James Brundage, *Law, Sex and Christian Society in Medieval Europe* (Chicago: University of Chicago Press, 1987), 378.

39 *Grettir's Saga*, chap. 75, 154.

40 Ibid., 155.

41 *Arrow-Odd: A Medieval Novel*, tr. Paul Edwards and Hermann Pálsson (New York: New York University Press, 1970).

42 Ibid., chap. 18, 58.

43 Ibid.

44 I mention above the case of the two boys "playing" Hrutr and mocking his failure to perform sexually with Unn.

45 *Arrow Odd: A Medieval Novel*, chap. 18, 58.

46 *Bosi and Herraud*, in *Gautrek's Saga and Other Medieval Tales*, chap. 7, 70.

47 Ibid.

48 Ibid., chap. 13, 83.

49 Ibid., chap. 11, 78.

50 *Eyrbyggja Saga*, chap. 15, 59.

51 *Njál's Saga*, chap. 17, 70; and in *Brennu-Njáls Saga*, 49: ". . . ok mælti þjóstólfr við Glúm, at hann hefði til engis afla nema b ǫlta á maga Hallgerði."

52 *Grettir's Saga*, chap. 17, 33.

53 *Egil and Asmund*, in *Gautrek's Saga and Other Medieval Tales*, chap. 5, 96.

54 Ibid.

55 Ibid., chap. 11, 107.

56 Ibid., chap. 12, 109.

57 Ibid.

58 Ibid.

59 Ibid., chap. 13, 111.

60 Preben Meulengracht Sørensen, *The Unmanly Man: Concepts of Sexual Defamation in Early Norse Society*, tr. Joan Turville-Petre, The Viking Collection: Studies in Northern Civilization 1 (Odense: Odense University Press, 1983), 15.

61 See Jesse Byock's recent translation: *The Saga of the Volsungs: The Norse Epic of Sigurd the Dragon Slayer* (Berkeley: University of California Press, 1990).

62 Preben Meulengracht Sørensen, *The Unmanly Man*, 15.

63 Ibid.

64 *Gautrek's Saga and Other Medieval Tales*, chap. 2, 29–30.

65 Ibid.

66 *Njál's Saga*, chap. 120, 249; and in *Brennu-Njáls Saga*, 305: "Er þér ok skyldara at stanga or tonnum þér razgarnarendann merarinnar, er þú ázt, áðr þú reitt til þings, ok svá smalamaðr pinn ok undraðisk, hví þú gerðir slíka fúlmennsku."

67 *Ale-Hood* in *Hrafnkel's Saga and Other Stories*, tr. Hermann Pálsson (Baltimore, Md.: Penguin Books, 1971), chap. 3, 90.

68 Ibid.

69 *Hreidar the Fool* in ibid., 106.

70   *Lokasenna*, in *The Poetic Edda*, tr. Henry Adams Bellows (New York: The American-Scandinavian Foundation, 1968), 155, verse 10.

71   *Bosi and Herraud* in *Gautrek's Saga and Other Medieval Tales*, chap. 11, 78.

72   *King Harald's Saga*, tr. Magnus Magnusson and Herman Palsson (New York: Penguin Books, 1966), chap. 66, 118.

73   *Íslendinga Saga*, in *Sturlunga Saga*, vol. I, chap. 174, 493: "Ok er Gizurr kom í kirkju, váru klæði borin at honum, ok vermði sú kona hann á lærum sér, er Hallfríðr hét ok var kölluð garðafylja . . . Omaði honum brátt."

74   *Bosi and Herraud*, in *Gautrek's Saga and Other Medieval Tales*, chap. 5, 67.

75   Sørensen, *The Unmanly Man*, 81.

76   Ibid., 82.

77   Ibid., 83.

78   *Íslendinga Saga*, in *Sturlunga Saga*, vol. I, chap. 44, 292: "Váru þar teknir prestar tveir ok geldir, Snorri ok Knútr."

79   *Helgakvitha Hjarvarthssonar*, in *The Poetic Edda*, 281, verse 20.

80   Jenny Jochens, "The Church and Sexuality in Medieval Iceland," *Journal of Medieval History* 6 (1980), 377–92.

81   *þorláks Saga Byskups* in *Byskopa Sögur*, vol. I, ed., Guðni Jonsson, (Reykjavík: Íslendingasagnaútgáfan, 1953). See also Einar Ol. Sveinsson's interesting discussion of Icelandic morality during þorlákr's episcopate and the following century: *The Age of the Sturlungs*, tr. Jóhann Hannesson (Ithaca, New York: Cornell University Press, 1953).

82   *Diplomatarium Islandicum*, vol. I, *Íslenzkt fornbréfasafn* (Copenhagen and Reykjavík: S.L. Möller and Hið íslenzka bókmentafélag, 1857–1952), 221 and 262.

83   *Hungrvaka* in *Byskupa Sogur*, vol. I, chap. 2, 4: "Hann hafði nauð mikla á marga vegu í sínum byskupsdómi fyrir sakir óhlýðni manna. Má þat af því merkja nökkut, í hverjum nauðum hann hefir verit fyrir sakir ótrú ok óhlýði ok ósíða sinna undirmanna, at lög[sógu] maðrinn átti mæðgur tvær ok þá lögðust sumir menn út í viking ok á herskap. . . ."

84   Margaret Schlauch, *Romance in Iceland* (Princeton, N.J.: Princeton University Press, 1934). An interesting account of Icelandic legendary fiction is given by Hermann Palsson and Paul Edwards, *Legendary Fiction in Medieval Iceland* (Reykjavik: Studia Islandica 30, 1971).

85   Stephan Kuttner, "St. Jón of Holar: Canon Law and Hagiography in Medieval Iceland," *Analecta Cracoviensia* 7, (1975), 375.

86   Sveinbjörn Rafnsson, *Studier i Landnamabok: Kritiska Bidrag til den Islandska Fristatstidens Historia* (Lund: Gleerup, 1974).

87   *þorláks saga* in *Byskupa Sögur*, vol. 1, chap. 5, 42–43.

88   Jón Hnefill Aðalsteinsson, *Under the Cloak: The Acceptance of Christianity in Iceland with Particular Reference to the Religious Attitudes Prevailing at the Time*, Acta Universitatis Upsaliensis, Studia Ethnologica Upsaliensia 4 (Stockholm: Almqvist & Wiksell, 1978). See esp. Aðalsteinsson's first four chapters, which attempt to deal with pagan influence in later Iceland.

"FAWN OF MY DELIGHTS":
BOY-LOVE IN HEBREW
AND ARABIC VERSE

Norman Roth

Those who have distinguished themselves ought to be permitted any handsome boy they like.

(Plato, *Republic* V. 463E)

This statement shows how far from any imagined "idealized love" were Plato's thoughts. Indeed, as R.G. Bury long ago pointed out, the true Greek ideal of love consisted of the twin concepts *eros pandemos*, "directed to women as well as boys, to the body rather than the soul, to unscrupulous satisfaction of lust," and *eros uranios*, which "seeks only such males as are noble and nearly mature in both mind and body."[1] One need only add that "nearly mature" meant under the age of eighteen, nevertheless.[2]

Nor, of course, is Plato our only or even our primary source for these practices. Greek literature, from philosophy to poetry and even history (Pausanius, *Description of Greece* III.xiv.6), is replete with details.

The famous *Greek Anthology*, largely the composition of Meleager of Gadara, is the most obvious source, and here we find poetry which is astonishingly akin in motif and style to the "boy poetry" of the Muslims and Jews of the Middle Ages. Apparently all lovers of boys detested the sprouting of hair which marred the innocent but seductive beauty of the youth and heralded the end of his appeal. Thus we find in the Greek poet:

> When you were pretty, Archestratus, and the hearts of the young men were burnt for your wine-red cheeks, there was no talk of friendship with me, but sporting with others you spoilt your prime like a rose. Now, however, when you begin to blacken with horrid hair, you would force me to be your friend, offering me the straw after giving the harvest to others (Book XI. 36).

Pseudo-Lucian, *Amores*, has the following: "Do you think it a hardship that you associate with women at their fairest and boys at the flower of their beauty?" This exactly expresses also the Muslim and Hebrew ideal: love of both women and boys. Typical also of the concern with facial (and body) hair is his statement about slave boys who remained with their master-lover "till the down first appeared on their faces" but were sent away when the beard began to show.[3]

We have mentioned Meleager, who was born and lived in Gadara, which is in the region south of the Sea of Galilee in Israel, across the Jordan River. Later he lived in Tyre. It is interesting to see how distinguished scholars who have dealt with the crucial Hellenistic period in Jewish history refer to the poetry of Meleager in the most circuitous manner so as to avoid mentioning the true subject matter. Thus Martin Hengel, a renowned authority, states that he "was a master of Hellenistic love poetry, which had perfect control of every degree of feeling," without even hinting at the nature of that poetry. He adds that "he also stresses 'holy' Tyre several times."[4] M. Stern, an equally renowned Israeli scholar, says of him only that in one of his poems "he mentions the cold sabbath: 'If thy lover is some sabbath-keeper no great wonder! Not even love burns on cold sabbaths,'" with no hint to the fact that Meleager is talking about a boy who is in love with a Jewish man![5]

Only one writer has dared at least to hint at the nature of this poetry, but even he "bowdlerized" it to say that Meleager complained of a Jewish "mistress" as rival for a boy's affections. The boy whom Meleager in fact loved, one Demo, preferred instead a "Sabbath-keeping Jew," according to the poet. And Meleager, indeed, refers to "holy Tyre" in the following line: "holy Tyre which has the perfumed grove where the boy-blossoms of Cyprus grow." While Meleager is thus an important source for the existence of boy-love among Hellenized Jews, it needs to be mentioned that he himself was not a Jew, as erroneously claimed by some authors.[6]

The "Scroll of the Wars of the Sons of Light and the Sons of Darkness" of the Essene community (written after 63 B.C.E.) reflects the continued practice of sex with boys in Palestine even after the peak period of Hellenistic influence, when in setting down rules for the soldiers preparing for battle it says: "And no young boy and no woman shall enter their camps when they leave Jerusalem to go into battle until their return" (VII.3–4); note that *after* their return from battle it is all right!

In at least two previous articles I have dealt in detail with the love of boys in medieval Arabic and Hebrew poetry.[7] There is no point in repeating here what has already been said, and the reader is urged to see those articles for details of themes and terminology as well as for previous bibliography and other examples of this motif in both Arabic and Hebrew poetry.

I only need to mention that, while there are some encouraging signs of an enlightened outlook and acceptance of the existence of this theme in Hebrew poetry among some contemporary Israeli writers, pietistic "objectors" continue to dissent, oddly enough in *this* country. For a point of view which is completely different from my own, one may consult an article by a non-scholar but well-known literary figure, Neal Kozodoy. This writer concludes that "we must wonder at every moment . . . whether the human love of which any particular poet speaks . . . is not really meant to do metaphysical duty for the love of God."[8] While certainly I disagree that we need to "wonder at every moment," it is quite true that there are some examples in medieval Hebrew poetry where the theme of love (whether of boys or of women) is used allegorically. The subject is not always God (as, for example, it invariably was in the religious poetry of the Muslim Sūfīs), but also includes the Messiah or even the Jewish people as the allegorical beloved. Elsewhere, I have dealt extensively with that poetry, showing that it is always easily recognizable as "religious" in nature, although the poetic genius lay in concealing the real nature of the "beloved" until the last possible moment.[9]

Sadly, I must also take issue with the views of a former teacher, Raymond P. Scheindlin, who apparently continues to view this poetry in an ambiguous manner. He mentions as a "peculiarity" of medieval Arabic and Hebrew love poetry that the beloved is "regularly" referred to in the masculine gender; implying that the beloved is actually, and usually, female (he refers to the "indefinite sexuality" of such poetry). The reference here to Arabic poetry is particularly puzzling, for all authorities acknowledge the existence of boy-love in Arabic poetry (indeed, given the very explicit scatological nature of that verse they could scarcely deny it!).[10]

However, it is important to note also that this writer has not fallen into the trap of "allegorizing" all such poetry, even the Hebrew; for later in the article he indeed acknowledges (though not apparently realizing how this contradicts his earlier statement) that such poetry really did exist and that it probably reflects a reality of actual conditions.[11] This conclusion he appears to have drawn from my previously cited article, but the point of the responsa (Jewish legal opinions) to which I there called attention is *not* that "official Judaism did not approve" of sexual relations with boys (and in spite of my careful argument to the contrary there, it is disconcerting to find authors still calling this "homosexuality"), but that on the contrary it did not *disapprove*; at least not very strongly. Oh, well; one grows accustomed to being misread and misinterpreted.

In fact there is no unified position of "official Judaism" (whatever that may be) on this question. Strict legal authorities, both in Islam and Judaism, certainly did disapprove vehemently, but there is no evidence that this had any effect on actual practice.[12]

Abraham b. Natan *"ha-Yarhiy"* (of Lunel), who lived also for a time in Toledo in the early thirteenth century, wrote that those who recite poetry other than at marriage feasts or other religious celebrations, but rather at a private meal or poetry which is "about a thing forbidden to look at," and rejoice and conduct themselves with levity, it is certainly prohibited. "And it does not need to be said that those young men who have gone from the path of [moral] instruction . . . and have written books concerning the love of women and of their deceit and frailty, I have no portion in them: not in their honey and not in their sting" (cf. Midrash *Gen. Rabbah* 20.9; here a clever pun on "honey," saliva of the mouth, in love poetry and "sting," their attack on women). Such writings deserve to be hidden away, for they have used scriptural texts and applied them metaphorically to "the abominations of women."[13]

While it is very probable that the author had in mind one particular book, the first of its kind as a satirical "attack" on women, there is no doubt that his general negative attitude to love poetry reflects a view held by more strict religious authorities.[14]

However, more than a century earlier, the great poet and philosopher Solomon Ibn Gabirol took a more realistic approach when he wrote:

> It is almost impossible for any man to be secure from this accident [lust], O God, save he whose intellect is master over his nature. None such exists; and if any [be found to] exist, he is undoubtedly one of the most excellent. . . . This quality [lust] is preferred by foolish men only because of the imminence (immediateness) of its delight and for the sake of the amusement and merriment and the hearing of mirthful songs [*aghanin*] which they get through it. . . .[15]

Interestingly, even Maimonides, whose opposition not only to pederasty, but to any kind of poetry is well known, quoted approvingly in one of his medical treatises the saying of Hippocrates: "The years of adolescence are the most excellent and agreeable."[16] However, as I already pointed out both in an earlier article and in my book on Maimonides, in a passage in which he specifically mentions *muwashshahāt* (poems in which the final couplet is in Romance or Arabic), Maimonides condemns especially the content of such poems:

> And know that poems made in any language are not examined except according to their subject, and their manner is as the way of speech, as we have already divided it. And I had to explain this even though it is simple because I have seen elders and pure (men) of our community when they were at a wine banquet, whether it is a wedding or some other place, and were a man to recite an Arabic poem, even if the words of that poem were praise of courage or generosity which is of the category of suitable (desirable), or praise of the wine, they would protest this with every manner of protest and not permit it to be heard; but if the poet were to recite a Hebrew *muwashshah* they would not protest it even though its speech (subject) is of the prohibited or despised category.

He concludes that if the subject matter is "vice," it is forbidden in any language, but that in his opinion it is even worse if the *muwashshah* is in Hebrew than in Arabic.[17]

In "Deal Gently," I pointed out that Saʿadyah Gaon, who was himself accused of sexual intercourse with boys on more than one occasion, used male references in discussing love in his "philosophical" (actually anti-philosophical) treatise. It is interesting to note that also Moses de León, the Spanish author of the *Zohar*, used as an example of kissing that between two males, and then expanded this to include "even more so" that between male and female:

> This is expressed in the love of kissing, how that kissing in love is only by the mouth, and spirit is united with spirit [so that] each one of them [masculine word forms] combines the two spirits, his spirit and that of his companion . . . and all the more so the masculine and the feminine in their combining.[18]

Finally, even in the fifteenth century, when Hebrew poetry (with exception of some in the kingdom of Aragón-Catalonia) had declined, the moralist Solomon Ibn Lahmis (or Lahmias, also called Al'amiy) wrote: "Take care against hearing poetry of lust and melodies of animal passion which arouse and lead to lechery which is disgrace and shame—also trampling and trouble [cf. Isa. 22.5]." Again, he warns more specifically:

> Take care against musicians [or singers] who are drinkers of strong drink, and of the poetry of fools—these are the vile cantors who interpose in the middle of the blessings sensual poems intermingled with the lusting of passion, with the meters of mockers, the Edomites [Christians] and Ishmaelites [Muslims], in order to find favor in the eyes of men of weak intellect and of *men who are similar to women, and in the eyes of the youths and capricious boys* [ta'lulim; even "naughty"]. These cantors are like idolaters.[19]

Even if it could be argued that the Hebrew poets might ignore the admonitions of contemporary legal authorities and moralists, the fact remains that the Talmud and early rabbinical literature certainly did not condone the writing of such poetry, much less the practices it praised. For example, Rabbi 'Aqiva (who elsewhere is credited with saving this book for the canon by allegorizing it) said that he who "shakes" his voice (sings) with the Song of Songs at taverns (or wine parties) and "makes of it a kind of song" has no part in the world to come.[20]

Yet not only was the Song of Songs routinely understood to be literally a love poem in Spain, it served as the fundamental source for the very imagery and terminology of love poetry.

Then, too, there was the example already set by some of the later *geonim* (heads of academies in Iraq and recognized as supreme legal authorities of the Jews). Thus, Judah Ibn Bal'am, one of the most important early grammarians and biblical commentators in Muslim Spain, says that he has seen erotic Arabic poetry cited by Sa'adyah and Hai Gaon.[21]

Also of crucial importance is the fact that, contrary to early erroneous assumptions (still maintained, e.g., by Scheindlin), there were very few if any "court poets" among the Hebrew poets; i.e., poets who were of an "aristocratic class" and who composed their poetry entirely for a wealthy benefactor who was in the service of a Muslim ruler. We know, indeed, that Hasdai Ibn Shaprut, a minister in the court of the caliph of Córdoba, 'Abd al-Rahmān III, did support a few such poets. After him Samuel Ibn Naghrillah, prime minister of the Muslim king of Granada in the eleventh century, may have supported the young Ibn Gairol for a very brief period (even this is far from certain), but aside from these there is absolutely no record of anyone that could remotely be called a "court poet."

Two things are of supreme importance about the stature of the Hebrew poets of Spain: they were almost all of the "working class," often desperately poor (as were Ibn Gabirol and Judah ha-Levy, the latter hardly a "doctor" as has been claimed), and they were almost without exception scholars of renown in fields such as philosophy, science, biblical exegesis, and even Jewish law. The list of the foremost Hebrew poets reads, indeed, like a veritable "Who's Who" of Jewish scholars: Ibn Gabirol, Abraham Ibn ᶜEzra, Judah ha-Levy, Moses Ibn ᶜEzra, Joseph Ibn Ṣaddiq, etc. Nor should we forget that Ibn Naghrillah himself won far more renown in medieval Spain, both in his lifetime and for centuries after, as an authority on Jewish law and apparently even on the Bible than he did as a poet (only in Egypt and in Yemen did any memory of his poetry survive). These facts certainly helped make, if not respectable at least acceptable, the theme of love—both of boys and women (no less objectionable to religious sensibilities).

We may now turn our attention to one more subject which again needs to be put to rest in the most emphatic terms: the "reality" of the poetry; i.e., did Jews in medieval Spain (and elsewhere, for that matter) actually engage in sexual practices with boys? Emphatically, the answer is yes. To a large extent, I thought I had already established this in the previous article.[22] However, it needs to be emphasized, especially in light of new evidence. Some of the Arabic poetry of the period itself reveals that Jewish boys, like boys in all cultures, were not above submitting to the advances of male lovers. A Muslim poet of Silves (in southern Portugal) during the Almoravid dynasty of the early twelfth century wrote a poem about a beautiful boy he encountered and who permitted him to kiss him: "I was then like Moses, who when he saw the light turned towards it with no other intent than to seek its warmth, and found there a secret colloquy with God."[23] Among the greatest of the Arabic poets of that period was a Jew, or possibly a convert to Islam, Abū Isḥaq Ibrāhīm Ibn Sahl al-Isrā'īlī (d. 1260), famous for his love poetry and particularly about two of his boy lovers, one a Jew named Mūsā (Moses) and the other a Muslim named Muḥammad. An even earlier Muslim poet, Abu ᶜAmir Ibn Shuhaid, whose work probably influenced Dante, wrote about a Jewish boy in Córdoba:

> There appeared a star [boy] in the Gate of the Jews
>   whose appearance eclipsed all beauty.
> When the Jews saw him at their gate
>   they thought him in his beauty to be Joseph.[24]

I have already previously given an example of a Hebrew poem about a Muslim boy, that of Moses Ibn ᶜEzra, and elsewhere I have quoted a similar poem from him about a Muslim woman (nor is that the only instance of such verses in Hebrew poetry).[25]

To muster now more positive evidence than the merely literary, the Muslim writer "al-Dabbī" (who cannot be the author of the same name who wrote a biographical encyclopedia in the twelfth century) reports that when he was in Almería, he was told by the *faqīh* (Muslim judge) in the year 1087–88 that he saw the Jewish *wazīr* (government minister; unfortunately not named) of the ruler Muhammad (not "Ahmad") al-Muᶜtasim in the baths with a Muslim youth named Muḥammad, whom the Jew affectionately called "Muḥammadell," with the diminutive suffix. The later al-Dabbī, Abū Jaᶜfar Ahmad b. Yaḥyī possibly a grandson, reports that the *faqīh* killed this Jewish *wazīr* for having thus insulted (the name of) the Prophet; but this is no doubt an apocryphal tale of his own invention, perhaps because he was scandalized by the obvious pederastic relationship with a boy who bore the Prophet's name.[26]

Nor are all the accounts of sexual activities with Jewish boys confined to Muslim Spain. In Christian Spain in the thirteenth century, probably in Aragón-Catalonia, some twenty Christian witnesses gave testimony before a Jewish court that two Jewish boys, one aged eleven and the other twelve, were engaging in sex with each other. The rabbi of the community asked the opinion of the great legal authority Solomon Ibn Adret as to whether the testimony should be accepted and what the punishment should be. Ibn Adret replied impatiently that he didn't need to give an answer about the testimony (obviously it should be believed). As to the punishment, a child younger than thirteen years and a day is not subject to punishment. If one were less than that (so, probably, the text should read) and the other older, the older is punished and the younger is exempt. But if the younger child is not yet nine years old, then even the older child is not punished because of him, for intercourse with one younger than nine is not considered intercourse.

What is astonishing about this ruling, aside from the extremely lenient attitude and not a word said about at least warning the boys not to engage in such behavior, is that the decision and supporting legal texts is based entirely on rules dealing with intercourse with females. He completely ignored the very clear and strict ruling of Maimonides which deals specifically with sex with boys and minors.[27]

Nor was such activity confined to Jews of Spain, of course. While we rarely hear of cases from other countries, this is due to the paucity of sources and to the undoubted effort to confine knowledge of such cases to the local communities involved. However, it happens that one of the most famous medieval Jewish rabbis, Ḥayyim b. Yiṣḥaq of Vienna (author of the important collection of responsa, Or zeruaᶜ), asked the opinion of Ibn Adret about a case that occurred in Vienna. The wife of a certain Rabbi Jonah had complained publicly in the market that her husband was a heretic and that she had seen him having sexual relations with his male slave and once even with his own son, and with others whom she had as witnesses. She even hired a Gentile to complain to the government and seek the penalty of burning her husband! Incredibly, perhaps, various rabbis who dealt with the case were inclined to judge her—as an informer. Ibn Adret was very reluctant to give an opinion, except to say that the woman's witnesses need have no fear of the threat of excommunication which Rabbi Jonah wished to impose upon them if they testified.[28]

At still a later date, we find the famous rabbi of Turkey, Elijah Mizrahi, has a responsum dealing with the sexton of a synagogue who engaged in sex with a boy in the synagogue—and so we have come full circle from the very similar case in eleventh-century Spain.[29] Homosexuality and pederasty existed, of course, among the Christians in Spain, just as it did elsewhere in medieval Christian Europe, but this is not the place to enter into that and I reserve the details for a future book.

As for Muslim society in Spain, the examples are too numerous to detail, and I will content myself with two interesting sources. The Arabic *maqāma* (a rhymed prose novella), *al-Maqāma al-Qurṭubiya*, falsely attributed to al-Fath Ibn Khāqān of Granada, reviles the famous philologist Ibn al-Sīd al-Baṭalyawsī of Valencia (1052–1127) in telling of his having to flee Córdoba after being sexually involved with three sons of influential citizens. The story is also reported by al-Maqqarī, who says they were not just sons of influential citizens, but sons of the ruler of Córdoba, Ibn al-Hajj.[30]

Boy prostitutes were also common, as we know from Rosenthal's book *Hashish* (cited in my "'Deal Gently'" article), but also in al-Andalus. In the Almoravid reign, they were ordered expelled from the city of Seville.[31]

Thus, while poetry does not always reflect the personal experiences of the poet, as was already observed by an early Muslim writer on poetics who wrote that a poet ought not be criticized if he says something morally objectionable, for he is only required to write good poetic description, we have nonetheless sufficient evidence to prove the existence of sexual activity between men and boys to justify the conclusion that this poetry is very real indeed.[32] More importantly, from a literary viewpoint at least, there is the evidence of our senses, for the sincerity and depth of the emotion expressed reflects a very real knowledge of boys and very real infatuation, at least, if not love.

Many of the traditional ideas about this (indeed, about many other things concerning Hebrew poetry) must simply be abandoned. These include such false notions as that Ibn Gabirol was "incapable" of loving women and never wrote love poetry about them at all, which as I have shown elsewhere is completely wrong.[33] So, for instance, the famous Israeli author Jacob Fichman, in his introduction to a collection of Hebrew love poems of all periods, claimed that Moses Ibn ᶜEzra's poetry was more lyrical, more emotional, that his imagery is "real" whereas the other medieval poets were only interested in displaying their technique.[34] Such claims betray an essential ignorance of medieval Hebrew poetry in general.

In the last century scholars were either particularly confused about this kind of poetry or deliberately sought to mislead their readers. Thus, Carmoly published Samuel Ibn Naghrillah's beautiful and clever poem about the "stammering boy," which I have translated and discussed in detail, and there he said it was about a woman! Abraham Geiger (*Salomo Gabirol und seine Dichtungen* [Leipzig, 1867], 151, Anm. 82) correctly recognized that the subject was masculine, and so also Luzzatto in the introduction to his edition of the *Diwan* of Judah ha-Levy (Lyck, 1864), except that he made the peculiar remark: "But I do not desire to copy here that poem and explain it in order not to mix the profane with the holy." A pious copyist of one manuscript "explained" the poem in the following way: "these lines were made by the wife of the *nagid* about her husband who stuttered." While ridiculing this, Jacob Egers totally ignored the sound interpretations of both Geiger and Luzzatto, both of which he cited, and perversely interpreted this and some other "boy" poems as referring to women.[35]

What was it that was considered beautiful and seductive about the boys who were the subjects of this poetry? The answer is, simply, exactly that which is found in all such poetry, whether Greek or Arabic or the poetry of medieval Christian Europe, and so down to our own day. Already Ḥayyim Schirmann, the greatest authority on medieval Hebrew poetry, observed, in a largely ignored article, that love in our poetry was exclusively *physical*, an ardent desire for the beautiful woman or boy, and not praise of the intelligence or character of the beloved. The only exceptions are one poem of Moses Ibn ᶜEzra and a couple of poems of Todros Abulafia, of which Schirmann says they reflect a kind of "spiritual love" but that this is foreign to medieval Hebrew style. No doubt Todros was influenced by the "courtly love" ideal of Christian poetry in his time.[36] However, Todros Abulafia certainly composed a great many love poems about the physical beauty of both women and boys, some fairly erotic. Nevertheless, I do not include a discussion of those here, for there is some doubt as to whether these poems are not, in fact, mere literary technique on his part.

No better example could perhaps be cited than the following lines of Judah al-Harizi concerning a boy:

Graceful gazelle, he is the image of Joseph in his beauty,
    And on his head like the crown of Helem [Zech. 6.14]
My soul is under the sole of his foot like a dot
    And he is haughty and proud above me like an exclamation point
I approached the garden of his face like a thief
    To gather the delights of his mouth and eat them,
    And the sun of his cheeks rose on me—
It is my "bloodguilt" and I will pay with my soul.[37]

(On the last line, cf. Ex. 22.2[3]. The point is that the lover must pay the penalty for his "theft" of the kiss.) The boy, "gazelle" (*ṣevy* in Hebrew, an image borrowed from Song of Songs), is compared to Joseph, the traditional image of beauty both in Hebrew and Arabic legend. The second line, while drawing from an obscure verse in Zechariah as its immediate source (the word Helem was necessary for the rhyme), relates also to Song of Songs 7.5, as the next-to-last line ("I approached the garden of his face like a thief") does to Song of Songs 4.16. The lover humiliates himself before the object of his desire, like a "point" (the poet used a term for a vowel point in Hebrew) under the sole of his foot. The haughtiness of the boy is also typical of our poetry. This is to be understood as a combination of adolescent bravado—which is at the same time vulnerability, seeking to protect himself in a world which he does not fully understand, and a seeming rejection of the advances of the would-be lover. When, in desperation, the poet "steals" a kiss, the cheeks of the boy turn red (embarrassment? anger?), which the poet turns into a metaphor for the sun of the biblical law concerning the thief: if the sun has risen on him, then there is blood-guilt.

This concludes, then, with yet another typical motif: the "martyrdom of love." The notion that the lover is willing to die, or is already dying from the frustration of unfulfilled desires, is very prevalent in Arabic and Hebrew poetry, dating in the former at least to Abū Nuwãs: "If you say 'Die,' I will die in my place / and if you say 'Live,' I will rise to life from my death." Already in the tenth century the famous Andalusian poet Ibn ᶜAbd Rabbihi wrote about a boy: "Oh, this in whose eyes is my illness and healing / and in his hand my death and my life."[38]

Love, passion, is a disease or madness (already, of course, in classical Greek and Latin literature), from which the lover may either go mad or "die." An example is found in one of Ibn Gabirol's poems:

Before my pain increases
   go, my brothers, hasten to Gilead [cf. Jer. 46.11]
And bring a balm for the pain of my heart;
   perhaps in it will be healing and support.
[One] perfect in beauty has trampled my heart
   when he trod, and stepped [on] the dust of the earth.
I shall await him, and my hope is deferred,
   and he draws my heart forever and ever.[39]

The cause of his "love-sickness" is a beautiful boy whose walk is likened to trampling on the poet's heart. "Hope deferred" immediately would call to the mind of the medieval reader Proverbs 13.12: "Hope deferred makes the heart sick."

Ibn Gabirol returned to the theme, and used the metaphor of "drawing the heart" in another way, in the following:

He steals the sleep of my eyes and I'm unaware—
   the like has never been seen nor heard!
I draw his heart, slowly, lest he be weary
   and he draws my heart, slowly, lest I pine away.
If doom [fate] comes to me, gently,
   and pity me, perhaps the evil will end.
Although I have not embraced you, for you is
   my desire nevertheless;
   strangers devour what I embrace.
I was asked to describe his form and said
   'Your soul has torn the sphere of the earth!'
Come, let us sing to the vine a song
   and in it, bow to God and to him bend down.[40]

This poem requires more explanation than the previous one. The opening line is undoubtedly "borrowed" from the famous poem of Ibn Naghrillah, "God, change please the heart of the dove who stole my slumber," etc., where there is the multiple pun of *gozal* (dove), *gazal* (stole) and (implied) *ghazãl* (gazelle in Arabic; boy), as I have elsewhere explained.[41] The term translated here as "doom," or fate is found in Ezek. 7.7, and the translation is dependent on medieval authorities. However, note also the same word apparently meaning a diadem of beauty (Isa. 28.5) and the very similar word *ṣafir* for a buck (Dan. 8.5). All this makes us wonder if the poet did not have different levels of meaning in mind: either, should my fate come to me, then deal gently with me (addressed, possibly, to the boy himself), or else: should I get the boy I desire, then (addressed to his companions, or even his rebukers), deal gently with me. Meanwhile, he laments his present fate: strangers devour (enjoy) what he can only hope for in vain. When asked to describe his beauty, the poet replies that this is impossible. Faced with that impossibility, and with the inevitability of his unfulfilled desires, he says to his friends "Come, let us drink," and so forget his sorrows (this is a "transition verse," and the remainder of the poem praises wine).

To return to our discussion of what was considered beauty, Ibn Naghrillah tells us very clearly:

> I see in you beauty like the sun in its brightness
> and splendor like the heavens with its moon shining.
> How goodly and how pleasant if it would be given you
> that your figure should last forever:
> Beautiful form, beauty and fortune and pure
> body, as the very heaven in its purity.
> Not good is the beauty of one who lies in
> the night of his death
> and is not roused, and does not see evermore the dawn.
> There is no good except a good name and good wine
> and singing
> well and a good companion to drink his merchandise.
> Bow to God by day, and bow down to the cup
> at night and drink it and forget sorrow.[42]

Here, beauty (hod; cf. Hos. 14.7) is also "manhood" (Prov. 5.9; Dan. 10.8), and "fortune" is not wealth but rather as in Prov. 12.27, where the *Targum* translates "luck, fortune" (cf. Ibn ᶜEzra's commentary there, and cf. *Taᶜanit* 29b). "Pure" is innocent (cf. Deut. 19.10, Ps. 24.4, etc.); hardly "clean" as Jarden apparently interpreted it. "Not good is the beauty of one who lies in death," etc. Here the poet contrasts the beauty and youth of the boy with the state of one "old" and near death (the lover himself); but as always, this is not to be taken literally, for "old" was a relative concept in love. The last line is an example of "audacity" in our poetry: here, worship God by day, but wine by night.

An even stronger example of audacity, and one which also discusses the theme of beauty in a boy, is the following poem of Ibn Gabirol:

> Lily upon a stalk like foliage
> are you upon a pillar a capital of gold.
> Sun upon [its] sphere slowly walking—ah!
> stealing gently the heart without breaking in.
> A fawn, embarrassed because of you—see
> pearl change its appearance to [a reddish stone].
> . . . .
> Write, brothers of instruction, my words
> upon the ark of testimony as a token
> For his heart—which, if the sons of Aaron find it,
> before it let them offer incense.

> If Aaron wrapped himself with a holy mitre, lo
>   the lock of your cheeks is a diadem of beauty.
> The form of a golden cherub with stretched-out wing
>   as the cherubim upon the covering.[43]

The boy, in the supple beauty of his body, is compared to a *shoshan* (Ar. *sūsan*), a lily, or possibly a narcissus, or to the sun slowly moving across the sky. These metaphors (gold, the sun) do not necessarily mean the boy has blond hair, although Arabic poets, and particularly in Spain, praised blond boys or women as the most desirable.

The meaning of the third line is that the boy, a "fawn" (young "gazelle"), is embarrassed when you look at him, and so his face changes to a reddish color (the meaning of *soheret*, cf. Esther 1.6, is uncertain; Ibn Janah renders it by the Arabic word *fūsfaisa*, apparently a kind of phosphorus—unless he meant *fusaifisā*, "mosaic pavement").

The audacity comes in the last lines where the poet says the holy mitre of Aaron, the priest, was nothing compared to the boy's locks (the word he uses, *ṣiyṣ*, can indeed mean "lock" as in Ezek. 8.3, but normally refers to a "fringe," as the ritual fringe on garments; Num. 15.38), which are . . . a diadem of beauty (here *ṣiyṣ* refers to the diadem of the high priest, on which the ineffable name of God was written; however, another meaning of the word is "blossom," and even this is associated with the blossoming rod of Aaron [Num. 17.23]). Finally, the beauty of the boy's body is compared to the cherubim on the ark (Ex. 25.20). Interestingly, Jewish tradition maintained that the faces of the cherubim in the Temple were those of boys.

Few poets expressed love of boys as beautifully as Moses Ibn ᶜEzra. In one of these poems he writes:

> The gazelle is like a branch of spices, and almost
>   because of his delicacy and tenderness
>   the wind shakes him,
> But a heart of stone is in him, pitiless for
>   the captive of lust, faint and weary of heart
> . . . .
> I asked of him to kiss his lips
>   in a mouth fragrant like spice, or like his body.
> He answered me: "Kiss my mouth and I will satiate you
>   from my tongue, its pleasant wine and honey."
> With his mouth he healed what he had wounded
>   with his eyes,
>   and he said that his deeds were smiting and healing.[44]

The appeal of the boy was that he was at once innocent and seductive, and we sense that these boys were fully aware of what was going on and very much in control of the situation. Here, the boy is frankly seducing the older lover.

Kissing, tasting the "wine of saliva" of the mouth, was not the only form of sexual involvement with boys, as seen in the following short poems of this same poet:

> Ah, for the time when its years
> in my eyes were, with the gazelle, a few days;
> Days when a fresh and an old body were united
> by the girdle of night until they were as one.[45]

Or this:

> A bough, onyx and light of the sun upon
> his face, which never departs;
> And offspring of the pomegranate are his fruits—
> but the hand of the lover does not feel them![46]

Abraham Ibn ᶜEzra, no relation at all to Moses but the father-in-law of Judah ha-Levy and perhaps the greatest biblical commentator of all time, also wrote poetry, among which are some of the "*seviy*" type. One of these is quite witty, but also extremely explicit:

> An old man of stooped stature, bent like a bow—
> A youth asked him, "What is the price of your bow?"
> He replied, "Quiet, my son; for if you live
> Freely will I give it to you when your time comes."[47]

What is apparently a quite innocent little epigram takes on a different meaning when we realize that the word *qeshet*, "bow," also means "penis." In the Talmud, *Sanhedrin* 92a, for example, we find the following: "R. Elᶜazar said, Whoever gazes upon one's shame, his virility shall be emptied, for it is written: Shame shall empty your bow [Habakkuk 3.9]." Incidentally, if memory serves, Shakespeare also has a speech in the last act of "Taming of the Shrew" in which "bow" is used to mean penis.

In the long history of sexuality, as old as man himself, there has always been room for much variety. In the medieval period men, Christian, Muslim and Jew, were rarely exclusively homosexual. It was, however, quite "normal" to enjoy the physical beauty and delights—and one might add also the exuberant joy and innocent seductiveness—of adolescent boys.

Notes

1   Plato, *The Symposium*, ed. R.G. Bury (Cambridge, 1932), viii.

2   See, for instance, Strato, *Musa Puerilis* 4, in the *Greek Anthology*, ed. and tr. W.R. Paton (Loeb Classical Library Series), IV, 285:

> I delight in the prime of a boy of twelve, but one of thirteen is much more desirable. He who is fourteen is still sweeter flower of the Loves, and one who is just beginning his fifteenth year is yet more delightful. The sixteenth year is that of the gods, and as for the seventeenth it is not for me, but for Zeus, to seek it. But if one has a desire for those still older, he no longer plays, but now seeks "And answering him back" [a common expression in Homer; i.e., he seeks a complete responsive love relationship.]

3   *Affairs of the Heart* (*Amores*), in the L.C.L. ed. and tr. of Lucian's complete works, vol. 8, 155, 165 (see there, 219–21, for an excellent statement as to what prompted the love of boys).

4   *Judaism and Hellenism* (Philadelphia, 1974), I, 84–85.

5   "The Jews in Greek and Latin Literature," in S. Safrai, M. Stern, eds., *The Jewish People in the First Century* (Philadelphia, 1976), II, 1123.

6   Norman Bentwich, "Of Jews and Hebraism in the Greek Anthology," *Jewish Quarterly Review* (n.s.) 23 (1932), 183, 184. Bentwich made Meleager an "apostate" Jew. Perhaps misled by this, F.A. Wright, *Poets of the Greek Anthology*, invented a "Greek father" and a "Jewish mother" for Meleager, as noted by Harold A. Harris, *Greek Athletes and the Jews* (Cardiff, 1976), 45.

7   "'Deal Gently with the Young Man': Love of Boys in Medieval Hebrew Poetry of Spain," *Speculum* 57 (1982), 20–51; and "The Care and Feeding of Gazelles: Medieval Arabic and Hebrew Love Poetry," in Moshé Lazar and Norris J. Lacy, eds., *Poetics of Love in the Middle Ages* (Fairfax, Va.: George Mason University Press, 1989), 95–118.

8   "Reading Medieval Hebrew Love Poetry," *AJS* (Association for Jewish Studies) *Review* 2 (1977), 111–29 (esp. 128).

9   "'My Beloved Is Like a Gazelle': Imagery of the Beloved Boy in Religious Hebrew Poetry," *Hebrew Annual Review* 8 (1984), 143–65.

10   "A Miniature Anthology of Medieval Hebrew Love Poems," *Prooftexts* 5 (1985), 110. This view is only slightly revised in his booklet *Wine, Women & Death* (Philadelphia, 1986), 86–88 (see my review in *Hebrew Studies* 28 [1987], 201–03).

11   Art. cit., 113–14 (a position he seems to have backed away from again in the book).

12   For Islam, see, e.g., the statements quoted in Franz Rosenthal, "Sex and Society in Islamic Popular Literature," in *Society and the Sexes in Medieval Islam* (Sixth Giorgio della Vida Biennial Conference, Malibu, Calif., 1979), 37. Moses b. Maimon (Maimonides), who though not a rabbi was perhaps the greatest medieval Jewish legal authority, severely condemned homosexuality also in his *Guide of the Perplexed* III. 49 (tr. Shlomo Pines [Chicago, 1963], 606).

13   *Perush Kallah Rabbatai*, ed. Barukh Toledano (Jerusalem, 1901), 20 (cf. Yitzhak Raphael's introduction to his ed. of Abraham's *Sefer ha-manhig* [Jerusalem, 1978], I, 18. Raphael believed the commentary to have been written in Toledo before the *Manhig*, which was written ca. 1204–05. On the contrary, it would appear that Toledano was correct in his carefully argued reasoning that it was written after the latter work (Raphael, 74).

14   This was the work known as *Minhat Yehudah* by Judah Ibn Shabbetai, the first draft of which was composed in 1188, rewritten in 1208 and revised in 1225. Thus, unless we assume the unlikely possibility that Abraham saw the first draft, there is no way he could have referred to the existence of such a work before he completed his *Manhig* in 1204–05. The *Minhat Yehudah*, incidentally, was dedicated to Abraham Ibn al-Fakhkhār, and Abraham b. Natan was a protegé of the rival Ibn Shushan family, both of Toledo (see on Ibn Shabbetai's book, and the genre of "deceits of women," my article "The 'Wiles of Women' Motif in Medieval Hebrew Literature of Spain," *Hebrew Annual Review* 2 [1978], 52–67).

15   *Improvement of the Moral Qualities*, ed. (Arabic) and tr. (English) Stephen S. Wise (New York, 1901), 26 (text), 69 (tr.).

16   Moses b. Maimon, *Pirqey Mosheh* ("Medical aphorism"), ed. Suessmann Muntner (Jerusalem, 1959) ch. 3.1 (38); Hippocrates, *De humana natura* 12.

17   Roth, *Maimonides. Essays and Texts. 850th Anniversary* (Madison, Wisc., 1985), 54–55, and cf. 114–15. I had earlier called attention to this passage and its significance in my article "Jewish Reactions to the ᶜ*Arabiyya* and the Renaissance of Hebrew in Spain," *Journal of Semitic Studies* 28 (1963), 81–82, of that article. I regret that James Monroe saw fit to plagiarize my work, including my original translation from the Judeo-Arabic text of Maimonides, in his article "Maimonides on the Mozarabic

Lyric," *La Corónica* 17 (1988), 18–32. That a scholar of this reputation needs to clothe himself in the work of others is unfortunate.

18   *Zohar* on Song of Songs 3 (*Zohar ḥadash* [Jerusalem, 1955], vol. 21. (Actually it is uncertain that this part is by Moses.)

19   *Iggeret musar*, ed. A.M. Habermann (Jerusalem, 1946), 24–25.

20   *Tosefta, Sanhedrin* 12.10; and cf. the talmudic tractate itself (*Sanhedrin* f. 101a): "the rabbis taught, he who reads a passage of Song of Songs and makes it like a song, or reads a passage in a tavern not at its time [i.e., in a secular manner] brings evil to the world," etc.

21   Commentary (Arabic) to Isa. 59.13; ed. Samuel Poznanski, "Hebräisch-arabische Sprachvergleichungen bei Jehúda ibn Bal^cām," *Zeitschrift der deutschen morgenländischen Gesellschaft* 70 (1916), 453.

22   "'Deal Gently'," 22–23; cf. also Yom Tov Assis, "Sexual Behavior in Medieval Hispano-Jewish Society," in Adda Rapoport-Alpert and Steven J. Zipperstein, eds., *Jewish History. Essays in Honour of Chimen Abramsky* (London, 1988), 50–51, citing my article (but not crediting me with the discovery of the responsum which I first brought to light there).

23   ^cAlī b. Mūsā Ibn Sa'īd al-Maghrībī, *Rāyāt al-mubarrizīn*, ed. and tr. Emilio García Gómez, *El libro de las banderas de los campeones* (Madrid, 1942), 158–59. The reference is to the burning bush, of course, but specifically to a Muslim tradition that Moses was on the road trembling with cold when he saw the light of what he thought was a bonfire, and turned aside to seek its warmth, without suspecting that God would speak to him.

24   Aḥamd b. Muhammad al-Maqqarī, *Nafh al-tīb* (*Analectes*), ed. R.P. Dozy (Leiden, 1858), I, 98; cf. *The History of the Mohammedan Dynasties in Spain*, tr. Pascual de Gayangos (London, 1840–43), I, 207 and 487, n. 20 (however, Gayangos translated the poem completely incorrectly).

25   ""Deal Gently,'" 44, and my "The Care and Feeding of Gazelles," 107.

26   The first story is told by José María Millás Vallicrosa, "Desinencias adjetivales romances en la onomástica de nuestros judíos, in *Estudios dedicados a Menéndez Pidal* (Madrid, 1950), I, 131. Unfortunately, he cited no source, but Millás was always entirely reliable. For the tale of the second al-Ḍabbī, see his *Bughyat al-multamis fī ta^crikh ahl al-Andalus*, ed. Francisco Cordera and J. Ribera (*Biblioteca arábico-hispana* III; Madrid, 1885), 332–33.

27   Ibn Adret, *She'elot u-teshuvot* V, No. 176 (Vilna, 1884; photo rpt., Jerusalem, 1976); Moses b. Maimon, *Mishneh Torah, Nashim, "Isurey biah"* 1.14 (cf. my "'Deal Gently,'" 23).

28   Ibn Adret, ibid., vol. I, No. 571 (Vienna, 1812; photo rpt. Jerusalem, 1976).

29   *She'elot u-teshuvot* I, No. 81 (Constantinople, 1610).

30   H. Nemah, "Andalusian Maqāmāt," *Journal of Arabic Literature* 5 (1974), 85; Aḥmad b. Muhammad al-Maqqarī, *Analectes sur l'histoire et la littérature des Arabes d'Espagne*, ed. (Arabic) R.P. Dozy, et al. (Leiden, 1858–61), II, 195, 310; see the translation of the poem he composed about the boys in A. R. Nykl, *Hispano-Arabic Poetry* (Baltimore, 1964), 236.

31   Muhammad b. Ahmad Ibn ^cAbdun, *Seville musulmane au début du XII siècle*, tr. E. Lévi-Provençal (Paris, 1947), but I cite the Spanish translation *Sevilla a comienzos del siglo XII* (Madrid, 1948), 157, sec. 170.

32   Qudāma Ibn Ja^cfar (d. ca. 922); see J.C. Bürgel, "Love, Lust and Longing: Eroticism in Early Islam," in the previously cited *Society and Sexes in Medieval Islam* (see n. 12 above), 84. Bürgel's otherwise excellent paper does not mention, except very briefly, the love of boys.

33   See, for example Ibn Gabirol's poems about women translated and discussed in my previously cited "The Care and Feeding of Gazelles," and in my "The Lyric Tradition in Hebrew Secular Poetry of Medieval Spain," *Hispanic Journal* 2 (1981), esp. 10–11.

34   Hayyim Toren, ed., *Shirey ahavah be-Yisrael* (Jerusalem, 1948), 6–7.

35   "Das stammeldne Mädchen," ᶜ*Ateret ṣevy. Jubelschrift zum siebzigsten Geburtstage des Prof. Dr. H*[einrich] *Graetz* (Breslau, 1887), 116–26.

36   "L'amour spirituel dans la poesie hébraique du Moyen Age," *Trudy XXV mezhdunarodnogo kongressa vostokovedov* (25th International Congress of Orientalists, Moscow, 1962), I, 395–401.

37   *Tahkemony*, Gate 50 (conveniently available in Hayyim Schirmann, ed., *ha-Shirah ha-ᶜivirit bi-Sefarad u-vi-Provens* (Jerusalem, 1954), II, 203–04, No. 3.

38   Abū Nuwās, *Dīwān* (Cairo, 1898), 368. For the poem of Ibn ᶜAbd Rabbihi and other examples, see Nykl, *Hispano-Arabic Poetry*, 39 and 236. See generally on this subject the excellent article of M.A. Manzalaoui, "Tragic Ends of Lovers: medieval Islam and the Latin West," E.S. Shaffer, ed., *Comparative Criticism*, A Yearbook (Cambridge, 1979), vol. I, 37–52.

39   *Shirey ha-hol*, ed. Dov Jarden (Jerusalem, 1975), 369, No. 215; *Shlomoh Ibn Gabirol shirey ha-hol*, ed. Hayyim Schirmann and H. Brody (Jerusalem, 1975), 89, No. 144.

40   Hayyim Schirmann, ed. *Shirimhadashim min ha-genizah* (Jerusalem, 1965), 175–78.

41   "'Deal Gently,'" 36.

42   *Divan Shmuel ha-nagid*, ed. Dov Jarden (Jerusalem, 1966), 291, No. 147.

43   *Shirey ha-hol*, ed. Jarden, 135–36, No. 64; ed. Schirmann-Brody, 143, No. 116.

44   *Shirey ha-hol*, ed. H. Brody (Berlin, 1935), 178, No. 179.

45   Ibid., 344, No. 1.

46   Ibid., 346, No. 18.

47   Ed. A.M. Habermann, ᶜ*Iyyun be-shirah u-vi-piyyuṭ* (Jerusalem, 1972), 77 (citing also Ms. Oxford 1986). I follow the preferable reading of the Oxford manuscript.

BESTIALITY IN THE MIDDLE AGES

Joyce E. Salisbury

In the past, there has been a broad range of attitudes toward bestiality. The classical tradition embraced nature to the degree that in mythology even Gods became animals to have intercourse with humans or humans disguised themselves as animals to satisfy their lust. The other extreme might be best expressed by the execution or incarceration of people for bestiality through the modern period. This essay will begin to explore this change by looking at the changing attitudes toward sexual intercourse with animals in the Middle Ages.

Medieval thinkers inherited the classical tradition with its view of the relationship between humans and animals. Since in mythology, Gods appeared as animals to have intercourse with humans, one assumes that such relationships were not completely forbidden. This view is reaffirmed in the classical "scientific" treatises on animals. Aelian's *On the Characteristics of Animals*, written ca. A.D. 170, was a popular, influential compendium of animal lore. Within his treatise, Aelian included more than a dozen examples of bestiality. He tells of a groom who fell in love with a mare, consummated the "strange union" and continued the relationship until he was killed by the mare's jealous foal.[1] A goatherd "under an erotic impulse lay with the prettiest of his goats" and was so pleased with the relationship that he brought the goat gifts and sweet herbs to make "her mouth fragrant for him if he should want to kiss her." In this case, too, jealousy was his downfall, for he was killed by an angry he-goat. The neighbors of the goatherd did not object to the relationship, but instead built the young man a fine tomb and deified the issue of the union, a goat with the face of a man. Aelian's moral of this tale was not to avoid such intercourse, but to recall that animals can be jealous just as humans can.[2]

Curiously, most of Aelian's anecdotes of bestiality identified the animals as the initiators in the relationships, and Aelian's catalogue includes a wide variety of animals. He tells us that "baboons and goats are lecherous, and . . . have intercourse with women. . . . And even hounds have assaulted women. . . . One woman in Rome was accused of adultery and the adulterer was a hound. Baboons are wanton and have fallen madly in love with girls and have even raped them."[3] In another instance, a snake fell in love with a girl and consummated the union repeatedly. The girl tried to escape his amorous overtures by leaving for a month, but upon her return, she discovered the snake was constant in his affections and angry at "being despised."[4] A ram and a goose fell in love with a beautiful woman musician.[5]

Men and boys were also objects of animal affection, but Aelian usually left the gender of the animal ambiguous, allowing for the possibility that he imagined some of these love affairs were homosexual. Aelian again showed the diversity of animals subject to such passion. "I am told that a dog fell in love with Glauce the harpist. Some, however, assert that it was not a dog but a ram, while others say it was a goose. And at Soli in Cilicia a dog loved a boy of the name of Xenophon; at Sparta another boy in the prime of life by reason of his beauty caused a jackdaw to fall sick of love."[6] In other instances, a goose fell in love with a handsome boy[7] and a female snake succumbed to passion with a gooseherd, and protected her beloved from the jealousy of the male snake.[8] Aelian continued his inventory describing the affections of a horse,[9] a dolphin[10] and a seal who was remarkable because its love object was an ugly diver. In the moral of this story, Aelian tells us not to be surprised at such an event, for people even sometimes fall in love with ugly people.

All these examples from Aelian yield some significant insights into Aelian's (and the classical) view of animals. Animals were not very different from people. They suffered the same emotions of love, anger, and jealousy; they had the same aesthetic appreciation for beauty, and were able at times to set aside that aesthetic to appreciate someone from the highest motives of love. Aelian tells us that the God of Love "does not overlook even brute beasts. . . ."[12] And as he summarizes, "So it seems that it is in fact a characteristic of animals to fall in love not only with their companions . . . but even with those who bear no relation to them at all. . . ."[13] There was so little distinction between humans and animals, that half-human/half-animal births were unremarkable, and the Gods could appear as animals without diminishing their power and stature. It seems to have been no threat to people's humanity to appear at times indistinguishable from animals.

As the early church fathers wrestled with the classical heritage and selected those elements suitable for Christians, they rejected this intimate relationship between humans and animals. The Bible was clear on maintaining appropriate distance between species: "You shall not let your cattle breed with a different kind; you shall not sow your field with two kinds of seed. . . ."[14] This prohibition also applied to bestiality: "You shall not lie with any beast and defile yourself with it, neither shall any woman give herself to a beast to lie with it: it is perversion."[15] With this clear directive, Augustine wrote with scorn of pagans who worshipped Gods who behaved so scandalously: "Jupiter himself is changed into a bull or a swan to enjoy the favors of some woman or other."[16] This rejection of such intimacy affected the selection of the classical heritage. Aelian's work was highly influential during the Middle Ages. It influenced the works of natural history and animal lore culminating in the bestiaries of the twelfth century. Yet, while copyists drew many of the interesting animal anecdotes from Aelian, including many sexual ones, such as that of the transsexual hyenas,[17] they did not reproduce the tales of bestial intercourse. The Middle Ages had its own tradition on the subject that drew more from Christian texts than from classical.

Christians and their animals were supposed to keep a greater distance than their classical counterparts. Like their classical predecessors, the early church fathers recognized the similarities between human and animal bodies, but for them the irreconcilable differences between the two kept humans apart from the animal world. The human soul was made in the image of God,[18] and with this soul came reason. As Augustine said, "Nothing else ranks me above the brute animal except the fact that I am a rational animal."[19] It was through this difference that people were given dominion over animals, and it was because of this ontological distance that churchmen believed people and animals should avoid sexual intercourse. Humans should not "brutalize" their rational and immortal souls.

The early medieval desire to prohibit bestiality came from Christian impulses that began with patristic reflections on human nature. The pagan Germanic tradition seemed to have lacked this concern. None of the early Germanic secular law codes prohibited bestiality. These codes suggest that for the early Germans animals were important as property and as food, and it was in these areas that they legislated. Such legislation was not aimed at preserving the boundaries between human and animal by restricting sexual contact.

Early Christian legislation in the West on sexual behavior developed from two main sources. First was formal conciliar decrees originating primarily in the East. Among its sexual regulations, the Council of Ancyra in 314 prescribed strict penalties against bestiality: fifteen years of penance for youths under twenty, twenty-five years for married people over twenty, and for a married person over fifty, he or she must wait until the end of life to receive communion.[20] This strict penalty seems to derive from patristic concern for maintaining the strict distinction between human and animal, rational and irrational, for the Council introduces its prohibition by writing "Of those who have acted or who act irrationally. . . ."[21] Humans were not to descend to the level of irrational beasts in their sexual lives. Basil of Caesarea continued Eastern prohibitions in his "Letter #217" written in 375, and which acquired the weight of conciliar decree in the Greek east by the sixth century[22] calling for fifteen years' penance.[23]

Evidence for the Eastern tradition on the subject was not limited to conciliar decrees. John Climacus the seventh-century monastic writer in the Holy Land addressed the question of bestiality with a realism and even compassion that the formal conciliar legislation lacked. John recognized the difficulties facing the celibate in their battles against lust. He joined patristic thinkers in stressing the distance between humans and animals, saying ". . . the height of lechery is that one raves even over animals and over inanimate things . . .,"[24] and told of the dangers of lust to men who were able to avoid temptation by women. He described a man who had been in charge of the monastery's donkeys and who "wretchedly fell under the

sway of wild donkeys and was deluded." The moral warning for John was that
". . . the sin of fornication does not require the availability of another
body."[25] Yet, for John the sin was not unredeemable, for he described a
bursar of the monastery who had fallen into sin with the monastery's
animals in his youth, confessed his sin, and was let go with a simple
reprimand.[26] This simple reprimand indicates that in spite of strict Eastern
conciliar legislation, the Greek church never feared bestial intercourse as
much as the West. It seemed no more disruptive to society than other sexual
alternatives, so churchmen repeatedly lowered the strict penances that
remained on the books from conciliar legislation.[27] In the West, however,
over time churchmen looked at the act with increasing concern.

The west combined Eastern legislation with its own penitential
tradition. The penitentials began in Ireland as a way to offer churchmen
manuals for healing the souls of their sinful parishioners. These handbooks
spread to Anglo-Saxon England, then to the Continent, and influenced the
important canonical collections of the eleventh century and later. As Pierre
Payer explained: "For 500 years the penitential literature continued to be
the principal agent in the formation and transmission of a code of sexual
morality."[28]

A review of the body of penitential legislation reveals that the history
of attitudes toward bestiality was more complicated than the clear-cut
Eastern prohibitions suggested. For example, the Eastern father Basil seems
to have considered sexual sins to be largely one category, linking
bestiality, homosexuality, and adultery together by assigning all three the
same penance.[29] However, most Western churchmen, including the authors
of the penitentials, thought sexual sins carried different weights, and that
opinion shaped the future of sexual legislation. Churchmen faced a number
of decisions about the mitigating and aggravating conditions of the act, and
in making these decisions, they shaped perceptions of both the sin of
bestiality and of the animals themselves.

All the secular Germanic law codes recognized age as a mitigating
factor in determining penalties,[30] and the penitentials continued this
practice. The age of maturity varied in the secular codes from ten to fifteen
years,[31] and the ecclesiastical legislation also varied from an unspecified
age of maturity to accepting the age of twenty as defined by the Council of
Ancyra. The Vinnian penitential gives a light penance of 100 days for a
"boy" who sinned with a beast before taking the sacrament[32] and the
Cummean Penitential confirms this penance and adds that a boy of fifteen
years would do penance for forty days.[33]

Age was linked to maturity and responsibility, and the codes further tie
this to matrimony. As the Council of Ancyra stipulated a longer penance for
anyone over twenty-five and married, so did the penitentials believe the sin
was greater if an individual violated the marital bond by having intercourse
with an animal. For example, even the mild penitential of Columbanus
required six months' penance for bestiality for a single man and double that
for a married man.[34] Churchmen might show some understanding for the

sexual sins of a youth (whether they be homosexual or bestial play), but once a man had taken up the responsibilities of age and marriage, his sexual energies were to be channelled only through the marital bond.

Ecclesiastical rank also brought additional responsibilities, the violation of which brought concomitantly greater penalties in ecclesiastical law. Churchmen were supposed to be even more spiritual than the laity, and thus even further from the beasts. Therefore, the sin of bestiality represented a greater crossing of boundaries. In the sixth-century Welsh Grove of Victory penitential and the penitential of Columbanus, clergy were to add one year to penalties for laity. In the case of bestiality, that would bring the penalty up to two and a half years or three years,[35] and these examples are representative of all the penitentials.

Factors of age, marital status, and ecclesiastical rank served to increase or decrease penances for all sexual sins. There were also mitigating factors specifically for bestiality, beginning with ecclesiastical attempts to define the nature of the act of bestiality. The character of the penitentials themselves required developing a hierarchical ranking of sins. For example, if adultery were worse than fornication, it received a greater penance. As churchmen determined bestiality's rank among the sexual sins, they began to reveal their view of the relation between humans and animals. The earliest penitentials ranked bestiality close to masturbation, making it a not very serious sexual sin. For example, the Columbanus penitential (ca. 591) directly equates "fornication with a beast" with one who "has defiled himself with his own hands." Both received a penalty of six months or a year, depending on marital status.[36] This penitential ranks other sexual sins more seriously: fornicating once received three years' penance, and sodomy received ten.[37] The influential Cummean penitential (ca. 660) reveals a similar ranking. A boy of fifteen engaging in bestiality or mutual masturbation before communion would receive forty days' penance in either case. Again for comparison, this penitential prescribes seven years for sodomy.[38]

By treating bestiality like masturbation, churchmen were in fact showing that they perceived animals to be profoundly different from humans. They rank almost as John Climacus' "inanimate things," hardly worthy of consideration. The mild penance also showed their security in the differences between humans and animals. When there was no threat of blurring the lines between species there was no need to regulate strictly the distinctions. The early Germanic world viewed animals primarily as property and food, and this attitude was reflected in the early Irish penitentials that sexual intercourse with animals was the same as sexual intercourse with nothing at all. This casual attitude toward animals and intercourse with them began to change as the conciliar legislation from the East began to influence the penitential compilers.

The Council of Ancyra equated bestiality with homosexuality: "Concerning those who . . . mix with cattle or who are polluted with males."[39] This association reached Visigothic Spain as early as the late sixth century with Martin of Braga who included the prohibition in his Canons appended to the Second Council of Braga.[40] This shaped the Spanish penitentials from the seventh or early eighth centuries, which gave a twenty-year penance for both those who committed sodomy and bestiality.[41]

The Irish penitentials slowly became influenced by the Council of Ancyra via the continental writings. As they were affected by the conciliar decrees, the insular penitentials shifted their perspective on the nature of bestiality. The ninth-century Carolingian capitularies directly quoted the Council of Ancyra linking bestiality with homosexuality,[42] and the English Bigotian penitential compiled no earlier than the late eighth-century, and heavily influenced by the continental material, completed the shift from treating bestiality as masturbation to treating it as homosexuality. It says, "One who often has intercourse with a male or with beasts, shall do penance for ten years."[43]

Equating homosexuality with bestiality not only escalated the penalty, but it expressed (and perhaps began to cause) a change in the way people looked at animals. Instead of being an inanimate, irrelevant object, the animal partner became just that, a partner in an "unnatural" act, just as homosexuality was an act between two partners. This shift raised the possibility of other mitigating or aggravating factors in the penalties for the act, the nature of the animal partner involved.

The eighth-century penitential of Egbert of York says the "Confessor ought to distinguish between the quality of the cattle [domestic animals] or of the men,"[44] but unfortunately, offers no advice on what "qualities" domestic animals might have that would affect the nature of the act. The Spanish penitential increased the penalty for intercourse with "small animals,"[45] but does not explain why. Were small animals considered more "bestial" than large animals? Was the size differential considered more "unnatural?" Was this a practical consideration recognizing the damage likely to be done to a small animal? The sources do not yield satisfactory answers to these questions, but the inclusion of the qualifier demonstrates the changing view of animals that saw them as something other than objects for masturbatory use. In this same spirit, the St. Hubert penitential of the mid-ninth century distinguished between sexual relations with "clean" or "unclean" animals, prescribing twelve years' penance for the former and fifteen years' for the latter.[46] The Eastern Slavic penitentials (influenced by the Council of Ancyra) also distinguished among animals, stipulating greater penalty for intercourse with a mammal than with a fowl,[47] again without explaining the reasons for the differentiation.

Once the animal was seen as a partner in the sin, the issue arose not only of varying the penalty depending on the animal, but of whether punishment was appropriate for the animal. The penitentials before the mid-eighth century, which dealt with bestiality as masturbation, thus effectively ignoring the animal, also ignored the prospect of penalty. After the animal became a participant in the equivalent of a homosexual encounter, churchmen turned to Leviticus and found the prescribed penalty for an animal involved in sexual contact: "If a man lies with a beast he shall be put to death; and you shall kill the beast."[48] The Canons of Theodore of Canterbury (ca. 741) elaborated on the biblical requirement. "Animals polluted by coitus with men are to be killed the flesh thrown to dogs. But what they give birth to may be used and the hides taken."[49] This was reaffirmed in the ninth century by Hrabanus Maurus in his response to the moral question of what to do with animals involved in bestiality. He quoted the Levitical condemnation, and reasserted the practical view expressed by Theodore, that there was no reason to waste the offspring of the animal.[50]

By the turn of the millennium, church law on the subject of bestiality had developed enough to have demonstrated a change in perceptions of animals and of sin. As churchmen increased their fear of the sin of bestiality, the animal participants were given greater importance. From nonentities, they had become participants that had to share in, indeed receive greater punishment than the human participant. Church legislation then influenced secular laws. The later Norwegian codes included its prohibition specifically as part of newly incorporated Christian legislation. The Norwegian laws of the eleventh century forbad men to have carnal dealings with animals "which is forbidden to all Christians" and which "destroys his rights as a Christian," and prescribed the severe penalty of castration and outlawry.[51]

The growing body of legislation on the subject left a complexity of laws that were often contradictory. This is, of course, inevitable as ideas change, but as early as the late eighth century, Egbert of York expressed his confusion with the penitential tradition on the subject: "He who has sinned with cattle or a mule, ten years; some [say] seven; some, three; some, one; some a hundred days as for boys."[52] The early canonists of the eleventh century inherited and continued the discrepancies observed by Egbert. Burchard of Worms (ca. 1020) and Ivo of Chartres (ca. 1090) repeated the previous prohibitions including the penalties ranging from forty days to twenty-five years' penance.[53]

In repeating the Levitical requirement that the animal be killed, Ivo added an explanation absent from the penitential tradition. He said that the animal must be killed to erase any memory of the act.[54] This reasoning seems to provide a corrective to considering the animals as partners bearing some responsibility and thus deserving punishment for the act. Ivo's explanation made the killing important to the surviving humans, not to punish any animal guilt. This explanation was continued by the later scholastics, who insisted that the separation between humans and animals was so great that animals did not have enough will for one to "attribute praise or blame to acts of animals. . . ."[55] However, Ivo's explanation of the necessity to execute the animal, and the subsequent reiteration of it[56] appeared because people had become more uncertain about the distance between human and animal natures. On the one hand, they believed animals to be sufficiently involved in the sexual act to deserve some punishment, but on the other hand to treat animals as equally blameworthy would be to violate the desired separation that was the point of much of this increasing legislation. In their uncertainty, they repeatedly asserted the differences in a way that had been unnecessary in the early Middle Ages when people took the differences for granted. By focusing on memory as the purpose for execution of "guilty" animals, medieval thinkers could have both punishment and distance.

In spite of Ivo's addition to the growing body of legislation on bestiality, the canonists by and large did not dwell on bestial intercourse. Burchard, Ivo, and the influential Gratian concentrated on legislation to solidify the marriage bond and increasingly to criminalize extra-marital sexual offenses.[57] As Professor Brundage summarized, in the eleventh century bestiality joined homosexuality and masturbation as "unnatural" offenses carrying "sanction of *infamia*" depriving the practitioners of respectable status in society.[58] However, in the eleventh and twelfth centuries outside the classrooms of the canon lawyers, people's views on the relationship between humans and animals was changing in a way that would cause the scholastics of the thirteenth century to rank bestiality as the worst of the sexual sins.

Throughout this period of growing sexual legislation against bestiality, there is no reason to think that the act was particularly curtailed. Modern surveys on bestiality reveal a fairly consistent pattern of activity in rural areas, and it is likely that it was so throughout the Middle Ages. Some non-legal sources report the activity in a fairly casual manner. For example, a tenth-century Spanish text describing famous physicians relates one anecdote from the career of Yahya' b. Ishaq, who practiced medicine in Cordoba. The author tells how a peasant came to Cordoba crying out in pain. The peasant told the physician he had been unable to urinate for several days. The physician ordered him to place his swollen penis on a flat rock and quickly punched it with his fist. The patient fainted in pain, but pus and urine flowed, curing the peasant. The physician explained his diagnosis: "you have cohabited in the anus of an animal and therefore a grain of animal feed was stuck in your urethra and caused the inflammation." The moral of the story as told by the author was not to avoid the dangers of animal contacts, but instead he said this anecdote showed the brilliance of the physician to make such an accurate diagnosis.[59]

Gerald of Wales, the twelfth-century chronicler reported instances of bestiality in his work the "Topography of Ireland." Gerald claimed that the Irish were so rural "living like beasts" that they were "particularly addicted to such abominations."[60] Gerald then proceeded to tell tales of men who had intercourse with cows and women with goats and a lion.[61] Gerald's anecdotes reveal a bit more than either his anti-Irish bias or popular belief of the prevalence of human/animal intercourse. Gerald recounts tales about half-human births generated from such intercourse. Men fathered half-human monsters on their cows or oxen, and Gerald stretches credulity to its limits by recounting an incident of a man who passed a calf from his bowels as "punishment attendant on some atrocious crime," presumably having been sodomized and impregnated by a bull.[62] These anecdotes caused Gerald to reflect upon exactly what it meant to be human rather than animal,[63] and this question is the significant one here. If some people in the twelfth century could tell stories of such births, then the lines that separated human from animal were beginning to blur. The penitential writers had seen no reason to kill the calves of animals that had been used for sexual intercourse, so great was the separation between the species. By the twelfth century, Gerald of Wales would wonder whether the killing of such an animal should be considered homicide since it was half human.[64] As the lines began to blur, legislation against bestiality began to increase to try to create more firm boundaries between human and animal when popular imagination was losing track of such barriers.

Also in the twelfth century, people seemed to worry more about demons than they had earlier, and this contributed to increasing ecclesiastical concern with bestial intercourse. While the early medieval world had its share of demons, churchmen did not believe they could physically interfere with humans, particularly sexually. Demons made of air were not substantial enough to have sexual intercourse with humans; such experiences were illusions or dreams.[65] By the twelfth century, that changed. Incubi and succubi seemed everywhere to seduce women and men who did not guard themselves against such attacks.[66] Jeffrey Burton Russell attributed this change to the development of scholastic theory,[67] and in addition to this, I believe, that it is not coincidental that the belief in substantial incubi coincided with the growth of the idea of purgatory in the twelfth century.[68] Just as souls were seen to be substantial enough to punish, demons were substantial enough to have intercourse with humans. Not only could demons have intercourse, they could beget offspring upon human women. Scholastic thinkers explained the process by which such generation could take place between species. Aquinas is representative in his explanation that ". . . for the purpose of generation, one and the same demon being succubus to a man and transferring the seed thus received by acting as incubus to a woman."[69]

The development of this idea (and this fear) was rapid. In the twelfth century Guibert of Nogent told of demons who lusted after women,[70] and even his mother was attacked by a lustful demon.[71] Also in the twelfth century, Gerald of Wales told of a man who was begotten by a demon upon his mother.[72] By the thirteenth century, the gossipy chronicler Caesarius of Heisterbach had so many stories of demons having intercourse with men and women that he could say "there is nothing wonderful that demons should make love to women. . . ."[73] In the thirteenth century, belief in such intercourse was manifested in the courts. In 1275 at Toulouse, Angèle de la Barthe was convicted for having intercourse for several years with an incubus. She was burned.[74] Courts were also prepared to protect society against the issue of such a union. In 1308, Guichard, Bishop of Troyes, was tried for sorcery, and among the charges was the claim that he was the son of an incubus.[75]

In virtually all the incubal appearances recounted in the sources, demons appeared as handsome men or beautiful women. But in the popular imagination, the devil and his followers were pictured as half or wholly animal. The devil could appear as almost any animal, but most frequently as serpent, goat, or dog.[76] Therefore, the word attached to the sin of demon intercourse was bestiality. Thus, the serious, heretical, crime of intercourse with the devil was linked with the earlier seemingly innocuous act of intercourse with an irrelevant object. As Professor Brundage showed, during the twelfth century all "unnatural" intercourse began to be linked with heresy,[77] and bestiality became inexorably joined with the heresy of dealing with the devil.

By the thirteenth century, the animal world seemed much more threatening than it had in the early Middle Ages, when animals were separated from humans by an unbreachable chasm of difference. Now, animals were believed to be able to mingle with humanity and create offspring, and the fearful world of demons was linked to the earthly menagerie. These ideas shaped the composition of the *Summae* that represented the highest development of medieval thought.

Thomas of Chobham (ca. 1158–1233) identified bestiality as a grave sin calling for extreme penalties. The human offender was required to do penance for fifteen years (twenty if married), and in addition, go barefoot throughout his or her life, never enter church, and permanently abstain from meat, fish and intoxicants. The animal participant was to be killed, burned and buried to prevent any memory of the crime to be renewed.[78] Alexander of Hales (d. 1245) continued Thomas' abhorrence, although in less detail. Alexander identified bestiality as the greatest sin against nature, for to sin with "another species" and with "things irrational" represents the furthest departure from human nature, and thus the most unnatural sin. The penalty for Alexander was simple and extreme: kill the human and the animal, and thus erase the memory of the act with the participants.[79]

The greatest of the schoolmen, Thomas Aquinas (1224–1274) continued this view of bestiality, but elaborated it into a more complete system. He said that "unnatural vice" was "contrary to the natural order of the venereal act as becoming to the human race." The four kinds of unnatural vice were masturbation, homosexuality, "unnatural manner of copulation," and bestiality.[80] Within these unnatural vices, Aquinas ranked bestiality as the worst, "the most grievous is the sin of bestiality, because use of the due species is not observed."[81] In Thomas' ranking one can see that the guiding principle was to observe and preserve the differences between humans and animals. The most grievous sin was to forget one's humanity while engaging in the act that along with consent defined marriage.

Although the schoolmen ranked bestiality as the most "grievous of sins," in practice the courts were more preoccupied with prosecuting homosexuality.[82] Yet, as these theorists increasingly legislated the exclusivity and the sanctity of the marital bond, they also solidified the idea of the evil of corrupting that bond by "unnatural" intercourse and the mingling of species.

The ideas of the theorists slowly found expression in the secular law codes. For example, the late thirteenth-century Spanish law code, the *Siete Partidas*, expresses the increasingly repressive attitude toward homosexuality and bestiality. It calls for the death penalty for both sexual crimes.[83] Such repressive legislation brought with it the idea that the separation between humans and animals was a matter that could not be taken for granted, and thus had to be actively preserved. This laid the groundwork for our attitudes toward the practice, as well as future prosecution of the act. As part of the late medieval and Renaissance active prosecution of homosexuality and sodomy, bestiality, too, became a matter for capital enforcement. In the fifteenth-century trial records of Majorca, several people were executed for the crime (no longer just sin) of bestiality,[84] and by 1534, bestiality had become a capital crime in England.[85] Through the seventeenth century there were a number of executions of both humans and animals for the crime.[86] Keith Thomas notes that these executions occurred because the early modern period was uncertain about the distinction between humans and animals: ". . . the separateness of the human race was thought so precarious, so easily lost, that the boundary had been so tightly guarded."[87] The occasional practice of bestiality seems to continue to be part of rural society. Kinsey calculated that forty to fifty percent of all farm boys experienced some sort of sexual animal contact,[88] and modern society's revulsion of this act has led to periodic imprisonment, commitment in mental institutions, or social ostracism.[89] It seems we have not given up the uncertainty of our place with respect to the animal world that developed in the high Middle Ages.

Notes

1 Aelian. *On the Characteristics of Animals.* trans. A.F. Scholfield (Cambridge, Mass., 1959), IV, 8, vol. 1, 223.

2 Aelian VI, 42, vol. 2, 59–61.

3 Aelian VII, 19, vol. 2, 127.

4 Aelian VI, 17, vol. 2, 31–33.

5 Aelian V, 29, vol. 1, 321.

6 Aelian I, 6, vol. 1, 21.

7 Aelian V, 29, vol. 1, 21.

8 Aelian IV, 54, vol. 1, 277.

9 Aelian VI, 44, vol. 2, 63–65.

10 Aelian VI, 15, vol. 2, 27–31.

11 Aelian IV, 56, vol. 1, 279.

12 Aelian VI, 17, vol. 2, 31–33.

13 Aelian VIII, 11, vol. 2, 195.

14 Lev. 19:19

15 Lev. 18:23.

16   Augustine. *City of God.* trans. by Henry Bettenson. (Middlesex, Eng., 1972), IV, 27, 169.

17   Aelian I, 25, vol. 1, 45.

18   Ambrose."Hexameron," in *Saint Ambrose: Hexameron, Paradise, and Cain and Abel.* tr. John J. Savage (New York, 1961), 256.

19   Augustine, "Divine Providence and the Problem of Evil" tr. Robert P. Russell, in *Writings of Saint Augustine,* vol. 1, *Fathers of the Church* (New York 1948), 326.

20   Pierre J. Payer, *Sex and the Penitentials* (Toronto, 1984), 45.

21   Payer, 45.

22   Basil, "Letter 217" in *Saint Basil: The Letters,* tr. R.J. Deferrari (Cambridge, Mass., 1962), xvi.

23   Basil, "Letter 217," 110.

24   John Climacus, *The Ladder of Divine Ascent.* tr. C. Luibheid and N. Russell (New York, 1982), 283.

25   John Climacus, 175.

26   John Climacus, 102.

27   Eve Levin, *Sex and Society in the World of the Orthodox Slavs, 900–1700* (Ithaca, N.Y., 1989), 205–06.

28   Payer, 5.

29   Basil, "Letter 217," 110.

30   Rudolf Huebner, *A History of Germanic Private Law.* tr. by Francis S. Philbrick (Boston, 1918), 54–55.

31   Huebner, 54–55.

32   Ludwig Bieler, ed. *The Irish Penitentials: Scriptores Latini Hiberniae,* vol. v. (Dublin, 1963), 75.

33   "Cumean," Bieler, 115 and 129.

34   "Columbanus," Bieler, 103.

35   "Grove of Victory," Bieler, 69, and "Columbanus," Bieler, 101.

36   "Columbanus," Bieler, 103.

37   "Columbanus," Bieler, 97.

38   "Cummean," Bieler, 115 and 129.

39   Payer, 45.

40   "Martin's Canons," in *Patrologiae Cursus Completus, Series Latina,* ed. by Migne (Belgium, 1844–55; hereafter cited as *PL*) 84, 585.

41   Severino Gonzalez Rivas, *La Penitencia en la Primitiva Iglesia Española* (Salamanca, 1949), 177.

42   "Cap. Ab Ansegise" *PL* 97, 513–14, "Benedicti Capitulam Collect Lib I," *PL* 97, 712.

43   "Bigotian," Bieler, 221.

44   Payer, 173, n. 153.

45   Gonzalez Rivas, 177.

46   Payer, 60.

47   Levin, 205.

48   Lev 20:15.

49   F.W.H. Wasserschleben, *Die Bussordnungen der abendländischen Kirche* (Halle, 1851), 213. See also Payer, 45.

50   Payer, 184, n. 91.

51   Laurence M. Larson, *The Earliest Norwegian Laws: Being the Gulathing Law and the Frostating Law* (New York, 1935).

52   Payer, 173, n. 150.

53 Burchard of Worms, *PL* 140, 924–926, 968; Ivo of Chartres, *PL* 161, 682, 686.

54 Ivo 9, 108, *PL* 161, 686.

55 Thomas Aquinas, *Summa Theologica*, tr. the English Dominican Fathers (New York, 1947), Q,6,2, 617.

56 This explanation for executing the animal extended beyond the canonists. For example, Gerald of Wales told of a lion which was executed for having intercourse with a woman. He said the lion was killed "not for its guilt, of which its nature as a brute exculpated it, but as a memorial. . . ." Giraldus Cambrensis, "Topography of Ireland," in *The Historical Works of Giraldus Cambrensis*, ed. Thomas Wright (London, 1887), 87.

57 See James A. Brundage, *Law, Sex, and Christian Society in Medieval Europe* (Chicago, 1987), 228 and 250.

58 Brundage, 207.

59 J. Vernet, "Los Médicos Andaluces en el *Libro de las Generaciones de Médicos*—ibn Yulyul," *Anuario de Estudios Medievales* 5 (1968), 456–57.

60 Giraldus, 124 and 85.

61 Giraldus, 344, 85, 86, 87.

62 Giraldus, 85 and 344.

63 Giraldus, 85.

64 Giraldus, 85.

65 Nicolas Kiessling, *The Incubus in English Literature: Provenance and Progeny* (Washington, 1977), 21.

66 See Jeffrey Burton Russell, *Lucifer: The Devil in the Middle Ages* (Ithaca, 1984), for the development in the 12th century of the idea of demons substantial enough for intercourse with humans. See also Kiessling, 21–28, for elaborations of the same theme.

67 Russell, *Lucifer*, 183.

68 Jacques LeGoff, *The Birth of Purgatory*, tr. Arthur Goldhammer (Chicago, 1981): "Purgatory did not exist before 1170 at the earliest," 135.

69 Thomas Aquinas, *On the Power of God*, II, 6,8, tr. English Dominican Fathers (Westminster, Md., 1952), 211.

70 Guibert of Nogent, *Self and Society in Medieval France* tr. J.F. Benton (New York, 1970), 223.

71 Guibert, 70.

72 Giraldus, 411.

73 Caesarius of Heisterbach, *Dialogue on Miracles*, tr. H. von E. Schott et al. (London, 1929), 134. See pages 134–39 for accounts of demon intercourse.

74 Kiessling, 24.

75 A. Rigault, *Le Procès de Guicard, évêque de Troyes*, (Paris, 1896), 111.

76 See Russell, *Lucifer*, 67, for an account of the devil's animal manifestations.

77 Brundage, 313.

78 Thomas of Chobham, *Summa Confessorum*, ed. F. Broomfield (Paris, 1968), 402–03. See also Brundage, 400, who discusses Thomas's *Summa* as "the most detailed treatment of bestiality in the early 13th century.

79 Alexander de Hales, *Summa Theologica. Tomus III*, Secunda Pars, Secundi Libri (Florence, 1930), 653–55.

80 Aquinas, *Summa* Q 154, art. 11, 1825.

81 Aquinas, *Summa* Q 154, art. 12, 1826.

82 Brundage, 473.

83 Scott, ed., *Las Siete Partidas* (Chicago, 1931), 1427.

84 Ramon Rossello, *Homosexualitat a Mallorca a L'dat Mitjana* (Barcelona, 1978), 13–14.

85 Keith Thomas, *Man and the Natural World* (New York, 1983), 39.

86 See Thomas, 119, for some examples.

87 Thomas, 135.

88 Alfred C. Kinsey, *Sexual Behavior in the Human Male* (Philadelphia, 1948), 671.

89 See Caldwell, *Animal Contacts* (Girard, Kans., 1948), for discussions of prosecution of the act in the twentieth century. See also R.E.L. Masters, *Forbidden Sexual Behavior and Morality* (New York, 1962), for other instances of prosecution.

THE STORY OF THE *VÖLSI*, AN OLD NORSE ANECDOTE OF CONVERSION

by Andreas Heusler*
[translated by Peter Nelson]

King Olaf II (d. 1030), who fortified Christianity in Norway, was a principal figure in Icelandic sagas. The events of his life have been passed down to us in a great many accounts. The latest and most elaborate of these, the *Flateyiarbók* (ca. 1390), presents a peculiar episode, the so-called *Volsapáttr* ("little story of the *Völsi*").[1] Its content, briefly, is as follows:

In northernmost Norway, in a remote area, stood a farmstead that was inhabited by a farmer, his wife, a son and daughter, a farmhand and a maid-servant. At this time the new Christian faith had yet to reach the area. Once, at the end of autumn, their fat and aged draught horse died, and as he was being skinned, to be eaten according to the heathen custom, the farmhand cut off the penis and was about to discard it; but the farmer's son took it and presented this "*Völsi*," as he called it, amid much laughter, to the three women in the farmhouse. Here he speaks one verse of the saga. The mother then took the *Völsi* for herself, dried it, wrapped it in a cloth, and sprinkled it with herbs so that it would not rot. By the power of the devil the *Völsi* grew in size and strength. The farmer's wife bestowed all her faith upon it, and it became her god. The others in the house also were lured through her to this erroneous belief. Every evening the *Völsi* was brought into the room and passed from one person to the next, each one speaking a verse over it.

The pious King Olaf, who had received word of this heathenism, sailed to the north country. There he anchored his ships in the vicinity of the farmer's house and ordered two of his companions to go with him to seek shelter there. The first one was a distinguished Norwegian, the other a loyal Icelandic skald for King Thormod. Disguising themselves with gray cloaks, they entered the farmstead unnoticed at dusk and seated themselves in the room. When the farmer's daughter came in to light the lantern, the men asked her for her name, and each of them called himself Grímr. The girl, however, seeing the gold jewelry and the costly garments that glittered beneath their cloaks, recognized the king. In a verse she revealed her knowledge, but Olaf ordered her not to betray them. Soon the others entered the room and began to converse with the strangers. Finally, when the table

187

was set and the meal was laid out, the farmer's wife came in with the *Völsi* in her arms. She pulled back the cloths covering it and presented it to her husband, speaking the following verse:

Empowered are you, *Völsi*,	lMay Mömir receive
and brought forth,	lthis sacrificial offering!
preserved in linen	lBut you, Farmer,
and sustained with herbs.	ltake the *Völsi* upon yourself!

Thereupon the farmer recited his verse and gave the *Völsi* to his son, who then passed it on to his sister; it then proceeded to the farmhand and then to the maid-servant, until finally it reached the three strangers, last among them Olaf himself. All in their turn spoke one verse of four lines. The structure of these verses remains the same as in our example: in the first half the speaker expresses personal sentiments, and in the concluding line turns toward the next recipient; the third line is an unaltered refrain. In the original text it went:

þiggi Mǫrnir	lþetta blœti!
[May Mornir receive	lthis veneration/offering]

The scene concludes with Olaf throwing the *Völsi* to the family's large dog, tearing off his disguise and converting all the inhabitants of the house to Christianity. One and a half verses spoken by the farmer's wife, expressing her outrage at their guest's blasphemy, accompany this concluding section.

The writer of the *Flateyiarbók* inserted this story in a quite improbable place: in the midst of the preparations for Olaf's last great battle, he writes, "King Olaf heard yet again that the land was still unchristian in some places. . . ." In this makeshift way, the collector of the Olaf stories created a context for this homey interlude. But on the next page he has changed his opinion of the time of the event, for he now writes, "Once, before King Olaf fled the land before King Canute, it had come to pass that. . . ." So the original source evidently had the simple beginning, "Once upon a time. . . ." Other clues also support the idea that the *Völsi* story passed into the larger corpus of the *Flateyiarbók* from a previous written account.

How is this mixture of prose and poetry to be interpreted? The assumption that the anecdote's source was a poem and that the verses inserted into it are parts of this poem cannot derive from the mere fact that the story begins with "As is reported in an old poem . . .," and that further on it refers to "the beginning of the poem" and to the "old poets." These expressions give the impression of a flourish that was common to certain fable narratives.[2] But even if they are intended seriously, they can prove only that a writer, perhaps our writer of ca. 1390, perceived an old poem as the basis of the episode.

One could just as easily base that assumption about its origins on the contention that the first of the inserted verses (which is thought to stand after the prose "in the beginning of the poem") is given as direct narrative:

Once there lived a farmer	who had a son,
and his elderly wife	with the goddess of gold
on a plot of land,	the hero—and a daughter
I know not where;	of shrewd sense indeed.

By any kind of analogy, these expository lines cannot have been created as an ornamental stanza, as a kind of *Lausavísa* [single-verse poems] for our anecdote. They presuppose a closed poetic narrative. But one should make clear: a coherent poetic account made up of verses of both narrative and speech would be a complete unit in Old Norse literature. What is told in prose form in this story would be inconceivable in verse form. According to the standards of Nordic alliterative poetry, the *Völsi* story is not song material. But judging from its content, that narrative verse, "Once there lived a farmer . . .," is general enough to belong to any other context. And the other verses, all of them dialogue verses, are proper *Lausavísur*. They create, together with the prose, a well-wrought whole; nothing supports the view that more verses existed at one time, and that the *Volsapáttr* ever was anything other than what it now is: a novella embellished with loose verses.

Whether the daughter's first spoken verse, which deviates metrically from the rest, was a later addition or revision, is no longer of importance. I consider the repositioning of the verse to the end of the text, as was done in the *Corpus poëticum boreale,* to be unjustified. (This verse and the first, i.e., narrative, verse are not considered in the quotations which follow.) Otherwise I wish only to make the following critical observation on the text: the surplus line 2 in the verse of the farmhand found its way in as a distant reminder of the *Rígspula 4,* and that the words "greatly to thrust" in the verse of the maid-servant should be considered an extraneous gloss on the verses.

The decided similarity of the first verse lines "Once there lived a farmer . . ." with the beginning of the "*Grettisfœrsla*," which G. Vigfússon was able to decipher thus:

A farmer did dwell,
Now note properly,

---

in the valley beyond

merely provides a further indication of the peculiar kind of folk poetry which flourished particularly in the sixteenth century, the "*sögukvœdi*" or "*sagnakvœdi*."[3] Our manuscript, the *Flateyiarbók,* places this type of poetry—or perhaps only these poetic openings—already in the fourteenth century, and it is conceivable that such an opening verse found its way into our text. But this sheds no light on the *Volsapáttr* itself or on the dialogued *Lausavísur,* which rightfully belongs to it; I therefore refrain from using the name "*Völsafœrsla*."

G. Vigfússon, in another place, has brought up the Penillion, the popular Welsh song quatrains. Any significant similarity with the *Völsi* verses, however, is not apparent to me.

An Icelandic folktale recorded in the seventeenth century contains a drastically rearranged and distorted form of the *Völsi* story, only without the verse addresses.[4] But this early descendant does nothing to explain the *Volsapáttr*.

Our entire episode is foreign to the older sagas of St. Olaf, and it likewise deviates completely from the Olaf conversion stories. Elsewhere the king appears "with open visor," i.e., without a disguise wherever he wishes to convert people, and he leaves no doubts that he will use force whenever kindly words prove ineffectual. Of the anecdotes about the older Olaf, too, which are generally of a more adventurous cast, only one is distantly comparable to the *Volsapáttr* (see below). Seen as a whole, our text is most likely an early work, let us say roughly from the thirteenth or fourteenth century. Its absence in Snorri and in the editor of the independent Olaf saga of ca. 1250 is hardly proof that no one told or knew of the story at that time; for a serious historian would have had to pass over it without comment. The possibility that some kind of real event from Olaf's life underlies it cannot be dismissed flatly, though certainly this historical kernel would have dissolved into fantastic motifs. Our summary of the contents shows plainly enough that the role of Olaf as well as the conditions in the farmhouse are the stuff of weightless fable.

The appearance of the King—the incognito visit with two companions;[5] their being recognized by the wise daughter, who perceives the gold underneath the plain cloaks; the command to say nothing; the striking gesture of throwing down the mask—these aspects of the tale could easily have been produced from the author's own imagination or his memories of folktales and folktale-like adventure sagas. However, the kernel of the anecdote, the *Völsi* cult, is another matter. This highly aberrant feature, which stands alone in Old Norse literature, cannot have been the invention of an Icelandic author of the thirteenth or fourteenth century. Apart from the general psychological impossibility, there is the fact that strange suggestions of customs of other times and peoples are evident. Moreover, the small tale harbors contradictions that indicate an errant or arbitrary application of stock narrative features.

This does not appear to be a case of borrowing from a foreign source. Nor is it possible, after what has been put forth above, to believe it to be a genuine descendant from conversion times. The story of the *Völsi*, I believe, was created in this way: the Icelandic author knew of a contemporary superstitious custom, probably practiced somewhere in Norway, a vestige of heathen times. This he shaped into the basis for an Olaf tale in which the King/Saint appears almost like a fairy-tale figure to put an end to the fabulous heathenism.

To get a general picture of this superstitious practice, let us take a close look at the following evidence of it.

In England in 1268, a *simulacrum Priapi* was set up and the hearths sprinkled with holy water: *intinctis testiculis canis in aquam benedictam.*[6] Likewise, a simulated phallus, supposedly human (*membra humana virtuti seminariae servientia super asserem artificiata)* was brought before a chorus of female singers, under *motus mimicus* and *verba impudica.*

In later folk customs we encounter the following: the sexual organs of a domestic animal slaughtered in the fall are severed and at mealtime are placed before the laborer who mowed or threshed the last stroke of the harvest;[7] or, the flesh is consumed communally but the genitalia are hung in the hallway.[8] Parts of the animal slaughtered at the harvest festival are preserved as holy objects until the end of the following harvest.[9] The tail of the ram prepared for the threshers' harvest meal is carried to the stove, specially roasted and cut into as many pieces as there are young girls present; the piece is presented to each amid much laughter.[10]

According to the Lauterbach statute of 1589, a pig which the tenantry was obliged to deliver to the feast of the Magi was led through the benches before it was slaughtered.[11] And the description of an Oxford custom, which in itself is not especially germane here, is notable for the peculiar rhyming refrain which was sung at the conclusion of each of three verses describing the serving up of a boar's head at the Christmas feast: *Caput Apri defero, Reddens laudes domino.*[12]

In these Christian customs the significance of the sacrifice has become more or less ambiguous. As a supplement, let us place against them the evidence of more distant rites.

In ancient Rome, the tail of a steed killed as part of an October sacrifice was cut off and carried directly from the Field of Mars to the royal house of Numa so that the still warm blood could drip onto an altar.[13]

In the Talmud, "a tradition is reported in which the tail of the Passover lamb is removed and presented, with the fat, to the priests, who passed it along from one to the next until it arrived at the altar, where it is salted and thrown into the fire."[14] Similar to this is the offering of the tail to the goddesses as part of the ancient Indian animal sacrifice.[15]

We should also observe the following conditions from Germanic heathen custom: the horse was considered the most esteemed heathen sacrifice,[16] hence the notions of eating horsemeat as an especially blatant relapse into heathen ways;[17] and the slaughter and disembowelment of horses as dishonest work.[18] The sacrifices of horses, dogs and humans performed in Upsala, according to Adamus Bremensis (4, 24), were accompanied by *neniae multiplices et inhonestae ideoque melius reticendae.* In Nordic sources, the only objects known to be passed around among participants in a feast are the horn or the cup (in the Minne drinking ritual). One of the regular Nordic sacrificial feasts took place in the fall.[19] After conversion, this celebration was retained by certain Norwegians in the form of a great invitation to a circle of friends.[20]

These observations, however, cannot finally give a satisfactory explanation of the *Völsi* cult, and the following outline of a theory can only be accepted speculatively. It was a rite practiced as part of the autumn sacrifice, in which the phallus of the sacrificed animal, the horse, was passed from hand to hand, each time a consecrating incantation was recited over it, until it finally completed the round and reached the altar, where it was burned (or held until the next autumn sacrifice?). A rite of this sort was maintained, in more or less diminished form and of increasingly obscure significance, into the thirteenth or fourteenth century, a by then inscrutable custom repeated as an ancient traditional communal entertainment at the beginning of winter. Out of this the author of the Volsapáttr, who was by no means unaware of the heathen undertones of this custom, forged a not quite repulsive but hardly flattering image of ancient idolatry which provoked ridicule. One wishes to say *in maiorem gloriam Sancti Olavi*, except that there is no doubt that the narrative, fabulous component of this work comes first and that the pious tendency is secondary, so much so that one would have to suppose a profane author, if only the line between clerical and lay views in Iceland were not so customarily indistinct. Out of the phallus, which originally had been a sacrificial offering, our author has made a fetish object worshiped by the peasants as their god, and he endows this fetish object with supernatural strength and stamina. Here he seizes on the contemporary notion of an inanimate object being miraculously empowered through the power of the devil,[21] a notion that belonged generally to the church's conception of heathen gods. He then omitted a sacrifice of the phallus, though it had probably already lapsed beyond recognition in the Norwegian practices from which it originated.

But here arises an odd contradiction in our story. In three places among the verses where the word blœti appears, it is evidently understood to be the *Völsi* itself.[22] From the refrain line already familiar to us,

þiggi Mǫrnir   þetta blœti

we gather that the blœti, the *Völsi*, is offered to a deity (Mǫrnir). "Mornir" must not be translated, as it might appear, as an appellation for the *Völsi*, from which would result:

May Mornir receive this veneration (homage)!

The *Völsi* is a sacrificial offering; this is the meaning which the word blœti obviously retains in the refrain:[23]

May Mornir receive this sacrificial offering!

If we examine those other three places individually, i.e., out of context, then one could indeed also translate with "sacrificial offering"; yet the more neutral meaning of "sacred relic" would also seem just as appropriate.

The narrator, however, who wants to depict the *Völsi* expressly as a deity of these peasants, must have thought of the word blœti in the sense of "sacred relic, i.e., divinely venerated object, fetish." From this standpoint, indeed, the lines 3, 3; 11, 4; and 11, 8 present no problems; however, the refrain line then renders the absurd notion that the deity *Völsi* is offered up to the deity Mornir—offered up, furthermore, in words and for appearances only. For, as we saw, it could never have amounted to a real sacrifice, even without Olaf's intervention.

Then, however, one cannot escape the further conclusion: this refrain line did not originate from the narrator, who misunderstood it, but was rather mechanically passed on by him. If our suppositions above are on the right track, then we can logically assume the following: the line was spoken at the very occasion of that superstitious custom. That Norwegians of the thirteenth or fourteenth century still clearly grasped its meaning—the summoning of a deity to receive a sacrificial gift—is very doubtful. It is more probable that the line goes back to a time when the entire practice was still alive and meaningful—in other words, that we are dealing with a genuine ritual formula from heathen sacrificial rites, the only one in all of Old Norse literature. Its characteristic stamp is without peer in Old Icelandic poetry; any sort of literary archaism is unthinkable here. On the other hand, foreign examples of invocations of divinity correspond very closely: consider the Lithuanian grain festival according to Matth. Prätorius:[24] "God and you Zeminele, we present to you this cock and hen, take them as a gift out of good will!" And especially the numerous passages in the Rigveda, e.g., ". . . accept this sacrifice, Agni!" (X 69, 4); ". . . Pause, o strong Indra, and savor your part!" (X 100, 1); ". . . Savor all this here, o eternal Agni!" (III 14, 7);

I 93,7	Partake of the drink offered,
	O bulls, o Agni-Soma, receive it, refresh yourselves!
III 28,1	Accept, Agni, our sacrifice,
	O all-knower, the baked offering
	with favor at the morning meal!
III 35,10	O Indra, by your own hand drink of the juice,
	O majestic one, or with the tongue of Agni;
	partake, o mighty one, of the sacrifice offered
	from the hand of your servant and from the pouring
	of the priest!

The first three of the following lines are like the verse in which the farmer's wife announces the passing of the holy object, while the fourth— the praise of the god—necessarily remains without its counterpart in the *Völsi*:

X 179,3	It is cooked in the kettle at the fire,
	this new sacrifice, nicely cooked I do believe;
	as a mid-day offering drink the whey, Indra,
	you who bring about much, rejoice, o you armed
	with lightning!

Yajya was the name of the verse spoken at the sacrificial offering to invite the god to partake.[25] Hence the old Indian *yajya* also finds a modest counterpart in Old Norse literature. We hear a faint echo of the "*neniae multiplices et inhonestae*," which in Iceland and elsewhere were treated all too much as "*melius reticendae*." It is peculiar that the single case of true refrain structure in Old Norse poetry—the refrains in skald songs are constituted differently—emerges in our liturgical verses 2–9. In observations on the Indian rites, Bergaigne poses the question, "could the origin of the refrain, at least in Vedic poetry, also be purely liturgical?"[26]

The question arises as to whether even more parts of the verses betray this liturgical origin. The concluding lines of verses 2–9, summoning the next person in line to take the *Völsi*, could, judging from its stereotypical structure, be imitating a ritual line, while their objective content presupposes the persons of the poem. If the line did appear in the heathen or semi-heathen practices, it must have had an unchanging form, for not all participants in a feast would have been able to find new alliterative rhymes! Line 4, 1. 2 deserves attention:

Carry the club		before the bride-women!
Berid ér beytil	/	*fyr brúdkonur!*

Brúdkona, according to the dictionaries, signifies only those women who sit with the bride on the women's bench (the pallr), the "bride's maids." But this meaning does not fit here. I do not know whether those who spoke, heard and wrote the line were able to interpret *brúdkonur,* for the sake of coherence, as "women folk" in general. The originator of the line will, in any case, have used the word with its correct meaning. Then, however, the verses were intended for a different context. We find support (if not absolute proof) for this in the plural imperative form *Berid ér . . .*: compared to the other lines, it is nevertheless conspicuous in this place, since the brother, as the third in line, receives the *Völsi* and simply passes it on to his female neighbor. The line seems like a formula spoken at a wedding banquet, in which *beytill* would have to signify an imitation priapus, as seen earlier in the English chronicle, as well as in the Roman Tutunus, *in cuius sinu pudendo nubentes praesident, ut illorum pudicitiam prior deus delibasse videatur*[27]*—cuius immanibus pudendis horrentique fascino vestras inequitare matronas et auspicabile ducitis et optatis.*[28] This line 4,1.2 causes one to think immediately of the line in the *Prymskvida* 30, 3.4:

Carry in the hammer,		to sanctify the bride!
Berid inn hamar,		/*brúdi at vígia!*

Here indeed a similar phallic origin is supposed, and yet the line is too distant for the line from the *Volsapáttr* to be a mere imitation of it. But I am unable to find further support for this combination; in the rich old Indian wedding ritual I have come upon no counterpart.[29] And likewise, as regards this line 4, 3.4:

they shall make wet		the handle tonight
pær skulu vingul		/*væta í aptan*

I cannot determine whether it constitutes the original continuation of the formula, nor where allegorical meaning ends and symbolic-literal meaning begins.

Several words which are not found outside of the *Volsapáttr also* support the possibility of an antecedent in these verses. *Blæti,* whose exact meaning the author has not retained, has been discussed earlier. Less problematic are *beytill* (club, pestle; 4, 1) and *andkæta* (mutual delight; 7,

4), as these could be new constructions from *bauta* and *kátr*, respectively. On the other hand, *vingull* (1, 3. 4, 3) and above all the word *völsi* itself are old constructions which did not descend from the Old Icelandic vocabulary. *Völsi* may have persisted, furtively, in semi-heathen oaths while dying out in the actual vernacular. This is not to say that the verses containing these words were created from the ritual source: the inventor of the *Völsi* scene took sufficient liberties to use these existing expressions in new verses.[30]

The *Völsi* tale as an almost farce-like extension of an actual superstition bears some resemblance to the tale which rightfully has often been cited as a valuable testament to the Nerthus cult:[31] the anecdote about Gunnarr Helmingr, who wrestles in Sweden with the diabolically enlivened *Freysbilde,* sits on a cart next to the heathen priestess and then plays the role of the god at the sacrificial rituals.[32] In this anecdote reliable reports of Swedish paganism, which extended well into the twelfth century, have been turned to good account here, fantastically and with no little humor; and again it arrives at the *pointe* of the Christian king (this time Olaf Tryggvason) triumphing over dark superstition. Undoubtedly also belonging to the conscious, adventurous embellishment here is how the pregnancy of the priestess is taken by the faithful Swedes as a good omen, ultimately strengthening their faith in God. Indeed the entire portrayal of the priestess as the god's wife was probably freely invented for the purposes of this tale. The Greek celebrations of "holy matrimony" have no equal.

The most substantial motif of the *Volsapáttr,* the actual sacrificial service, was not "phallic" in the sense that "the phallic god *Völsi*" was worshiped (as has been asserted by some scholars). Rather, this was only a misinterpretation, or reinterpretation, on the part of the fourteenth-century narrator. In reality the *Völsi* was no godhead; it was not the object, but rather the means of worship. This Icelandic anecdote is in no way evidence of a Germanic fetish ritual.

However, it is certainly plausible that the godhead, in whose worship the phallus was passed around and (originally) presented on an altar, was a phallic god, a god of fertility. One thinks immediately of Freyr, commended in the much-cited testimonial of Adam von Bremen,[33] and named as a god receiving sacrificial offerings at the harvest feasts, sometimes alone[34] and sometimes among other gods,[35] and in whose name, moreover, horses were blessed.[36]

But what is the meaning of *Maurnir* (the word as found in the manuscript), who is summoned in the refrain line to receive the *Völsi*? For the author of the *Volsapáttr* "*maurnir*" was certainly no more than a mere sound, as the author provides no explanation for the entire line in which it is found. Hence "*maurnir*" is not of Icelandic origin; but the extant (Norwegian) text could have substituted an unobjectionable name for the name of a heathen god. Therefore it is by no means certain that the underlying cult was one which worshiped a god by the name of "*maurnir*"; on the contrary, the name could be an remnant of an old heathen tradition.

I have failed to arrive at a satisfactory interpretation of "maurnir." Linguistically, one would most likely see *mornir* as a feminine plural noun: "the giantesses." But this is a highly dubious construction when seen in context. I am unable to support *"maurnir"* as an epithet for Freyr. For those who wish to examine this matter further, it may be useful to see here what has been determined about the words *"morn"* and *"mornir."*

In Old Norse poetry there are two substantives *morn:* the first signifies "river" and is related to the name of the French river Marne; this word is of no importance to us here. The other is the proper name of a giantess, or a generic name meaning "giantess." This use appears in a number of Old Norse examples.[37] In this way *mornir* in the *Volsapáttr* could be a nominative plural form of the feminine *morn* "giantess." The refrain line would then be summoning "giantesses" to accept the sacrificial offer; this indeed is the meaning rendered in the Lp. translation:

> *monstra gigantea   hoc sacrificium accipiant!*

Clearly, then, it is hardly possible to think of this as a genuinely heathen expression. For a cult of giantesses or giants has not been credibly established (Maurer, Bekehrung 2, 43), not even by the findings in E.H. Meyer (Mythol.§ 211). The often-mentioned "sacrifice to the goddess" is not to be related to gigantides! In the reports about Þorgerðr Holgabrúdr and Irpa, to be sure, both these things do coincide: there are giantesses, *trollkonur,* and sacrifices are made for them. Bugge considers the entire figure of the Þorgerðr Holgabrúdr to be a fiction of the Christian era, ca. 1050, and he traces the Þorgerðr back to the *Sváva* of Helgi Hiorvarzson.[38] I am not convinced by his assumption that the purely human episode of Thora and Helgo (Saxo, 116f.) represents an earlier stage of the *Porgerdsage* than that found in Iceland (334). But even if one does accept a divine worship of the Þorgerðr in the Haloga lands, one would probably have to concur with G. Storm's view[39] that this was a giant figure only to outsiders and to Christian posterity, but was not referred to by its own worshipers as *morn,* i.e., by the name applied to the giantesses who were engaged in battle by Thor. Moreover, the sister of the Þorgerðr, Irpa, appears to be a later invention, and hence a plural *mornir* would find no explanation here.

A masculine *mornir*—or perhaps *mornir,* from *maruniz*—is encountered in two places. In one, it appears as one of many expressions for "sword." The word also appears in the Heimskringla in a satirical verse written by the Icelanders about the Danish King Harald Blauzahn, because the Danes had appropriated the freight of a wrecked Icelandic ship. The line in question, in prose form, goes as follows: *þá er mordkunnr Haraldr í faxa ham sparn sunnan á mornis mó*[40] [When the death was known, Harald rode the pony south with agitated pining]. One suspects that behind *mornis mór* lies some contextually germane but veiled allusion. But what it alludes to escapes my knowledge. For this reason we do not know whether the word *mornir,* in this second location, means "sword" or something else. I know of no way to relate it to the god Freyr.

I cannot take leave of the *Volsapáttr* without saying a few words about its narrative style. To be sure, our author was no outstanding literary master among his countrymen, but he has unmistakably taken on the general heritage of the Icelanders, the dexterity in treating a simple dispassionate event epically. The skill lies in the clear exposition, in the articulate, realistically observed reporting and in the depiction of individuals. The narrator begins with the peasant family and informs us of the origin of the daily practice of their *Völsi* service. Then Olaf enters the story, and what follows can be presented in a smooth epic flow, without any regressions or commentary to hinder it. The six inhabitants of the farmhouse are presented in an orderly manner, yet without names, as in a folktale; the parents and children also get a brief, direct characterization. Authentically Icelandic characteristics are the careful mentioning and naming of the dog, which only at the very end intervenes in the action, and the explicit statement that the farmstead lay in a quite remote area, yet near a navigable harbor. Thus the king's landing occurs all the more believably and inconspicuously.

The narrative proceeds tersely and smoothly; the notion of religious conversion is subordinated to the narrative depiction of life, just as one would expect of a pupil of profane sagas. A few stilted sentences (on 332, 6f., 25f.) produce a dissonance, partly because of diction and syntax, and may have resulted from a religious copyist, whose contributions are most conspicuous in the more evangelical turns of phrase at beginning and end (the manuscript concluded in a nice folktale-like way with "and held well to their faith ever since"). On the other hand, the narrator treats the strange and astonishing elements in the story dryly as forgone conclusions, as though here as in a folktale anything is possible. The sober exactitude with which he reports the farmer's wife's care of the *Völsi* almost suggests the appearance of documentary historiography. The prose lingers longest on the arrival of the three guests in the room: how they seat themselves, how the daughter comes with the light, how the rest of them then take their places—these things are intimately revealed to us, and these many small individual brush strokes are not bad in conveying the impression that a man is telling us something experienced himself. The borrowed motif of the daughter recognizing their eminent guest is not developed any further and only contributes to narrative color and probably also to narrative tension: now one of the participants has the same knowledge as those listening to the story. As soon as the *Völsi* is again present on the scene, the narrator retreats almost completely behind the verse dialog of his characters; in the short prose interludes he only gives carefully weighed stage directions to prepare the next character's brief dramatic entrance. On the whole, the conduct is homey, good natured in a a peasant sense, with a constant undertone of gentle humor. It borders on the style of many New Icelandic folktales. Of all the medieval *Sögur*, no tale in such a manner can be named except the *Gautapáttr* in the *Gautyrekssaga*, which itself contains so many folktale elements.

However, our narrator gives his very best in differentiating characters, or shall we say, their roles. Each of the three couples in the farmhouse—father and mother, son and daughter, servant and maid—form an antithesis based on their relation to the *Völsi*. The author does not define them as merely being for or against it, but rather he portrays the attitudes of each of the six differently. The old farmer's wife with her jealous, almost pathetic fanaticism; the farmer, who says "if it were up to me, we'd leave it alone"; the son, who rather relishes the chance to joke coarsely with the women; the daughter, painfully moved in her virginal shame; the servant, who would rather have a good loaf of bread than these useless remains from a slaughtered animal; and finally the maiden, who willfully lets her imagination be aroused by the mystery: these are presented perspicuously, one by one, in the six stanzas. Of the three guests, it is the Icelander who distinguishes himself by looking at the *Völsi* very carefully and smiling (one thinks involuntarily: just as the narrator would have done in his place). Finally it is the King whose elevated speech:

> Ruler I was
> and captain at the stern
> and leader of the army
> of the entire nation,

makes for hilarious contrast when he then surprises all by calling the dog of the house! An epic creative power completely subdues the indecency occasioned by the subject matter, never allowing it to obtrude. Only in the two stanzas of the son and in that of the maid—i.e., in places where it has a foundation in the roles—is a tone of obscenity discernible. The narrator himself stands above it all and skillfully orchestrates the crude with the wholesome and the astonishing and, finally, the edifying to render a nicely unified little picture.

The heroic epics and the historic sagas in Old Norse literature, such serious, grandiose monuments so imbued with heroic spirit, cast their shadows far over the lowlands, over the more modest products of a younger and more commonplace spirit. The story of the *Völsi* is one of the many such stories lying in the shadows. It is included in the records of Nordic literary history only for the sake of completeness. But for just a moment let us ask the question: what wouldn't the other medieval literatures give for such an anecdote! Among the fableaux and *Schwänke* of the fourteenth century, how greatly would our little conversion story stand out!

*This article originally appeared as Heusler, Andreas, "Die Geschichte vom *Völsi*, eine altnordische Bekehrungsanekdote." *Zeitschrift des Vereins für Volkskunde* (Berlin), 13 (1903), 29–35.

Notes

1   In the *Flateyiarbók* edition, vol. 2 (Christiania 1862), 331–35; also in the collection entitled *Bárdarsaga Snæfellsáss* . . ., ed. G. Vigfússon (Copenhagen 1860). The verses are also found in the *Corpus poëticum boreale* 2, 380 ff.

2   Cf. *Fas.* 3, 363; *Flateyiarbók* 1, 529f.; *Stjörnu-Odda draumr*, 116–20; *Bergbúa Pättr*, 124, 128; *Bósasaga*, 15.

3   *Jón Porkelsson*, Om Digtn.þå Island i det 15.og 16.årh., p. 201 ff, Jón Ärnason, Pjódsögur 1, 171.

4   See Jón Ärnason, Pjódsögur 1, 176f.; Maurer, *Volkssagen*, 310f.; Rittershaus, *Die neuislandischen Volksmärchen*, 289f.

5   Cf. *en hvárteggi kvazt Grimr heita* of the two envoys of Gudmund af Glasisvollum, in *Helga Páttr Pórissonar* (*Flateyiarbók* 1, 360).

6   According to the *Chronicle of Lanercost*; see Kemble, *Die Sachsen*, 1, 294f.; Jahn attempts a closer explication in *Die deutschen Opfergebräuche*, 31, 134.

7   Panzer, *Beitrag* 2, 218, No. 401; *Bavaria* 3, 2, 969.

8   Kuhn, *Märkische Sagen*, 368.

9   Found in Dauphiné; Manhardt, *Mythologische Forschung*, 164.

10   From Normandy; Mannhardt, 186.

11   Jahn, *die deutschen Opfergebräuche*, 264.

12   Hone, *The Every-Day Book* 1, 1618f.; 3, 85; cf. Jakob Grimm's reference to it, *Myth.* 1, 178.

13   Mannhardt, *Mythologische Forschung*, 156f., 183; cf. the *offa penita*, 183, and E.H. Meyer, *Anz. für d.Alt.* 11, 158f.

14   Mannhardt, 176; cf. Mannhardt's supposition, 191, about the Shrovetide custom in the province of Saxony in which "the tail of the deer is passed around."

15   Schwab, *Das altindische Tieropfer*, 159f.

16   Maurer, *Bekehrung* 2, 198f.

17   E.g., in the *Hervarar-Saga*, 297.

18   In Norway and Sweden: Storaker, *Norsk hist. Tidsskr.* 1, 478.

19   *haustbod at vetrnóttum*, Gísla-Saga, 27; *Blótveizla um haustit at vetri*, Hkr. 1, 191, cf. 2, 219. Víglagl. c. 6, 16.

20   Hkr. 2, 242.

21   Cf. *Flateyirbók* 1, 213, 292, 337; *Fas.* 3, 237.

22

Verse 3:	Mundi eigi,	I	blœti þetta
	ef ek um réda,	I	borit í aptan . . .
Verse 11:	Hvat er pat manna	I	hefik mik um hiarra
	mér ókunnra,	I	ok á hurdása,
	er hundum gefr	I	Vita ef ek borgit fae
	heilagt blœti?	I	blœti 'nu helga.

23   The *Egilssaga* (ed. AM. 1809, 209) translates correctly by the word "*victima*," the Lp. s.v. *mörn* 2 with "*sacrificium*."

24   17th century; Mannhardt, *Wald- und Feldkulte*, 2, 250.

25   Oldenberg, *Religion des Veda*, 309f., 328, 387.

26   *Jornal asiatique*, 8, série 13 (Paris 1889), 154f.

27   Lactantius inst. div. 1, 20, 36.

28   Arnobius 4, 7. These and further passages are found in *Roshers Lexikon der griechischen und römishcen Mythologie* 2, 204f.; cf. Holtzmann, *Deutsche Mythologie*, 110, and Liebrecht, *Zur Volkskunde*, 396f.

29   Excepting, perhaps, verse 1 of the *Epithalamium Atharvaveda* 6, 11. From
Bloomfield's translation in *Sacred Books of the East* (XLII, 97f.): "The açvattha
(*ficus religiosa*) has mounted the çami (*mimosa suma*): then a male child was
produced. That, forsooth, is the way to obtain a son, that do we bring to (our) wives."
The verse was spoken while agitating the fire made from rubbing together the wood of
both the açvattha and the çami.
30   The word *vingull* is common in New Icelandic usage. According to Björn
Haldorsen it has the meanings of (1) *funis contortus*, (2) *mobile quid pendens*, (3)
homo fatuus, vertiginosus; according to Oxford, (1) an oaf, (2) botan festuca;
according to Jón Thorkelsson Suppl. III, festuca, Svingel; for an etymology, see
Brím Arkiv 11, 10. *Volsi* is associated with the Russian hearth god Volos in Fritzner,
Norst hist. Tidsskr. 1, 181. Heinzel, *Ostgot. Heldensage*, 82; defined as "*potens scil
membrum*" (from *valor, Valerius*) by v. Grienberger (*Zeitschrift f.d. A.*, 36, 309).
Detter-Heinzel, Beitr. 18, 552f. Much, *Festgabe für Heinzel*, 275f. Its connection to
the *Volsunagr* has been alluded to by Fritzner (ibid.; Beitr. 18, 553), to which I would
only add that "ancestor *Völsi* (Freyr)," at least in the *Volsapáttr*, finds no support in
light of the above. *Hellquist Arkiv* 7, 148. 156 considers its relation to *volr* ("staff")
or the Greek *phállos* (root *ghal*). —Tkhe hap.leg. *nosi* 5, 4 is rendered by Fritzner
Orbdog as *hredr, hesthredr*, and Oxford alludes to the Danish *nosse* "*testiculi*." I doubt
whether this meaning for *nosi* is acceptable: in the speech of the farmer's daughter
one would expect some kind of euphemistic expression; cf. the prose passage behind
verse 1: *en bóndadóttir bad hann út bera andstyggd pessa.*
31   Golther, *Mythologie*, 229f.; Müllenhoff, *D Ak.* 4, 470.
32   *Flateyiarbók* 1, 338.
33   Munch, *Norr.Gude- og Helte-Sagn*, v. 2, 19; Bang, *Den norske kirkes hist.*
9.; Detter-Heinzel, ibid.
34   *Gísalsaga* 27.
35   *Hkr.* 1, 187.
36   *Flateyiarbók* 1, 401; *Hrafnkelssaga* 5.
.37   See original article, 36, for examples from the Old Norse literature.
38   *Helgedigtene*, 321–38.
39   *Arkiv* 2, 133.
40   See the original article, 37, for a fuller discussion of the manuscript
orthography and of the controversy surrounding the use of the phrase.

Public Implications

SAINTS AND SEX, CA. 500–1100: STRIDING DOWN THE NETTLED PATH OF LIFE

Jane Tibbetts Schulenburg

What is carnal love but horror, and the origin of sins; one who loves much gets heated as with the heat of fire; it is a hurtful thing, an odious thing, which draws one to punishment. Let it not burn thee, nor the fierce desire of poison urge thee . . . .

Life of Saint Illtyd

Although by far the most outstanding of his deeds is that he preserved his chastity to old age. For it is chastity alone which imitates the purity of angels.

The Life of Saint Gerald of Aurillac

When one thinks of a medieval saint, the topic of sex does not immediately spring to mind. In fact, the juxtaposition of "saint" and "sex" might appear as essentially antithetical in nature, as representing two quite different and irreconcilable spheres, that of the sacred and profane. For in their pursuit of the *vita* perfecta, saints have been portrayed as other-worldly beings, "impatient angels"—"dead to earthly desires, breathing only heavenly affections."[1] They have been perceived as virginal or celibate, untouched by sexual thoughts or experiences. However, despite this initial impression, many saints' lives are in fact very much concerned with sex. From "womb to tomb" sex appears as a prevalent theme in the *vitae* of the holy dead.

From a collective study of saints' lives of the Latin West from the sixth through the eleventh century, enough information is available to form a rather rough evaluation of ecclesiastical attitudes toward sex. Although the *vitae* in their edifying intention are rich in fantasy and contradiction and must therefore be used with caution, they also inadvertently provide scholars with an incredible wealth of historical information—a solid core of social and personal detail not found in any other documentation for this period. The sheer numbers of *vitae*, the hundreds of lives of saints, afford us an unsurpassed view of changing attitudes, values, and moral concerns, as well as practices of the period. They also provide us with an opportunity to compare these attitudes and experiences as they refer to gender.

The *vitae* were written to glorify the lives of the holy dead—to make a case for an individual's worthiness of sainthood. They offered models of both exemplary behavior and improper deportment. They were essentially works of propaganda intended to promote the popularity and cult of the

203

candidate for sanctity. As such, the *vitae* documented the public roles and virtues of saints;[2] however, hagiographers were also interested in providing information for the faithful on the more private or personal aspects of their protagonists' lives: the elements of renunciation and self-denial, asceticism, and especially celibacy or virginity.

Beginning with the injunctions of St. Paul, followed by the Church Fathers and early monastic writers, the concept of the superiority of virginity became firmly implanted in the mentality of the Latin West. Over time the Church established the notion of a hierarchy of sexual perfection with the distinct grades measured in terms of the degree of a person's denial or withdrawal from sexual activity.[3] According to this scale of values, there were three separate levels or states of chastity: virgins were accorded the highest value, followed by widows; those who were married occupied a distant third. In the writings of the Church Fathers, these three states were traditionally compared to the hundred-fold, sixty-fold, and thirty-fold fruit found in the biblical parable. However, the Anglo-Saxon Bishop Aldhelm, (d. ca. 709) in his treatise *De Virginitate*, introduced in place of widowhood a new category called "chastity" which he defined as including those who had once been married but had now rejected this marriage in order to pursue a religious life. According to Aldhelm, ". . . virginity is (that) which unharmed by any carnal defilement continues pure out of the spontaneous desire for celibacy; (and) chastity on the other hand which, having been assigned to marital contracts, has scorned the commerce of matrimony for the sake of the heavenly kingdom; or conjugality which, for propagating the progeny of posterity and for the sake of procreating children, is bound by the legal ties of marriage."[4]

In general, from the hagiographic point of view, a chaste, ascetic life was therefore of paramount importance in making a case for one's individual sanctity. In fact, for many of the candidates, without this special virtue there would have been insufficient evidence of their worthiness of sainthood. Thus, as might be expected during the period from the sixth through the end of the eleventh century, the majority of saints won recognition for their chaste lives. And particularly for female saints, the status of *virgo intacta* was nearly a prerequisite for sanctity.

Therefore, one of the major accomplishments underscored by the hagiographers was their protagonist's lifelong maintenance of sexual purity. For many of the saints, this reputation began with their miraculous, "untainted" birth. As youths, they declared their firm commitment to the chaste life and, frequently acting against the wishes of their families, they adopted various strategies to avoid forced marriages and loss of their *integritas*.[5] Subsequently, confronted by temptations of the flesh and accusations of sexual improprieties or scandal, these saints were forced to resort to heroic measures in order to maintain or redeem their reputations of sexual purity. Also, according to their hagiographers, these same saints, during their lifetimes or posthumously (as apparently experts in the field), were called upon to assist or admonish the faithful in their own personal problems with sex. Thus the lives of saints are unique documents which provide us with remarkable detail about sexual attitudes and activities of this early period.

Coitus Sacer and the Procreation of Saintly Offspring

A number of *vitae* of this early period begin by identifying the saint's "noble" genealogy—frequently providing the names of both the mother and father as well as other notable family members. The purpose of this summary of the saint's lineage was to glorify the candidate's parentage.

The lives also frequently describe the special circumstances surrounding the conception and birth of the saint. In their attempts to distance their protagonist from ordinary conceptions involving sexual intercourse, lust, and pollution, these episodes are frequently explained metaphorically and/or assume the form of a vision.[6] They also incorporate some rather fantastic or folkloric explanations of procreation. This emphasis on the denial of sexual intercourse and any type of pollution in the conception of the saint seems to have been especially prevalent with monastic saints or lives shaped or written by monastic reformers. These legends then tend to accentuate the miraculous aspect of *coitus sacer*: they describe, for example, conceptions coinciding with the appearance of a bright light, "extra-vaginal" conceptions, miraculous erections, types of "immaculate conceptions," and conceptions among those advanced in years, convinced of their infertility.

A number of early Irish saints' lives, in the tradition of the bright light motif, relate the occurrence of fiery manifestations during intercourse. Some saints were described as having actually been conceived of fire. One Irish *vita* tells of a saintly conception in terms of a mother who dreamt that her breasts were filled with gold and glowing with a bright light.[7]

Several early Irish saints' lives describe a vision of a star falling into the mother's mouth at the time of conception. According to the life of St. Maedoc of Ferns, the parents of the future saint went to Drumlane to fast with the purpose to obtain an heir. Here the mother of the saint saw a vision of the moon entering the mouth of her husband the king, and the king saw a star entering the mouth of the queen. This was interpreted to mean that an eminent birth would emerge from this couple.[8] The mother of St. Finan of Kinnity was said to have seen a vision of a red-gold fish entering her mouth at the time of conception. However, in another version of this story, St. Finan is said to have been conceived through intercourse of a "red-gold salmon" with his mother while she was bathing in Loch Lein. Another Irish source notes the wonderful case of a saint owing his conception to the ink of Comgall of Bangor which his mother fortuitously drank.[9] While these miraculous, extra-vaginal descriptions of conception were written to enhance the sanctity of the future saint, they also seem to reveal a misogynist rejection of female genitals as polluting. It is interesting that a number of these early *vitae* also deny paternity to a human male.

A rather detailed and fascinating description of the conception of a tenth-century saint can be found in the Life of St. Gerald of Aurillac, written by St. Odo of Cluny. According to this vita, Gerald's father "was so careful to conduct himself chastely in his marriage, that he frequently slept alone far from the marriage bed, as though for a time giving himself to prayer according to the word of the Apostle [I Cor. vii. 5]." Odo then notes that during his sleep one night, Gerald's father was said to have been warned that he should know his wife because he would beget a son. His son was to be called Gerald, and he would become a man of great virtue. When he awoke from his dream "he was full of joy at the vision." Odo continues his explanation of Gerald's miraculous conception noting: "Having fallen asleep again it seemed to him that a rod grew up from the big toe of his right foot, which gradually grew into a great tree, which burst into leaf and spread itself on all sides. Then seeming to call workmen he ordered props in the form of forks or poles to be put underneath it. And even when it grew very great, he felt no weight on his toe." Odo then concludes with the following observation: "In truth visions of dreams are not always vain. And if faith is to be put in sleep, it seems that this vision agrees in its result with future events. He knew his wife, who conceived a son as the vision foretold." And finally, no doubt aware of this rather far-fetched account and of pushing the credulity of his audience perhaps a bit too far, Odo adds: "The dream may perhaps be doubted, but the mark of virtue evidently followed."[10]

In contrast, the Life of St. Odo of Cluny, written by John of Salerno, assures us that Odo was a product of sexless regeneration or immaculate conception. Odo tells us that his father "was accustomed to celebrate the vigils of the saints throughout the night." Thus, one Christmas night, while he was celebrating the watch in tears and prayers, he decided in the name of the Virgin birth, to ask God to give him a son. "And by the insistency of his prayers he merited that his wife should bear him one, though past the age when that might be expected." And according to St. Odo, "My father often related that in no other way had my nativity been brought about."[11]

Another case which denies sexual intercourse in the conception of a saint concerns the saintly Aleth, mother of St. Bernard of Clairvaux. According to one of St. Bernard's *vitae*, all seven of this saintly woman's children were in fact the result of "immaculate" conceptions, that is, they were venerated not by her husband, but by God alone ("*septem quippe liberos genuit non tum viro suo quam Deo*")![12]

A number of the vitae, following in the biblical tradition, describe the parents of the saint as advanced in years, sterile and unfruitful. As noted in the Life of St. Columban by Jones (in regard to the childlessness of Duke Waldelen and his wife Flavia) this occurred "in order that," as Juvencus says of Zachariah and Elizabeth, "the gift might be more welcome to those who had already given up hope."[13] Desperately wanting children, these couples sought out confessors and bishops, or visited the tombs of special saints to ask for assistance in conceiving a child. They were then provided with prayers and assurances that they would soon give birth to their much desired offspring.

The contemporary *vita* of St. Benno II (eleventh century) notes that his parents had waited many years for a child. They then made a pilgrimage to Rome and brought with them a votive offering of a little doll made of silver. They also promised that if God answered their prayers and provided them with a son, they would dedicate him to the Church—a promise which they ultimately carried out.[14]

The Life of St. Beino (a Welsh saint of the late sixth/early seventh century) notes that his parents were aged and without heirs, for they had slept together twelve years without sexual intercourse. However, one evening as they were talking they saw an angel approach. The angel then told them that God had heard their prayer and "Let there be sexual intercourse tonight between thee and thy wife, and she will become pregnant, and from that pregnancy, a son will be born to thee, and he will be honorable with respect to God and man." And according to the *vita*, "and as the angel ordered them, they did; and Eeren was rendered pregnant that night, and from that pregnancy, a son was born to her, and to that son they gave the name of Beino."[15]

Thus many of the saints of this period can perhaps be best described as "miracle babies," that is, born of parents seemingly infertile and advanced in years who had against all odds finally conceived their special child. Included in this tradition of saints born of aged parents are, for example, Saints Remi, Donatus, Lioba, Samson, Odo of Cluny, Hildegund, Sirude, Odilia and others. The conceptions of many of the other saints also participated in miraculous or folkloric traditions and were frequently described in metaphorical terms incorporating bright light motifs, "extravaginal" conceptions, miraculous erections, and immaculate conceptions.

Sexual Temptations and Saintly Strategies

After a discussion of the saint's birth and early years, one of the pervasive themes found in the early medieval *vitae* is that of the young saint's renunciation of the world and espousal of a life of virginity. It is then in the attempt to live as "impatient angels"—"dead to earthly desires"—that the saints found themselves frequently challenged by various temptations.

Some of the most vivid illustrations of sexual attitudes and strategies for sexual avoidance can be found in the lives of male saints who had been recruited from the eremitic and monastic milieu. Many of these *vitae* underscore a basic contempt for the human condition, hatred of the body and a concern, or, in some cases, an obsession with virginal maintenance. In part motivated by fear of their own weakness and susceptibility to female seduction, these holy men fled to the "desert," i.e., the wilderness of the hermit or the cloister of the monk, to shield them from these struggles with sexuality.[16] In these saints' lives, woman is portrayed as the handmaid of the devil or, for the Irish, man's "guardian devil."[17] As the source of perpetual temptation, she must not be trusted. The mere sight, touch, or sound of a woman was thought to be potent enough to provoke concupiscent thoughts or worse, instant fornication.[18] These *vitae* then focus at some length on the would-be saints' heroic struggles with female temptation and the persistent demon of fornication. While again many of these episodes appear to be highly imaginative constructs and thus difficult to validate historically; nevertheless, they serve a very important role as indirect indexes of the religious mindset of the period. The strategies of these holymen, as described by their hagiographers, thus ranged from fleeing from temptation, or, actively courting temptation (with the intent to extinguish lust), mortifying the flesh, or receiving miraculous release from temptation.

Some of the *vitae* portray blatant examples of female temptation with the intent to dissuade these holymen from their profession. Especially during the period of conversion to Christianity, pagans were described as employing a clever sexual strategy with the intent to force churchmen off their lands. "Lewd and lascivious women" were specifically sent as a type of "secret weapon" to disturb the peace of the monks and to drive them out. For example, in the Life of Saint David, written by Rhigyford (d. 1099), a fire is lit by Christian missionaries in the region with smoke seeming to encompass the whole land. A pagan man named Raia, holding a fortress in the area, was disturbed by the smoke, for he was convinced that "he who kindled that fire will surpass all men in power and glory, for, as if by some omen, this smoke predicts fame."[19] After an abortive attempt to get rid of the holymen, Baia's wife then assumed command and attempted to drive these usurpers out of their land. According to the *vita*, this woman, "afire with a jealous spite," called her maids and said: "Go where the monks can see you, and with bodies bare, play games and use lewd words." The maids obey, they play immodest games, imitating sexual intercourse and displaying love's seductive embraces ("*impudicos exercent ludos, concubitus simulant, blandos amoris nexus ostendunt*"). The minds of some of the monks they entice away to lust, the minds of others they irritate. The monks endeavor to abandon the place." However the holy father, St. David, remained steadfast and encouraged the ascetic resolve of his disciples. And soon these problems disappeared: Baia was killed, and his wife became mad. Thus St. David and his monks remained to establish a successful monastery at this spot in Wales.[20]

The early Irish saints, as portrayed by their hagiographers, seem to have been especially fearful of female temptation, concupiscent thoughts and fornication. In this tradition they are shown fleeing after hearing the mere sound of a cow or sheep because of the association of cattle with women. A *vita* of an early Irish holyman notes: "In this place I will not go, for where sheep, therein a woman; where a woman, therein sin; where sin, therein the devil, and where the devil, therein hell."[21] Thus one of the strong messages of these lives was an exaggerated fear of sex and the necessary avoidance of females at all costs.

The *vita* of the Celtic saint Columban, abbot of Luxeuil and Bobbio (d. 615) provides another description of a heroic struggle against the temptations of the flesh. According to his biographer, Jonas, the devil aroused within Columban the lust of certain *lascivae puellae*, "especially of those whose fine figure and superficial beauty are wont to enkindle mad desires in the minds of wretched men." Therefore the young saint found himself strongly tempted to yield to their undisguised wishes. However, in the midst of this moral crisis, he consulted a local woman who had lived for twelve years as a hermit. After listening to his dilemma, she counseled Columban to flee the temptation, even if it meant leaving his homeland. Then, according to Jonas, she warned the young saint with the following: antifeminist tirade: "Out of weakness you lend your ear even against your own will, to the voice of the flesh, and think you can associate with the female sex without sin. But do you recall the wiles of Eve, Adam's fall, how Samson was deceived by Delilah, how David was led to injustice by the beauty of Bathsheba, how the wise Solomon was ensnared by the love of a woman? Away, Oh youth! away! flee from corruption, into which, as you know, many have fallen. Forsake the path which leads to the gates of hell." 30 St. Columban then received this timely warning as a call to flee the fleshy world which is "nought but filth and vileness," and to withdraw to the cloistered life.[22]

In contrast to these dramatic examples of holymen fleeing sexual temptation, we can also find in our sources a few cases of male saints deliberately courting temptation with the intent to "deaden their flesh" or subdue their lust. These examples concern the rather dangerous trials of chastity or ordeals of the flesh—experiments which essentially involved male ascetics chastely sharing their beds with virgins. In these heroic tests of endurance, these male saints attempted to prove their miraculous asceticism or self-control by actively seeking out or confronting sexual temptation. (These challenges also seem to underscore the apparent "perverse" enjoyment of some of these saints in defying social or moral conventions as well as becoming the focus of scandalous accusations.) Variants of this ancient practice known as *agapetes, syneisactism, virgines subintroductae, mulierum consortia,* etc., had been condemned as immoral by a number of churchmen including Irenaeus of Lyons, Cyprian, Jerome, John Chrysostom, St. Patrick, Caesarius of Arles, as well as by various church councils.[23] However, this experiment is described in some detail in a rarely cited legend of the Celtic saint Scothin (Scuthin), a disciple of St. David. According to this account, St. Scothin customarily shared his bed every night with "*duas pulcherrimas virgines*" or maidens with "pointed breasts" so that the "battle with the Devil might be greater for him."[24] St. Brendan, learning of this rather risky practice, questioned whether Scothin was in fact committing an act which went against the laws of morality. In his own oblique defense, Scothin challenged Brendan to try this experiment. The following night he was introduced to the two virgins who, as proof of their chastity, arrived with their laps full of glowing embers which did them no harm. They then spilled these embers in front of Brendan and got into bed with him. Brendan then asked them, "What is this?" They replied that they did this every night. However, we learn that Brendan was unable to sleep because of his sexual attraction to these women. They then said to him, "That is imperfect, o cleric, he who is here every night [Scothin] feels nothing at all. Why goest thou not, O cleric, into the tub [of cold water] if it be easier for thee? 'Tis often that the cleric, even Scothin, visits it." Brendan responded that "It is wrong for us to make this test, for he is better than we are." Thus convinced that Scothin had attained a higher level of spiritual perfection than he had, Brendan was satisfied that there was no violation of morality in this arrangement.[25]

A similar case can be found in William of Malmesbury's *De Gestis Pontificum Anglorum.* Here he describes the ordeal of chastity undertaken by the Anglo-Saxon St. Aldhelm, Abbot of Malmesbury/Bishop of Sherborne. According to this account, Aldhelm deliberately sought out beautiful women to tempt him sexually so that ultimately he would be crowned in heaven for his perseverance of the chaste life. (William of Malmesbury then cites as "proof" of Aldhelm's love of the celibate condition, his famous work, *De Virginitate.*)[26] However, in regard to this saintly exemplum, Giraldus Cambrensis warned: "let us not presume to attempt such things, therefore, according, to the example of St. Aldhelm of Malmesbury, who, it is said, lay between two maidens every night, one on one side and the other on the other side, so that he might be defamed by men, but his continence rewarded the more copiously in the future by God, who understood his conscience."[27]

Perhaps the most famous example in this tradition of self-induced temptation, namely, the ordeal of chastity, is that of Robert of Arbrissel (d. 1117), founder of the Monastery of Fontevrault. According to our sources, Robert was said to have slept chastely with the nuns of his foundation. In a letter written ca. 1098–1100, Marbode, Bishop of Rennes, accused Robert of his scandalous behavior in taking pleasure in the *mulierum cohabitatio.* For Robert, apparently greatly affected by the Gregorian reform ideals of celibacy, the *mulierum cohabitatio* was said to have been a type of ordeal which helped him to expiate for his past transgressions.[28]

In contrast to patterns of flight from temptation/women or that of courting temptation, many of the *vitae* of male saints describe these holymen quietly adopting programs of mortification of the flesh. They attempted to extinguish their sexual urges by adopting rigorous programs of fasting or sleep deprivation. They believed that an abundance of blood was associated with lust and desire; therefore the amount of blood in the body needed to be reduced by fasting or blood letting.[29]

Other saints resorted to more dramatic means of mortification of the flesh, namely, inflicting on themselves sharp physical pain to counteract their concupiscent thoughts. One of the most famous episodes in this tradition can be found in the life of the Father of Western Monasticism, St. Benedict of Nursia (d. ca. 547). According to his *vita*, written by Pope Gregory the Great, while Benedict lived hidden in a smell cave at Subiaco, temptation arrived in the form of a blackbird. As recorded by Gregory the Great, "The moment it left, he was seized with an unusually violent temptation. The evil spirit recalled to his mind a woman he had once seen, and before he realized it his emotions were carrying him away. Almost overcome in the struggle, he was on the point of abandoning the lonely wilderness, when suddenly with the help of God's grace he came to himself. Just then he noticed a thick patch of nettles and briers next to him. Throwing his garment aside, he flung himself naked into the sharp thorns and stinging nettles, There he rolled and tossed until his whole body was in pain and covered with blood. Yet once he had conquered pleasure through suffering, his torn and bleeding skin served to drain off the poison of temptation from his body. Before long the pain that was burning his whole body had put out the fires of evil in his heart." Thus, as Gregory noted, it was "by exchanging these two fires" that Benedict triumphed over sin so completely that he never experienced another temptation of this type.[30]

The life of the reformer St. Wulfstan, Bishop of Worcester (d. 1095), relates a similar cure adopted by a holyman confronted by sexual temptation. According to his *vita*, written by Colman (Wulfstan's own chaplain or chancellor), from the time of his youth Wulfstan loved sexual purity. However, on one occasion, "a local girl offensively set about the shipwreck of his modesty and his temptation to sensuality. To be brief, she was in the habit of squeezing his hand, giving some come-hither looks and making other lewd gestures which are signs of lasciviousness and loss of virginity." One day "with the accompaniment of a harp [she] began to dance in front of him with lewd gestures and shameless movement such as might gratify the eyes of a lover. And he, whom neither words nor touches had weakened, now panted with desire, completely reduced by her disarming gestures. He immediately came to his senses, however; and bursting with tears, fled away into some rough undergrowth and prickly scrub." For some time Wulfstan remained here, and after falling asleep in those "prickly scrubs," he awakened to find himself fully cured. He then described this divine miracle to his friends, saying: "just then I was burning with huge goadings of fleshly urges; but now, watered with divine dew, both my guts and all my vital parts are cool. I hope that from now on with the aid of God's mercy, to be free from fleshly arousal and no longer troubled by such disturbance." And in the wake of his prophetic words, we are assured that "from that time on no marvelous figure excited either his mind or eye; nor was the peace of his sleep disturbed by wet dreams."[31]

Other eremitic or monastic saints, when confronted by concupiscent thoughts, mortified their flesh by adopting the ordeal of burning coals.[32]

The events of the life of St. Leoban of St-Etienne de Fursac (6th c.) describe this tradition of self-mortification. St. Leoban followed the eremitic life in the mountains of Limoges. According to the legend, one night some young men sent a prostitute with the intention to corrupt this holy man. However, under the eyes of this courtesan, the saint lay down on a bed of burning coals while begging her to join him. Because of his chaste state, the fire did not cause any harm to the saint, and this was viewed as a miracle. Witnessing this, the woman fled in haste, while the young men who had arranged this seduction came to beg the saint's forgiveness.[33]

The Abbot-Saint Odilo of Cluny (d. 1048) was also renowned for his chastity. He was called the Virgin or *"virgo centenarius"*—because of his longevity, as well as the temple of the holy spirit/tabernacle of purity. According to a tradition held at the Cluniac Priory of Souvigny, Countess Ermengardis of Bourbon had one day apparently incited the holy abbot to sin. However, in response to this temptation and in order to frighten the Countess, Odilo rolled on smoldering coals. These coals were then kept in the sacristy of the Priory of Souvigny as relics associated with the holy Abbot Odilo.[34]

A final example of this type of mortification of the flesh concerns the late eleventh century St. William Firmatus. According to his *vita*, while living as a hermit in a forest near Laval, some licentious young men along with a woman of ill repute attempted to disturb his peace and assail his virtues. One night the woman came into his cell and began seducing the holyman. However, William, in her presence, took a burning fire-brand and applied it with such force to his arm that he kept the scar from this burn for the remainder of his life. The woman, apparently impressed by this heroic act, threw herself at the knees of the hermit and begged his forgiveness. Those who had planned this assault also witnessed William's miraculous defense of his chastity and spread his fame.[35]

Many of the Celtic saints were especially well known for their rigorous avoidance of women and their extreme mortifications of the flesh. We learn from the *vitae* that some of these saints regularly practiced ascetic immersions in icy water during the night.[36] They accompanied these exercises with psalms and prayers. A few of the sources note that this method of bodily mortification was specifically practiced to tame the flesh or suppress sexual desire. Giraldus Cambrensis, for example, relates that the early Welsh saint Dogmael (5–6th c.) regularly plunged himself into the river near his hermitage. And he notes that this rite was done specifically *"ad domandam libidinem."*[37] One of the legends of St. David of Wales relates a similar practice: "Also he sought cold water at some distance, where by remaining long therein, and becoming frozen, he might subdue the heat of the flesh."[38] The life of the sixth-century St. Kentigern, Bishop of Glasgow, describes in some detail the manner in which this holyman conquered his problems with concupiscence and lust. The *vita* notes that Kentigern immersed himself in icy water "because the law of sin, which wars within the *membris pudendis*, thus was weakened, and the fire of desire having ceased and extinguished, in order that no corruptness of wanton flesh might pollute or soil the lily of his chastity in waking or even in sleeping." The life of St. Kentigern also notes that following this "cold water treatment," he enjoyed absolute immunity from temptation even by the most beautiful women.[39] The reformer Saint Peter Damian, Cardinal-Bishop of Ostia (d. 1073) was known for his great austerities and sexual purity. We learn that when he was attacked by temptations of the flesh during the night, he plunged his body in icy waters, remaining there until he obtained the relief which he sought.[40] A popular episode in the Life of St. Bernard of Clairvaux notes this same method of extinguishing temptation and lust. According to this account, realizing that he was deriving an inordinate amount of pleasure from looking at a woman as well as entertaining concupiscent thoughts, he threw himself into a pool of icy water.[41]

A number of other sources mention the ascetic immersions of these early saints (both male and female); however, they do not specifically connect these activities with the need to suppress sexual desire. Such is the case, for example, of the Irish female saint Moninne. According to her *vita*, Moninne was accustomed to sit in an icy spring in water up to her breasts while saying her psalter and imposing a blessing with her staff or bachall.[42] St. Brigid, along with a young companion, was said to have immersed herself in a pond one winter night, while praying and shedding tears.[43]

Other male saints were described as receiving miraculous salvation or cures in response to their problems with sexual temptation. In his *vita* of the nobleman St. Gerald of Aurillac, St. Odo of Cluny provides us with an interesting example of this type of miraculous defense. Odo notes that Gerald, in his youth, was attacked by the devil who "constantly suggested lustful thoughts to him therefore, for that is his first and greatest means of leading mankind astray." But when Gerald completely repelled them, he had to resort to "the instrument of deception by which Adam and his posterity are often led astray—I mean woman." Then, according to Odo, the devil brought "a certain girl before his eyes and while Gerald incautiously took notice of the colour of her clear skin, he was softened to take delight in it. O, if he had at once understood what lay hidden beneath the skin! For the beauty of the flesh is nothing but the thin disguise of the skin. He averted his eyes but the image impressed on the heart through them remained. He was tortured therefore, allured, and consumed by a blind fire." Overcome at last by concupiscent thoughts, Gerald sent word to the girl's mother that he would come to their house that night. However, reminded of the "sweetness of divine love," Gerald prayed that he not be "entirely swallowed up by this temptation." When he arrived at the house and the girl entered the room, she appeared to him so deformed that he hardly recognized her. Gerald then understood that this transformation and his salvation had occurred only through divine intervention.[44]

The *vita* of the Irish saint Mochuda also notes a case of miraculous intervention. According to this legend, Mochuda was the most handsome man of his time. "Thirty maidens loved him so passionately that they could not conceal it. This was grievous to Mochuda, and he prayed to God to turn this love into spiritual love, and He did so. And Mochuda made nuns of these maidens, and they were serving God till they died."[45]

While many of the *vitae* of male eremitic or monastic saints focus on the need for female avoidance, ordeals of chastity, various creative strategies to ward off sexual temptation and temper the flesh, there does not seem to be a similar obsession in the lives of contemporary female saints. Jonas' Life of St. Columban notes, for example, that such care was taken at the Monastery of Faremoutiers that one of the nuns died without having learned that there was in fact any difference between the sexes ("*ut nullatenus inter sexuum noverit diiudicare naturam; aequae enim marem ut feminam putabat, aequae feminam ut marem.*").[46] The lives of these women saints, at least as officially portrayed by the hagiographers, appear to be on a more even keel, or more practical or enlightened in regard to male/female relationships. Although we can find examples of women saints who "guarded their eyes" while in the presence of men, or adopted rigorous regimens of fasting and sleep deprivation, immersions in cold water, etc., these ascetic practices do not seem to have been tied to their fear of susceptibility to male seduction and concupiscence. This apparent difference in emphasis may be due in part to the fact that in the practice of their religious life and pursuit of holiness, these women saints simply could not get along without men. There was a required male presence. They were dependent on priests, confessors, abbots and bishops, male *advocati*, procurators, workmen, and others. These *mulieres sanctae* did not have the same "luxury" that male saints had of being able completely to close out of their lives members of the opposite sex. Therefore, we see the development of many close friendships between female saints and bishops, abbots, and priests, etc.

This difference in emphasis might also be explained by the fact that the *vitae* were invariably written by churchmen who saw their protagonists from a protective and deferential distance, as essentially asexual virgins or widows. Thus in their descriptions of the activities of these women, who were in some cases their biological or spiritual mothers, sisters and their saintly associates, they seemed to assume that these special women, in contrast to ordinary women, i.e., daughters of Eve/temptresses, etc., remained unaffected by sexual temptation, lust, and sex. From their perspective, these types of concerns were simply not in the vocabulary of these female saints. However, when the hagiographers do treat women saints and sex, these women are frequently placed in dire situations where their virginity or chastity is threatened by sexual assault. They then find themselves forced to resort to various heroic strategies of virginity or to die as virgin/martyrs.

It is then in this tradition that we find the legend of the virgin/martyr St. Dympha. According to a later tradition, she was the daughter of an Irish king and lived during the seventh century. After her mother's death,

Dympha's father developed an incestuous desire for her. He began to woo her and promise her glory, riches and honor if she would become his wife. According to the *vita*, she answered him "that she would never consent to that impiety: adding that by no law nor right, the daughter might defile her father's bed, nor by such shameful wickedness stain and infame all her stock and posterity forever." To escape from this "guilty lust" of her father, Dympha fled to Antwerp with Gerebern, her priest, and her father's jester and his wife. They then settled down in Ghele near the church of St. Martin where they lived a life of prayer and fasting. After three months, her father discovered them and tried to win Dympha back. Gerebern, the priest then admonished the king calling him a "most abominable and horrible man, that would seek to defile his own daughter." Her father then killed Gerebern. And after a strong defense of her virginal intentions and refusal to offend her only lover, Christ, by polluting her body, the king, with his own hands, cut off his daughter's head. Later, when her body was rediscovered, a local cult grew up around the tomb of this virgin/martyr.[47]

The legend of the ninth-century virgin/martyr Saint Solangia also concerns a victim of an attempted sexual assault. According to this story, Solangia was a shepherd and watched over her father's sheep. One day as she was alone with her flock, the son of the Count of Poitiers attempted to carry her off and rape her. She resisted and was then stabbed to death by the nobleman.[48]

While there are a number of other examples of these types of virgin/martyrs during this period, it is also within this same context that we can perhaps see one of the most arresting strategies in the heroics of virginity; namely that of sacrificial self-mutilation. I have treated this subject in some detail in another study. However, very briefly, there are two separate cases (an eighth-century Frankish example and the other, a ninth-century Anglo-Saxon case) which describe the responses of female religious when confronted by the certainty of sexual assault by troops of Viking or Saracen invaders. According to our sources, these saintly abbesses, along with their nuns, disfigured themselves by cutting off their noses and lips. This strategy, we learn, was adopted out of desperation in order to physically disgust the invaders and thus prevent them from raping these women whose lives had been dedicated to virginity.[49]

Thus we can see in the *vitae* different pattern of attitudes toward sex and sanctity based on the gender of the saint. Many of the early lives dealing with male saints were very much concerned with sexual temptation and strategies for avoiding women and concupiscence; the lives of virgins, on the other hand, focused on very real threats of physical violence and sexual assault. Not infrequently did these women, in defense of their virginity, become candidates for martyrdom.

Saints and Chaste Marriages

While the majority of the "holy dead" from this period were unmarried and were noted for their lives of virginal perfection, a number of those recognized for their sanctity—although perhaps at somewhat of a spiritual disadvantage—had in fact been married, with some, as we have noted, producing saintly offspring. Other saints adopted chaste lives within marriage, and, as noted by Aldhelm, although they were assigned to marital contracts, they "scorned the commerce of matrimony for the sake of the heavenly kingdom."[50] The hagiographers are then interested in the relationships of married saints and are informative in their discussions of sanctity, marriage, and sex.

The ideal relationship within marriage, as articulated by the Church, was that of chaste lovers. Gregory of Tours in his *History of the Franks* as well as his *Glory of the Confessors* relates the famous exemplum of the two lovers.[51] According to this story, a marriage ceremony took place between a young man and woman from senatorial families of Clermont-Ferrand, each was an only child. As customary, after the ceremony the two were placed in the same bed. The young bride then "turned her face to the wall and wept bitterly." After her husband begged her to tell him what was troubling her, she proceeded with a "sermonette" on the glories of chastity and the transitoriness of life and material possessions. She told him: "I had determined to preserve my poor body for Christ, untouched by intercourse with man. Now to my great sorrow I am deserted by Him and I have not had the strength to achieve what I wanted so much; for on this day, which I could have wished never to see, I have lost that which I have preserved from the beginning of my life. I am forsaken by the sempiternal Christ, who promised me heaven as my dowry, for now it is my fate to be the consort of a mortal man. . . . How unhappy I am! I should have had heaven as my reward, instead I am plunged into hell." Then after a long diatribe on the uselessness of wealth and earthly existence, her young husband won over to her point of view, responded: "If you are determined to abstain from intercourse with me, then I will agree to what you want to do." She answered him: "It is difficult for a man to make such a compact with women. All the same, if you can agree that we shall remain unsullied in our human existence, then I will share with you the dowry which is promised to me by my spouse, the Lord Jesus Christ, to whom I have vowed myself as handmaiden and bride." Her husband then crossed himself and said: "I will do what you ask." According to Gregory of Tours, they went to sleep hand in hand, "and for many years after this they lay each night in one bed, but they remained chaste in a way which we can only admire, as was revealed when the time came for them to die." The couple died within a short time of each other. And although their tombs were placed by different walls within the church, when people came to visit the following morning, they found the two tombs had moved together and were now side by side. Gregory then noted that this miracle provided further proof of their chastity.[52]

The concept of chaste marriage and problems surrounding this practice can also be found in a number of saints' lives of the fourth through seventh centuries. Several of these *vitae* concern bishop saints who had been married but had had to renegotiate their relationships or "put away their wives" on acceptance of ordination. These saints' lives reflect a major concern of the Church (especially during the sixth and seventh centuries) with the growing need for sexual purity among priests and prelates. The issue, particularly for bishops, was whether they should be allowed to continue to sleep with their wives or, because of the sacral nature of their office, they were now required rigorously to avoid all sexual contamination.[53] The councils of the period warn, for example, that "the bishop must treat his wife as his sister." They also rather ingeniously conclude that if a cleric does have intercourse with his wife—especially resulting in children—he was guilty of incest and must be removed from his office.[54] In this same tradition, the councils provide increasingly strict prohibitions of domestic space which forbid any type of contact between priests or prelates with women with whom they were not closely related. The *vitae* then reflect this difficult period of transition in the values and policies of the Church regarding clerical marriages and problems of cohabitation.

Gregory of Tours provides a number of vivid, early examples of married bishop saints. In his *Glory of the Confessors*, he dwells in some detail on the fourth-century Bishop Simplicius' chaste marriage. He notes that although their completely chaste life was known to God, it was unknown to men. He then relates: "After Simplicius accepted the rank of bishop, his blessed sister [i.e., wife] who had previously been united to her husband not by lust but by chastity did not allow herself to be removed from the bishop's bed. Instead she approached the bed of her most chaste husband with as pure a chastity as before, untroubled in the conscience of her holy mind and knowing that she could not be aroused with the heat of a lustful fire." Nevertheless, the citizens of Autun became suspicious of their cohabitation and a scandal ensued. They accused the bishop's wife saying: "It is unbelievable that a woman united with a man cannot be defiled, for a man joined to the limbs of a woman cannot refrain from intercourse. For so the proverbs of Solomon say: 'No one,' he says, 'can be pure after touching tar.' Nor will someone who carries fire in his breast not be burned. We see you both lying in one bed, and can we imagine anything else except that you are having intercourse together?" Provoked by this, the bishop's wife went to her husband and repeated this accusation. Then to prove her chastity, she placed burning coals in her cloak for almost an hour without harming her garment. The bishop also took the coals, and his garment remained unharmed. They thus demonstrated to the crowds through this miracle "that the flames of wantonness" had been extinguished between them.[55]

Gregory of Tours provides further insight into contemporary views of episcopal marriage and the need for celibacy in the following example from his *Glory of the Confessors*. According to Gregory, an unnamed cleric of Nantes was ordained bishop, and "in accordance with the requirement of catholic custom he had set his bed apart." However, he notes that the bishop's wife did not accept this separation and each day she argued with her husband to no avail that they might sleep in one bed. Then one day, angered and feeling rebuffed, she decided to go into his chamber while he was taking his afternoon nap and see "that he is not perhaps sleeping with any other woman for whose love he has rejected me." And as she approached his bed, she was terrified with the vision that met her: for lying on his breast was a lamb of overpowering brightness. According to Gregory of Tours, this miracle then provided the episcopa or bishop's wife, and any other skeptical persons, with irrefutable evidence of the chastity and holiness of the bishop.[56]

In his *History of the Franks*, Gregory of Tours provides another example of a married bishop and problems related to cohabitation. Bishop Urbicus of Clermont-Ferrand (fourth century) was a convert from a senatorial family and was married. However, as Gregory notes, "according to the custom of the church, his wife lived as a religious, apart from her husband. They both devoted themselves to prayer, charity and good works." All went well until the woman became "filled with the Devil's own Malice, which is always hostile to holiness: for he inflamed her with desire for her husband and turned her into a second Eve. She burned so hot with passion, and was overwhelmed by dark thoughts of such a sinful nature," that one night she made her way to the church-house or bishop's palace. Discovering that the complex was locked up for the night, she beat on the doors and shouted something like the following: "Bishop! How long do you intend to remain asleep? How long do you propose to refuse to open these closed doors? Why do you scorn your lawful wife? Why do you shut your ears and refuse to listen to the words of Paul, who wrote: 'Come together again, that Satan tempt you not.' I am here! I am returning to you, not as to a stranger, but to one who belongs to me." After apparently listening to these and similar shouts for some time, the Bishop "forgot his religious scruples and ordered her to be admitted to his bedroom, where he had intercourse with her and then said that it was time for her to go." Later, according to Gregory, he grieved for the sin which he had committed and went to a monastery in his diocese to do penance. "With lamentation and tears" he atoned for his serious misdeed and then returned as Bishop of Clermont-Ferrand. Although they remained separated in this life, Gregory of Tours notes that later, the tombs of the bishop, his wife and daughter (whose conception had taken place on that night) were located next to one another.[57]

Another saintly anecdote which underscores the difficulty these early married bishops experienced in their attempts to refrain from sex with their former wives can be found in Flodoard's *History of the Church of Rheims*. It concerns the sixth-century St. Genebaud who was consecrated first bishop of Laon by St. Remi. A learned nobleman, he had left his wife (who was said to be the niece of St. Remi) to lead the religious life. However, according to

Flodoard, overly self-confident because of his past life and his high rank as bishop, Genebaud imprudently permitted his wife to visit him too often. We learn that the frequent visits (made under the pretext of receiving his teachings), and the sweet talk of his wife, softened the new bishop's heart, which had up to then been firm and incorruptible to the pleasures of the senses. And thus, like a rock, he was hurled from the summit of sanctity into the mire of lust. At the promptings of the devil, Genebaud allowed himself to be devoured by the flames of concupiscence, and he resumed sexual relations with his former wife. Out of this, they had a son who was called Larron, so named because he was begot by larceny or petty theft. For fear of giving rise to suspicion, the bishop wanted to conceal his sin; he therefore forbad his son to stay at his house, although his wife continued her visits. Later, we learn, a daughter was born of this sinful relationship: she was given the name Vulpecule, so designated as she was conceived under the false pretenses of a cunning and sly mother! Finally, overcome by guilt of his sinful life, Genebaud sought repentance. He begged St. Remi to come to Laon where he then heard Genebaud's complete confession. For his penitence, St. Remi determined that Genebaud was to spend seven years enclosed within a small cell, lighted by a small window with an oratory, which he built near the church of St. Julien of Laon. After the seven years had passed, Genebaud returned to his episcopal position at Laon, and he lived the remainder of his life in sanctity. And at his death, Genebaud transferred his bishopric to his son, who, following in the footsteps of his father, also came to be recognized as a saint.[58]

A final example of the hardship and suffering found among married bishops who had to "put away" their wives can be noted in the *vita* of St. Faro (7th-century Bishop of Meaux). Faro had married early in his career. However, after a long discussion with his sister, St. Fara, he decided to renounce his former life and separate from his wife Blidehilde. They separated by mutual consent: Blidehilde took the veil and adopted the life of a hermit, and Faro entered the clergy of Meaux, where he was ultimately chosen bishop. It is reported that one day Faro was strongly attacked by fond memories of his wife. He invited her to come to visit him on three separate occasions. When she finally agreed to come, in order not to expose this servant of God as well as herself to the snares of Satan, she cut off her hair, put on ugly clothing and a haircloth vest. This strategy, which successfully negated Blidehilde's attractiveness, made Faro reconsider his original intentions. He became embarrassed by his own weakness of the flesh. The *vita* adds that Faro admired the wisdom and virtue of Blidehilde, whom he then sent away.[59]

Chaste marriages are also a frequent motif in the *vitae* of royal saints who are praised for their continence within marriage. In his description of Queen/St. Etheldreda, Bede notes that "Although she lived with him [King Egfrid] for twelve years, she preserved the glory of perpetual virginity." He then adds for the skeptics in the audience, "This fact is absolutely vouched for by Bishop Wilfrid of blessed memory, of whom I made enquiry when some people doubted it." As proof of this chaste relationship, Wilfrid told Bede that the King had promised to give him estates and much wealth if he could persuade the queen to consummate their marriage.[60]

There are a few other cases of kings and queens who were said to lead chaste lives within marriages. The seventh-century St. Kineswide, daughter of King Penda of Mercia and virgin/ abbess of Dormancaester, was married to King Offa. According to tradition, although married, she left her royal marriage bed for the single and chaste life. "For getting her king and husband's consent, they with mutual devotion, did often attend upon Christ lying as brother and sister, serving in the spirit not in flesh."[61]

The late seventh-century Frankish saints Bertha and Gonbert were also married. However, according to the sources, they lived together in perpetual continence. Later in their lives, desiring to give themselves more completely to God, they separated from one another: Gonbert went to Ireland, where he built a monastery, and Bertha constructed two monasteries in the neighborhood of Reims.[62]

St. Aya, daughter of the Count of Ardennes (d. 707), married Hidulphe, who was related to her. After spending their youth in perfect innocence, they married and continued to live in continence. They regarded one another as consecrated to God. Hidulphe retired to become a monk at Lobbes, and Aya became a nun at Mons.[63]

There are other cases in the tradition of the chaste marriage which are perhaps more problematic. Two eleventh-century examples are of special interest. One concerns the eleventh-century German imperial couple, Saints Cunegund and Henry. According to a relatively late biography, written with a view to Cunegund's future canonization, this couple took a vow of chastity on their wedding day. Cunegund, for example, is praised in the following terms: "*O coniugium non voluptate, sed bona voluntate copulatum! O sanctum matrimonium, ubi una fides inviolate castitatis. . . .*"[64] This commitment to chastity could then conveniently be used by supporters to explain this imperial couple's childlessness, although there is no reliable evidence to support this statement of their chaste marriage.[65]

A similar case in which chastity was connected with childlessness, can be found in the *Life of King Edward the Confessor*, written by an anonymous author between 1065–1067. According to the *vita*, Bishop Brihtwald had experienced a vision in which the future king, Edward, would come to the throne, adopt a life of celibacy and leave no offspring.[66] The anonymous author of the life notes that Edward "preserved with holy chastity the dignity of his consecration, and lived his whole life dedicated to God in true innocence."[67] In Osbert of Clare's later rendition (1138), Edward is described as a "temple of virginity." He like the blessed confessor Alexius, was kept by God "all the days of his life in the purity of the flesh." Osbert of Clare also notes that Queen Edith "preserved the secret of the king's chastity of which she had learned, and kept those counsels that she knew."[68] The discrepancy in age between Edward and his Queen was apparently quite substantial: she was at least fifteen or perhaps even twenty years younger than Edward. Their relationship is depicted by the anonymous author to have been that of a father with his daughter: "She called him father and herself his child."[69] In his dying words he addressed his consort, who was sitting at his feet, saying that "she has served me devotedly, and has always stood close by my side like a beloved daughter."[70] Thus this life of Edward the Confessor stresses the "positive/holy" concept of abstinence and chaste marriage as the explanation for the critical failure or incapacity of the royal couple to produce offspring.[71] However, as in the case of Sts. Cunegund and Henry, the actual evidence for Edward and Edith's commitment to lifelong celibacy is not very strong.

A rather famous example of a married saint who later espoused a chaste monastic life, is that of the sixth-century Frankish queen and saint Radegund. Although neither of her biographers attempt to argue that her marriage was in fact chaste, Fortunatus does mention her disdain for the marriage bed. According to Fortunatus, while Radegund shared the royal bed at night, she always managed under some pretext to get up and leave the room. She would then retire to her oratory to pray. Wearing a haircloth shirt, the queen would remain in the oratory for a long time where she lay on the cold floor as if she were dead. When she returned to the bedroom, it was only with great difficulty that she warmed herself with the heat of the hearth and bed. According to Fortunatus, someone mentioned her inappropriate marital behavior to the king, noting: "It is a nun and not a queen that you have for your wife."[72]

The *vitae* also furnish a number of examples of married couples who renounced sex after having had children. The sixth-century Welsh saints, Gwynllyw and Gwladys, parents of St. Cadoc, for example, were encouraged by their son to separate in order to pursue a chaste life. Gwynllyw retired to live on a mountain and his wife built a dwelling within a furlong or one-eighth of a mile from her husband's cell. Here they both followed austere lives, mortifying their bodies by wearing haircloths, fasting, etc. According to Gwynllyw's life, "They were accustomed to restrain the desires of the body by washing themselves in the coldest water; and they did not more seldom wash themselves in the frosty season of winter than in the heat of summer; they rose from their beds in the middle of the night, and after a bath returned to the coldest apartment, put on their clothes, and visited the church, praying and kneeling before the altars until it was day." However, becoming increasingly worried about his parents' spiritual health, Cadoc warned them that they should not be such close neighbors, "lest carnal concupiscence should, through the persuasion of the unseen enemy, pervert their minds from inviolable chastity." He therefore exhorted his mother to leave her residence. Thus, following his advice, she departed from that place to another where she served God with a group of nuns.[73]

We can also find in the *vitae* a number of accounts of female saints unjustly accused by their husbands of adultery. One rather interesting case concerns the ninth century Empress St. Richardis, wife of Charles the Fat.

She was accused of unfaithfulness by her husband, who also named as her accomplice, Liutward, Chancellor and Bishop of Vercelli. Appearing together before the imperial assembly, they denied these allegations. Bishop Luitward took an oath and St. Richardis proved her innocence by resorting to the Judgment of God, specifically, the ordeal by fire. According to our sources, the Empress was wrapped in linen cloth, which had been soaked with inflammable liquid. The linen was then set on fire at its four corners, and although it burned completely, Richardis remained miraculously unharmed. She was also said to have walked with bare feet across the burning embers without receiving any lesions. After this dramatic proof of her innocence, Richardis was allowed to separate from the king and to leave the court. She then retired to the Abbey of Andlau, which she had founded.[74]

Although the majority of the holy dead were recruited from among those who were virgins or never married, there were also a good number of married saints found during this early period. The ideal relationship within marriage, according to the church, was that of chaste lovers. During the fourth through seventh centuries, when the church was especially concerned with the need for sexual purity among its priests and prelates, the lives of bishop saints frequently describe in miraculous terms the chaste relationships adopted by these men with their "former wives." Saints recruited from among royal and noble families also won high praise for their abstemious behavior within marriage. Hagiographers appear to be in agreement that for all saints—whether married or single—concupiscence and sex were very hard to avoid. Indeed, one had to be quite remarkable to do without sex. And in general, the *vitae* seem to be consistent in their views of what works to avoid sex: to flee from temptation, practice bodily mortification, and hope for miraculous intervention. As we have seen, their recommendations are essentially the same for married people as well as singles.

Saintly Interventions in Sexual Problems of the Faithful

While many of the saints cultivated reputations of perpetual virginity and displayed a violent disdain for sex, they were, nevertheless, frequently called upon by the faithful to assist them in their own rather specific and intimate marital problems. In fact, a number of these virginal saints, despite their lack of "life experience" in sex, were looked to as experts in the field; as perhaps early marriage counselors or sex therapists. While this might appear to be an odd paradox (although bishops/priests as confessors or nuns as spiritual advisors have served in this capacity for centuries); no doubt for the faithful, this did not pose a problem.[75] They were after all seeking supernatural or divine intervention which often took the form of a miracle—definitely a saintly prerogative.

As one might expect, the advice or punishment which these holy advisors dispensed, or the miracles they performed, often reflected various moral reform ideologies of the period and attempts at sexual behavior modification. Therefore, we can find in the lives and miracles of the saints, as well as chronicles, and other sources of the period, illustrations of sexual problems and saintly interventions. It appears that the saints were especially invoked to reconcile estranged couples, to assist with problems of infertility, and to cure cases of excessive lust. They also intervened to warn the faithful of the need for periodic continence in their sexual relationships.

The *vita* of St. Brigid of Ireland describes in some detail a case of marital difficulty and the saint's successful assistance in furnishing the couple with a love potion. According to this account, a certain man came to ask St. Brigid for her help since his wife would neither eat nor sleep with him, and had threatened to leave home. Brigid blessed water for him and said: "Put that water over the house, and over the food, and over the drink of yourselves, and over the bed in the wife's absence." We learn that when he had accomplished this, "the wife gave exceeding great love to him, so that she could not keep apart from him, even on one side of the house; but she was always at one of his hands."[76]

Adomnan's *Life of St. Columba* also recounts this saint's success in reconciling an estranged couple through prayer. According to the *vita*, while the saint was visiting the island of Rathlin, he was approached by a certain layman who "complained regarding his wife, who, as he said, had an aversion to him, and would not allow him to enter into marital relations." Hearing this, Columba began chastising the woman saying, "Why, woman, do you attempt to put from you your own flesh? . . ." She replied: "I am ready to perform all things whatsoever that you may enjoin on me, however burdensome: save one thing, that you do not constrain me to sleep in one bed with Lugne [her husband]. I do not refuse to carry on the whole management of the house; or, if you command it even to cross the seas, and remain in some monastery of nuns." The holyman reminded her that since her husband was still alive, she was bound by the law to remain with him, as it was forbidden for her to separate from him. Columba then suggested that the three of them fast and pray—which the couple agreed to do. Also, on the night following the fast, the saint prayed for them. The next day we learn that under Columba's questioning, the wife admitted that she knew the saint's prayer had been heard by God. "For him whom I loathed yesterday I love today. In this past night (how, I do not know) my heart has been changed in me from hate to love." Thus, concludes the *vita*, "From that day until the day of her death, that wife's affections were indissolubly set in love of her husband; so that the dues of the marriage-bed, which she had formerly refused to grant, she never again denied."[77]

As we have already noted in regard to the conception and birth of saints, infertile couples frequently sought out saints to help them with this problem. This type of difficulty is mentioned often in the *vitae*. In the

Miracles of Saint Martin, for example, Gregory of Tours notes the case of a certain Blideric. He had been married for thirty years without any offspring. He finally visited the Church of St. Martin and promised the saint (church) all of his inheritance. Gregory then notes, during that same night that he gave his property to the church, he knew his wife and conceived a son. Later they had other children. One does not doubt, Gregory assures us, that this man owed his ability to have children to the power of the saint.[78] We learn of another man named Charimond who was described as impotent. He was also cured of this problem by the power of St. Martin.[79]

The miracles of King Edward the Confessor describe another case relating to problems of infertility. According to this miracle, a young married woman who had no children, contracted a severe infection of the throat and area under the jaw. "These had so disfigured her face with an evil smelling disease that she could scarcely speak to anyone without great embarrassment." She was then informed in a dream that if she had her neck washed by the king's hands she would be cured of this troublesome disease. She went to the palace, and the king himself, who "did not disdain to help the weaker sex, dipped his hand in a dish of water and "with the tips of his fingers he anointed the face of the young woman and the places infected by the disease. He repeated the action several times, now and then making the sign of the cross." A speedy recovery followed. And within a year, this woman became pregnant by the same husband. (Thus this case of scrofula, which hindered the woman's ability to conceive, was cured by the royal power of touching for the "king's evil.")[80] William of Malmesbury, in his rendition of this miracle, notes that within a year this woman became the mother of twins which "increased the admiration of Edward's holiness!"[81]

Problems associated with excessive lust were also brought to the saints. According to the life of the Irish St. Carthach (Mochuda), this saint possessed a wonderful girdle or belt of gold which had miraculous powers. The belt blessed by the holy saint was placed around the genital organs of a man called Fergus, who was afflicted by a grave case of lecherousness or lust. He was immediately relieved of his problem and restored to health.[82]

A number of saint's lives deal with issues concerning the need for periodic continence among married couples and problems of impurity following sex. The *Dialogues* of Gregory the Great record the case of a noblewoman from Tuscany, who, along with her newly married daughter-in-law, was invited to the dedication of the oratory of the martyr/saint Sebastian. According to Gregory the Great, "the night before this solemnity, overcome with carnal pleasure, she could not abstain from her husband; and though in the morning her former delight troubled her conscience, yet shame drove her forth to the procession, being more ashamed of men than fearing the judgment of God." She then attended the dedication with her mother-in-law. However, immediately, as the relics of St. Sebastian were brought into the oratory, a wicked spirit possessed the young wife which tormented her before everyone present. The priest, witnessing this, took the white linen altar cloth and covered her with it; he in turn was immediately attacked by the devil. After a long struggle, this young woman was ultimately freed of this possession by the prayers of the venerable Bishop Fortunatus.[83]

Gregory of Tours notes another case which warns of divine punishments inflicted on those unable to refrain from having sex at times prohibited by the Church. According to the *Miracles of Saint Martin*, a woman in Berry gave birth to a son who was severely malformed: "he was more a monster than a being imitating the human form." When the mother was asked how she had given birth to such an infant, she confessed while crying that he had been conceived during a Sunday night. And not daring to kill him, as mothers were accustomed to do, she raised him the same as if he had been well formed. Gregory of Tours then cautions his readers that this happens to parents as punishment for their sin and because they have violated the "*noctis dominicae.*" He warns that there are enough other days to give themselves over to "*voluptati,*" sensual pleasure; they should spend Sunday in praise of God and in purity. And if spouses insist on having sex on Sunday, the children born of this union will have crippled limbs, epilepsy, or leprosy. They should learn from this case, lest the evil committed in the course of a single night endures for many years.[84]

Through a collective study of several hundred saints' lives, a wide variety of information on ecclesiastical attitudes toward sex is available. This rather vast compilation of examples found in the *vitae* provides compelling evidence of the great interest in sex, or perhaps more accurately in denying sex, found among the churchmen of this early period. Although this study has only begun to scratch the surface, certain initial patterns can be discerned. Since the majority of those recognized as saints during this early period cultivated reputations of sexual purity, many of the *vitae* appear as essentially anti-sex tracts. They focus on the negative virtues of self-mortification, sexual renunciation, heroics of celibacy/virginity, and the necessary avoidance of women. Also, as we have noted, there appear to be some important gender-based discrepancies in the emphasis or perspectives on sex in the vitae. During various periods of reform (e.g., that of the early Irish Church, Carolingian, Cluniac, and Gregorian), saints' lives—especially those of male saints—provided convenient vehicles to promote programs of severe asceticism and celibacy for churchmen and women. The agendas promoted in the saints' lives were in turn closely corroborated by the canons of church councils, penitentials, and sermons of the period.[85]

On another level, the lives and miracles of saints also recognized the central importance of sex to all of those who had not adopted the chaste life; namely, the majority of the faithful. We therefore find many of these same virginal saints assuming roles of marriage or sex counselors and assisting laymen and women with their problems. They are depicted advising estranged and infertile couples as well as coming to their aid with saintly miracles. Again, with an end to modifying sexual behavior, the saints are shown punishing those who failed to respect the moral laws of the church.

However, in making the case for an individual's membership among the spiritual elite, the chaste, ascetic life remained of primary importance. Perpetual chastity, from "womb to tomb," provided these holy men and women with a moral advantage, a spiritual edge, a proven strength or power over ordinary members of the Christian community. This life of bodily mortification, of heroic renunciation and withdrawal from all sexual activities, was viewed as perhaps a minor miracle in itself by the faithful.

Frequently, the saint's lifelong preservation of sexual purity was miraculously validated even after death. In his description of Gerald of Aurillac's death, Odo of Cluny provides us with a wonderful story about the holyman's continued concern with the perfection of chastity. He tells us that "When his body had been stripped for washing, Ragembertus and other servants who were performing the duty put both his hands on his breast, when suddenly his right arm extended itself, and his hand was applied to his private parts so as to cover them. Thinking this had happened by chance they bent the hand back to the breast. But again it was extended in the same way and covered his private parts. They were amazed," Odo notes, "but wishing to understand the matter more carefully they bent the arm back a third time and put the hand back with the other on his breast. Immediately with lightning speed it sought the same parts and covered them. Those who were laying him out, struck at once by admiration and fear, realized then that this was not happening without divine power. Perhaps it was being divinely shown that this flesh when alive was always anxious to preserve the modesty of chastity. They quickly covered the body, and when it had received a covering the hand no more stretched out."[86]

William of Malmesbury, in his *History of the Kings of England*, and of *His Own Times*, includes a number of cases of the miraculous incorruptibility of the body or its "private parts" as proof of the perpetual virginity of a saint. He notes, for example, in regard to Saints Etheldreda and Ethelberga's preservation of virginity: "It is well worthy of remark, that as both sisters had subdued the lusts of the flesh while living, so, when dead, their bodies remained uncorrupt, the one in England and the other in France; insomuch, that their sanctity, which is abundantly resplendent, may suffice to irradiate both poles."[87] In his description of the Virgin/Saint Edgitha, William of Malmesbury provides us with another example of posthumous virginal incorruptibility. He discloses that Saint Edgitha was known to habitually stretch out her right thumb and make the sign of the cross on her forehead. In response to this, Dunstan exclaimed, "May this finger never see corruption." After Edgitha's death, miracles occurred at her tomb. Her body was then translated to a more honorable location and "the whole of it [i.e., the body] was found resolved into dust, except the finger, with the abdomen and parts adjacent." Some discussion arose about the meaning of this. Afterward the virgin herself appeared in a dream to one of those who saw her remains saying "It was no wonder if the other parts of the body had decayed, since it was customary for dead bodies to moulder in their native dust, and she, perhaps, as a girl, had sinned with those members; but it was also highly just, that the abdomen should see no corruption which had never felt the sting of lust; as she had been entirely free from gluttony or carnal copulation."[88]

The life of subjection of the flesh, of renunciation of sex, was then the *vita* perfecta adopted by many of the early medieval saints. While focusing their primary attention on becoming worthy of membership in the celestial kingdom, these "impatient angels" first needed to prove themselves by "suffering" through the many ordeals of life in this world. And as Odo of Cluny so aptly argued in his promotion of Gerald of Aurillac to sainthood, "For it is chastity alone which imitates the purity of angels."[89]

Notes

1 William of Malmesbury, *The History of the Kings of England, and of His Own Times* in *The Church Historians of England*, tr. Rev. John Sharpe, rev. Rev. Joseph Stevenson. (London, 1854), vol. III, pt. I, 29, no. 5.

2 See Schulenburg, "Female Sanctity: Public and Private Roles, ca. 500–1100," in *Women and Power in the Middle Ages*, ed. Mary Erler and Maryanne Kowaleski (Athens, Ga., 1988), 102–25.

3 Peter Brown, *The Body and Society: Men, Women, and Sexual Renunciation in Early Christianity* (New York, 1988), 359.

4 Aldhelm, *"De virginitate,"* in *Aldhelm: The Prose Works*, ed. and tr. Michael Lapidge and Michael Herren (Totowa, 1979), 55.

5 For the importance of virginity in the making of saints see Schulenburg, "The Heroics of Virginity: Brides of Christ and Sacrificial Mutilation," in *Women in the Middle Ages and the Renaissance: Literary and Historical Perspectives*, ed. Mary Beth Rose (Syracuse, 1986), 29–72. Barlow, for example, also emphasizes the critical importance of virginity in regard to the spiritual dossier of Edward the Confessor. Frank Barlow, ed. and tr., *The Life of King Edward who rests at Westminster, attributed to a monk of St. Bertin* (London, 1962), lxxv.

6 Carolus Plummer, *vitae* Sanctorum Hiberniae (Oxford, 1910), vol. I, clvii–clviii.

7 Ibid., cxxxvii, n. 9; clviii, n. 2.

8 Charles Plummer *Lives of the Irish Saints* (Oxford, 1922), vol. II, 177.

9 See Plummer, *Vitae Sanctorum Hiberniae*, I., clviii, and n. 4 for all these incidents.

10 Dom Gerard Sitwell, tr. *St. Odo of Cluny: Being the Life of St. Odo of Cluny by John of Salerno and the Life of St. Gerald of Aurillac by St. Odo* (London and New York, 1958), bk. I, ch. 2, 95.

11 Ibid., bk. I, ch. 5, 8.

12 "S. Bernardi vita prima," *Patrologiae Cursus Completus*, 185, J.P. Migne (henceforth *PL*), bk. I, ch. 1, 227 (1063).

13 Jonas, "The Life of St. Columban," in *Translations and Reprints from the Original Sources of European History* (Philadelphia, 1902), vol. II, no. 7, c. 22, 13.

14 *"Vita Bennonis II Episcopi Osnabrugensis"* by Norberto abbate Iburgensi, *MGH Scriptorum*, vol. XII, ch. I, 61.

15 W. J. Rees, ed. and tr., "The Life of Saint Beino," in *Lives of the Cambro British Saints* (Llandovery, 1853), 299–300.

16   Brown, *The Body and Society*, 213–40.

17   Kathleen Hughes, *The Church in Early Irish Society* (London, 1966), 177.

18   Brown, *The Body and Society*, 242.

19   *Rhigyfarch's Life of St. David*, ed. and tr. J.W. James (Cardiff, 1967), ch. 15–16, 34. See also Plummer, *Vitae Sanctorum Hiberniae*, I, clxvi; clxvi, n. 2.

20   *Rhigyfarch's Life of St. David*, c. 17–20, 35.

21   Plummer, *Vitae Sanctorum Hiberniae*, I, cxxi, n. 5.

22   Jonas, *Life of St. Columban*, ch. 7–9, 3–4. See also *Vitae columbani abbatis discipulorumque eius, MGH, SRM*, vol. IV, bk. i, c. 3, 68.

23   See esp. Roger E. Reynolds, *"Virgines Subintroductae* in Celtic Christianity," *Harvard Theological Review* 61 (1968), 547–66, L. Gougaud, "Mulierum Consortia: Étude sur le syneiaktisme chez les ascètes celtiques," *Eriu* 9 (1921–23), 147–56, Elizabeth Clark, "John Chrysostom and the *subintroductae*," in *Ascetic Piety and Women's Faith: Essays on Late Ancient Christianity* (New York and Toronto, 1986), 265–90, and Clark's *Jerome, Chrysostom and Friends* (Lewiston, 1979), Rosemary Rader, *Breaking Boundaries: Male/Female Friendship in Early Christian Communities* (New York, 1983), H. Achelis, *Virgines subintroductae* (Leipzig, 1902).

24   Reynolds, "*Virgines Subintroductae*," 563, 559. For this episode, see also J.H. Todd, *St. Patrick, Apostle of Ireland* (Dublin, 1864), 91, n. 1. I would like to thank Isabella Moreira for bringing this wonderful case to my attention.

25   Reynolds, "*Virgines Subintroductae*," 559.

26   William of Malmesbury, *De Gestis Pontificum Anglorum, Libri quinque*, ed. fr. ms. by N.E.S.A. Hamilton (London, 1870, reprint, 1964), pt. III, no. 213, 358–59; Gougaud, "Mulierum Consortia," 148–49; Reynolds, "*Virgines Subintroductae*," 559.

27   Reynolds, "*Virgines Subintroductae*," 563; Gougaud, "Mulierum Consortia," 149–50; Giraldus Cambrensis, *Gemma Ecclesiastica*, ed. J.S. Brewer (London, 1862), II, 15, 236–37.

28   See esp. Jacques Dalarun, "Robert d'Arbrissel et les femmes," *Annales, Economies, Sociétés, Civilisations* (1984), 39, no. 6 (Nov.–Dec.), 1140–60, esp. 1147–48; Gougaud, "Mulierum Consortia," 150–51.

29   Brown, *The Body and Society*, esp. 224–25, 269; for a superb treatment of the practice of fasting by holywomen, see Caroliine Walker Bynum, *Holy Feast and Holy Fast: The Religious Significance of Food to Medieval Women* (Berkeley, Los Angeles, London, 1987).

30   Gregory the Great, "Life and Miracles of St. Benedict," *Book Two of the Dialogues*, tr. Odo J. Zimmermann and Benedict R. Avery (Collegeville, Minn., n.d.), ch. 2, 7–8. In regard to the "historicity" of this episode, see P. Courcelle, "Saint Benoît, le merle et le buisson d'épines," *Journal des savants* (1967), 161, and M. Doucet, "La tentation de saint Benoît: relation ou création par saint Grégoire le grand?," *Collectanea Cisterciensia* 37 (1975), 63–71. Both of these scholars seriously question the historical validity of this episode.

31   Michael Swanton, tr. *Three Lives of the Last Englishmen*, in *The Garland Library of Medieval Literature*, vol. 10, ser. B (New York and London, 1984), 94–95. See also 99–100 where Wulfstan is again shown successfully resisting female temptation.

32   Gougaud notes the significance of saints adopting ordeals involving fire and burning coals as proof of their chastity. He cites the tradition found in Proverbs VI, 27–28 "Can a man carry fire in his bosom and his clothes not be burned? Or can one

walk upon hot coals and his feet not be scorched?" Gougaud, "Mulierum Consortia," 153.

33   *Acta Sanctorum* (henceforth *AASS*), vol. 6 (October 13), 227.

34   See Dom Jacques Hourlier, *Saint Odilon Abbé de Clumy: Bibliothèque de la revue d'histoire ecclésiastique*, No. 40 (Louvain, 1964), 130–31.

35   *AASS April*, vol. III, (April 24), ch. 8, pp. 337–338. See also, Dominique Iogna-Prat, "La femme dans la perspective pénitentielle des ermites du Bas-Maine (fin XIème–debut XIIème siècle)," *Revue d'histoire de la spiritualité* 53 (1977), 57–62.

36   See Dom Louis Gougaud, *Devotional and Ascetic Practices in the Middle Ages,* ed. G.C. Bateman (London, 1927), 159–78.

37   Giraldi Cambrensis, *Gemma ecclesiastica* in *Rerum Britannicarum medii aevi scriptores* (Rolls Series), ed. J.S. Brewer (London, 1862), 21, 2, ch. X, 216. In this chapter Giraldus also includes other dramatic examples of saintly struggles against temptation such as Gregory the Great's description of St. Benedict and the wonderful story of the twelfth century St. Godric of Finchale.

38   Rees, *Lives of the Cambro British Saints,* 431.

39   Gougaud, "Mulierum Consortia," 147–48.

40   *AASS*, Feb., vol. III (Feb. 23), ch. II, 424.

41   "S. Bernardi Vita prima" *PL*, 185, bk. 1, ch. III, 230 (1065). On this rather popular episode in St. Bernard's life see: Jean Leclercq, *Women and St. Bernard of Clairvaux* in *Cistercian Studies Series: 104*, tr. Marie-Bernard Said, (Kalamazoo, 1989), pp. 116–17.

42   Gougaud, *Devotional and Ascetic Practices,* 162; also, *AASS*, Julii, vol. II (July 6), ch. 2, n. 21, 300.

43   Gougaud, *Devotional and Ascetic Practices,* 160.

44   Sitwell, *St. Odo of Cluny,* ch. 9, 102–03.

45   Plummer, *Lives of Irish Saints,* ch. xv (24), 286.

46   *Vitae columbani abbatis discipulorumque eius, liber II, MGH, SRM,* vol. IV, No. 13, 133.

47   *The Lives of Women Saints of Our Contrie of England, Also Some Other Lives of Holie Women Written by Some of the Auncient Fathers* (The Early English Text Society), ed. C. Horstmann (London, 1886), 43–49.

48   *AASS*, Maii, vol. II (May 10), 589–91.

49   Schulenburg, "The Heroics of Virginity," 29–72, esp. 46–49.

50   Aldhelm, *"De Virginitate,"* 75.

51   Gregory of Tours, *The History of the Franks,* tr. Lewis Thorpe (Harmondsworth, 1974), bk. I, ch. 47, 95–97; Gregory of Tours, *Glory of the Confessors,* tr. Raymond Van Dam (Liverpool, 1988), ch. 31, 45.

52   Gregory of Tours, *The History of the Franks,* bk I, ch. 47, 95–97.

53   See esp. Brian Brennan, *"Episcopae*: Bishops' Wives Viewed in Sixth-Century Gaul," *Church History* 54, No. 3 (Sept. 1985), 311–23, and Suzanne Wemple's classic study, *Women in Frankish Society: Marriage and the Cloister, 500–900* (Philadelphia, 1981), esp. 130–36.

54   E.g. Council of Clermont (535), Council of Tours (567), etc. The Council of Clermont also concluded that clerical incontinence was in fact a form of incest and thus required the deposition of the cleric. See Wemple, *Women in Frankish Society,* pp. 132–33. Brennan, *"Episcopae,"* 314–15.

55   Gregory of Tours, *Glory of the Confessors,* ch. 75, 78–80.

56   Ibid., ch. 77, 81.

57   Gregory of Tours, *History of the Franks,* bk. I, ch. 44, 93–94.

58   Frodoard (Flodoard), *Histoire de l'église de Rheims: Collection des mémoires relatifs à l'histoire de France*, ed. M. Guizot (Paris, 1824), bk. I, ch. XIV, 47–51.

59   *AASS*, Octobrius, vol. 12 (October 29), pp. 609–616.

60   Bede, *A History of the English Church and People*, bk. IV, ch. 19, 238.

61   *The Lives of Women Saints of Our Contrie of England*, p. 71.

62   *AASS*, Maii, vol. I (May 1), chs. 2–3, 117; Frodoard, *Histoire de l'église de Rheims*, bk. IV, ch. XLVII, 595–97.

63   *AASS*, Aprilis, vol. II (April 18), 576.

64   *Vita S. Cunegundis, MGH, Scriptorum*, IV, 822, 824.

65   *The Life of King Edward*, ed. Barlow, lxxviii.

66   Ibid., 8–9, appendix 85–87.

67   Ibid., 60–61

68   Ibid., 15.

69   Ibid., 60.

70   Ibid., 79.

71   Ibid., lxxvii.

72   Fortunatus, *De Vita Sanctae Radegundis* Liber I, *MGH, SRM*, II, bk. I, ch. 5, 366–67.

73   *Lives of the Cambro British Saints*, 451–56.

74   *AASS*, Septembris, (September 18), 794–98; Agnes B. C. Dunbar, *A Dictionary of Saintly Women* (London, 1905), II, 186.

75   See Jane Bishop, "Bishops as Marital Advisors in the Ninth Century," in *Women of the Medieval World*, ed. Julius Kirshner and Suzanne F. Wemple (Oxford and New York, 1985), 53–84.

76   *Anecdota Oxoniensia Lives of Saints from the Book of Lismore*, ed. and tr. Whitley Stokes (Oxford, 1890), p. 192.

77   Adomnan, *Adomnan's Life of Columba*, ed. and tr. Alan Orr Anderson and Marjorie Ogilvie Anderson (London, 1961), bk. II, ch. 41, 436–41.

78   Gregory of Tours, *Libri Miraculorum aliaque Opera Minora*, tr. H.L. Bordier (Paris, 1860), II, bk. IV, ch. XI, 286–89.

79   Ibid., bk. IV, ch. xxiii, 302–03.

80   *The Life of King Edward*, 61–62. In this miracle we see an early example of the English king's thaumaturgic power of touching for the "king's evil." Barlow notes that "it seems that the cult was largely French in inspiration and that it had a fluctuating influence on English belief" (*Life of King Edward*, 123). See also Marc Bloch's classic study, *Les Rois Thaumaturges (Publications de la Faculté des Lettres de l'Université de Strasbourg*, XIX (Strasbourg, 1924); William A. Chaney, *The Cult of Kingship in Anglo-Saxon England: The Transition from Paganism to Christianity* (Berkeley and Los Angeles, 1970), 73, 83.

81   William of Malmesbury, *History of the Kings*, ch. 222, 209.

82   Plummer, *Vitae Sanctorum Hiberniae*, I, 184.

83   Gregory the Great, *The Dialogues of Saint Gregory*, ed. Edmund G. Gardner (London, 1911), ch. 10, 38–39. For this topic see also Jean-Louis Flandrin, *Un Temps pour embrasser: Aux origines de la morale sexuelle occidentale VIe–XIe siècle)* (Paris, 1983).

84   Gregory of Tours, *Libri Miraculorum*, II, ch. XXIV, 131–33.

85   The importance of saints promulgating programs of public policy has been underscored in Kathleen Mitchell's interesting study, "Saints and Public Christianity in the *Historiae* of Gregory of Tours," in *Religion, Culture, and Society in the Early*

Middle Ages: Studies in Honor of Richard E. Sullivan, ed. Thomas F.X. Noble and John J. Contreni (Kalamazoo, 1987), 77–94.

86   Sitwell, *St. Odo of Cluny*, bk. III, ch. 10, 170.
87   William of Malmesbury, *History of the Kings*, ch. 214, 205.
88   Ibid., ch. 218, 207–08.
89   Sitwell, *St. Odo of Cluny*, bk. II, ch. 34, 160.

PENIS CAPTIVUS

Penis Captivus: A Historical Note

J.D. Rolleston, M.D.*

DEFINITION. In the present paper the term "penis captivus" is applied to incarceration of the organ in the vagina due to psychogenic spasmodic contraction of the *levator ani*, and not to the condition resulting from insertion of the penis into rings and similar inanimate objects.

Although references to the condition are to be found in the works of Bloch, Hühner, Kisch, Moll and Stoeckel, and isolated cases have been recorded by Scanzoni, Hildebrandt, Piltz and others, the literature on the subject, as will be seen by consulting the three series of the Surgeon General's Catalogue under the heading of Penis and Vaginismus is remarkably scanty[1]). It was particularly surprising to find no mention of penis captivus in Gould and Pyle's well-known "Anomalies and Curiosities" of Medicine, especially as this work contains a remarkably well-documented chapter on surgical anomalies of the genito-urinary system. Moreover, personal inquiry of many eminent London gynaecologists, urologists, venereologists, sexologists, general surgeons and medical antiquarians revealed the fact that they had not only never seen any cases of the kind but knew little or nothing of the literature of the subject which most of them seemed to regard as unworthy of serious consideration.

My attention was first drawn to the subject during a recent search for references to venereal disease in mediaeval belletristic literature when I came across certain passages describing the condition in the Early English Text Society's publications, which have not hitherto, as far as I can ascertain, found any notice in medical literature. The first passage is in the poem of Robert of Brunne, alias Robert Mannyng (1264–1340) entitled "Handlyng Synne", which is a free translation made in 1303 of William of Wadington's "*Manuel des Pechiez*", the English and French texts being given in parallel columns in the E.E.T.S. publication edited by F.J. Furnivall. "Handlyng Synne" is a series of metrical homilies dealing among other subjects with the Seven Deadly Sins illustrated by stories from various sources. The passage in question which exemplifies the evil results of lechery relates how a man named Rychere (Fr. Richer) with his wife sought refuge from his enemies in a monastery where the abbot gave him a chamber close to the church with the following result:

O nyt thyr was, he knewe hys wyfe
Of fleshely dede, as fyl here lyfe
And God was nat payd, and wide hyt not,
So ny be charche, swyche dede were wroght;
*They myghte no more be broughte a-sondre
*Than dog and byche that men on wondre.
The monks were then summoned
*To praye for hem yn orysun
*That they myghte be undoun
And God almyghty graunted hyt sone.

[One night it happened that he took his wife in carnal intercourse, like a concubine her lover, and God was not pleased, not at all pleased that such deeds be done so near the church; men wondered at the fact that they could no more be separated than a dog and a bitch. The monks were then summoned . . . to say prayers for them that they might be uncoupled, and God Almighty soon granted it.]

According to Furnivall, in the Harleian MS, the lines marked with an asterisk "were inked over and scraped out by some ancient jigleafite." The passage ends with the warning that:

moche more dampnacioun
Wyl falle of fornycacyun
And yet more for avowtrye (adultery)
Of prestys or wyves lecherye,
Whan God toke wreche that many of spake
For a dede that was do yn ryt wedloke.

[much more hellish punishments will result from fornication—and even more so from the adultery of priests or of lecherous wives—considering the widely known penalty God imposed for an act done in lawful wedlock.]

How a more severe penalty (in the form of exposure to the public and self-castigation) than that inflicted on Richer and his wife did actually overtake unwedded couples guilty of a similar sacrilege is related as follows in two consecutive chapters of "The Book of the Knight of La Tour-Landry," a work written in French by Geoffrey de La Tour-Landry for the instruction of his daughters in 1372, of which an English translation printed by Caxton appeared in 1484,
    Chap. 35:

Hit happed in a chirche on an even of oure lady, one that was called Pers Lenard, whiche was sergeaint of Candee on the night delt fleshely with a woman on an auter, and God of his gret might wolde shewe that they dide evelle, tyed hem faste togedre dat night and thee morw all day in the sight of the pepill that come thedir into the towne; and all the contre there about come downe and sawe hem. And thei might never parte, but were fast like a dogge and a biche togedre, that night and the morw all day until the tyme that the pepill yode a procession about for them to pray to God that that orrible sight might be ended and hidde and atte the last, whanne it was night thei departed. And after the chirche was halowed or ever there were saide therein ani masse. And they that dede the dede were ioyned to penaince to go naked afore the procession thre sondayes beting hem self and recordyng her synne tofore the pepill. And therfor here is an ensaumple that no body shudde do no suche filthe in the chirche, but kepe it clene and worshipe God there inne.

Chap. 30:

There was an abbey in Peytow called Chimfere, the whiche abbey was
fortefyed for werres and the prioure of that abbey had a monke there, that
was his nevew, that hight Pigreet, the whiche atte a tyme might not be
founde: and he was lost and atte the laste thei fonde hym in a comer of a
chirche behinde a wyche (hut) on a woman, and they might not parte that
one from that other and than all folke came thedir to see hem; of the whiche
sight the sely monke was sore ashamed of and full of sorw, and so was his
uncle and all other monks and after, whaune it was the will of god, thei
parted, and the monke Pygreet went and fledde a-wey oute of the abbey for
shame.

Commenting on this passage the editor Thomas Wright remarks that "a
similar miracle is related in several of the mediaeval religious legends. In
one a Welsh king and his queen are the offenders. Robert De Brunne dwells
at length on the greatness of the offence in a manner than would lead us to
suppose it is not uncommon."

Although the passages which I have quoted appear to be the fullest
description of *penis captivus* in early literature, brief allusions to the
condition are to be found in much older works.

Apart from the entanglement of Mars and Venus in the net prepared by
Vulcan and their exposure to the "inextinguishable laughter" of the gods on
Olympus, while the goddesses modestly held aloof (Homer, Odyssey VIII,
266 *et seq.*), which may be regarded as an allegory, there is the following
passage in Lucretius (IV, 1195–1201) describing the adhesion during coitus
which takes place in dogs preceded by two lines which may possibly refer to
a similar process in mankind:

Nonne vides etiam quos mutua saepe voluptas Vinxit, ut in vinclis
communibus excrucientur? In triviis non saepe canes disceders aventes,
Divorsi cupide summis ex viribu' tendunt, Cum interea validis Veneris
compagibus haerent? Quod facerent nunquam, nisi mutua gaudia nossent:
Quae lacere fraudem possent vinctosque tenere.

[See you not too how those whom mutual pleasure has chained are often tortured in
their mutual chains? How often in the highways do dogs desiring to separate eagerly
pull different ways with all their might, while all the time they are held fast by the
strong fetters of Venus. This they would never do unless they experienced mutual
joys, strong enough to force them into the snare and hold them in its meshes.]
(Munro's translation)

Another mediaeval writer who alludes to *penis captivus* is Saxo
Grammaticus, the Danish historian who flourished in the second half of the
twelfth century. This writer states that some of the inhabitants of Karenza
(the modern Garz) in the island of Rügen were punished by the gods for their
debauchery by inseparable cohesion in sexual congress after the manner of
dogs and were exposed in this ridiculous position on poles to the gaze of the
multitude. The occurrence according to Saxo was regarded as a miracle
subsequently commemorated by the erection of obscene statues.

All the passages hitherto quoted are by lay writers, but Schurig (1656–
1733) in that storehouse of sexological lore, entitled "Spermatologia" has

collected the following cases reported by contemporary physicians as well as the passage in Saxo Grammaticus.

In a case reported by Borel the man's imprisonment is attributed either to excessive heat of the swollen genital organs or to the application of civet to the glans on the advice of a friend for the sake of increasing his pleasure. Borel remarks that separation in such cases can be effected by the frequent administration of clysters. Schurig also quotes a similar case due to the application of civet reported by C.F. Lange, Daniel Ludwig's case in which on the first night of marriage not only the glans but the whole of the penis was constricted and Paullini's case in a citizen of Jena, about which no details are given. Diemerbroeck, the well-known seventeenth century anatomist also gives the following account of a case:

> When I was a Student at Leyden I remember there was a young Bridegroom in that Town that being overwanton with his Bride had so hamper'd himself in her Privities, that he could not draw his Yard forth, till Delmehorst the Physician unty'd the Knot by casting cold Water on the Part.

In some but by no means all of the recorded cases, as wrongly stated by Stoeckel, the spasm has occurred during illicit intercourse, but the cases reported by Diemerbroeck, Ludwig, Scanzoni and Hildebrandt as well as those already alluded to in mediaeval literature show that married couples are not exempt.

Although since the days of Homer the condition of the imprisoned couple has appeared so supremely ridiculous as even to raise a doubt as to its actual occurrence, it is difficult to imagine not only the acute mental and physical suffering of the unfortunate victims during their conjunction but also their feeling of shame after release which in the following case reported by Piltz led to double suicide.

> We remember a case of vaginismus with penis captivus which occurred in 1923 at Warsaw and ended by double suicide. It was in the spring, a couple of young students stayed behind in the garden after closing time. In the midst of their amorous sport a violent spasm occurred imprisoning the penis. The keeper alarmed by the desperate cries of the young man ran up. The doctor of the municipal ambulance after giving an anaesthetic to the woman separated the couple. The matter might have been forgotten, but the journalists in their greed for sensational facts did not fail to publish the adventure. The next day two revolver shots put an end to the mental sufferings of the two lovers.

Under the circumstances the question of treatment deserves some consideration. At the present-day administration of chloroform to the female partner is usually necessary to relax the vaginal spasm. In the pre-anaesthetic era the release of the imprisoned organ apart from aspersion of water in Diemerbroeck's case must have been spontaneous, as in the cases reported by the mediaeval and seventeenth-century writers, as well as in the following case reported in 1872 by Hildebrandt relating to a man married to a very excitable young woman:

How many minutes the imprisonment lasted he could not say, but its duration seemed to be interminably long, until finally the obstacle gave way by itself and he became free.

Henrichsen, who has recorded a case of vaginismus without any history of *penis captivus*, in which the spasm was relaxed by insertion of the finger through the anal sphincter, has suggested that this procedure should be employed in cases of penis captivus, but I have not found the report of any case where this suggestion was put into practice. According to Stoeckel even in the cases in which chloroform has been used, forcible introduction of the finger into the vagina is necessary to release the swollen and discoloured organ.

*This article first appeared in *Janus*, vol. 39 (1936), 196–201. Reprinted courtesy of *Janus*. My thanks to Professor Michael Murphy of the University of Wisconsin–Green Bay who translated the Middle English passages.

Notes

1   I have been unable to obtain Dr. Foucault's Paris thesis entitled "Note sur cinq cas de penis captivus," 1881, listed in the first series of the Surgeon General's Catalogue, s.v. Vaginismus.

References

Bloch, I. "The Sexual Life of Our Time." 1909, 433, footnote.
Henrichsen, K., *Arch. F. Gyn.* 23 (1884), 59.
Hildebrandt. *Arch. F. Gyn.* 3 (1872), 221.
Hühner, M. *A Practical Treatise on Disorders of the Sexual Function in the Male and Female.* 3rd ed. 1929, 183.
Kisch, E.H. The Sexual Life of Woman. Tr. M. Eden Paul. 1910, 340.
La Tour-Landry. *The Book of the Knight of La Tour-Landry.* E.E.T.S., Orig. Ser. 33. 1906. 51–53.
Moll, 1A. *Handb. d. Sexualwissenschaften.* 1913. 722.
Piltz, A. Thèse de Paris, 1931, Mo. 376.
Robert of Brunne. *Handlyng Synne* E.E.T.S., Orig. Ser. 123. 1903. Pl. II, 281–82.
Saxo Grammaticus. *Historiae Daniae* 1644, Lib. XIV, 327–28.
Scanzoni. *Beitr. z. Gebartsk. u. Gyn.* 7 (1873), 141.
Schur gius, D.M. "Spermatologia"; 729, 314.
Stoeckel, W. "Lehrb. Gyn" 4 Aufl. 1933, 162.

Postscript

I am indebted to Dr. J. Beattie, who has recently succeeded Sir Arthur Keith as conservator of the Royal College of Surgeons' Museum, for having drawn my attention to the passage in Harvey Cushing's *Life of Sir William Osler* (1926, i. 2450) alluding to a case described by "Egerton Y. Davis," a pseudonym mischievously adopted by Osler on various occasions. The case which was reported in *Medical News* 45 (1884), 673, though entirely fictitious, so closely resembles those described by previous writers that it has been quoted in some standard works on sexology such as those of Kisch and Hühner.

Three Cases of Vaginism

C. Grant Loomis**

Hagiological records contain many a strange and unexpected item. An occurrence which is apparently miraculous is often a recognized phenomenon in more enlightened days. The three excerpts brought together here from different sources, which date roughly from the twelfth to the fourteenth centuries, may be of interest to the student of medical history. The first two accounts seem to be sufficiently explicit to warrant a definite assumption about their real nature. The third derives credulity by analogy. We must premise, of course, that we are dealing with a real occurrence and not with a hagiologist's fiction. Since vaginism is a perfectly recognizable and not unusual phenomenon, we may presume that we are interpreting in these cases a real fact.

In the life of Saint Clitaucus we find the following:

> Potens quidam die dominico cum uxore ad audiendum dei seruitium in ecclesia sancti Clitauci veniens, super ripam fluminis, non longe ab ecclesia positam, cum uxore sua concubuit, et peccato commiso, ab illa separari non potuit, immo iunctus uxori inseparabilis remansit. Et exclamans sodalibus voce magna dixit: "Ite ad sepulchrum martyris Clitauci, et pratum istud, a me vi et iniuste ablatum, sibi restitui promittite, et pro me suppliciter queso intercedite." Quo facto, ab horribili ligamine statim liberatus est.[1]

[A certain man along with his wife were coming on Sunday to hear the servants of God in the church of Saint Clitaucus, and on the riverbank not far from the church, he had intercourse with his wife, and having committed this sin, he could not be separated from her, indeed remained inseparably joined to his wife. So calling out to his comrades, he said loudly: 'Go to the grave of the martyr Clitaucus and promise to be returned to him that very site (meadow) I had taken forcibly and unjustly, and intercede, I beg you, humbly on my behalf.' When this was done, he was immediately freed from this horrible bind.]

A similar happening is told in the life of Saint Guignerus. Here we have an interesting physical moral variant:

> Super sarcophagum venerabilis cuiusdam Episcopi, qui contubernalibus fuerat Regis Clitonis, corruptor quidam gremia cuiusdam mulieris incestare præsumpsit; qui more canum in ipso opere turpitudinis inseparabiliter copulati, nulla poterant ratione ab inuicem separari.

Adducuntur tandem ad memoriam martyris gloriosi Guigneri, ubi merito testis Christi & intercessione fidelium liberantur.[2]

[Over the coffin of a certain old bishop who had been the comrade of King Clitonus, a particular corruptor was eager to invade the lap of a certain woman. As they were inseparably coupled in the fashion of dogs in this dishonorable work, they could in no way be separated from each other. At last they were led to the memory of the renowned martyr Guignerus, where by the good work of Christ's witness and the intercession of the faithful, they were freed.]

A third brief statement suggests a similar situation:

Miraculum de quadam muliere quae viro conjugato adhæsit et eum non sinebat ad uxorem propriam remeare.[3]

[There's a miracle about a certain woman who stuck when joined with a man and did not let him return to his own wife.]

**This article first appeared in *Bulletin of the History of Medicine* 7 (1939), 97–93. Reprinted courtesy of *BHM*. My thanks to Professor Clifford Abbott of the University of Wisconsin–Green Bay who translated the Latin passages.

Notes

1 Horstmann, *Nova Legenda Anglie*, Oxford, 1901, vol. I, 190.

2 *Acta Sanctorum*, Bollandist Society, Antwerp, 1643—, March, vol. III, 459, col. 2. Auctor se Anselmum nominat. Ex MS. Parisiensi S. Victoris (early 12th century?).

3 *Analecta Bollandiana*, vol. VIII, 188 (Bibl. Civit. Carnot. Codex 212. Saec. XIII). This appears in a list of the miracles of the Virgin Mary.

THE POLITICS OF SODOMY: REX V. PONS HUGH DE AMPURIAS (1311)

James A. Brundage*

Among the litigation records in the Archives of the Crown of Aragon in Barcelona reposes a small file containing a dozen paper folios, in fragile condition.[1] The records in this file consist of the testimony in a criminal proceeding brought by King James II of Aragon (1291–1327) against Count Pons Hugh IV of Ampurias (1277–1313) on a charge of sodomy. This paper will examine both the law and what little is known of the facts of this case, which was far from the routine criminal prosecution on a morals charge that it might at first glance seem to have been.

The opening document in the file sets forth the prosecution's theory of the case and the rationale on which the charge was alleged to be based:

> Friday, the sixth of August, in the year of the Lord 1311 in the city of Barcelona. Since through [common] fame and [general] knowledge certain matters have come to the attention of Us, James, by the grace of God King of Aragon, Valencia, Sardinia, and Corsica and Count of Barcelona, We can no longer ignore [this situation] without scandal or tolerate [it] without danger. [We have learned that] it has happened often, indeed very often, that some persons in the Diocese of Gerona cultivate that sort of debauchery which is against nature. Because of this God's wrath fell upon the sons [of Lot] and He consumed with fire five cities where Venus was changed into another form. . . . Nor does it seem that We, who hold Our office, lands, and kingdoms from on high [can allow] such criminal, vile and horrid [deeds] because of the danger that is known to befall cities and their inhabitants [from such activities]. For, on this account, earthquakes, famine, and pestilence increase, the air becomes infected and disturbed. . . . Accordingly we began diligently to inquire about the aforesaid matters in the following manner.[2]

What follows is the record of the testimony of twelve witnesses who were interrogated on this matter, some of them under threat of torture. Upon examining their depositions, it quickly becomes clear that one central figure appears in all of this testimony. He is Pons Hugh IV, Count of Ampurias, who is alleged by one witness after another to have made sexual advances to other men. Some witnesses stated that they had observed the Count's homosexual activities.[3] Others testified that they had been approached by the count with sodomitical intentions, but that they had repulsed his advances.[4] One witness, when threatened with torture, broke down and gave a detailed account of his own involvement as one of the

Count's lovers, although he maintained that the Count had only secured his cooperation under coercion.[5] Such in summary are the facts of the prosecution's case, so far as they are known to us, for at this point the depositions abruptly break off. The evidence, such as it is, seems relatively clear-cut, although we are certainly entitled to doubt the credibility of evidence secured under threat of torture and also to be a trifle skeptical of the value of a witness' recollection of events in the distant past—one deposition relates to an episode that had taken place thirty-two years previously. Still there is a case of sorts—enough, at least on the surface, to sustain a prosecution.

Nonetheless a question remains: why should the King of Aragon have bothered himself personally with this matter? And why did he choose to prosecute this defendant on this charge at this time? The rationale advanced in the prefatory document is not very convincing, especially since a good part of it is simply standard vituperative rhetoric, borrowed from well-known sources.[6] In any case it is difficult to accept the proposition that so seasoned a skeptic as James II really believed that homosexuality caused earthquakes or that the cities of Aragon and Catalonia were in imminent danger of destruction because of the deviant sexual preferences of the Count of Ampurias.

The charges against the Count of Ampurias were exceedingly serious. No category of sexual offense was treated more harshly by medieval law than sodomy, which was a general term used to describe any and all varieties of male homosexual activity.[7] Both Roman law, whence some of the rhetoric in the charges against Pons Hugh was derived, and also the customary law of Catalonia treated sodomy as a capital crime.[8] The canonists did not treat sodomy as a capital crime, since canon law in principle altogether rejected capital punishment, but the canonists applied to sodomy the most severe penalties available to them.[9] Moreover the crime of sodomy in the early fourteenth century was closely allied with the equally serious canonical crime of heresy and there was a tendency for canonists to link the one crime with the other, so that proof of unnatural sexual preferences might imply guilt of heresy as well, and vice versa.[10]

It is not, I think, entirely coincidental that among the charges brought against the Knights Templars in 1307, just four years prior to the prosecution of the Count of Ampurias, accusations of sodomy and heresy were especially prominent.[11] Although James II had been a shade more reluctant to institute proceedings against the Templars than had been Philip IV of France (1285–1314), he had ordered their property in Aragon to be seized in November 1307, well before receiving instructions on the matter from Pope Clement V (1305–1314), to the pope's great displeasure.[12] It also may not be coincidence that one of the few lay nobles who resisted the king's actions against the Templars was Count Pons Hugh of Ampurias.[13]

The Count's reluctance to cooperate with King James's proceedings against the Templars was the more notable because of the record of earlier support for the Aragonese monarchy by the Counts of Ampurias in general and by Pons Hugh IV in particular. Pons Hugh was one of the few major Catalan noblemen who had refused to join the unsuccessful conspiracy against the King in 1280, and he had given numerous other evidences of his loyalty to the crown.[14] His support of James II had been poorly rewarded, however, and as James's ambitions led him to move with increasing vigor against the independent-minded noblemen of Aragon-Catalonia, Pons Hugh found himself increasingly at odds with his king. A breaking point came in 1293, when James commenced construction of a series of fortifications close to the boundaries of the County of Ampurias. Pons Hugh sought royal permission to build some castles of his own in the border region, but this James refused to allow. Later James seized the Viscounty of Bas, which Pons Hugh had held previously, although he later allowed the Count to buy it back in partial exchange for Pons Hugh's assistance against James of Mallorca.[15] This episode marked the beginning of a series of squabbles between the two over Bas. James confiscated the Viscounty once more in 1300, only to return it shortly thereafter; he repossessed it again in 1315. After Pons Hugh's death[16] James's actions against the Count of Ampurias became increasingly brusque and authoritarian, and his interventions in the internal affairs of Ampurias became more frequent.[17] In 1308, however, when James once more needed Pons Hugh's services in an attack on Granada, there was another reconciliation, during which James appointed Pons Hugh admiral of the Catalan fleet.

Perhaps as a result of his increasing friction with King James, Pons Hugh increasingly turned his attention to naval adventures and to regions far removed from Aragon-Catalonia. Whatever the reason, he appointed his eldest surviving son, Malgauli, as heir to his claims in Ampurias and in 1309 left Catalonia for good to undertake a successful career as a pirate and merchant-adventurer in the eastern Mediterranean.[18] In 1310 he outfitted a fleet of five galleys with which he set out on his new career.[19]

His fresh field of activity did not, however, keep Count Pons Hugh out of Aragonese-Catalonian politics. On the contrary he soon became more deeply embroiled than before. In 1310 he captured a Venetian prize ship that, contrary to repeated papal prohibitions against such commercial activity, was engaged in trade with the Saracens. The Venetians were notable offenders against this ban. Indeed, in the previous year Pope Clement V had singled them out for special censure as habitual suppliers of strategic war material to the Muslims. Accordingly, Count Pons Hugh's capture of the Venetian ship was welcomed by the pope, while the Venetian authorities were outraged by this attack upon their trade. The Venetians soon complained to James II about the activities of Pons Hugh, who was still James' vassal. Although James defended Pons Hugh's action, he promised to bring the matter to the attention of his court and meanwhile ordered that the prize cargo be turned over to his own agents. The pope at this point granted Pons Hugh papal protection, while James prepared to undertake legal proceedings against the count. The king claimed first that the captured Venetian ship and its contents had been taken by Pons Hugh using vessels that were in fact the property of the Aragonese-Catalan monarchy. Second, in consequence, the prize really belonged to the king and was being illegally detained by the count. Third, Pons Hugh's actions had broken the peace between Aragon-Catalonia and Venice. Finally, the king contended that the count had failed to respond to the king's summons to appear at a royal court to answer for his actions.[20]

The sodomy prosecution against Pons Hugh commenced in the midst of all this controversy over the Venetian ship. The complaint in the sodomy case dated from the sixth of August, 1311, the height of James's fevered correspondence with the pope and the Venetians over the captured vessel. On the twenty-eighth of August, James was complaining to the Venetians about Pons Hugh's failure to appear to answer the charges against him. Three days later, in another letter, he advised the Venetian Doge that he had taken action to seize Pons Hugh's property, had attacked and burned one of this castles, harried the Count's lands, *et alia etiam dampna multiplicata contulimus*.[21] Pope Clement, for his part, protested James's actions against Ampurias. One royal emissary declared that he had even observed tears in the pope's eyes when they discussed the royal proceedings against Pons Hugh.[22]

We have little further information about the outcome of this affair. There was an additional exchange of correspondence between Clement V and James II on the matter, in which the king intimated that he believed that the pope and the Venetians had reached an understanding with one another and promised for his part to respect the pope's wishes.[23] In the summer of 1312, the diplomatic correspondence on the subject broke off abruptly and Pons Hugh was apparently deserted toward the end even by his own brothers.[24] He ultimately paid a large indemnity to James II, mainly by ceding to the king several castles and other property.[25]

In this context, the prosecution of Count Pons Hugh for sodomy begins to make sense in (dare I say?) a perverse sort of way. It is apparent that this prosecution might have played a role in James II's strategy for dealing with the problem of that captured Venetian ship. Granted that James was proceeding separately against Pons Hugh on that matter, the sodomy prosecution might still have seemed a likely ploy for strengthening his case against the Count of Ampurias. For if Pons Hugh were convicted of sodomy, the monarch's hands were freed to proceed against him and, more important, against his possessions, regardless of whether Pons Hugh ever returned to face the charges directly connected with the Venetian ship or not. There was no question in law that a person convicted of sodomy was tainted with infamy, and so stood to lose all public offices and positions of trust.[26] If Pons Hugh could be convicted on the sodomy charge, the king would have more than adequate basis for claiming that the Count had forfeited his rights to the County of Ampurias, as well as to any lands that he held in fee, or as allodial property, or by any other title. Thus, James could with impunity launch those attacks on Pons Hugh's castles of which he boasted to the Venetians. Moreover, if Pons Hugh were judicially found guilty of sodomy, there was little likelihood that the other barons of Aragon-Catalonia would be tempted to come to his aid or even to protest the king's encroachments on his property. Beyond this, a sodomy conviction would deprive Pons Hugh of his claims to papal protection and would force Clement V to retract the letters by which he had directed the Archbishop of Tarragona and the Bishop of Valencia to safeguard Pons Hugh's lands and other properties.[27]

Beyond all of this, I suspect that there lies a further layer of significance in this sodomy case. As mentioned earlier, there may be a connection between this prosecution and the actions taken against the Knights Templars. James II of Aragon-Catalonia had evidently learned, as had Philip the Fair of France, that the connection between sodomy and heresy that had proved so devastating to the Templars might equally well be employed against other antagonists of the monarchy. By the beginning of the fourteenth century, it was widely accepted that the Cathar heretics of southern France and Catalonia were as prone to deviant sexual behavior as they were to deviant beliefs. The Templars, like the Cathars, were charged with holding that homosexual relationships were sinless between members of their own group. Given the juxtaposition in time between a reinvigorated campaign against the Cathars in southern France, the proceedings against the Templars, and the prosecution of the Count of Ampurias, it is difficult to believe that the Ampurias case is not a part of a larger pattern and very likely inspired by it. The proceedings against the Templars began in 1307 and in 1311–12 the order was suppressed by the Council of Vienne.[28] It is also worth recalling that the mass detention of the population of Montaillou on an apparently well-founded suspicion of Catharist activities began in 1308.[29] It may also be significant that there was a continual interchange of persons between Montaillou and its environs and Catalonia, notably the seasonal migrations of shepherds between the two areas.[30] It is highly unlikely that the anti-Cathar drive in the Diocese of Pamiers had escaped the notice of royal and ecclesiastical officials in Aragon-Catalonia.

This body of circumstantial evidence suggests that the prosecution of the sodomy charges against the Count of Ampurias in 1311 represents another episode, hitherto unknown, in the political use of sodomy as an instrument of royal as well as ecclesiastical power.

*This article first appeared in *In iure Veritas: Studies in Canon Law in Memory of Schafer Williams*, edited by Steven Bowman and Blanche Cody (Cincinnati: School of Law, 1991). Reprinted with permission of the editor.

Notes

1 Barcelona, Archivo de la Corona de Aragón Cancilleria real, procesos, serie II legajo 5, proceso 24 (*olim* Gerona, Sant Feliu 210; hereafter ACA). The documents

are fairly well preserved, save that the upper right portion of all of the folios has been badly worm-eaten and in some cases completely destroyed.

2   ACA fol. 2r: "Die veneris viii idus aug. anno domini mccc°. undecimo in ciuitate Barchinonis. Cum ad audienciam nostram Jacobi dei gratia regis arrangonensis, ualencie, sardinie, et corsice ac comes barchinonensis per famem . . . et c[lam]orem . . . quam et quem diuicius sine scandalo dissimulare non possemus vel sine periculo tolerare sepe ac sep[iu]s pervenisset ut nonullos in diocesis Gerundensis illa incontinentia laborare que contra naturam est, propter quod venit ira dei in fili[os] . . . et quinque ciuitates igne consumpsit ubi uenus mutatur in aliam formam, ubi amor queritur, nec uidetur nos qui ex officio ab alto n . . . tenemus regna et terras meas criminosis ac maxime tam nefandis et orribilibus expiare . . . quibus ciuitates cum hominibus periculum perisse leguntur et terre motus fames et pestilencie multiplicare increspescant et aere pestilens redditur et turbatur ne, quod absit, predicta a nostris manibus requirantur sed ea conuiuentibus ecclesiis transiremus. Incepimus super premissis inquirere sub forma que sequitur diligenter."

3   Thus for example R. de Trumella de Yunuglio swore that he had seen the count having intercourse with another man. R. declared that he had witnessed this activity surreptitiously, while peeking through a window into a room where he had heard peculiar noises. ACA fol. 2r.

4   Such was the testimony of Sir James de Coniliano, who gave a detailed account of an encounter that, he said, had taken place thirty-two years earlier. While on campaign with the Count, he states, he and Pons Hugh chanced one night to share the same bed. "Et comes predictum uoluit quod his testis jaceret cum eo in eodem lecto, quod fecit, et cum ambo intrassent lectum uidelicet dictus comes in camisia et femoralibus et his testis cum camisia et femoralibus. Dictus comes dixit isti testis quod [de]poneret femoralia, quia pars estatis erat et multi iacent sine ipsis, quod his testis fecit. Quo facto dictus comes comensa a processigat lo dicto Ja en la cuya et el flanch en menes en joc ab ell: Et iste testis dixit et quod non faceret, et dormiret, quia media nox fiebat in illo tempore et tunc ipsi comes desinit. Postmodum cum his testis erat guri in casu quod uolebat dormire, idem comes posuit alteram manuum suam in membro uirili ipsius testis ei ipse testis senciens hoc cum manu sua inpulit manum predictam comitis super dictum et prolongauit ipsam ab ipso lecto et dixit dicto comiti, 'ho que diamy es ays,' et dictum comes dixit tunc, 'somiaua et eram uiars, que uos ceugesses so mu membre et in comuen' ipse testis accepit sui femoralia et calciauit ex sibi." Sir James testified further that he subsequently heard rumors about the Count's homosexual adventures with several different partners. ACA fol. 2v–3v.

5   This witness was one Bartholomew, not otherwise identified, but apparently a young man of humble social status. Summoned, sworn, and questioned on his homosexual involvement with Count Pons Hugh, Bartholomew at first denied everything. The judges, not satisfied with his story, informed him that they would continue their interrogations under torture. After Bartholomew's hands had been tied for this purpose, he broke down and promised to tell all, provided that he might be spared the torture. The judges agreed to this and he was then questioned in the king's presence, "absque tormens et metu tormentorum." In his testimony Bartholomew related how he had been seduced by the Count. One night the two of them chanced to share a bed. Their initial encounter involved mutual masturbation; this led to further intimacies, including anal intercourse, although according to Bartholomew's story, all of this was accomplished under coercion. Thus for example he reports one episode: "Et tunc dictum comes dixit ei, 'si non fas al man, te penyar.' Et tunc ipse deponens dixit ei, 'a senyor, por amor de diu, no sia.' Et comes dixit ei, 'per lo cap de ma mar,

sic fac si non fes.'" ACA, fol. 7v–8v. The record of the case ends abruptly following Bartholomew's deposition.

6 Notably *Nov. 77*.1 pr. 1 and *Nov.* 141.

7 John T. Noonan, Jr. *Contraception: A History of Its Treatment by the Catholic Theologians and Canonists* [Cambridge, Mass., 1865], 226, notes that "sodomy" may be used to denote variant forms of heterosexual intercourse, as well as any variety of male homosexual behavior; see also John Boswell, *Christianity, Social Tolerance, and Homosexuality* [Chicago, 1980], 316, n. 48.

8 *Nov.* 77 and 141; *Costums de Tortosa* 9.24.3. ed Oliver Bienvenido in *História des derecho en Cataluña, Mallorca y Valencia*, 4 vols. (Madrid. 1876–1881), vol. 4, 433.

9 C. 32 q. 7 c. 11–14; see also *glos. ord.* to C. 32 q. 9.4 c. 12 *ad v. polluerentur*, as well as to C. 32 q. 7 c. 7 ad v. *sodomita* and to C. 13 ad v. *que si omnes* and *perversitate.* A lengthy and detailed exposition of the canon law on this matter is furnished by Egidio Bossi, *Tractatus varii qui omnem fere criminalem materiam excellenti doctrina complectuntur*, tit. *De stupro detestabili in masculis* (Venice, 1574), fol. 189v–190r. Although Bossi wrote at the beginning of the sixteenth century his discussion of the subject draws heavily on thirteenth- and fourteenth-century sources.

10 This association has frequently been noted. For recent discussions of it see Michael Goodrich, *The Unmentionable Vice: Homosexuality in the Later Medieval Period* (Santa Barbara, 1979), 7–10; E. William Monter, "La sodomie á l'epoque moderne en Suisse romande" *Annales: Economies, sociétés, civilisations* (1974), p. 1024; and Boswell, *Christianity, Social Tolerance and Homosexuality*, 283–286.

11 Georges Lizerand, ed., *Le dossier de l'affaire des Templiers* (Paris, 1923), 18, 26–27, 32, 40.

12 Heinrich Finke, *Papsttum und Untergang des Templerordens* 2 vols. (Munster, 1907), vol. 2, 63–66 (doc. 42); A.J. Forey, *The Templars in the Corona de Aragon* (London, 1973), 366, n. 19.

13 J.N. Hillgarth, *The Spanish Kingdons, 1250–1516.* 2 vols. (Oxford, 1976), vol. 1, 96–97; J. Lee Schneidman, *The Rise of the Aragonese-Catalan Empire, 1200–1350* 2 vols. (New York, 1970), vol. 1, 63; Finke, *Papstutum und Untergang des Templerordens* 2, 66 (doc. 42).

14 Hillgarth, *Spanish Kingdoms*, vol. 1, 252–255; Schneidman, *Rise* 1, 34.

15 Hillgarth, *Spanish Kingdoms*, vol. 1, 264–265; Schneidman, *Rise* 1, 163.

16 Schneidman, *Rise*, vol, 1, 180, n. 76.

17 Schneidman, *Rise*, vol. 1, 62.

18 Schneidman, *Rise*, vol. 1, 163.

19 Schneidman, *Rise*, vol. 1, 164, vol. 2, 348; for a recent study of this episode based on documents in the Archivo Ducal de Medinacelli in Seville, see Maria Isabella Simó Rodriguez, "Un conflicto entre Ponce Hugo IV Conde de Ampurias y los Venecianos," *Historia, documentos, instituciones*, 4 (1977), 583–96. Simó Rodriguez does not mention the sodomy charge.

20 For the pope's version of the ship case see *Registrum Clementis Papae V editum cura et studio monachorum Ordinis Sancti Benedicti*, 9 vols. (Rome, 1885–1892), vol. 6, 14–15, no. 6438. Heinroch Finke, *Acta Aragonensia: Quellen der deutschen, italienischen, französischen, und spanischen zur Kirchen und Kulturgeschichte aus der diplomatischen Korrespondenz Jaymes II. (1291–1327)*, 3 vols. (Berlin, 1908, repr. Aalen, 1968), vol. 2, 658–659, doc. no. 417.

21 Finke, *Acta Aragonensia*, vol. 2, 659; Finke, *Papsttum und Untergang des Templerordens*, vol. 2, 244 (doc. 126); Francisco I. Miguel Rosell, *Regesta de letras*

pontificial del Archivo de la Corona de Aragón (Madrid, 1948), Nos. 365, 370 (121, 192–194).

22   Finke, Acta Aragonensia, vol. 2, 659.

23   Finke, Acta Aragonensia, vol. 2, 659–660; Finke, Papsttum und Untergang des Templerordens, vol. 2, 263 (doc. 133).

24   Finke, Acta Aragonensia, vol. 2, 660.

25   Simó Ridriguiz, "Un Conflicto," 589–92; Jose Pella y Forgas, Historia del Ampurdan (Barcelona, 1883), 517–518.

26   Peter Landau, Die Entstehung des kanonischen Infamiebegriffs von Gratian bis zur Glossa Ordinaria (Köln, 1966; Forschungen zur kirchlichen Rechtsgeschichte und zum Kirchenrecht, vol. 5), 48–49, 97–102.

27   Finke, Acta Aragonensia, vol. 2, 658.

28   Conciliorum oecumenicorum decreta, ed. J. Alberigo et al., 2nd ed. (Basel, 1962), 312–336.

29   Emmanuel Le Roy Ladurie, Montaillou, The Promised Land of Error (New York, 1978), xii.

30   Ladurie, Montaillou, 69–135.

NOTES ON CONTRIBUTORS

JAMES A. BRUNDAGE is Professor of History at the University of Kansas. His many publications include *The Crusades, The Chronicle of Henry of Livonia, Medieval Canon Law and the Crusader,* and most recently *Law, Sex, and Christian Society in Medieval Europe,* which traces sexual legislation in the Middle Ages and points to its longstanding influence.

CATHY JORGENSEN ITNYRE is in the doctoral program at Rutgers University. She spent two years in Reykjavik, Iceland, on a Fulbright scholarship, and currently teaches European medieval history at the College of the Desert, Joshua Tree, California.

JENNY JOCHENS is Professor of History at Towson State University. Focusing on medieval Scandinavia, she has published numerous articles on the history of women, sexuality, marriage and the family in journals such as *The American Historical Review, Annales: Economies Sociétés Civilisations, The Journal of the History of Sexuality, Scandinavian Studies, Journal of English and Germanic Philology,* and *Arkiv för Nordisk Filologi.* She is currently at work on a book on the perception of women in the Old Norse tradition.

RICHARD KIECKHEFER is a professor of the History and Literature of Religions at Northwestern University. His publications include *European Witch Trials: Their Foundations in Popular and Learned Culture, 1300–1500* (London: 1976), *Unquiet Souls: Fourteenth-Century Saints and Their Religious Milieu* (Chicago, 1984), *Magic in the Middle Ages* (Cambridge, 1989). Currently he is completing a study of *A Necromancer's Manual from the Fifteenth Century.*

CHRISTOPHER KLEINHENZ teaches Italian at the University of Wisconsin-Madison, where he is also Chair of the Medieval Studies Program. In addition to books on textual criticism and the early Italian sonnet, he has published numerous articles on medieval Italian literature and is currently working on a study of Dante and the Bible.

ESTHER LASTIQUE is a graduate student in history at New York University. Her field of concentration is Women's History; she has prepared an article on Women and the Temperance Movement in the American South.

HELEN RODNITE LEMAY is Associate Professor of History at the State University of New York at Stony Brook. Her translation of Pseudo-Albertus

Magnus' *De secretis mulierum* will appear in the SUNY Press Series in Medieval Studies. Professor Lemay's next major project is a critical edition of Guillaume de Conches' *Glosae super Macrobium*.

PETER NELSON is a former Lecturer in German at the University of Wisconsin-Green Bay. He is a freelance translator and indexer of a wide variety of German and English materials, and is currently a graduate student in Library Science at the State University of New York at Albany.

PIERRE J. PAYER is a Professor of Philosophy at Mount Saint Vincent University. His publications include translations of Peter Abelard, *A Dialogue of a Philosopher with a Jew, and a Christian* (1979), and Peter Damian, *Book of Gomorrah* (1982), and an influential analysis of early sexual attitudes, *Sex and the Penitentials* (1984). He will continue his work on history of sexuality with a forthcoming book *The Bridling of Desire: Ideas of Sex in the Later Middle Ages*.

NORMAN ROTH is Professor of Jewish history, literature and thought at the University of Wisconsin–Madison. He specializes in Jewish civilization of medieval Spain and has written on Hebrew poetry, Jewish philosophy, and the history of Jews in Spain. He is also the author of *Maimonides. Essays and Texts* (Madison, 1985), and co-editor of the forthcoming *Encyclopedia of Medieval Iberia*.

JOYCE E. SALISBURY is Professor of History at the University of Wisconsin–Green Bay. In addition to articles on various topics of medieval religious history, she is the author of *Iberian Popular Religion, 600 B.C. to 700 A.D.* (1985), *Medieval Sexuality: A Research Guide* (1990), *Church Fathers, Independent Virgins* (1991). Currently she is working on a book-length study of the relationship between people and animals in the Middle Ages.

MARGARET SCHLEISSNER is Associate Professor of German at Rider College. Her fields of research are medieval German literature and medieval women's medicine. Her edition (with commentary) of Pseudo-Albertus Magnus, *Secreta mulierum cum commento*, deutsch is forthcoming in Würzburger medizinhistorische Forshungen.

JANE TIBBETTS SCHULENBURG is Professor of History in the Department of Liberal Studies at the University of Wisconsin–Madison. In addition to many articles on saints in the Middle Ages, she is currently completing a book entitled *Forgetful of Their Sex: Female Sanctity and "Deviancy" ca. 500–1100*, and is beginning a project on medieval women and proscriptions of sacred space.

INDEX